Michael Roll has put together a path-breaking volume that is certain to become the standard reference on its subject. Addressing the unjustly neglected topic of 'pockets of effectiveness' in otherwise under-performing states, it sets a stimulating agenda for future research.

David Booth, *Overseas Development Institute*

It is easy to show that the reigning 'more market, less state' ideas about economic development strategy over the past three decades have at most a partial empirical validity. It is a lot more difficult to give implementable, non-obvious prescriptions for how to make state agencies work more effectively. Michael Roll's edited book does just that. Combining case studies with determined induction, Roll and co-authors present a clear analytical framework in terms of which they answer a question familiar to many who have encountered government agencies in middle-income countries: why do some (a few) agencies work effectively, while the majority do not? And how can a government go about creating and sustaining 'pockets of effectiveness'? Anyone who is concerned about improving the development prospects of middle-income countries – and who enjoys the company of articulate and provocative authors – should pay attention to its arguments.

Robert H. Wade, *London School of Economics and Political Science*

Surprisingly, pockets of effectiveness can emerge in the public sectors of even the worst governed countries. It is hugely important for reform that we understand why and how these exceptions emerge. In this volume Michael Roll brings together the latest research on 'pockets of effectiveness' in developing countries, work done both under his direction and by independent scholars of the subject. In doing so, Roll is able to synthesize conclusions that take our understanding of the topic to a new level.

David K. Leonard, *Professor Emeritus, University of California, Berkeley*

Debates on the public sector in developing countries are dominated by a combination of deep pessimism and calls for market reform. In this valuable and innovative comparative study Michael Roll provides an answer to why and how 'pockets of effectiveness' emerge in certain public organizations and why they persist. It is a breath of fresh air and a must read for academics and public servants. It should become a standard text book for students in the field of public management.

Edward Webster, *Professor Emeritus, University of the Witwatersrand, Johannesburg*

Whereas most public sector organizations in developing countries (and reforms to such) fail, Michael Roll reminds us that there are successes. And that these examples could be the key to more widespread success; through the lessons they offer, the inspiration they provide, and more. This timely book should have an important place on the shelf for anyone interested in governance and government in development.

Matthew Andrews, *Harvard University*

This book is an apt reminder that the blanket gloom through which we often judge the institutions of developing countries is in need of some critical re-examination. It offers invaluable insights into some institutional dynamics in the countries that are covered, especially Nigeria. Taking us beyond the anodyne prescription of 'good governance', it offers examples of institutional contexts in which positive and progressive change is possible. By addressing the key questions of how and why some public institutions function well, it opens the possibility to more fundamental change in African bureaucracies and beyond in the future.

Abdul Raufu Mustapha, *University of Oxford*

When assessing the role of the African state in the process of development today often observers emphasize incidents of bad governance, state failure and corruption. However, this process is complex and in remarkable cases it involves good governance and the effective performance of governmental institutions in the delivery of public goods. This book goes a long way towards disentangling this process in developing countries, teasing out evidence of 'pockets of effectiveness' in the delivery of public goods. It is destined to broaden the discussion on state effectiveness in the context of development.

Edmond J. Keller, *University of California, Los Angeles*

This innovative book analyses rare cases of well-performing public organizations in developing countries. It offers fascinating insights for researchers and inspiration for reform-minded practitioners.

Peter Eigen, *Founder of Transparency International*

This welcome and important volume begins to address our lack of knowledge about public agencies in developing countries that do well despite the most difficult of contexts. It examines the 'how' and 'why' of the emergence, and importantly the persistence, of these 'pockets of effectiveness'.

Colin Talbot, *University of Manchester*

The Politics of Public Sector Performance

It is widely believed that the state in developing countries is weak. The public sector, in particular, is often regarded as corrupt and dysfunctional. This book provides an urgently needed corrective to such overgeneralized notions of bad governance in the developing world. It examines the variation in state capacity by looking at a particularly paradoxical and frequently overlooked phenomenon: effective public organizations or 'pockets of effectiveness' in developing countries.

Why do these pockets exist? How do they emerge and survive in hostile environments? And do they have the potential to trigger more comprehensive reforms and state-building? This book provides surprising answers to these questions, based on detailed case studies of exceptional public organizations and state-owned enterprises in Africa, Asia, the Caribbean, Latin America and the Middle East. The case studies are guided by a common analytical framework that is process-oriented and sensitive to the role of politics. The concluding comparative analysis develops a novel explanation for why some public organizations in the developing world beat the odds and turn into pockets of public sector performance and service delivery while most do not.

This book will be of strong interest to students and scholars of political science, sociology, development, organizations, public administration, public policy and management.

Michael Roll is a University Fellow in the Department of Sociology at the University of Wisconsin–Madison, USA.

Routledge Research in Comparative Politics

1. Democracy and Post-Communism
Political change in the
post-communist world
Graeme Gill

2. Sub-State Nationalism
A comparative analysis of
institutional design
*Edited by Helena Catt and
Michael Murphy*

3. Reward for High Public Office
Asian and Pacific Rim States
*Edited by Christopher Hood and
B. Guy Peters*

**4. Social Democracy and Labour
Market Policy**
Developments in Britain and
Germany
Knut Roder

5. Democratic Revolutions
Asia and Eastern Europe
Mark R. Thompson

6. Democratization
A comparative analysis of
170 countries
Tatu Vanhanen

**7. Determinants of the
Death Penalty**
A comparative study of the world
Carsten Anckar

**8. How Political Parties Respond to
Voters**
Interest aggregation revisited
*Edited by Kay Lawson and
Thomas Poguntke*

9. Women, Quotas and Politics
Edited by Drude Dahlerup

10. Citizenship and Ethnic Conflict
Challenging the nation-state
Haldun Gülalp

**11. The Politics of Women's
Interests**
New comparative and international
perspectives
*Edited by Louise Chappell and
Lisa Hill*

**12. Political Disaffection in
Contemporary Democracies**
Social capital, institutions
and politics
*Edited by Mariano Torcal and
José Ramón Montero*

13. Representing Women in Parliament
A comparative study
Edited by Marian Sawer,
Manon Tremblay and Linda Trimble

14. Democracy and Political Culture in Eastern Europe
Edited by Hans-Dieter Klingemann,
Dieter Fuchs and Jan Zielonka

15. Social Capital and Associations in European Democracies
A comparative analysis
Edited by William A. Maloney and
Sigrid Roßteutscher

16. Citizenship and Involvement in European Democracies
A comparative analysis
Edited by Jan van Deth,
José Ramón Montero and
Anders Westholm

17. The Politics of Foundations
A comparative analysis
Edited by Helmut K. Anheier and
Siobhan Daly

18. Party Policy in Modern Democracies
Kenneth Benoit and Michael Laver

19. Semi-Presidentialism Outside Europe
A comparative study
Edited by Robert Elgie and
Sophia Moestrup

20. Comparative Politics
The principal-agent perspective
Jan-Erik Lane

21. The Political Power of Business
Structure and information in public policymaking
Patrick Bernhagen

22. Women's Movements
Flourishing or in abeyance?
Edited by Marian Sawer and
Sandra Grey

23. Consociational Theory
McGarry and O'Leary and the Northern Ireland conflict
Edited by Rupert Taylor

24. The International Politics of Democratization
Comparative perspectives
Edited by Nuno Severiano Teixeira

25. Post-communist Regime Change
A comparative study
Jørgen Møller

26. Social Democracy in Power
The capacity to reform
Wolfgang Merkel,
Alexander Petring, Christian Henkes
and Christoph Egle

27. The Rise of Regionalism
Causes of regional mobilization in Western Europe
Rune Dahl Fitjar

28. Party Politics in the Western Balkans
Edited by Věra Stojarová and
Peter Emerson

29. Democratization and Market Reform In Developing and Transitional Countries
Think tanks as catalysts
James G. McGann

30. Political Leadership, Parties and Citizens
The personalisation of leadership
Edited by Jean Blondel and Jean-Louis Thiebault

31. Civil Society and Activism in Europe
Contextualizing engagement and political orientation
Edited by William A. Maloney and Jan W. van Deth

32. Gender Equality, Citizenship and Human Rights
Controversies and challenges in China and the Nordic Countries
Edited by Pauline Stoltz, Marina Svensson, Zhongxin Sun and Qi Wang

33. Democratization and the European Union
Comparing Central and Eastern European post-communist countries
Edited by Leonardo Morlino and Wojciech Sadurski

34. The Origin of Electoral Systems in the Postwar Era
A worldwide approach
Krister Lundell

35. The Globalization of Motherhood
Deconstruction and reconstructions of biology and care
Edited by Wendy Chavkin and JaneMaree Maher

36. Parties, Elections, and Policy Reforms in Western Europe
Voting for social pacts
Kerstin Hamann and John Kelly

37. Democracy and Famine
Olivier Rubin

38. Women in Executive Power
A global overview
Edited by Gretchen Bauer and Manon Tremblay

39. Women and Representation in Local Government
International case studies
Edited by Barbara Pini and Paula McDonald

40. The Politics of Charity
Kerry O'Halloran

41. Climate Policy Changes in Germany and Japan
A path to paradigmatic policy change
Rie Watanabe

42. African Parliamentary Reform
Edited by Rick Stapenhurst, Rasheed Draman and Andrew Imlach with Alexander Hamilton and Cindy Kroon

43. The Politics of International Law and Compliance
Serbia, Croatia and The Hague Tribunal
Edited by Nikolas Rajkovic

44. The Funding of Political Parties
Edited by Keith Ewing, Joo-Cheong Tham and Jacob Rowbottow

45. Parliamentary Oversight Tools
A comparative analysis
Riccardo Pelizzo and Frederick Stapenhurst

46. Inclusion and Exclusion in the Liberal Competition State
The cult of the individual
Richard Münch

47. New Challenger Parties in Western Europe
A comparative analysis
Airo Hino

48. Metropolitan Governance and Policy
Jen Nelles

49. Rewards for High Public Office in Europe and North America
Edited by B. Guy Peters and Marleen Brans

50. International Security, Conflict and Gender
'HIV/AIDS is another war'
Hakan Seckinelgin

51. Young People and Politics
Comparing Anglo-American democracies
Aaron J. Martin

52. Immigration and Public Opinion in Liberal Democracies
Gary P. Freeman, Randall Hansen, and David L. Leal

53. Russia's Regions and Comparative Subnational Politics
Comparing Anglo-American democracies
Edited by William M. Reisinger

54. Protecting Immigrant Rights in Mexico
Understanding the state-civil society nexus
Laura Valeria González-Murphy

55. The Politics of Public Sector Performance
Pockets of effectiveness in developing countries
Edited by Michael Roll

The Politics of Public Sector Performance

Pockets of effectiveness in developing countries

**Edited by
Michael Roll**

LONDON AND NEW YORK

First published 2014
by Routledge
2 Park Square, Milton Park, Abingdon, Oxfordshire OX14 4RN

and by Routledge
711 Third Avenue, New York, NY 10017

First issued in paperback 2015

Routledge is an imprint of the Taylor & Francis Group, an informa business

© 2014 Michael Roll, selection and editorial matter; contributors their contributions.

The right of Michael Roll to be identified as editor of this work has been asserted by him in accordance with the Copyright, Designs and Patent Act 1988.

All rights reserved. No part of this book may be reprinted or reproduced or utilised in any form or by any electronic, mechanical, or other means, now known or hereafter invented, including photocopying and recording, or in any information storage or retrieval system, without permission in writing from the publishers.

Trademark notice: Product or corporate names may be trademarks or registered trademarks, and are used only for identification and explanation without intent to infringe.

British Library Cataloguing in Publication Data
A catalogue record for this book is available from the British Library

Library of Congress Cataloging in Publication Data
  The politics of public sector performance : pockets of effectiveness in developing countries / edited by Michael Roll.
     pages cm. – (Routledge research in comparative politics)
  Includes bibliographical references and index.
  1. Public administration–Developed countries. 2. Government business enterprises–Developed countries. 3. Administrative agencies–Developing countries–Evaluation. I. Roll, Michael, 1976-
  JF60.P677 2013
  352.3'6091724–dc23
                          2013022534

ISBN 13: 978-1-138-95639-1 (pbk)
ISBN 13: 978-0-415-64361-0 (hbk)

Typeset in Times New Roman
by Taylor & Francis Books

Contents

List of illustrations	xiii
List of contributors	xv
Preface and acknowledgements	xvii

1 Introduction   1
MICHAEL ROLL

2 Pockets of effectiveness: review and analytical framework   22
MICHAEL ROLL

3 Pockets of effectiveness: lessons from the long twentieth century in China and Taiwan   43
JULIA C. STRAUSS

4 An enduring pocket of effectiveness: the case of the National Development Bank of Brazil (BNDE)   74
ELIZA J. WILLIS

5 Turning Nigeria's drug sector around: the National Agency for Food and Drug Administration and Control (NAFDAC)   97
AITUAJE IRENE POGOSON AND MICHAEL ROLL

6 Taming the menace of human trafficking: Nigeria's National Agency for the Prohibition of Traffic in Persons and Other Related Matters (NAPTIP)   128
ANTONIA T. SIMBINE WITH FRANCA C. ATTOH AND
ABUBAKAR O. OLADEJI

7 'Confidence in our own abilities': Suriname's State Oil Company as a pocket of effectiveness   147
WIL HOUT

xii   *Contents*

8   Defying the resource curse: explaining successful state-owned
     enterprises in rentier states   173
     STEFFEN HERTOG

9   Comparative analysis: deciphering pockets of effectiveness   194
     MICHAEL ROLL

     Bibliography   242
     Index   267

List of illustrations

Figures

5.1	Model for how pockets of effectiveness emerge	123
5.2	Model for how pockets of effectiveness persist	123
6.1	Factors explaining how NAPTIP emerged and persisted as a PoE	137
7.1	*Staatsolie*'s financial results, 1990–2010	159
7.2	Return on investment, *Staatsolie*, 1990–2010	161
8.1	Profit margins of selected Gulf SOEs (net income/sales)	178
8.2	Populism and central administrative control of SOEs	182
9.1	Model for the emergence of pockets of effectiveness	217

Tables

1.1	Overview of the public organizations covered in this book	17
1.2	Government effectiveness in countries in which PoE are located	18
2.1	PoE research questions primarily addressed in previous research	33
3.1	Salt Inspectorate net tax receipts, 1913–1927 (in standard silver dollars)	53
3.2	Salt Inspectorate collections under the National Government, 1928–1937	54
5.1	Categories and factors explaining NAFDAC as a PoE	102
5.2	Income, sources of income and expenditure of NAFDAC, 2000–2007	115
5.3	New categorization of factors	122
6.1	Number of convictions and rescued trafficking victims achieved by NAPTIP	135
6.2	Budget allocations and international and domestic development partners' contributions to NAPTIP, 2004–2009 (June), in million Naira	140
7.1	*Staatsolie's* contribution to the Surinamese economy, 1990–2010	160
8.1	The leading successful SOEs in the GCC	177
8.2	SOE successes and failures: overview	190
9.1	Factors behind the establishment of pockets of effectiveness	195

xiv *List of illustrations*

9.2	Categories and factors that explain how pockets of effectiveness emerge	200
9.3	Truth table scores for PoE cases	216
9.4	Government effectiveness in the countries covered in Portes and Smith (2012a)	226
9.5	Truth table scores for selected institutions in Colombia and the Dominican Republic	227
9.6	Factors that explain how PoE emerge and corresponding factors from Portes and Smith (2012a)	228

Contributors

Franca C. Attoh is a lecturer in the Department of Sociology, University of Lagos, Lagos.

Steffen Hertog is associate professor in comparative politics at the London School of Economics and Political Science. He was previously Kuwait Professor at the Chaire Moyen Orient at Sciences Po/Paris. His research interests include Gulf politics, Middle East political economy, political violence and radicalization and he has published in journals such as *World Politics, Review of International Political Economy, Comparative Studies in Society and History, Business History, Archives Européennes de Sociologie,* and *International Journal of Middle East Studies.* His book about Saudi state-building, *Princes, Brokers and Bureaucrats: Oil and State in Saudi Arabia* was published by Cornell University Press in 2010.

Wil Hout is Professor of Governance and International Political Economy at the International Institute of Social Studies, Erasmus University Rotterdam. His research interests relate to international relations, development assistance and issues of ('good') governance. He is the author of *Capitalism and the Third World* (Edward Elgar, 1993), *The Politics of Aid Selectivity* (Routledge, 2007) and (co-)editor of six volumes and special journal issues, most recently of *Governance and the Depoliticisation of Development* (with Richard Robison, Routledge, 2009) and *EU Strategies on Governance Reform: Between Development and State-building* (Routledge, 2013). He has published articles in, among others, *Acta Politica, Critical Asian Studies, Development and Change,* the *European Journal of International Relations,* the *Journal of Development Studies* and *Third World Quarterly.*

Abubakar O. Oladeji is a research fellow at the Nigerian Institute of Social and Economic Research (NISER), Ibadan.

Aituaje Irene Pogoson is a senior lecturer in the Department of Political Science, University of Ibadan, Ibadan. She was a governance policy analyst at the Independent Policy Group (IPG), a think tank to President Olusegun Obasanjo, and is a member of numerous learned societies including the Nigerian Society of International Affairs and the Mo Ibrahim Index xvi *Contributors*

Advisory Council. She has published articles, book chapters and monographs both in Nigeria and internationally. Her research interests are governance and development, women and gender studies, international politics and foreign policy.

Michael Roll is a PhD student and University Fellow in the Department of Sociology at the University of Wisconsin–Madison. He worked for the Friedrich-Ebert-Stiftung (FES) in Johannesburg and Berlin and was their Resident Representative in Nigeria until 2009. He holds degrees in social anthropology and sociology from Stellenbosch University and Bielefeld University, respectively. His research interests include comparative sociology and politics, development, institutional and structural change and democratization.

Antonia T. Simbine is a Research Professor at the Nigerian Institute of Social and Economic Research (NISER), Ibadan and an associate lecturer on the Peace and Conflict Studies Programme, Institute of African Studies, University of Ibadan. She has varied research interests, including government and politics in Nigeria, corruption, development and gender. Some of her publications include 'The Role and Performance of State Legislators in Nigeria' (*African Journal of Public Administration and Management* 2009) and 'Corruption in Nigeria', in *State, Economy and Society in Post-Military Nigeria*, published by Palgrave Macmillan (2011).

Julia C. Strauss is Professor of Chinese Politics at the Department of Politics and International Studies at The School of Oriental and African Studies (SOAS), University of London. Her research interests are state and institution building, governance and environmental policy in China. She is the former editor of *The China Quarterly* and her publications include the edited volumes *China and Africa: Emerging Patterns in Globalization and Development* (Cambridge University Press, 2009), *The History of the People's Republic of China* (Cambridge University Press, 2006) and the monograph *Strong Institutions in Weak Polities: State Building in Republican China, 1927–1940* (Clarendon, 1998). Her articles have appeared in, among others, the *Journal of Asian Studies, Comparative Studies in Society and History, The China Quarterly* and *Modern Asian Studies.*

Eliza J. Willis is a professor of political science at Grinnell College. Her research interests encompass decentralized governance, state development banking in Brazil, and the impact of globalization on democracy. Her work has appeared in *Journal of Latin American Studies, Latin American Research* Review, *World Politics* and *Latin American Politics and Society.* Her current research project, in cooperation with Janet Seiz, explains the reasons behind the intense conflict over the ratification of the Central America Free Trade Agreement (CAFTA) in Costa Rica and its larger significance for current debates over globalization, state retrenchment and democracy.

Preface and acknowledgements

The process that led to this book was a journey of close to five years with a large number of temporary fellow travellers, funders, advisors, and other supporters. The first phase began while I was the Resident Representative of the Friedrich-Ebert-Stiftung (FES) in Nigeria. My initial motive for looking into the phenomenon that I later termed 'pockets of effectiveness' was to go beyond the widespread lamentation about Nigeria's permanent crisis of governance. While this crisis is real and prevents millions of Nigerians from developing their full potential every single day, only looking at what does *not* work did not seem very constructive to me. Instead, I wanted to focus on those things that actually *do* work, and that work where one would least expect them to do so but where it matters most: right in the heart of the Nigerian state, in its public sector. It seemed to me that if we could find out why and how these pockets of effectiveness emerge and manage to persist, these would be valuable lessons that others could use to make public sector organizations more effective in providing desperately needed public goods and services.

The first two people I shared this idea with encouraged me to pursue it further. I thank Adele Jinadu and Jan Kees van Donge for that. In December 2008 a meeting with a small group of Nigerian scholars took place in Lagos where we discussed the idea. The initial reactions were not encouraging. The tenor was that effective public organizations did not exist in this country. But then again, they were all Nigerian academics and as such they were looking at the world – and even more so at their country – in the most critical way imaginable. Toward the end of the meeting we agreed that a very small number of relatively effective public organizations *did* exist. All members of this initial meeting became involved in the primarily FES-funded research project 'Pockets of Effectiveness in Nigeria' that ran from 2009 until 2010.

Starting in early 2009, we met again, identified potential pockets of effectiveness in Nigeria's public sector in long and structured but still heated debates. We identified particularly qualified Nigerian junior researchers to work with us on this project and at the same time improve their analytical and research skills. While most of the fieldwork was carried out later that year, we continued to meet regularly for training and discussion workshops in Abuja, Lagos, Ibadan, Ile-Ife and Sokoto. I thank all researchers who were involved

xviii *Preface and acknowledgements*

in this project for their commitment, the hard work and perseverance they put into their fieldwork while simultaneously trying to reconcile German financial guidelines with Nigerian realities: Adele Jinadu, 'Lai Olurode, Antonia Simbine, Irene Pogoson, Fatima Adamu, Abubakar Momoh, Charles Ukeje, Idongesit Eshiet, Kehinde Olayode, Franca Attoh, Rasheed Akinyemi, Jane-Frances Agbu, Elias Wahab, Jubril Jawando, Musa Abutudu, Suraj Mudashiru, Azeez Olaniyan, Abubakar Oladeji, David Enweremadu and Aliyu Yahaya.

When the research teams had written up the first drafts of their reports, we invited an outstanding group of Nigerian and international scholars to Lagos to critically discuss and review them with us. I am deeply grateful to this group of not only brilliant academics but also unpretentious and most supportive individuals. Despite all the rain that just did not stop pouring on us during these days, this was a wonderful exchange of ideas and a unique learning opportunity for all of us well beyond the project. For their rich advice, constructive criticism and encouragement at the workshop and beyond I thank David Leonard, Ed Keller, Adigun Agbaje, Raufu Mustapha, Thomas Bierschenk, Jibrin Ibrahim, Otive Igbuzor, Christian von Soest, Omano Edigheji and Joe Abah.

In order for others to benefit from our research until then and to provide us with external input and advice, we had invited some experts to this review workshop in Lagos and benefited greatly from their contributions. I am thankful to David Omozuafoh, Nnamdi Obasi and Christiana Famro. For written input and comments at various stages of the project, I owe thanks to Ladipo Adamolekun, Dele Olowu, Joseph Ayee, Daniel Bach, Judith Tendler, Tunji Olaopa and Matías Cociña.

Like so many other things, this research project could not have been realized without the hard work of the FES Nigeria team in Abuja and Lagos at the time. My sincere appreciation and thanks go to Adeyinka Adekeye, Faith Adogame, Yosola Afutu, Gbenga Akindeju, Juliana Anosike, Simon Asoba, Cornelia Cole, Ife Esho, Remi Ihejirika, Henry Okotie, Godwin Okpa, Festus Omofemiwa, Nadia Nata, Stephen Omudu, Sanni Salihu, Monday Sanni, Yakeen Teslim, Tunde Ukanah as well as my fellow *oyibo* in the office, Sebastian Sperling, and my successor Thomas Mättig.

Funding is a necessary condition for research. In addition to the funds provided by FES Nigeria the project received financial support from the United Nations Development Programme (UNDP) Nigeria as well as from the Institute of International Education (IIE), based on a recommendation from the Ford Foundation West Africa – many thanks to Adhiambo Odaga for this. This support is greatly appreciated.

The second phase of the process that led to this book was not as interactive and the acknowledgements are therefore shorter. I am grateful to the authors who contributed chapters on pockets of effectiveness from countries other than Nigeria to this book. In their previous works, many of them had seen the potential for comparative research on this phenomenon. I am delighted that they have worked with me to realize this project.

Preface and acknowledgements xix

I appreciate Thomas Bierschenk's and Jean-Pierre Olivier de Sardan's invitation to contribute a chapter on pockets of effectiveness to their forthcoming book *States at Work. Dynamics of African Bureaucracies* which forced me to think and write about the findings from this study sooner than I had planned to. Two anonymous reviewers provided helpful comments on the concept for this book when it was under review with Routledge. On two occasions, audiences asked critical questions and suggested changes that improved the quality of the book, first at the European Conference on African Studies (ECAS) in Uppsala in June 2011 and second at the Sociology of Economic Change and Development colloquium at the University of Wisconsin–Madison in November 2012, coordinated by Gay Seidman. In the chapters I am responsible for, all remaining shortcomings and errors are of course my own.

Some of the chapters in this book are based on previous publications. We thank the respective publishers for allowing us to use this material. The first part of Julia Strauss' chapter draws heavily upon material from: Julia C. Strauss (2008) 'Rethinking institutional capacity and tax regimes: the case of the Sino-Foreign Salt Inspectorate in Republican China', in Deborah A. Bräutigam, Odd-Helge Fjeldstad and Mick Moore (eds) *Taxation and State-Building in Developing Countries. Capacity and Consent* (pp. 212–34), © Cambridge University Press, reproduced with permission. Wil Hout's chapter is a substantially revised, adapted and extended version of: Wil Hout (2007) 'Development under Patrimonial Conditions: Suriname's State Oil Company as a Development Agent', *Journal of Development Studies* 43: 1331–50, © Taylor & Francis, used with permission. Steffen Hertog's chapter is an abridged and adapted version of a prior article and therefore draws heavily upon material from: Steffen Hertog (2010) 'Defying the Resource Curse: Explaining Successful State-Owned Enterprises in Rentier States', *World Politics* 62: 261–301, © Trustees of Princeton University, published by Cambridge University Press, reproduced with permission. I am grateful to Alejandro Portes and Lori D. Smith for allowing me to reproduce parts of the truth tables from their 2012 book *Institutions Count: Their Role and Significance in Latin American Development* (pp. 34–35), © University of California Press, used with permission.

More than to anybody else, I am indebted to my family. Without Anne's understanding and support in countless ways and in often challenging environments, this book could have never been realized. And without Simon's and Ella's natural insistence on their own worlds, doing so would have been much more tedious.

M.R.
Madison,
March 2013

1 Introduction

Michael Roll

States in developing countries are not necessarily weak. Neither are they entirely 'fragile', 'failing' or 'neopatrimonial', to mention just a few of the most frequently used labels to describe states in the developing world. While these adjectives may capture key elements of the respective political and administrative systems, they are dangerous because they conceal the enormous variation both between the states thus labelled and within them. This book is about a particular phenomenon that has been largely ignored or only mentioned in passing precisely because it contradicts such general categorizations and labels: it is about public organizations that deliver public goods and services relatively effectively in contexts of largely ineffective government. Such exceptional organizations have been called 'pockets of productivity' (Daland 1981; Leonard 1991), 'pockets of efficiency' (Geddes 1990a) or 'islands of excellence' (Therkildsen 2008). We refer to them as 'pockets of effectiveness' (PoE) throughout this book since it is their *effectiveness* in fulfilling their official mandate by providing the public goods and services they are supposed to provide that differentiates them from other public organizations in their environment.[1]

Before we present our research questions, the methodology and the case studies, we take a step back to locate our research within the recent academic and policy debates about governance in developing countries. We do this by giving a selective and to some degree stylized overview of perceptions of and reform approaches to governance and the state as well as the public sector in developing countries.

A stylized overview: governance, the public sector and development since 1990

Governance, the state and politics

After a short period of optimism that all countries would now converge towards liberal democracy after the collapse of communism (Fukuyama 1992), both academics and policy makers realized that this was not happening. What emerged instead was a world that did not fit into the ready-made

2 Michael Roll

concepts and categories. States that were guaranteed sovereignty by international law but lacked essential features of 'empirical statehood' (Jackson and Rosberg 1982) were therefore labelled 'weak states' (Reno 1998), 'quasi-states' (Jackson 1990), 'fragile states' (OECD-DAC 2007), 'failed states' (Rotberg 2003) or outright 'collapsed states' (Zartmann 1995). How to classify them and even more so how to deal with them became a major concern of development policy and at least since 11 September 2001 also of security policy and international politics more broadly. 'State-building' and modernized versions of 'nation building' rose to prominence in both academic and policy circles (see, for example, Fukuyama 2005 and Hippler 2005).

With regard to the regime question the third wave of democracy (Huntington 1991) also led to more heterogeneity and defied existing frameworks and theories. In political science, the transition paradigm first flourished (Diamond and Plattner 1996), then faltered and eventually collapsed (Carothers 2002). Gone were the underlying assumptions of teleology and the binary framework. Based on the confusing empirical realities that emerged new concepts were proposed such as 'delegative democracy' (O'Donnell 1994), 'illiberal democracy' (Zakaria 1997), 'electoral authoritarianism' (Schedler 2002), 'competitive authoritarianism' (Levitsky and Way 2002), 'semi-authoritarianism' (Ottaway 2003), 'defective democracy' (Merkel 2004) or 'hybrid regime' (Diamond 2002), to mention but a few. Some of these concepts that Collier and Levitsky have so aptly labelled 'democracies with adjectives' (Collier and Levitsky 1997) grasped key features of the emerging 'democratic grey area' (Croissant 2002) regime subtypes. However, overall the sheer number and diversity of attempts to categorize them illustrate that both academics and policy makers found it hard to make sense of the new post-1990 forms of governance in the developing world.

For different reasons but just in time for this political and conceptual confusion, the World Bank had begun to use a concept that was to serve as an umbrella term for the coming decades precisely because it was broad and nonspecific: 'governance' (World Bank 1989).[2] Since the World Bank was not allowed to get involved in politics, it preferred technical and seemingly apolitical terms like this one. The normative blueprint for what should be achieved in this domain followed three years later: 'good governance' (World Bank 1992). This concept basically included all dimensions and reforms regarded as critical for development. Its very broadness and lack of prioritization was one of its main weaknesses. Attempts to trim the agenda down, focus on minimal conditions of governance in the sense of 'good-enough governance' (Grindle 2004) and offer tools to operationalize it (Grindle 2007) have only had limited success in addressing this problem. In part, this success was limited by the second major flaw of the good governance concept: its normative character which was based on a historically specific (Anglo-American) model of liberal political, social and economic development. While the World Bank preferred technocratic language, others have argued that – a third major problem – the good governance framework ignored the essentially political nature of the issues it addressed.[3]

This is also true for the new 'development architecture' that began to emerge at the end of the century. Debt relief, poverty reduction and eventually the Millennium Development Goals (MDGs) began to dominate the development debate. At the same time, donor organizations finally began to look more critically at their own role in development cooperation and in development more generally. The *Paris Declaration on Aid Effectiveness* (OECD 2005) formalized this process. Attached to these shifts was the move of some donor organizations from project to programme-based aid. Budget support, sector-wide approaches, ownership and donor coordination were some of the catchwords of the time.

Another notable development related to governance was the growing focus of the donor community on civil society, participation and social capital since the mid-1990s. These factors were regarded as crucial for democracy and development in their own right. However, with growing discontent about the stubborn resistance of states in the developing world to converge towards the models that development professionals had in mind, in part they began to see them as functional substitutes for many of those things states and governments failed to do (Houtzager 2003).

In broad strokes a normative governance framework, a technocratic approach to poverty reduction and a tendency by some donor organizations to bypass the state and the political process and instead focus on civil society were some of the main features of development policy roughly since the mid-1990s. In contrast to that, especially staff of development organizations working 'on the ground' in the country offices had 'longstanding concerns … about the intractability of governance problems, and the failure of traditional reform approaches to make much impact' (Dahl-Østergaard *et al.* 2005: 6). In response to these concerns, some organizations began to initiate detailed analyses, focussing on the 'political and institutional factors that shaped development outcomes' (ibid.: iv) in the early 2000s. The British Department for International Development (DFID) and the Swedish Development Cooperation Agency (SIDA) directly addressed 'Drivers of Change' and power issues, respectively (see ibid.: iv). Even the World Bank's Institutional and Governance Reviews explicitly included a focus on political issues and motives. While it is difficult to judge to which degree these political or political economy analyses have changed the policies, strategies and operational work of these organizations, they clearly signalled the demand for a better understanding of how governance, the state and politics were actually working in the developing world. While this was in part due to the very complexity of governance in developing countries, it was also a reaction to the prevalence of strong theoretical and normative assumptions and frameworks that had dominated the development debate on governance since the end of the Cold War.

Many researchers have been trying to improve our understanding of what is going on in terms of governance in developing countries in general – to the degree that this can be generalized – and in specific countries in particular. However, much of the research that ended up shaping policy in this field from the mid-1990s until the mid-2000s was based on cross-country regression analyses, often to the detriment of more context-sensitive qualitative or mixed method comparative studies. The latter did not receive much attention in policy circles during this period. With the mounting critique of the good governance paradigm and the realization that our understanding of fundamental social and political processes in developing countries is limited this has changed in recent years. This is important because both kinds of research tend to produce different kinds of knowledge and often recommend different strategies of action. New research that is based on the latter type of research design challenges much of our common knowledge about governance and development. Below, we make reference to selected findings from two recent research projects that used this approach. These projects are the Centre for the Future State (Centre for the Future State 2010a) and the Africa Power and Politics Programme (Booth 2012).[4] We reproduce these findings here for two reasons: first, to illustrate the point we have just made: how fundamentally this kind of research can challenge prevailing assumptions and beliefs about governance and development. The second reason is that we used a comparable research approach and our findings and theirs are often complementary and sometimes very similar. For the sake of brevity, for encouraging readers to consult the original reports and briefs and because these excerpts largely speak for themselves, we do not discuss the findings of these projects here in more detail:

Centre for the Future State:[5]
- 'The global environment creates perverse incentives for political elites to perpetuate fragile states' (Centre for the Future State 2010a: 70).
- '"Good governance" is a flawed approach' (CFS 2010b: 4).
- 'Instead of "state building" and "state capacity", think about "public authority"' (CFS 2010a: 9).[6] 'Public authority can be created in unexpected ways' (CFS 2010b: 8).
- 'States matter, but state building need not follow Western models' (ibid.: 4).[7]
- 'State-society bargaining underpins the creation of effective, accountable public authority' (ibid.: 7). '[G]overnments' need for tax revenue has driven implicit or explicit bargaining with citizens, with the potential to enhance accountability' (CFS 2010a: vii, 59–68; see also Bräutigam, Fjeldstad and Moore 2008).
- ' ... informal institutions and personalised relationships are pervasive and powerful and can contribute to progressive outcomes in poor countries' (CFS 2010a: 70).

African Power and Politics Programme:
- 'Good Governance ... is *not* a precondition for successful economic transformation' (Africa Power and Politics Programme et al. 2012: 6; emphasis in original).[8]

- Kelsall describes what the programme refers to as 'developmental patrimonialism': ' ... provided rent management can be centralised and oriented to the long term, neo-patrimonialism is compatible with strong economic performance' (Kelsall 2011: 84).[9]
- 'The right approach to governance for development is "best fit", not "best practice"' (Booth 2011b: 1).[10]
- '[D]emocracy is a desirable long-term goal but not a reliable route to better public policies in the short and medium term' (ibid.: 2).
- 'The critique of principal-agent, demand-supply, thinking ... should become the central idea for the next generation of governance specialists in development agencies' (Booth 2012: 94). Instead, 'a diagnostic approach based in the theory of collective action' (ibid.: 94) is suggested.

What can we take away from this stylized overview of the debates on governance, the state and politics in developing countries since the 1990s? After the 'second world' had collapsed, academics could not quite make sense of the 'third world' anymore and to some degree this conceptual confusion continues until today. Policymakers and development practitioners developed a normative agenda, based on ideology, theory and pieces of evidence and swarmed out of their headquarters to implement it. Others complemented this approach with spread sheet and workflow style development management for reducing poverty. However, many have realized that both approaches have not really delivered as expected, especially in the fields of governance and public sector reform. To an important degree this is because, apart from certain areas perhaps, our understanding of how governance and politics works in developing countries is often still flawed. This is the problem that the two projects referred to above and a large number of researchers elsewhere are addressing.[11] While many of the findings and recommendations quoted above call into question explicit or implicit assumptions that many governance experts held in the 1990s and are therefore controversial, this is not their most important contribution. Most important is that they fundamentally challenge our assumptions and prompt us to rethink 'governance'. Instead of thinking about what the world *should* look like it is perhaps better to analyse it as it is in particular places and under specific conditions, paying attention to the underlying political dimension, and then build on that. Doing all that in a systematic comparative perspective even allows us to arrive at findings that apply to a much wider range of cases. This book tries to contribute to that broader movement for a very specific governance phenomenon in developing countries.

Public sector and reform

Moving closer to our object of study, public sector organizations, we can now take a look at how the debates about the public sector and its reform in developing countries have changed over more than the past two decades.[12] In

6   Michael Roll

the early 1990s it was slowly realized that simply downsizing the state to its absolute minimum to allow market forces to take over in the context of structural adjustment programmes ('first generation' reforms) did not produce the desired results. Especially the performance of the public sector in sub-Saharan Africa had not only not improved but parts of it had virtually collapsed due to severely decompressed wage scales and radical downsizing.

Coinciding with the rediscovery of the state and the emergence of 'governance' and the Good Governance paradigm, it became increasingly accepted during the 1990s that instead of a 'minimal state' a 'capable state' was needed for development (World Bank 1997). It was in this context that the World Bank's rather recent explicit focus on public sector performance and service delivery emerged in the mid-1990s (Larbi and Bangura 2006: 283; Therkildsen 2006: 59–61). The focus of their civil service programmes correspondingly shifted from retrenchment to human resource management (World Bank 2008: 52–54) in combination with increasing attention to institutional development and capacity building. The so-called 'second generation' public sector reforms from the mid-1990s onwards were based on the reform model of 'New Public Management' (NPM) (Hood 1991). While the public sector should remain small, it should at the same time become more capable through the introduction of market forces, competition and other supposedly performance-enhancing private sector management approaches to the state.[13, 14]

Based on theoretical inputs from public choice theory, new economic institutionalism, new management theories and the principal-agent model, this approach claimed universal validity. It was thus often applied in a 'one-size-fits-all' manner with little attention to local context and history. A significant number of researchers studied this experiment of applying advanced private sector management techniques to public sectors on the verge of collapse.[15] Given their limited capacities, Batley and Larbi find it paradoxical (2004: 233) that the public sectors in developing countries were now expected to perform new roles such as indirect management that were often more demanding and complex than previous roles (ibid.: 221, 236). Other authors argue that successfully internalized 'old public administration' principles and mechanisms, which often did not exist in developing countries, are a precondition for shifting to NPM administrative principles (Schick 1998; Batley and Larbi 2004: 219; Bangura and Larbi 2006a: 21). Confusion and conflict about as well as resistance against NPM reforms were also widespread in developing countries (Batley and Larbi 2006: 123; Therkildsen 2006: 70–71) since they touched upon essential political, power and livelihood questions. Moreover, NPM reforms often added another layer to already existing generations of administrative institutions in a process of institutional 'sedimentation' (Bierschenk and Olivier de Sardan 2003; Bierschenk forthcoming). This also led to conflicts and coordination problems which prevented effective implementation.

Many of these problems were not specific to the developing world. Even in advanced economies the evidence for the very claim that NPM is superior to non-NPM style administration is mixed (Boyne et al. 2003; Pollitt and

Bouckaert 2004; Pollitt, Van Thiel and Homburg 2007). To date, NPM reform implementation in developing countries remains patchy and selective and its impact limited and ambivalent (Batley 1999; Manning 2001; Batley and Larbi 2004: 235; Larbi and Bangura 2006: 279). The World Bank's independent evaluation of its public sector reform support between 1999 and 2006 confirms this assessment by concluding that especially '[c]ivil service reforms, despite modifications in approach, have remained a relatively difficult and often unsuccessful area of the Bank's assistance' (World Bank 2008: 54).[16]

In his review of public sector reform in Africa, Ayee identifies a 'third generation' of reforms (Ayee 2008: 59–65), following the publication of the World Development Report 1997 on the 'state in a changing world' (World Bank 1997). According to him a new feature of these reforms is their focus on the improvement, responsiveness and effectiveness of service delivery to citizens (Ayee 2008: 60; see also World Bank 2003a). While he concedes that these '[n]ew generation programmes since the millennium [are] … still falling very much within the NPM paradigm' (Ayee 2008: 60), the NPM paradigm has been adjusted and 'reframed' by the new poverty agenda since 2000. The focus on achieving the Millennium Development Goals by 2015 has put more emphasis on the delivery of public services while the overall NPM framework remains (see also World Bank 2003a).

Irrespective of how many public sector reform generations we distinguish, the change in strategies, approaches and instruments has seen more continuities and generally has been more fluid and overlapping than described here. There is also a variety of donor organizations which have pursued different strategies over the years. Nevertheless, if we look at the past two decades of public sector reform, the situation on the ground in many developing countries remains dreadful. Despite billions of US-Dollars invested, especially in sub-Saharan Africa, the provision of even the most basic public services remains patchy in many countries. This suggests that the proposed reform models were definitely not the 'best fit' in most developing countries.[17] What Stevens and Teggemann (2004: 70) find for the largely unsuccessful introduction of Performance Improvement Funds (PIF) in some African countries holds true for many ambitious public sector reform programmes: they were 'building[s] without foundation' (Stevens and Teggeman 2004: 70). It is hard to believe how reform programmes were designed and promoted for so long without paying sufficient attention to this fundamental insight. Another reason why public sector reform results in developing countries have been disappointing is the predominance of a technocratic reform approach, which neglects the fact that public sector reform is essentially about the renegotiation of power and the redistribution of resources and therefore is an inherently political process.

These major flaws of public sector reform policy in recent decades have a common root. The reform blueprints that policymakers developed and then tried to implement were based on the belief in abstract universal principles of human behaviour. That is why all reform strategies for developing countries

8   *Michael Roll*

simply mirrored the reform paradigms that dominated in 'the West' at that time and did not bother to pay attention to local contexts and the motives and interests of actors in these contexts.[18] The public sector was regarded as a kind of 'machinery' that needed technical fixes if it did not function properly. This fundamentally ideological approach is distinct from but comparable to the debates about governance and the state in developing countries discussed above. Similar to what happened there, these major shortcomings have been realized in recent years. A new World Bank document that outlines the organization's approach to public sector management and reform from 2011 until 2020 admits the faults identified above and can partly be read as a response to them (World Bank 2012a). Many of the points made in this document reflect the general insights about governance and the state in developing countries from the two research projects discussed above. This is interesting but not surprising since the directors of both projects were members of an advisory group to the World Bank for updating its approach on public sector management and reform (ibid.: ii). Again, for the sake of brevity and for illustrating how strongly the understanding of the nature of the public sector and approaches to reforming it have changed in recent years, I quote selected statements from this document:

- 'Changes to formal arrangements are often critical, *but ultimately PSM* [public sector management] *reform is about changing the informal de facto behaviors of agents within the public sector*' (World Bank 2012a: 3, emphasis in original).
- 'The Bank has yet to put "best fit" fully into practice. In its interventions, the Bank ... has made significant strides in implementing the shift in thinking towards "best fit" in PSM reform' (ibid.: 6).
- ' ... there has been a strong move away from "Washington Consensus"-style theorizing about PSM reform, entailing broad claims about PSM reform contents that should work across a number of different contexts, towards the idea that "what works" in PSM reform is highly context-contingent' (ibid.: 10).
- 'PSM reform is seen as an "adaptive" challenge that cannot be solved through "perfect fit" "technical" solutions developed on a whiteboard – but ultimately as a political and behavioral problem which can only be resolved in a carefully managed process' (ibid.: 10).

The report even goes to the heart of the matter in acknowledging that 'there is more willingness to *expose the assumptions* underlying PSM reform approaches in order to make them testable and open to improvement today than there was in the past' (ibid.: 10, emphasis in original). Considering the policies for and approaches to public sector reform the World Bank had favoured for decades, these statements are remarkable.

In conclusion, we find that on governance, states and politics in general as well as on public sector reform more specifically, academics and policymakers have begun to challenge preconceived beliefs, to reflect on implicit ideological and normative ideas and question long-held assumptions. New systematic and often explorative research is suggested for learning more about why the processes on the ground work as they do, and how so.[19] While a significant body of literature already exists on governance and the state in developing countries and deserves to be rediscovered, on public sector reform the World Bank report notes that '[b]eyond the broad trend towards recognizing that "context" and "process" matter, explicit theory about "what works" in PSM reform in developing countries and supporting evidence remains scarce compared with other policy fields' (ibid.: 12). One of the strategies that the report suggests for addressing this shortage is to promote 'high quality inter-disciplinary case studies and theory development on the political dynamics and impact of public sector reform' (ibid.: 18). This description comes pretty close to the design and approach adopted for this study as we show in the following section.

Pockets of effectiveness are not the kind of comprehensive public sector reform the World Bank and other international organizations are often talking about. Whether they can contribute to 'triggering' such broad reforms is one of the questions we are trying to answer in this book. But in light of the complexity and eventually the unlikeliness of successful comprehensive reforms not only in developing countries, the importance of PoE as 'small-scale public sector reforms' should not be underestimated, both in terms of actual service provision for citizens and for academics and policymakers to learn from.

Research questions and methodology

Having located our research project in the recent debates about governance and development, we see that research on a phenomenon like pockets of effectiveness is highly topical. Academically, it contributes to the growing body of analytical work that is revisiting fundamental questions of governance and changes in governance in developing countries based on detailed and comparative case studies. To date, more is known about why governance fails than under which conditions it succeeds in challenging environments.[20] As a counter-intuitive phenomenon, organizations that defy the odds and *do* work in such environments hold particular promise to challenge common preconceptions and contribute to a more nuanced understanding.

Given the inadequacy of much recent development policy and practice to the realities of governance on the ground, knowing more about why and how particular 'home-grown' initiatives and small-scale reforms like pockets of effectiveness – with or without external support – have worked in the past can also give us some hints for better policy and practice in the future.

Mick Moore and his colleagues from the Centre for the Future State have made the case for using the term 'public authority' when thinking about what is commonly referred to as 'state building' and 'state capacity' (Centre for the Future State 2010a: 9–10). Among other reasons, they argue that the sources of public authority go beyond the state and that including non-state actors is

10 *Michael Roll*

therefore crucial for an appropriate understanding of governance in developing countries (ibid.: 9–10). While we agree wholeheartedly, we still use the terms 'organization', 'bureaucracy', 'state' and others rather than 'public authority' for two reasons. First, in analytical terms both our framework and our approach are open enough to include contributions made to their functioning by non-state actors as the case studies will show. Second, we contend that the public sector holds a key position for effecting comprehensive social, economic and political change (Evans and Rauch 1999). It therefore deserves to be the main focus of empirical investigation.

Our four research questions on pockets of public sector effectiveness are:

1. *Why* do some public organizations emerge as pockets of effectiveness?
2. *How* do public organizations become pockets of effectiveness?
3. How do these organizations manage to *persist* as pockets of effectiveness in hostile environments?
4. Do these organizations *trigger* positive transformations of other public organizations or even the broader governance environment and if so, how?

While question one looks at the factors that explain why public organizations are either established as or transformed into relatively effective organizations, question two focuses on the process of this transformation. Obviously, the answers to both questions are strongly interrelated but distinguishing between them makes analytical sense and clarifies our argument. If public sector performance is the exception rather than the rule in a given environment, it is likely that a variety of actors will challenge these pockets of effectiveness. Question three is therefore concerned with how PoE manage to survive in a hostile environment despite these challenges. The last question looks at whether PoE trigger positive transformations of either other public organizations or the wider administrative, political and social environment. While questions one to three are addressed in each of the case study chapters, this is not the case for question four where our evidence is limited. We will come back to this discussion in the comparative analysis chapter.

Answering these research questions for seven very different case studies across space and time separately as well as for all of them together in a comparative perspective was a major challenge. That is why we spend some time now on specifying and reflecting upon methodological issues, especially our approach, the aims and the analytical focus of this study. We continue with the selection of the case studies and discuss critical features of this unusual sample and the implications. We end with some comments on the strengths and weaknesses of our analysis and the nature of the claims we are therefore able to make.

As the next chapter will show in more detail, the literature on PoE and related phenomena in developing countries is scarce.[21] Despite a first attempt to come up with an inventory of previous findings in this field and categorize them into meta-hypotheses (Leonard 2008, 2010), we argue that our knowledge of why and how PoE emerge and persist is still very limited. Our approach is therefore qualitative and explorative. This is most appropriate for discovering and assessing new factors and the way they interact with each other.

The comparative analysis of the case studies has three aims. First, it should test and demonstrate the usefulness of the analytical framework that we describe in the next chapter. The second aim is to identify crucial factors and mechanisms that answer our research questions. The third contribution we are hoping to make is to generate middle range theoretical explanations that can be used for formulating hypotheses for future research. The three aims of our research carry equal weight. In the final chapter we also compare our results to findings from similar studies in a first step of testing how well our analysis travels.

In combination with these aims, our research questions led us to adopt a particular analytical focus on processes and mechanisms. Whenever we talk about 'factors' that explain why PoE emerge or persist, we describe them as part of a particular process. We do so because we assume that it is the inter-action of individual factors in processes and specific mechanisms that holds most explanatory value, rather than isolated factors. This focus is also reflec-ted in our analytical framework in the next chapter.

While we do not consistently adopt the language and concept of 'causation' it is helpful here for differentiating between different possible foci. Reformu-lated in that language, therefore, our focus is more on 'causal mechanisms' than on 'causal effects' (Gerring 2004: 348–49). That means that, based on our case studies, our analysis establishes a structured and plausible argument for how certain developments are systematically related to and lead to other developments. However, causal mechanisms and effects are of course inex-tricably linked and one can therefore not talk about one without the other.

This focus on processes and mechanisms is especially important since we look at the performance of organizations. While the relevant literature in sociology, political science, economics and development studies is rich in attempts to explain the development failure or success of countries, organi-zations often remain black boxes. To a significant degree, our project is pre-cisely about what is going on *inside* these organizations and how that is related to their interactions with their respective environments.[22]

Explaining our selection of case studies requires more information about the history of this project. This history is somewhat unusual. The project grew out of the two-year research project 'Pockets of Effectiveness in Nigeria' that has been conducted in Nigeria from 2009 until 2010. Twenty senior and junior Nigerian social scientists and I have been involved in this project which covered seven case studies of relatively effective public organizations in the country.[23] After the project in Nigeria had been concluded I developed a more elaborate analytical framework for comparative research on PoE. Its final version is presented in the next chapter. With this framework in mind, I then started looking for researchers who had worked on phenomena similar to what I had defined as PoE. My aim was to go beyond Nigeria and study

12   *Michael Roll*

PoE from a broader, more comparative perspective. However, I had not imagined coming up with a sample as diverse as what is now presented in this book. It includes case studies from Africa, Asia, the Caribbean, Latin America and the Middle East, two of them being case studies of historical PoE. In this context 'historical' means that they existed as effective organizations for several decades, of course allowing for performance 'ups' and 'downs' during these periods. This is an unusual sample since comparative researchers commonly try to 'hold constant' or 'control' for as many messy context variables as possible for preventing that they interfere with the (causal) relationships they are trying to establish between independent variables and the dependent variable.

So how did we select the case studies and how can we justify this sample? My literature research on existing studies of PoE and related phenomena in 2010 revealed three striking features: first, studies on that phenomenon were rare and if they existed, they usually did not refer to each other. Part of the reason for that was that they were usually presented in an area studies context. Second, the few studies that had been carried out on this phenomenon looked at organizations in very different parts of the world and they looked at both historical and contemporary cases. But, third, despite being rare and focussing on different parts of the world, their findings were surprisingly similar in many aspects. This suggested that irrespective of all the differences, a common set of mechanisms might be at work here. The untapped potential for comparative analysis seemed promising. Digging deeper into these studies I also found that despite all their differences, the relevant environments in which these PoE-like phenomena were situated were also similar. The qualification 'relevant' is crucial here. Many comparative studies take the 'country' with its socio-economic characteristics as the relevant context for their units of analysis. We claim that for this study of public organizations, that would not be appropriate. While most but not all countries we look at were relatively poor and had a low level of socio-economic development during the period under investigation, that is not immediately relevant for the public organizations. Neither are all the other enormous differences between (and often also within) these countries in terms of culture, social structure or demographic profile. However, what *is* relevant for how these organizations emerge, persist and work is what we call their 'politico-administrative environment' or the 'politico-administrative system'. This is the set of political and administrative institutions and the dominant logics according to which they operate as far as they are relevant for and impact on public organizations and their (non-) effectiveness. As the case studies will show, the features of the politico-administrative environments of all public organizations were fairly similar. The heads of state were powerful, the state apparatus, especially the civil service, was primarily used as a source of patronage and prebends while its potential functional contribution was neglected, both of which, in the aggregate, led to a largely dysfunctional public service in terms of public goods and service provision (see chapter 2 for a more extensive discussion).

The case studies for this book were selected based on four criteria that the public organization had to fulfil: relative effectiveness in providing the public goods and services the organization was mandated to provide, the capacity to provide these public services or goods throughout the country, a service delivery mode that is in line with human rights and the country's laws and a minimal period of persistence as a PoE of five years (see next chapter for more details). For allowing us to also analyse PoE in a long-term perspective and answer our fourth research question about the potential trigger effects of PoE, we deliberately included historical case studies. When I had found authors who were willing to work with me on this project, I shared the analytical PoE framework with them and asked them to write their chapters. Since some of these chapters are based on prior publications, the authors were asked to return to their data and use the analytical framework. The draft chapters were then discussed and commented upon and revised accordingly. This book is therefore a collaborative project, held together by the framework presented in the next chapter. While some aspects of this framework are more present in some chapters than in others, overall the case studies provided a great empirical foundation for the comparative analysis presented in the last chapter.

As we have argued above, overall, the relevant structural environments of the organizations in the countries in which our PoE are located are sufficiently similar to compare these organizations to each other. While this is generally true, we have to add one qualification and three remarks to enable the reader to better understand how we arrived at this bold claim in light of all the differences between these countries.

Obviously, the cases of the Republic of China and Taiwan are exceptional since during the period under investigation, civil war raged in the country, territorial sovereignty was contested and colonial powers such as Japan as well as other foreign actors like the foreign banks that set up the salt tax inspectorate were very powerful. While this difference in context conditions *did* matter for some features of both organizations in the case study, it did not do so for others. These countries' dysfunctional public sectors that were dominated by patronage were largely comparable to those in the other case studies. The most important difference of the politico-administrative environments of the organizations was the lack of a strong head of state. However, for the purpose of our study, there was a consortium of foreign banks for one organization and an unusually tight network of agricultural experts for the other that to some degree acted as functional substitutes. Therefore, we decided to include the case study with these two organizations.

Due to their character as oil rentier monarchies, one could argue that the countries in the Middle East are also qualitatively different from the other cases in this book. While this is true at the political level, we found that with regard to the public administration and the embeddedness of public organizations in the political system, there are no major qualitative differences that would lead us to exclude them from our sample.

14   *Michael Roll*

Why two case studies from Nigeria? The pragmatic reason is that this is where the project started. However, the initial decision to carry out this kind of research project in Nigeria was based on careful considerations which still hold true and therefore justify the inclusion of two case studies from this country. In a recent book on the role and significance of mostly public institutions in Latin America (Portes and Smith 2012a) only one African country is mentioned: 'It is possible that not all governmental agencies and quasi-governmental institutions in Nigeria are hopeless' (Portes and Smith 2012b: 25). While explicitly challenging the assumed uniformity of the quality of institutions within countries, their statement reflects Nigeria's image in the academic world and beyond:[24] it is regarded as the prototype of a 'bad governance', 'neopatrimonial' country.[25] With this image and the sad reality of pervasive corruption and the persistent failure of public service provision, Nigeria is therefore a country in which one would least expect to find PoE.[26] Yet, they *do* exist which makes studying why and how they emerged and persist in this particularly hostile environment especially promising for our analysis.

We also need to justify why we think we can meaningfully compare public organizations which provide public goods and services with state-owned enterprises operating in the private sector and in a profit-making mode. We argue that at least with regard to our sample, the differences in names ('state-owned enterprise' vs. 'public organization' or 'agency') are bigger than in actual institutions. While the two groups of state-owned enterprises covered in this book (state oil company in Suriname, non-oil sector enterprises in the member countries of the Gulf Cooperation Council (GCC)[27] still retain close links to the state, the service-providing organizations covered in the other chapters have been granted at least a semi-autonomous status from the state. Both groups of agencies therefore enjoy a relative autonomy from the state. As the case studies show in more detail, all organizations in our sample were autonomous with regard to personnel decisions and had separate salary and benefits systems that were higher than in the regular civil service. Some of these organizations could even retain their income and thereby consolidate a certain degree of financial autonomy. While the differences between state enterprises and public organizations are important, in our sample they were differences in terms of degree, not substance.[28] We therefore claim that they did not systematically distort our analysis.

While the research approach for all the case studies was qualitative and explorative, the methods that the authors used for conducting research and analysing their data are described in the chapters. The comparative analysis of the case studies was carried out by way of qualitative coding and analysis, using the Grounded Theory approach (Strauss 1998). Analytical codes are abstract terms that the researcher develops in order to capture the theoretical phenomenon a particular piece of data is pointing to. In an iterative process, codes are generated and 'tested', compared with new and old empirical data to see whether they are analytically adequate or not. They are constantly reformulated, sub-coded, grouped into analytical categories and related to each other to analytically reconstruct processes. Most relevant in this process is to systematically search for data and patterns that challenge the emerging explanations or 'theory' in order to develop it further. The focus of our analysis was on identifying patterns with regard to factors and mechanisms that were relevant for answering our research questions. The aim of this process was to develop middle range theoretical explanations that are based on and 'controlled' by the data, therefore pieces of a *grounded* theory (ibid.).

Since this is a comparative study, it is important to understand that the Grounded Theory approach facilitates the development of analytical codes at a certain level of theoretical abstraction while explicitly paying attention to the contexts of the phenomena on which the codes are based. That allows for a 'non-cannibalistic comparativism' (Steinmetz 2005: 149) in the sense of not simply rejecting certain factors or mechanisms because they are not present in all cases irrespective of the context. Rather, it facilitates the search for systematic differences in context conditions of these phenomena or whole cases that could explain why certain factors are not present but the outcome is or the other way round. The approach therefore uses the comparison of the presence and/or absence of 'determinants' of outcomes as a heuristic device that remains sensitive to context. To be able to do this in a systematic and transparent way, the qualitative data analysis and research software Atlas.ti was used. Chapter 9 of this book is based on the codes and categories, their interrelations and connections that were developed through this analysis.

We can now turn to the strengths and weaknesses of our approach and the nature of the analytical and theoretical claims we are able to make. The strengths of the approach we have chosen include the systematic discovery of new factors and mechanisms, a more detailed understanding of the processes through which PoE emerge and persist and the generation of new hypotheses. We have already dealt with one of the major methodological limitations that one could claim this study has when looking at the diversity of its sample. A second objection based on the design of this study could be that we selected our cases on the dependent variable (here: effective public organizations). This often attracts critique (see, for example, Geddes 1990b, 2003 and King, Keohane and Verba 1994). However, since we are focussing on the processes and mechanisms through which PoE emerge and persist, including cases where PoE did *not* emerge would not have been useful. The selection bias critique also does not apply because our primary concern was to determine whether the factors and conditions we identified were *necessary* but not whether they were *sufficient*. Dion (1998) has argued that for identifying necessary conditions, selecting cases on the dependent variable is appropriate (see also Collier, Mahoney and Seawright 2004; George and Bennett 2005). While the distinction between necessary and sufficient conditions is often less clear in empirical research than in theory, this certainly is a limitation of our study. However, especially given the limited knowledge about PoE in developing countries and our focus on the workings of processes and mechanisms, our findings about necessary conditions are an important contribution to the

16   *Michael Roll*

literature.[29] Dion confirms that 'necessary conditions will be most helpful when they are rarely satisfied. In such cases the phenomenon under investigation will rarely be observed, because the necessary conditions for it are seldom realized' (ibid.: 142). PoE certainly belong to this group of phenomena.

To conclude the methodological discussion, we summarize the analytical and theoretical claims we are able to make, based on the research design and approach adopted in this study. First, the factors we identify in our comparative analysis are necessary factors for the emergence and persistence of PoE in the particular kind of environment we have briefly described above. Based on a systematic and detailed examination of the cases we are also able to describe how some of these factors relate to each other and interact in processes and mechanisms. Third, we derive empirically substantiated arguments for why and how PoE emerge and persist that may prove useful for generating new hypotheses and theories to be tested and qualified in future research on PoE. The answers to our fourth research question on whether PoE can trigger positive transformation or not are merely suggestive due to limited relevant empirical material and therefore require further research.

Structure and case studies

The next chapter provides the common analytical framework for all the case studies and the comparative analysis. The chapters that follow are detailed case studies of effective public organizations in environments in which the great majority of public sector organizations were not effective. Table 1.1 gives an overview of some of the most important features of the organizations analysed in this book and the countries they are located in at the point in time when the respective PoE were established. Table 1.2 presents the World Bank's Government Effectiveness indicators for the countries in which the PoE are located and, where available the years in which they were established. This indicator complements the information provided in the case studies, showing that overall, the governments and public sectors in the countries concerned were not effective and the public organizations we analyse therefore were indeed isolated 'pockets' of public sector effectiveness.[30]

Chapter 3 covers two case studies over several decades, both of which emerged in the Republic of China. Both the Sino-Foreign Salt (tax) Inspectorate on mainland China and the Joint Commission on Rural Reconstruction in Taiwan were remarkably successful despite having very different organizational structures. These organizations are not only the oldest ones included in our study but they are also special in the sense that colonialism and other foreign powers still had a strong impact on them.

The chapter that follows also looks at a historical case study, this time in mid-twentieth century Brazil. Brazil had just returned to democratic rule when the new nationalist government established several organizations for promoting industrialization and development. The National Bank for

Table 1.1 Overview of the public organizations covered in this book

Organization (country)	Task area[a]	Degree of autonomy[b]	Environment: regime and state capacity[c] (new regime in power since)	Year established (effective since)
Sino-Foreign Salt Inspectorate (Republic of China)	Finance	Semi-autonomous	Weak authoritarianism, collapsed state (1912)	1913–28 and until 1949 (1913)
Joint Commission on Rural Reconstruction (Republic of China/Taiwan)	Service delivery	Semi-autonomous	Weak authoritarianism (martial law), weakly institutionalized state (1945/49)	1948–79 (1948)
National Bank for Economic Development (Brazil)	Finance	Semi-autonomous	Young presidential democracy, institutionalized state (1951)	1952 (1952)
National Agency for Food and Drug Administration and Control (Nigeria)	Regulation	Semi-autonomous	Young presidential democracy, weakly institutionalized state (1999)	1994 (2001)
National Agency for the Prohibition of Traffic in Persons etc. (Nigeria)	Regulation	Semi-autonomous	Young presidential democracy, weakly institutionalized state (2003)	2003 (2003)
State Oil Company of Suriname (Suriname)	Profit	Autonomous	Military dictatorship, weakly institutionalized state (1980)	1980 (1982)
Several (several, GCC)[d]	Profit	Autonomous	Monarchies, patrimonial administration	Miscellaneous

Notes: [a] The following task area classification was used: service delivery, regulation, finance (taxation, banking), profit (state-owned enterprises that are supposed to make profits through private business-like operation which, in part, flows back to the government).
[b] The following degrees of autonomy were used: not autonomous (civil service rules and regulations apply, part of civil service hierarchy), semi-autonomous (separate rules and regulations, part of civil service hierarchy), autonomous (separate rules and regulations, not part of civil service hierarchy). The classification is valid for the year in which the respective organization was established (see last column).
[c] Earlier in this chapter, we have seen that the classification of political regimes and state capacity is difficult. The pragmatic solution we have resorted to is to describe them as briefly and accurately as possible for the year in which the respective organization was established (see column to the right).
[d] Gulf Cooperation Council: members are Bahrain, Kuwait, Oman, Qatar, Saudi Arabia and United Arab Emirates.

18   *Michael Roll*

Table 1.2 Government effectiveness in countries in which PoE are located

Country (Organization)	Years of interest	World Bank Government Effectiveness indicator (Percentile rank)
Brazil (BNDE)[a]	1996	-0.15 (50.7)
	2011	-0.12 (49.8)
Nigeria (NAFDAC and NAPTIP)	2002	-1.06* (11.7)
	2003	-0.96 (15.6)
	2011	-1.08* (13.7)
Suriname (Staatsolie)	1996	-0.80 (22.4)
	2011	-0.11 (50.2)
GCC:[c] Saudi Arabia	1996	-0.26 (46.3)
	2011	-0.32 (44.1)
GCC: Qatar	1996	0.47 (68.3)
	2011	0.78 (75.4)
GCC: United Arabian Emirates	1996	0.63 (72.7)
	2011	1.06* (82.0)
GCC: Bahrain	1996	0.63 (72.7)
	2011	0.55 (68.7)

Notes: *More than one standard deviation above or below the mean of zero.

According to the World Bank, the Government Effectiveness indicator is 'capturing perceptions of the quality of public services, the quality of the civil service and the degree of its independence from political pressures, the quality of policy formulation and implementation, and the credibility of the government's commitment to such policies' (Kaufmann, Kraay and Mastruzzi 2009: 6). The Worldwide Governance Indicators (WGI) are aggregate indicators which, for the countries included in the table, are based on between two or three data sources in the earlier years up to a maximum of 11 data sources in more recent years. The units of measurement follow a normal distribution with a mean of zero and a standard deviation of one. Almost all scores therefore lie between -2.5 and 2.5, with higher scores indicating better, and lower scores poorer outcomes. For the percentile rank each country is ranked among all other countries included in that particular year. It ranges from 0 until 100 with 0 corresponding to the lowest and 100 corresponding to the highest rank. We argue that, notwithstanding the many shortcomings of this indicator for our purposes and more generally, it provides a useful approximation.

The earliest year for which the WGI data are available is 1996. This limits the usefulness of the indicator for our purposes even further. Our years of interest are the years in which the organizations were either established or reformed. If this was before 1996 we report the indicator for 1996 and, for each country, the latest available indicator at the time of writing (2011). Due to the very long time lag between the organization's establishment and 1996 we excluded China and Taiwan.

[a] Since one of our periods of concern is the 'turning period' of the bank in the 1990s, our year of interest is 1993. Since the data are only available starting in 1996, we used the data for this year.

[b] NAFDAC's reform and emergence as a PoE began in 2001, which is why this would have been our year of interest. Because no WGI data are available for this particular year, we used the data for 2002.

[c] Gulf Cooperation Council: members are Bahrain, Kuwait, Oman, Qatar, Saudi Arabia and the United Arab Emirates. We only look at the four countries with the most important state-owned enterprises, according to table 8.1. Since the case study is not about any particular company but about state-owned enterprises more generally, we also do not focus on specific years.

Source: World Bank (n.d.).

Economic Development (BNDE) was one of the most effective and enduring of these organizations. The chapter tells us why.

Chapters 5 and 6 are based on the original research project in Nigeria which led to this book. Both studies look at remarkably effective regulatory organizations, both of which were established or reformed in the early 2000s. The first of them regulates Nigeria's drug and food sectors (National Agency for Food and Drug Administration and Control, NAFDAC) while the second one tries to prevent and police human trafficking (National Agency for the Prohibition of Traffic in Persons, NAPTIP).

The two subsequent chapters both cover PoE in oil rentier states. The first one looks at Suriname and its oil company State Oil Company of Suriname (*Staatsolie*). In many rentier states, state oil companies are a major source of rents and the organizations are therefore often anything but bureaucratic and effective. In Suriname, while the general politico-administrative system was dominated by patronage and clientelism when *Staatsolie* was established, the organization has managed to persist as a PoE.

As chapter 8 shows, the same has happened in some state-owned enterprises outside of the oil sector but based in and owned by oil rentier monarchies in the GCC area. This chapter is different from the others in that it is in itself a comparative study of effective and ineffective state-owned enterprises in several countries.

The last chapter presents the findings from the comparative analysis of the case studies. It answers our four research questions, compares our findings to those of other researchers and draws conclusions for theory and policy.

Notes

1 This book is a collective enterprise. However, while all authors used the analytical framework presented in chapter 2, not all of them may agree with all aspects. This is even more true for what I write in this chapter and in the comparative analysis (chapter 9). The 'we' that I use in these chapters should therefore be read as a compromise. While I would not have been able to arrive at the conclusions without the author's contributions, these three chapters present my own thinking with which they may or may not agree.

2 The concept emerged in the World Bank's 1989 report *Sub-Saharan Africa: From Crisis to Sustainable Growth* in which a serious crisis of governance in most countries was identified as the key factor for the continent's development problems.

3 For more detailed critical discussions of the concept and of attempts to implement it, see Leftwich (2000: 116–26), Weiland, Wehr and Seifert (2009) and Grindle (2010).

4 We do not provide a full summary of their findings here but selected only those points which speak most directly to the preceding overview of the governance and development debate since the 1990s.

5 For an interesting review of the Centre for the Future State's final report *An Upside-down View of Governance* by David Booth, the then director of the Africa Politics and Politics Programme, see Booth (2011a).

6 The report gives several reasons for this advice which is key to both their approach and their findings (see Centre for the Future State at the Institute of Development Studies 2010a: 9–10). Some of them are that they want to use an approach that does not implicitly refer to the historical process of state building in Europe, that

20   *Michael Roll*

they want to look at formal as well as informal institutions and that, according to them, the sources of public authority cut across the state-society boundary which tends to be weak in development countries anyway (ibid.: 9–10).

7 It should be noted that the document from which this quote is taken is directed at policymakers and therefore uses both the familiar concept of 'state building' and 'public authority', which the authors prefer.

8 Note that with regard to many of these insights, the Africa Power and Politics Programme researchers do not claim to be the first to make this point (see, for example, Khan 2010 and Khan and Jomo 2000). However, it contradicts core elements of and justifications for the good governance agenda of the past two decades so strongly that it is still disturbing news, especially for many policymakers.

9 For more details and research on 'developmental patrimonialism', see Crook (1989), Booth (2012: 22–30), Booth and Golooba-Mutebi (2012) and Kelsall (2013).

10 For the African Power and Politics Programme, 'best fit' implies 'building on existing institutional arrangements that have recognisable benefits' and 'a shift from direct support to facilitating local problem-solving' (Booth 2011b: 1).

11 For a paper that also raises some but not all of the issues discussed in the two research projects outlined above, see Carothers and de Gramont (2011).

12 Since I am most familiar with the history of public sector reform in sub-Saharan Africa, this section draws on that particular history. However, in varying degrees the general features also apply to other 'developing' world regions.

13 Batley and Larbi summarize three core tendencies of NPM reforms as follows: '[o]*rganisational restructuring* ... to shift resources ... to decentralized management', '*increasing use of market-type mechanism*' and '*increasing emphasis on performance* ... towards "getting results"' (Batley and Larbi 2004: 222; emphases in original).

14 Other approaches of public sector reform which were either related to or overlapped with the implementation of NPM such as capacity-building and capacity-development, decentralization, privatization or public-private partnerships since the 1990s are not discussed in this chapter. See Turner and Hulme (1997), Economic Commission for Africa (2003), Batley and Larbi (2004), African Development Bank (2005) and Ayee (2008: chapter 5) for more details.

15 See Turner and Hulme (1997), Schick (1998), Minogue, Polidano and Hulme (1999), Manning (2001), McCourt and Minogue (2001), Batley and Larbi (2004), Bangura and Larbi (2006b) and Anders (2010). On NPM implementation in Africa, see the special issue of *Africa Development*, edited by Dele Olowu (2002).

16 The 2008 evaluation covered various reform areas. While World Bank-supported reforms on tax administration were rated 'satisfactory' and public expenditure and financial management 'moderately satisfactory', direct anticorruption and transparency, civil service and administration as well as integration and consistency across themes only achieved 'moderately satisfactory' results (World Bank 2008: 72). The World Bank's Independent Evaluation Group team also identified some relapses into previous reform patterns and did not mince its words when commenting on them: 'in other places the Bank (often with the IMF) continued to support simplistic retrenchment programs of the same sort that failed in the past' (World Bank 2008: 73).

17 See Polidano (2001) for reasons why civil service reforms fail and Long and van der Ploeg (1989) for a critique of mechanical models of planned intervention and reform implementation as well as an alternative, more complex sociological understanding.

18 The following conclusion from the World Bank's Independent Evaluation Group on the organization's contribution to 'first generation' public sector reforms confirms this point: ' ... this focus [on retrenchment and salary decompression] often overlooked indications that these actions were *politically unrealistic* and also *assumed without evidence* that these changes would bring about improved public administration. This approach usually failed ... ' (World Bank 2008: 52; my

Introduction 21

emphasis). While the paradigm changed somewhat with the shift to the 'second generation' reforms, evidence suggests that the underlying approach did not.

19 For more interesting examples, in addition to the two research projects presented above, see the mostly ethnographic contributions in Blundo and Le Meur (2009) and Bierschenk and Olivier de Sardan (forthcoming). From a political science perspective, see Holmberg and Rothstein (2012).

20 This approach of looking at governance- or rather public authority-related success stories and at 'what works' in a respective context is in line with an emerging body of literature which includes, among others, Tendler (1997), Hilderbrand and Grindle (1997), Bebbington and McCourt (2007), Manor (2007), Robinson (2007), Tsai (2007), Grant, Hudson and Sharma (2009) and Melo, Ng'ethe and Manor (2012). From a very different perspective and focussing more on the societal than on the governance dimension, see Hall and Lamont (2009).

21 However, as of late, the interest in what we call pockets of effectiveness is growing. We refer to some of the most recent literature and ongoing research in the final chapter.

22 However, our case studies vary in the degree to which they do that. One example is Hertog's chapter which is in itself comparative and focusses more on the interaction of organizations with their respective environments rather than on what is going on inside the organizations.

23 Apart from the two case studies presented in this book, the case studies included the Economic and Financial Crimes Commission (EFCC), the Federal Inland Revenue Service (FIRS), the Ministry of Environment of the Lagos State Government (a state-based public organization), the *Punch* newspaper (a quasi-public but privately owned organization) and the Fahimta Microfinance Bank (another quasi-public organization).

24 The authors make this statement after discussing studies using either cross-country regression analysis or building indices for assessing the quality of institutions across countries. They find out that '[n]ot surprisingly, African countries, such as Nigeria, rank at the very bottom of this scale ... ' (Portes and Smith 2012b: 25) and argue that 'studies at closer range are needed to develop nuance and bar tautology' (ibid.). Their perspective and approach are therefore quite similar to ours.

25 Another example is Kohli (2004: part IV) who chose the case of Nigeria for outlining the general features of a neopatrimonial system or Smith (2008) who describes Nigeria's 'culture of corruption'.

26 The studies in the following short and by no means exhaustive list shed more light on how 'things fell apart' (adapted from Achebe 1958) in Nigeria: Panter-Brick (1978), Achebe (1984), Ake (1985), Joseph (1987), Soyinka (1996), Ibrahim (1997), Osaghae (1998), Kohli (2004: part IV), Olurode and Akinboye (2005), Olurode and Anifowose (2005), Agbaje, Akande and Ojo (2007), Jega (2007), Lewis (2007), Oyekanmi and Soyombo (2007), Falola and Heaton (2008) and Smith (2008).

27 The member countries of the GCC are Bahrain, Kuwait, Oman, Qatar, Saudi Arabia and the United Arab Emirates.

28 For an overview of empirical research on the differences between and similarities of public and private organizations, see Rainey and Bozeman (2000).

29 Despite the general scarcity of literature, prior studies of PoE and PoE related phenomena have of course already found out much about why they exist, even if they have not used the necessary/sufficient terminology. We review some of these contributions in the next chapter.

30 While we found that, overall, the indicators corresponded with our assessments of government and public sector effectiveness for the countries in the years concerned, this is not true for the three GCC countries Qatar, United Arabian Emirates and Bahrain (see table 1.2). While one of the problems with the indicator is that the first year for which it is available is 1996, see Hertog for a discussion and his assessment of the quality of government and the public sector in these countries in chapter 8.

2 Pockets of effectiveness
Review and analytical framework
Michael Roll

Pockets of effectiveness are not just organizations that perform better than others. Unlike the companies that Thomas J. Peters and Robert H. Waterman studied for their management classic *In Search of Excellence: Lessons from America's Best-Run Companies* (1982) for example, pockets of effectiveness (PoE) do not perform better in an environment in which many other companies or organizations also perform relatively well. PoE are effective public organizations in environments in which almost all other public organizations do *not* perform well at all. The reason for this is that these organizations operate in politico-administrative systems that are primarily based on personal loyalty and informal networks instead of a substantial degree of impartiality and formal, law-based rules.[1] Organizations aiming at being even modestly effective in the sense of carrying out their official mandate in such an environment have to work against all sorts of odds. What distinguishes them from other organizations in the same environment is that they somehow manage to defy the prevailing systemic constraints and perverse incentives that usually lead to poor performance. PoE are scattered islands in seas of administrative ineffectiveness and corruption.

Considering its counterintuitive nature and its importance, the phenomenon of PoE has only received little academic attention to date and remains poorly understood. Studies of PoE exist but they are rare. Some of them focus on historical cases in early modern Europe.[2] Others focus on current developing countries as the literature review in this chapter will show. Most PoE studies are based on a particular region or country. To our knowledge, only three comparative cross-country analyses of PoE exist to date (Israel 1987; Hilderbrand and Grindle 1997; Barma, Huybens and Viñuela 2012). While some of the single country PoE studies also draw more general conclusions we hope to be able to offer new insights based on our study design which is comparative with regard to both time and space (see chapter 9).

We see four reasons why comparative studies of PoE in developing countries are scarce to date, two of them epistemological and the other two methodological. The first reason is the strong focus on developing indicators for various dimensions of governance at the country level since the 1990s. Organizations such as the World Bank as well as researchers have tried to measure, compare and track governance with indicators such as the 'Worldwide Governance Indicators' (World Bank n.d.). These and similar indicators but also qualitative governance assessments usually focus at the country level at the expense of attention to in-country variation. The second epistemological reason is that many academics and policymakers working in and on developing countries focus on deficits. In these studies, institutions in developing countries are either explicitly or implicitly compared to 'Western' normative standards (e.g. good governance), against which the majority of them perform poorly. This deficit-focus is often so dominant that empirically existing variation escapes the attention of the observers.

The two other reasons for the scarcity of comparative studies of PoE in developing countries are methodological. One of them is that no coherent terminology has been established for describing, let alone comparatively studying, PoE and related phenomena. The fourth reason is the absence of an analytical framework for studying PoE. In this chapter we seek to make a contribution to filling the last two gaps. It provides the common framework for the case studies that are presented in this book, as well as for the comparative analysis. Beyond our own study, we hope that it will inspire others to study PoE and related phenomena elsewhere by using, modifying and improving the framework.

Given the lack of a common PoE terminology the next section provides definitions and clarifications, followed by a discussion of some criteria for how PoE can be identified. The chapter continues with a review of four studies of PoE in the developing world. Their findings are brought together with three general hypotheses for why and how such pockets emerge. Our analytical framework is then presented in the final section.

Terminology

As the review of the PoE studies below will show, no coherent terminology has been established for the phenomenon we call 'pockets of effectiveness' in this book. While Daland (1981) and Leonard (1991) prefer to call them 'pockets of productivity',[3] Geddes's use of 'pockets of efficiency' (1990a, 1994) goes back to an expression for exceptionally well-performing public organizations in Brazil in the 1950s and 60s. Making reference to Geddes, Peter Evans has further popularized this term (1992, 1995). Other designations such as 'islands of excellence' (Therkildsen 2008) or 'islands of effectiveness' (Crook 2010) have also been employed.

While some authors use these and similar terms for exceptionally well-performing *organizations*, others apply them to policy programmes or development projects. In his 'propositional inventory' of PoE (Leonard 2008, 2010), David Leonard has suggested to classify these studies according to their focus (Leonard 2008: 9). He finds six different foci, namely studies focussing on successful organizations, others on exceptional managers, public policies, successful policy reform initiatives, World Bank projects and finally studies that are cross-cutting (for references, see Leonard 2008: 9). For our study we have chosen public organizations as our unit of analysis, although we pay close attention to the context in which they are embedded and to their interaction with it.

Public organizations are state-owned organizations which have the mandate to provide public goods and services. This includes regulatory functions and natural resource management. Our understanding of 'public organizations' comprises both administrative government agencies and state-owned enterprises. We contend that the differences between these two ideal types of public organizations have to be established empirically and cannot be simply assumed (see Rainey and Bozeman 2000). In the introduction we argued that for the purpose of this study and given the characteristics of the organizations in our sample we can justify including and comparing both kinds of organizations.

We define 'pockets of effectiveness' as public organizations that are relatively effective in providing the public goods and services the organization is officially mandated to provide, despite operating in an environment in which effective public service delivery is not the norm. In such environments, PoE may emerge in several ways. A first crucial distinction is whether they are the result of deliberate action or more the unanticipated consequence of purposive political action (adapted from Merton 1936). Second, PoE may either be the outcome of top-down action or they may emerge bottom-up or from within the larger administrative system as niches of 'subcultural bureaucracy' (see McDonnell 2012). All PoE in our sample were the result of deliberate and targeted top-down political decisions and actions.[4] We therefore claim that our analysis applies to this particular type of PoE.

Like we said in the introduction, the environments in which the PoE in our sample exist(ed) shared similar features. They had powerful heads of state in presidential systems while the state apparatus, especially the civil service, was often used as a source of patronage and prebends. Prominent features of this type of politico-administrative system are a high degree of personalization, a particularistic and relationship-based orientation, constant competition for the distribution of resources and their appropriation by groups and individuals, and other kinds of informal, non-bureaucratic relationships. Formal rules and laws do exist, are referred to in rhetoric and practice but the degree to which they are implemented and to which they actually serve as guidelines for political and administrative action varies strongly. Their relevance is most adequately described as inconsistent, fragmented and frequently not the dominant frame of reference in the politico-administrative system. The combination of both the patrimonial use of the civil service and the neglect of its potential functional contributions by politicians leads to a situation in which the preconditions are absent for a public sector to work in a predictable way through bureaucratic procedures that are based on impartial criteria. That is why most public organizations in this type of environment are dysfunctional and perform poorly in terms of producing public goods and services.[5]

Public organizations are essential parts of the infrastructure of politico-administrative systems in these environments. Having authority over them gives groups and individuals access to public funds and allows them to award public contracts as well as jobs in the public sector. They are therefore major sources of power and patronage. For being able to provide public goods and services relatively effectively based on their mandates, public organizations have to avoid being at least completely instrumentalized for political or private purposes. Because politicians are usually trying to do that in these environments we can say that these PoE exist in 'hostile' environments. Since effective public service delivery was not the overriding motive of most politicians in these environments, patrimonial demands, political interference and political capture were constant threats for PoE.

In this book, 'effectiveness' refers to whether or not a public organization is successful at doing what it is mandated to do.[6] Organizations which are supposed to provide public services are only classified as 'effective' if they actually *do* provide these services to a meaningful extent. This definition is further clarified in the following discussion of criteria for PoE.

Criteria for pockets of effectiveness

We suggest the following four criteria for identifying public organizations that qualify as PoE:[7]

A. Relative effectiveness in providing the public goods and/or services the organization is officially mandated to provide.
B. Capacity to provide this public good or service throughout the country.
C. Mode of public good or service delivery that is in line with human rights principles and laws of the country concerned.
D. Period of persistence of at least five years.

Relative effectiveness is the core criterion and has to be fulfilled for an organization to be a PoE. The tricky question is what 'relative' means. We opted for a strongly context-dependent conception which means that the more hostile the environment and the less effective other public organizations in the same environment are, the less effective an organization needs to be in 'absolute' terms to pass this criterion. A public organization in Somalia may therefore be less effective in absolute terms than an organization in Ghana, for example, but may still count as a PoE. However, the bottom line is that the respective public goods or services have to be provided by that organization. It is not sufficient if the organization works well internally but does not produce any output. With regard to our sample, this criterion did not pose a problem. All the organizations we selected were clearly effective not only in relative but often also in absolute terms, based on indicators and qualitative accounts that are presented in the chapters.

26   *Michael Roll*

An organization also has to have the capacity to provide a public good or service not only in the capital or a metropolitan area but across the whole country. Depending on the task of the organization it does not necessarily have to have a network of offices or agents across the country but it has to cover the whole country with its services (e.g. a development bank).

The third criterion applies particularly to law enforcement agencies. In many developing countries their human rights records are devastating.[8] By including this criterion we wanted to exclude public organizations that could be regarded as 'effective' based on the first two criteria but are so in part because they use illegal means and/or violate human rights.

The last criterion is crucial. An organization should be considered a PoE only if it has continued to exist as a PoE for a certain period of time. For their analysis of successful public policy programmes, McCourt and Bebbington (2007) have suggested that the programmes should have endured for at least ten years or have survived a change of government in a competitive electoral system (ibid.: 6). We argue that the length of time that a public organization should have persisted as a PoE also depends on the respective context and the history of the country. When we started to work on this project in Nigeria, a period of ten years would have excluded all organizations since Nigeria only returned to civilian and democratic rule in 1999. The regime change eventually led to a reorganization of the public sector and the establishment of new organizations or, less frequently, the reform of 'old' ones. We therefore decided that having existed as a PoE for more than five years and therefore more than half as long as the new regime was in place, would be a strong criterion. However, given the relative youth of the Nigerian organizations we decided to include two historical case studies (China and Brazil) in our comparative sample as we could look at them in a long-term perspective and answer our fourth question about their potential 'trigger' effect.

These criteria were mainly helpful for us for *identifying* potential PoE. One of the main tasks of the research teams or individual researchers was then to find appropriate indicators and supporting evidence to substantiate our decision to include the organization as a PoE. The evidence is presented in the case study chapters.

We now take our definitions and criteria and take a look at the literature which at least implicitly shares our understanding of PoE. What do these studies tell us about why and how PoE emerge, how they persist and whether they have a trigger effect on other public organizations?

Pockets of effectiveness: a review of marginal monologues

Unfortunately, 'marginal monologues' captures the state of the PoE literature well. 'PoE literature' refers to the academic literature that deals with PoE and PoE-related phenomena in line with the definition provided above, irrespective of the specific terms that are used. The literature that focuses on them explicitly is very limited. Other studies sometimes mention this phenomenon when discussing public sector reform issues more broadly.

The PoE literature is 'marginal' because it is neither in the mainstream of academic development studies and social sciences nor of current development policymakers' debates. We also refer to it as 'monologues' because a coherent terminology has not been established so far and authors often work in isolation from each other, not making reference to related literature.

In 2008, however, David Leonard published a 'propositional inventory' in which he reviewed, structured and condensed the then existing PoE literature (Leonard 2008, 2010). Since he provides a comprehensive overview of the literature, our review concentrates on a more narrow body of work. We look at studies that either share our focus on public organizations or are of particular relevance for PoE studies with this focus. This implies that we do not include other potentially insightful studies such as those on 'co-production' arrangements for service delivery in developing countries (see Ostrom 1997; Evans 1997; White and Robinson 1998; Joshi and Moore 2004), for example.

We also exclude studies with a narrow explicit or implicit focus on leadership and individual managers (Krishna et al. 1997). Studies that do not primarily focus on public organizations but civil society, community or religious organizations are also left out (Esman and Uphoff 1984; Jain 1994; Uphoff 1994; Krishna, Uphoff and Esman 1997; Uphoff, Esman and Krishna 1998). That leaves us with four PoE studies to review. The authors of these studies are Arturo Israel (1987), David Leonard (1991), Judith Tendler (1997), and Merilee S. Grindle (1997) together with Mary E. Hilderbrand and Grindle (1997).

Specificity, competition and institutional development: Arturo Israel

Arturo Israel's contribution is the oldest and at the same time the most abstract one reviewed here. In his study he tries to identify universal features that make organizations perform more or less effectively, especially in developing countries. In the late 1980s when 'institutions' began to return to academic and policy debates, the then head of the World Bank's Public Sector Management and Private Sector Development Division published his book in an attempt to better explain institutional development and performance in developing countries. His findings are based on his own experiences as well as ex-post evaluation studies and other documentation of World Bank financed development projects from the 1960s to the 1970s, in which 159 principal institutions are covered. Apart from some 'standard explanations'[9] (Israel 1987: 31–32) the focus of his study is on two alternative explanations: specificity and competition.

Two groups of elements define 'specificity' for Israel. The first one contains the extent to which objectives, the methods for achieving them as well as ways of controlling these achievements can be defined. The second group of elements includes the *effects* of the activity in terms of intensity, temporal immediateness or time lag, the number of people affected and realistic possibilities of tracing these effects (ibid.: 4–5). His hypothesis is that 'the higher the degree of specificity, the more intense, immediate, identifiable, and focused will be the effects of a good or bad activity' (ibid.: 49). This implies that the positive or negative incentives for better performance are also stronger and more direct. To Israel, specificity therefore is an "'automatic" determinant of institutional performance' and 'imposes a discipline [on actors] which is derived from the intrinsic nature of the activity' (ibid.: 49). Two of his main conclusions on specificity are that it is independent of other internal and external factors and that a higher degree of specificity produces better organizational performance.

The second factor in Israel's study, competition, includes alternative dimensions apart from the traditional economic market 'competition'. These 'competition surrogates' (ibid.: 89) are pressures produced by clients, beneficiaries, suppliers, the political establishment, controlling and regulatory agencies and an internal competitive atmosphere created through managerial measures. While Israel argues that competition might produce strong incentives for better performance, he sees it as a 'double-edged sword' (ibid.: 101) which could at the same time also bring about negative results.

Israel concludes that the incentives produced by specificity and competitiveness are so powerful that they have a critical impact on the performance of organizations.[10] Therefore, sectors, organizations and activities with a high degree of specificity and strong competitive elements are likely to perform better than those with low specificity and weak competitive elements. He refers to technical and financial activities such as jet engine maintenance and other high-technology activities or banking as examples for strong specificity and high competitiveness. Educational counselling or agricultural extension work are listed as examples for low specificity and low competitiveness. Based on his findings, Israel also recommends managerial strategies for producing surrogates for specificity and competition in low specificity and weak competition sectors.

Successful rural development in Kenya: David K. Leonard

David Leonard's study *African Successes: Four Public Managers of Kenyan Rural Development* (1991) traces the professional and non-professional biographies of four civil servants in rural development. It is based on extensive fieldwork and is extraordinarily rich in terms of historical and biographical contextualization. While Leonard's focus is on successful leaders, it is included here because his findings are much more comprehensive and include conclusions about exceptional organizational performance in a hostile environment.

Leonard's argument contains two elements, one focussing on the individual dimension of managers and another one looking at the political economy context. On the first and more important one, Leonard stresses two more general points, describes eleven attributes of successful managers or organizations and finally highlights three of them as most important, all influenced by one common factor.

The two general points Leonard makes are the importance of good institutional inheritance (ibid.: 254) as well as the fact that the successful managers did not passively receive inputs from the political context but rather 'exhibited ... leadership and skill at manipulating the environment of their organizations' (ibid.: 253) and thereby actively shaped it. Against this background he identifies eleven attributes of successful management.

The first attribute is 'political connections and organizational development', which Leonard uses to describe the fact that all managers used political connections up to the president to protect the autonomy of their organizations, ensure support and use this autonomy and resources to carry out their responsibilities professionally. Attribute two is 'professional concern with public policy and organizational mission' and indicates that the administrators had well-defined organizational missions, were entrepreneurial, concerned about the public interest and pursued internal administration as part of the larger goal of their organizations and their place in a larger professional conception of public service. In short: they were 'committed professionals' (ibid.: 259) with strong professional identities.

They also shared attribute number three, 'professional integrity' in the sense of strong ethics they adhered to, although there was some variation with regard to this factor. Almost all of them were good at acquiring donor resources and managed the 'Africanization' of their respective organizations fairly well so as to avoid accusations of ethnic bias. Attribute six 'being a "nationalist"' also refers to remaining above ethnic ties and not compromising the organization's performance for it. 'Staff management' is attribute number seven and refers to the selection of staff, setting high standards but also protecting and supporting staff with good performance records, being accessible and caring about staff's problems. In return, the managers enjoyed staff loyalty and effort.

Competition in combination with the effective use of Management Information Systems (MIS) is attribute eight while some degree of delegation is number nine, but not all were effective at that. Next is 'risk taking' which refers to making crucial decisions or policy suggestions that are important for the organizations. The four managers did this because they believed in their judgement and had the financial independence as well as alternative job options, allowing them to risk losing their present jobs. The final attribute Leonard finds is 'drive' for hard work which includes working long hours and with a strong degree of self-discipline.

Leonard emphasizes three of these attributes as most critical for managerial effectiveness: 'organizational mission, professional integrity, and risk taking [which] are all influenced by professionalization' (ibid.: 272). Rigorous training and socialization within a professional discipline, according to him, produce strong professional values that are ideally nurtured in professional associations and produce ethical and effective professional leaders.

The second element of Leonard's framework is political economy. He argues that for a pocket of administrative performance to exist there has to be a political demand for the very service this organization provides (ibid.: 300). He sees both a 'professional group sustaining its values' (ibid.: 300) and political demand as necessary conditions for administrative performance.

30 *Michael Roll*

Sectoral turnarounds in Brazil's periphery: Judith Tendler

Judith Tendler's study (1997) looks at the success of sectoral policy reform programmes (preventive health, employment, agricultural extension and public procurement) but organizations are of crucial importance to her study. One of the outstanding features of her book is that she masters the challenge of linking contextual factors with internal organizational developments and vice versa.

Tendler starts by criticizing mainstream development thinking for focussing on poor governance and importing reform concepts from completely different contexts to developing countries. Moreover, she claims that in the literature existing studies of the improved performance of organizations in OECD (Organisation for Economic Co-operation and Development) countries are often ignored and even contradicted. She refers to this body of work as the 'industrial performance and workplace transformation' (IPWT) literature which has identified the importance of worker dedication through greater autonomy, self-management, multitask jobs and participation (ibid.: 4–5).

Tendler identifies five central themes that explain good performance in her case studies. The first one is exceptionally strong dedication of workers to their jobs. This dedication came about as a result of being appreciated by the communities which they served and a growing trust-based relationship between them and these communities. The creation of a sense of 'calling' and 'mission' is the second theme. This was achieved through public information campaigns, performance awards, public screening for recruits, orientation programmes and the popularization of the success through the media. Tendler stresses that these were partly unintended results of government action.

A large variety of tasks that workers carried out is theme three. Workers had greater autonomy and used it to respond to their clients' needs. They carried out tasks which were not immediately part of their responsibilities. This was combined with new accountability mechanisms. An informal source of accountability was the motivation of civil servants not to disappoint the newly gained trust by their clients. Another part was contributed by stronger monitoring of service delivery and civil servants by communities, whom the government provided with information about their rights and about how public services should work.

The final theme five that explains improved performance contradicts common assumptions about decentralization because Tendler identifies an unorthodox three-way dynamic of an activist state government, local governments and civil society. The state government carried out some tasks that are not usually regarded as higher level government's responsibilities such as outreach to poor people, hiring and training of municipal workers and encouraging and assisting the establishment of civic associations. These associations in turn demanded better performance from local and state governments which contributed to increasing capacity on both sides and improving accountability. Tendler shows how these five elements were closely related to each other which was often the result of deliberate planning but sometimes also an entirely unintended outcome. Eventually however, and in combination with each other, these elements led to better public service delivery and improved accountability.

Organizational culture and performance in developing countries: Merilee S. Grindle

Merilee S. Grindle's work together with Mary E. Hilderbrand (1997) as well her own article (1997) are based on a World Bank-funded set of studies on capacity building in six developing countries from Africa, Latin America and South Asia.[11]

Grindle's work has the most explicit PoE focus. While Israel (1987) looks for universal factors that make organizations perform well, Leonard (1991) focuses primarily on leadership and Tendler (1997) on public policy programmes, Grindle specifically asks why 'there are organizations that perform relatively well, despite dauntingly unfavourable contexts and despite overall poor public sector performance' (1997: 481). In a nutshell her answer is: because of their exceptionally positive organizational culture:

> These organizations are characterized by cultures that emphasize commitment to organizational goals, a strong sense of professionalism, efficiency, elitism, and hard work. A strong sense of mission, effective managerial practice, and high expectations about employee performance were factors that led organizations to perform well, while some autonomy in personnel matters allowed a mission to be identified and enabled skilled managers to have some room to manoeuvre in setting standards for their organizations.
>
> (ibid.: 491).

Three aspects of her work are emphasized here because they offer new and surprising insights. The first aspect is that instead of strong hierarchies and control mechanisms the factors that contributed to good organizational performance were wide consultation with staff, participation, teamwork, leading by example and open non-hierarchical styles of interacting with staff, in combination with clear rules and procedures (ibid.: 489–90).

Second, Hilderbrand and Grindle (1997) make an important point about the relevance of specific skills training and capacity building on which so many development interventions have focussed and continue to focus on. They find that 'human resource constraints are more likely to derive from the failure to provide people with meaningful jobs and to utilize their skills effectively than from problems related to training per se' (ibid.: 34). The importance of meaningful work and the motivation it provides compared to the emphasis of donor-sponsored training programmes on often contextless training and capacity building is striking.

32   *Michael Roll*

The third aspect is that the sense of mission or 'mystique' (Grindle 1997: 488–89) was more important for explaining performance than rules, regulations, or even remuneration and control (Hilderbrand and Grindle 1997: 56). Members of staff of such organizations shared professional norms, cherished the reputation of their organizations, believed that they were selected because of their skills and had a strong sense of service to their country (Grindle 1997: 489). Grindle concludes that these features created a positive 'organizational culture' that even offset resource shortage and poor working conditions.

From monologues to dialogues

By concluding this literature review we do not attempt to integrate these findings into a single coherent framework but rather to point out what they have in common and how they challenge public sector performance and reform orthodoxy. Due to its rather functionalist approach, Israel's study will only play a marginal role in this discussion.

Perhaps most interesting is what these studies have identified as *not* being important or of secondary importance for explaining organizational performance. This includes formal organizational structures and hierarchies, monetary incentives, control and – apart from Israel – competition. While these factors are by no means irrelevant, the authors agree that they are not decisive.[12] Public sector reform orthodoxy on the other hand has long regarded these factors as critical for better performance, and many public sector reform programmes were based on these assumptions.

Leonard, Tendler and Grindle on the other hand find that positive motivational factors, which give the individual civil servant professional as well as personal satisfaction and that are nurtured in a team where certain values and expectations are shared, explain exceptional performance. They refer to similar factors such as a sense of mission, professional values, skill- and performance-orientation and a general sense of public service. Hierarchy, formal organizations and monetary incentives are important but at least above a certain threshold they are the foundation based on which these other factors then do or do not make a difference.

A third commonality is the finding that political demands and organizational autonomy are seen as facilitating rather than directly contributing factors. While improved performance might not be possible without them, their existence is no guarantee either. While the authors agree on this they differ in how explicitly they include external factors in their analyses and pay attention to the interaction of external and internal factors. Leonard and Tendler put more emphasis on this than Grindle, who focuses almost exclusively on internal factors.

Which of our four research questions are being addressed and to some degree answered by these five authors? Question one on 'why' PoE emerge is explicitly addressed only by Israel (1987) and to some degree by Leonard (1991). Tendler also provides some thoughts on this. On the other hand, all three authors deal with and partially answer question two on 'how' PoE emerge. Many of their findings on this are quite coherent.

The issue of 'persistence' as an effective organization is not explicitly addressed by the authors. The same is true for our research question four which asks whether PoE can 'trigger' more comprehensive change. Nevertheless, Grindle and Leonard are optimistic that their explanations hold great potential. Grindle speculates that they could be the '"missing ingredient" in the disappointing results of many civil service reforms' (Grindle 1997: 491). Leonard also thinks that his findings could be 'the keys to the successes Africa has already experienced' and 'the means for creating more of them' (Leonard 1991: 301).

It turns out that the four studies under review contribute most strongly to answering the 'how' question and that many of their findings support or complement each other (see table 2.1). To a lesser degree, the studies present findings that help to answer the other three questions. While we hope to contribute new answers to these relatively understudied questions, on how PoE emerge, we already have a strong and relatively coherent body of literature with which we can then compare our findings.

Three hypotheses on PoE

Based on his comprehensive review of the PoE literature, Leonard (2008) condensed the findings into five 'mega-hypotheses'. They summarize the major factors that researchers have identified as crucial for explaining why and how PoE emerge. For our purposes, we have further condensed Leonard's five into three 'mega-hypotheses':

Table 2.1 PoE research questions primarily addressed in previous research

	Why do PoE emerge?	How do PoE emerge?	How do PoE persist?	Trigger function
Israel (1987)	X (function)	(X)		
Leonard (1991)	(X)	X (internal/external)	(X)	
Tendler (1997)		X (external/internal)	(X)	
Hilderbrand and Grindle (1997); Grindle (1997)		X		

Note: If two criteria are mentioned in brackets in the 'emergence' column, the first one mentioned is what the respective author emphasizes or refers to primarily.

34   *Michael Roll*

- Hypothesis 1 (internal factors): An organization's effectiveness in a challenging context is determined by *leadership and management* – i.e. how it does its tasks (based on Leonard 2008: 15).

The hypothesis is that the impact that these practices have on public organizations' performance is independent of function and political context. These managerial attributes include good management practices, performance-based personnel systems, meritocratic recruitment, adequate resource mobilization and competent and honest resource management, goals that give the organization external and internal legitimacy, flexibility in setting and implementing goals and strong commitment, amongst others. Of the PoE studies discussed above, Grindle (1997) and Hilderbrand and Grindle (1997) support this hypothesis while Leonard (1991) does so with qualifications.

- Hypothesis 2 (external or political economy factors): The underlying *political economy* in which an organization is placed ultimately will overcome and dominate all other causal factors and thus determine what effectiveness is possible (based on Leonard 2008: 25).

This hypothesis is about how the political system is organized, which logics, incentives and whose interests dominate and how various groups are incorporated into this process. It assumes that these factors that are external to the organization have a direct impact on the organization's performance. Interest groups seem to be particularly important, since effectiveness is more likely to arise if the potential beneficiaries are organized based on their interests and not in patron-client networks. Although most PoE authors admit that this factor has some relevance, only Leonard (1991) and Tendler (1997) include it more systematically.

- Hypothesis 3 (function or task-related factors): The *function* an organization performs determines the degree of specificity of the benefits it delivers and the incentives it provides to its staff and therefore an organization's effectiveness (based on Leonard 2008: 18).

According to this hypothesis, function works through the specificity of its benefits, its technological attributes, the type of workforce it attracts and the incentives it provides to staff. It assumes that function is independent of management and political context and eventually also more powerful. This is basically Arturo Israel's argument (1987) although Leonard (1991) also applies parts of this explanation.

In conclusion, three possible groups of factors seem to exist that may be helpful for explaining why PoE emerge, based on our interpretation of Leonard's propositional inventory (2008): internal factors, external or political economy factors and function- or task-related factors. Most research on public sector reform focuses exclusively on management-related factors while political and functional aspects have often been ignored. However, it is obvious that explaining 'real world' PoE is not such a clear cut issue in which two of these hypotheses will be rejected and the remaining one explains why and how PoE emerge and persist. It is more likely that a sequence of interactions of factors will provide the best answer.

The condensed hypotheses provided some direction for our original study in Nigeria. While we chose an explorative qualitative instead of a hypothesis-testing research approach, the hypotheses provided a heuristic framework and inspiration for thinking more systematically about PoE, especially during the earlier phases of our research.

A framework for pockets of effectiveness research

In this section we outline our analytical framework for studying PoE. We begin with a key insight from organizational sociology that is useful for understanding and conceptualising the interaction of different factors that may explain the emergence and persistence of PoE. We then single out analytical dimensions and distinctions that may be essential for our study. Following on from that, we suggest a broader political sociology perspective for this study.

Organizations and environments

How do organizations and their environments and how do external factors, functional and internal factors interact? Organizational sociology provides some insights that we can build our conceptualization on. The most important insight for our study is on the relationship between organizations and their environment.

In the 1960s the open system model entered organizational sociology (Thompson 1967; Weick 1969). The environment of organizations was no longer ignored or regarded as determining the actions and performance of organizations. Different kinds of relationships, exchange and influence were studied and conceptualized such as 'loose coupling' (Weick 1982/2001). One of the key insights of this literature was that within their respective contexts, organizations do have considerable autonomy and agency to perform irrespective of how adverse or supporting their environments are. Organizations can block, let through, transform, selectively process and implement but definitely shape environmental inputs as well as to some even the immediate environment itself.

While this agency also exists in developing countries it might be more fragile there because the rule of law and administrative procedures are often not as strongly institutionalized which makes direct interventions by powerful actors easier. We conclude that although contextual challenges exist, organizations and their leaders can have significant agency depending on how well they 'manage' and are able to transform their environment by skilfully using the resources at their disposal in the respective context.

36 *Michael Roll*

Analytical dimensions and distinctions

Based on theoretical considerations and the PoE literature review, we arrived at four key analytical dimensions and distinctions that warrant special attention.

Emergence and persistence: For analytical purposes, we decided to distinguish the two phases of the emergence of an organization as a PoE and its persistence. Leonard calls these phases 'initiation' and 'consolidation' (Leonard 2008: 10). We use 'emergence' instead for the period where the PoE becomes a PoE in line with our definition and the criteria. We prefer 'persistence' over 'consolidation' to emphasize that in a politico-administrative environment that does not encourage public sector effectiveness, a PoE has to permanently fight for survival and defend its mode of work and performance. It is therefore often struggling to persist against the odds. It is our assumption that PoE and their managers have to explore all sorts of creative strategies and means in order to manage to persist as a PoE. Depending on whether an organization is just emerging as a PoE or struggling to persist as one, the importance of the same factors such as leadership, political protection and others might vary considerably. That is why this distinction is crucial for the analysis.

Relative effectiveness and internal variation: The *relative* nature of the PoE's effectiveness is part of our definition. They are effective, relative to the context they operate in and relative to other public organizations in the same context. Media and international organizations tend to 'hype' reasonably effective organizations when they find them, which makes it difficult but even more necessary to carefully examine whether the organization is actually performing sufficiently well to qualify as a PoE or not. Another aspect is the internal variation with regard to effectiveness within PoE. Some departments and organizational units may be much more effective than others. A detailed examination of the internal workings of an effective organization would allow us to study the factors that led to some units performing better than others. While some of our case studies managed to analyse the internal structures and workings to some degree, this turned out to be particularly difficult and would have required either a more long-term ethnographic approach or careful survey research, both of which were not part of our research design. However, for future research we think that more attention to internal diversity in terms of power and performance is essential for really understanding the 'black box' that public organizations, including PoE, tend to remain in most research.[13]

Dynamic 'lifecycle' perspective and 'turning points': Apart from emergence and persistence there are other phases that a PoE might pass through throughout its organizational lifecycle. A PoE can but does not necessarily have to degenerate from a PoE into a 'regular' organization that is as ineffective as others in the same environment. Moreover, it is likely to have its up and down phases while struggling to persist. Therefore, a dynamic analytical research perspective that pays attention to process, time and sequence is required. This lifecycle perspective is of a heuristic nature and does not presume any particular sequence of specific phases. It should not be confused with the business lifecycle models with clearly defined subsequent phases that are prominent in management studies. Two additional time-related issue need to be raised: institutional inheritance and 'turning points'.

Organizations with a positive institutional inheritance and reputation for performance have a considerable advantage over those with a negative inheritance. However, this effect does not necessarily last indefinitely and can weaken or even become a burden over time.

We use the concept 'turning point' to refer to points in time or rather periods of time in which organizations either emerge as PoE or degenerate from a PoE into a 'regular' and ineffective organization (see Abbott 1997). These phases are strategically important for our analysis since they narrow down the focus for identifying which contextual or organizational factors have led to increased or decreased effectiveness. Therefore, 'turning points' provide a useful analytical focus.

Leadership: Are PoE basically just 'pockets of good leadership'? Many studies on organizational success, particularly in management studies, seem to suggest that. We argue that this is due to the fact that these studies typically look at the cases from a 'leadership perspective', largely ignoring or even misinterpreting other, possibly relevant factors. While we certainly do not underestimate leadership as an explanatory factor, we share Judith Tendler's reservations. Her study showed that many of the achievements she found were 'not attributable to strongly intentional leadership' (Tendler 1997: 14). Instead, many of the performance improvements rather emerged as indirect side-effects of the 'real' reforms (Tendler 1997: 17). She continues that 'good leadership' could also not explain why some organizations had good leaders and did not perform well and why some organizations continued to perform well despite a change in leadership while others did not (Tendler 1997: 18).

How then do we deal with this ambivalent factor? First, as much as possible we tried to get first-hand accounts of how organizations developed historically in order to avoid ending up with ex-post rationalizations of motives and strategies. Such 'intentionalist' accounts tend to overemphasize the importance of leadership to the detriment of more complex social processes, such as the interactions of actors with other actors and institutions that produce results that were at least partially unintended. PoE in public sectors could be such unintended outcomes. Furthermore, from the very beginning of our study we were cautious and reflected on the danger of neglecting other explanatory factors and mistakenly simply attribute effectiveness to leaders. That is even more important in countries where, like in many developing countries, leaders are celebrated and a 'personality cult' is created around them. This makes it very difficult to analytically disentangle the various factors and account for the actual contribution of leadership.

We therefore agreed before the research was undertaken that whenever the question of leadership arises in the field, we would continue to ask interviewees but also ourselves and the data more detailed and 'deeper' questions such as the following ones: How and why did that particular person manage

38 *Michael Roll*

to turn the organization around while others did not? Which contextual circumstances allowed this person to introduce change? Which organizational procedures and rules did the person introduce and actually implement, why did he or she do that and how? Are the changes that have been introduced sufficiently institutionalized to be sustainable, so that the organization can continue to perform well as a PoE when this particular leader leaves the organization?

We paid particular attention to this last point of leadership change. What happens when the leader, especially a somewhat charismatic 'founding' leader, hands over to his or her successor? Does it affect the effectiveness or other features of the organization? If it does, how so and if not, then why not? Individuals *are* important, particularly if an organization is newly established and has to find its feet and both consolidate internally and build a reputation externally. In our analyses we account for that but go beyond individuals to look at social, institutional and organizational mechanisms and innovations which made public organizations more effective in hostile environments.

Triggering change and state-society bargaining

So far we have focussed on the public organizations and PoE themselves as our units of analysis. We now put them into a broader context and call this our political sociology perspective. After all, public administration and its reform are inherently political processes through which power is exercised, distributed and shifted. This is what we want to focus on. The first part of our political sociology perspective looks at the politico-administrative environment in which PoE operate. In line with our fourth research question we ask whether the very existence of PoE within this environment may also have an effect on the institutional and operational logics that shape this environment. Did PoE trigger changes of other public organizations in this very environment or even the politico-administrative environment itself? We see three possible mechanisms of how this could work.

The first mechanism is the *demonstration mechanism*. It could be argued that a well-performing public organization that provides public goods and services in an environment in which most public organizations do not do that will attract considerable attention. Whether that attention is created internally within the government or publicly through the media or NGOs does not really matter. For various reasons the government could then decide or be successfully lobbied to take measures that allow selected other public organizations to copy some of the key features of that organization and try to also become more effective.

The second possibility, the *contagion mechanism*, is more direct. If civil servants see another organization performing well in the same politico-administrative environment under the same restrictions and with similar resources, they might want to improve their own organization's performance as well, independent of government intervention. If we assume some degree of

PoE: review and analytical framework 39

organizational autonomy, intra-administrative competition and some general commitment to the country's development this is a plausible mechanism.

The final channel could be called the *transplantation mechanism*. In that case the members of staff of the PoE are moving to other public organizations, take up other powerful positions in the media or the private sector or go into politics. In their new positions they could use their expertise, reform-mindedness and PoE experience and credibility to try to reform another organization along similar lines. These three mechanisms do not cover all possibilities but they seem to be the most plausible ones and we will continue to work with them.

The second part of our political sociology framework goes beyond the confines of the politico-administrative system. It is broader both in terms of time and in terms of the actors its looks at. It asks what the contribution of PoE could be to (re)building state-society relations and eventually maybe even accountability and a minimal degree of state legitimacy in the medium to long run. In many developing countries citizens perceive the state as incompetent, non-responsive, careless, corrupt, self-interested and often outright illegitimate. It is usually the very police officers, customs officials, market supervisors, doctors and other civil servants who are supposed to provide public services that make life more difficult and certainly more expensive, especially for poor people. As a response 'the state' is either approached strategically (Roll 2004) or avoided wherever possible; people opt for 'exiting from the state' (Osaghae 1999).

Rebuilding state-society relations in these countries is a precondition for accountability, state legitimacy and democracy and for improving the everyday lives of citizens in these countries in the long run. On the basis of the processes through which representation and accountability have emerged in early modern Europe, we argue that the most likely way that this can happen is through some form of state-society bargaining. Following historical examples, this essentially involves two processes: the extraction of resources from society by the state and some degree of political participation and public goods or service provision in return. The issue of taxation and its paramount importance for state-building and democracy in developing countries has entered the mainstream of development research and policy in recent years (see Moore 1998, 2001, 2004; Moore and Rakner 2002; Bräutigam, Fjeldstad and Moore 2008; DFID 2009; OECD 2010; Prichard 2010; Prichard and Leonard 2010).[14] In its most basic form the argument is that state-building and accountability between state and society only emerge if they are forced to bargain about resources with each other. On the demand side of bargaining, the early modern European state needed resources from private wealthy groups and individuals, primarily to fight wars. On the supply side are these wealthy groups and individuals who requested political participation in exchange for their contributions.[15] The famous slogan 'no taxation without representation' that was coined during the Boston Tea Party, captures this essence well. At a later stage, basic public goods and services such as security

40 *Michael Roll*

were also demanded. While governments no longer collect taxes for waging wars and parliaments have long become institutions in their own right, the basic logic still holds: in return for extracting taxes from citizens the state has to legitimize itself through governance and the provision of public goods and services. Taxation may then provide an incentive for citizens to demand representation, accountability and public services from the state (see Ross 2004; Prichard 2009). While these authors have convincingly argued that taxation is of crucial importance for state building in today's developing countries, the same point has not been made for the provision of public goods and services. What long-term political relevance does the provision of public goods and services by the state have in developing countries for the process of state building? And what role do the public organizations that actually provide or are supposed to provide these goods and services play in this context?

We suggest that the provision of basic public goods and services in these countries may be as crucial to the process of state building as is taxation. It could be a key ingredient to the crucial process of '(re)building' the state in developing countries. States earn part of their legitimacy from providing public goods and services to the general public. Especially in largely discredited states and bureaucracies the provision of essential public goods and services such as the rule of law, security and public order, freedom of speech – not to talk of drinking water, health services and education – could help to 'reaffirm confidence in public authority' (Joshi 2006: 125). While taxation can be seen as the 'bottom up' incentive for citizens to bargain with the state for political participation and public services, the increasingly effective provision of these public services could be a kind of 'top down' teaser to begin to bridge the enormous trust and legitimacy gap that exists between the state and citizens. Or, as Joshi puts it, 'effective delivery of services can lead citizens to re-engage with the state and can be a path towards a virtuous cycle of engagement and accountability in the broader political sphere' (2006: 125).[16] Banerjee and Duflo (2011) have recently made a very similar point when arguing that if 'the governments start to deliver, people will start taking politics more seriously and put pressure on the government to deliver more, rather than opting out … ' (Banerjee and Duflo 2011: 262).

While taxation may provide the stronger incentive for citizens to bargain with the state, the importance of overcoming the distrust and suspicion towards public authority in developing countries should not be underestimated. This is even more relevant given the fact that taxation in developing countries often implies excessive or arbitrary extraction of money from citizens (see Fjeldstad and Therkildsen 2008), which then further delegitimizes the state.

While both incentives are therefore important in their own right, their impact is likely to be strongest when they are combined and citizens feel that there are responsible public managers who transform their contributions into goods and services from which they benefit. Whether or not this scenario is too optimistic and too much at odds with the empirical situation on the ground in developing countries remains to be seen. We can only give a first hint at that in the last chapter of this book, where we return to the question of the broader societal and political transformative potential that PoE might or might not have.

Notes

1 On impartiality and government, see Rothstein and Teorell (2008).
2 See, for example, on the British Navy during the age of fighting sail, Fischer and Lundgren (1975) and more recently Allen (2002).
3 Through his involvement as an international peer reviewer in the FES Nigeria 'Pockets of Effectiveness in Nigeria' project, David Leonard has also started to use the term 'pockets of effectiveness' since 2009 (see Leonard 2010 and Prichard and Leonard 2010; personal communication).
4 While that means that all PoE in our sample were created through deliberate decisions, it does of course not imply that all public organizations that were intended to be effective, actually became PoE.
5 We deliberately avoid calling this a 'neopatrimonial' system. While we acknowledge the contributions of the concept that is especially popular in African Studies (Eisenstadt 1973; Eisenstadt and Lemarchand 1981; Médard 1982, 1991; Clapham 1982; Bratton and van de Walle 1994; Erdmann and Engel 2007; von Soest 2007; von Soest 2009) but increasingly also in other fields and area studies (see von Soest, Bechle and Korte 2011; Bach 2011; Bach and Gazibo 2012), it is still fraught with problems. Some of the main problems include a vague definition, the absence of a convincing operationalization, and the fact that many studies use it to assume instead of examine the systemic features the very term is supposed to capture (see Therkildsen 2005; Pitcher, Moran and Johnston 2009). While suggestions have been made in recent contributions for addressing some of these problems (Beekers and van Gool 2012; Therkildsen forthcoming), for the purpose of this study it is not necessary to engage in this debate in further detail.
6 For a comprehensive overview and discussion of theories of organizational performance and service delivery improvement with a focus on public organizations, see Talbot (2010). He also provides an overview of the 'organizational effectiveness' literature that dominated organizational studies, public administration and management from the mid-1940s until the early 1980s (ibid.: 145–51).
7 The list we wanted to use for identifying PoE originally also included the criteria 'strong mission to contribute to the public good', 'public accessibility', 'responsiveness/accountability' and 'efficiency'. This original list was based on Heredia and Schneider (2003: 7). We dropped these criteria in order not to narrow our focus and therefore our analysis prematurely.
8 For the case of Nigeria, see Human Rights Watch (2010) on the role of the police and Human Rights Watch (2012) on the security forces more generally. However, while Nigeria's police can hardly be regarded as effective, this claim is sometimes made with regard to the military in local newspapers.
9 The 'standard explanations' Israel finds and discusses are, in order of increasing relevance: exogenous factors, outstanding individuals or groups of individuals, effective planning and implementation of institutional development programmes, effective application of management techniques, adequate relative prices, and sufficient political commitment (Israel 1987: 31–32).
10 The similarities of his conclusions with the New Public Management agenda are obvious. Although he works with similar theoretical approaches and models like New Public Management proponents, his analysis is rooted in his data from developing countries rather than based on OECD country experiences and reforms.
11 The study countries were Ghana, Morocco, Tanzania, the Central African Republic, Bolivia and Sri Lanka.

42   Michael Roll

12 Owusu (2006a) deviates from this consensus. In his study of poor and well-performing public organizations in Ghana, he identifies two major differences between the two groups: well-performing organizations offered higher remuneration and used competitive recruitment procedures. However, without discussing this in more detail and with reference to Grindle's work he concedes that changes in the organizational cultures of the poorly performing organizations are necessary in order for them to improve their performance (Owusu 2006b; see also Owusu 2012).
13 See Therkildsen (forthcoming) for a fascinating study based on a survey of public servants, complemented by focus group discussions, about management and motivation in the public sector in Tanzania and Uganda. For the study, organizations were selected based on their relative performance, and one organization was chosen that performed above and another one that performed below average in each category.
14 This comes at the same time as sociology and especially historical and comparative sociology re-discover taxation and 'fiscal sociology' (see Martin, Mehrotra and Prasad 2009) which used to be one of the major topics of early political economists, especially Joseph A. Schumpeter (1918).
15 For important contributions to the historical and comparative sociology and social sciences of state formation in early modern Europe in which these points are made, see Levi (1988), Tilly (1990) and Ertman (1997), among others.
16 There are indications that different public goods and services impact differently on the legitimacy of new democracies. Bratton and Lewis (2007) use data from Nigeria to show that political goods, especially civil and political rights as well as trustworthy leaders, are more durable than previously thought, even in contexts where socioeconomic development is not forthcoming. However, the importance of governance performance on implementing specific economic policies which provide socioeconomic benefits increases over time. The crucial point is that they complement rather than replace political goods in impacting on the legitimacy of democracy, according to Bratton and Lewis.

3 Pockets of effectiveness

Lessons from the long twentieth century in China and Taiwan

Julia C. Strauss

Introduction

The contemporary phrase 'pockets of effectiveness' is very much of its own early twenty-first century period, and as such its evolution is worth reflecting on. Notions of effectiveness, and its closely related cousins, efficiency and productivity, are key components in a cluster of attributes that at their core comprise the institutions of markets, legal orders and bureaucratic organizations. Legal and bureaucratic orders by definition require impersonality: that individuals be processed by an impersonal order that subjects everyone to the same rules, and that breaks down holistic categories (work, personhood) into measurable and divisible units measured against a particular standard (a rule, a law, a precedent).

However personalized or distorted the operation of particular markets might be in practice, markets are almost always conceived of as an impersonal set of transactions (the sum of individual decisions made in the pursuit of self-interest). Although the legal order might be skewed in favour of those with property and financial resources, and those with social status or political power might be able to sidestep bureaucratic rules, as ideal types, the trio of institutions of impersonal law, bureaucracy, and markets is so firmly associated with 'modernity' that the relative absence of any of these elements is labelled corrupt, ineffective, and neo-patrimonial.

'Effectiveness' does not by definition require an impersonal order, and historically effectiveness was not particularly tied to impersonal orders. The term came in to the English language as early as the fourteenth century (Oxford English Dictionary n.d.). One only needed to be as 'effective' as customary norms dictated, or in action more effective than the competition. Generals won and lost battles; states rose and fell because of their relative effectiveness in their own time and circumstances, often without particular efficiency, productivity, or recourse to impersonality. In contrast, the administrative concept of 'efficiency' as a ratio of inputs to outcomes only came into its contemporary common usage in the early twentieth century, with the institutionalization of economics as a discipline, and it assuredly does presuppose impersonality.

44   *Julia C. Strauss*

The term 'productive' bridges both notions of effectiveness and efficiency; with its roots in the medieval period via Norman French, 'productive' originally referred to bringing something about, the creation of concrete goods or ideas, and, from the time of Adam Smith onward, that which creates economic or commercial wealth (Oxford English Dictionary n.d.). For most of recorded history, governments were certainly not efficient, and were often not even particularly effective. They only needed to be more effective than their neighbours and effective enough to internally cohere and maintain a degree of social order in the territories over which they ruled. Defined by this rough rule of survival, Charles Tilly usefully reminds us that the vast majority of states in Europe from the late medieval through the early modern periods were patently ineffective – they failed and were absorbed by more effective neighbours (Tilly 1975). Of those that did survive, behaviour that we would now call corrupt, suspect, patrimonial, wasteful, and deeply inefficient was the norm even for states that in the nineteenth and twentieth century went on to export significantly more rigorous notions of efficiency and effectiveness.

Thus any discussion about pockets of effectiveness must ask at the outset: are we primarily concerned with efficiency, which lends itself to at least relatively transparent criteria of measurement, or productivity, which encompasses elements of efficiency and effectiveness? In practice, the kinds of policy areas that lend themselves to counting and credible claims about 'efficiency' may or may not also lend themselves to 'effectiveness'. Conversely there are any number of policy areas of great importance (in public health, in women's emancipation, and in environmental conservation and restoration) ratios. In other cases, parts of wider projects that do lend themselves to determinations of efficiency may end up displacing equally important parts of wider core state goals. For example, since 1998 the government of the People's Republic of China has taken very seriously its profound issues of deforestation, soil erosion, desertification and environmental destruction. Its response has been to intensify tree planting campaigns to get trees into the ground quickly in vulnerable areas. In terms of measurable and countable efficiency it has done a remarkable job of reversing forest destruction, increasing its carbon sink, and dramatically increasing its forested area. The rush to get quick growing trees into the ground has also resulted in huge tracts of monocultural stands that have so ruined biodiversity, wiped out wildlife, and are at risk for disease that in the eyes of their critics they are nothing more than 'green deserts' (see Strauss 2009). Depending on venue, officials in the Bureau of Forestry and in the national government claim that these tree planting campaigns display the core desirable programmatic features of efficiency, productivity, and effectiveness. In this context, efficiency is measured by per unit cost in labour and seedlings. Productivity refers to the ways in which the particular incentives for the farmers engaged in the planting have been deployed. And effectiveness is affirmed by stating the total number of acres planted and acreage of vulnerable watershed uplands now protected against erosion. Critics point to a wider mandate that values biodiversity, and concede efficiency and narrowly defined standards of productivity, but argue that the Forestry Bureau's very success in tree planting campaigns undercuts the effectiveness of the Forestry Bureau's environmental mandate.

Thus, conceptualizing what is, or even might be involved in pockets of effectiveness is far from straightforward. Inherent to all public policy are questions of measurement. Assessing efficiency requires defining the standard against which a given policy can be measured. Judging effectiveness needs agreement on what is a desirable set of goals to aspire to in the first place, and a reasonable set of criteria as to how one would determine whether those goals have been met in whole, in part, or not at all. And questions of scale continue to plague many development projects. Small pilot projects and/or restricted policy domains might well be both efficient and effective in terms of productivity, while scaling up to larger programs, larger numbers of officials, and larger territories covered might well not only end up in failure, but even result in undercutting an originally successful smaller scale venture.

The experience of Republican China (1911–49 on the mainland of China; after 1949 in Taiwan) offers two particular case studies through which to explore these issues of strategy, implementation, measurement, and scale for particular types of government productivity. Each of these case studies also engages the ways in which foreign aid, personnel, and modes of organization have an impact on that organization's effectiveness and prestige in policy space. Although we are at present accustomed to thinking of China as strong, unitary, and well organized, for the first half of the twentieth century China was more reminiscent of the weak states of sub-Saharan Africa, albeit without the ethnic and religious tensions of many states in this world region. After the fall of the Qing Empire in 1911, China was proclaimed a Republic, but beyond agreeing on the new name, the political and military elites of China could form a consensus on little else. Fractious civilian politics quickly gave way to military involvement in politics, and the more the military intervened, the weaker civilian governments became. At an early stage in this process, Yuan Shikai, the one strong man potentially able to impose his dominance on the rest of the country by force after the fall of the dynasty, drastically miscalculated the depth of opposition to his rule in the central and southern regions of China. The inability of the opposition to Yuan Shikai to agree amongst itself and oust him, in combination with Yuan Shikai's inability to impose his will on central and south China, led to ever deepening waves of militarization which set the stage for eventual state fragmentation and warlordism. State collapse invited an upswing in colonial pressure, particularly from Japan, which in turn sparked the rise of mass movements of protest in both city and countryside. Outer border lands not historically populated by the Han Chinese majority in practice fell away. This environment characterized by militarization, insecurity, state fragmentation, foreign pressure, and frustrated mass nationalism in turn provided the seed bed for the rise of the Leninist Guomindang (Nationalists) and Chinese Communist Party. Their

46 *Julia C. Strauss*

slightly different versions of party-state-military led to nearly a quarter century of bitter civil war. These two nationalist-Leninist parties would go on to dominate Chinese politics throughout the remainder of the twentieth century.

Throughout the Republican period, from 1911 until 1949, with the Guomindang's decisive defeat at the hands of the People's Liberation Army, China as a polity was riven with corruption, incredibly weak governmental institutions, and armed violence. This remained the case for large parts of the country even after the Guomindang succeeded in nominally unifying the country in 1927–28. At this time, the rival Communists had been temporarily defeated but not completely vanquished. Even nominal unification of the country had been accomplished largely by including warlords in the government. The government only had solid control over two and a half provinces in the triangle of territory centred on Shanghai-Hangzhou-Nanjing. While this lower Yangzi region was and is unusually well endowed in terms of agriculture, commerce, and wealth, it was both geographically smaller than and atypical of the rest of the country. In short, if ever there was a case of a government in sore need of 'pockets of effectiveness' – pockets that had the potential for diffusion at large to other government organizations – Nationalist China in the Republican period was it.

This article focuses on two very different organizations that operated in China and Taiwan in the twentieth century; the Sino-Foreign Salt Inspectorate (1913–28, and then with various name changes, until 1949), and the Joint Commission on Rural Reconstruction (JCRR) (1948–79), at which point it was amalgamated into the Ministry of Agriculture. These two institutions were quite different, and neither was a conventional 'pocket' in the sense of being a geographically proximate cluster of individuals and networks. In geographical distribution the Salt Inspectorate was more skeleton than pocket; its prefectural offices and sub stations were thinly spread across some of the most insalubrious locations in the rural hinterland of China. The JCRR was an almost acephalous team of agricultural economists and development specialists who were, aside from a very small managing board and record keeping centre, almost entirely project based: most of the JCRR's time and efforts was spent working with the local and regional rural organizations who requested funds and expertise for particular projects. They were formed at opposite ends of the Republican period, shortly after the fall of the dynasty for the Salt Inspectorate, and at the very end when the Guomindang was on the verge of losing the civil war for the JCRR. The policy areas in which they worked were also very different. The Sino-Foreign Salt Inspectorate was a tax organization and the JCRR was specifically geared towards a range of rural development projects – from its signature program of land reform to fertilizer provision, hygiene, experimenting with new seed strains, and establishing the material and moral incentives for the recreation and institutionalization of rural farmers' associations. The ways in which historical contingencies forced these two organizations to scale up and down were mirror images. Formed at the very outset of the Republican period, the Salt Inspectorate was pushed (along with all other Guomindang government organizations) to rapidly expand during the Sino-Japanese War (1937–45), setting in train a process that permanently impaired the organization. The JCRR was formed at the opposite end of the Republican period under nearly unimaginable conditions. The civil war with the Communists was then nearing the endgame of disastrous defeat for the government; the JCRR decision to follow the Nationalist government into exile to the relatively safe haven of Taiwan led to dramatic scaling down rather than expansion.

For all their many differences in timing of creation, goals, structure, scale and trajectory, and significance for the larger process of state building, the Sino-Foreign Salt Inspectorate and the JCRR had some important features in common. Each was in its own time and place considered to be an unusually effective and efficient organization in a wider environment of chaos, patronage, and profound ineffectiveness. The language to describe these successes at the time was different, but both are recognizable cases of unusually strong and effective organizations. They both performed services deemed to be so important to the state that they were both afforded a great deal of autonomy from the normal politics of their times, which were rife with political interference. How each was formed and then protected its autonomy from the norms of regular politics was different, but in each case a direct foreign presence in the organization was an important factor, as was the steady flow of protected resources that the foreign presence guaranteed in the organization's all important starting up and early institutionalization. But because of their very differences, the experiences of both suggest that the way to effectiveness and high performance is varied, not singular, and there may well be different ways in which to formulate, insulate, and then build on organizational effectiveness in different policy areas for contemporary states.

Taxing matters: the curious case of the Sino-Foreign Salt Inspectorate[1]

Republican era governments in China were weak for many reasons, not the least of which was their near total loss over centralized taxation. After the fall of the dynasty in 1911–12, most provinces simply stopped remitting funds to the central government. Some 15 years later, in 1927–28, the Guomindang government had almost no revenue outside two institutions set up by foreigners to guarantee the international loans taken out by earlier governments (both Qing dynasty and warlord governments). Tax is especially vital for states as it is simultaneously a key *enabler* of other aspects of state building, as well as a reflective *indicator* of the state's institutional capacity. Unless it has recourse to unlimited funds from the outside there is not much that a state can proactively accomplish by way of programs without a steady flow of tax receipts coming in. Strong and pro-active states for the most part also have strong and pro-active capacity to raise revenue, either through direct levies, and/or the creation of financial institutions that enable the state to

48 *Julia C. Strauss*

borrow significantly from its own citizens. But many states outside the Organization for Economic Co-operation and Development (OECD) are characterized by a basic institution building dilemma: how to expand the capacity of state institutions (including those to tax effectively and fairly) when the administrative and institutional base for so doing is insufficient. Aspiring state builders are frequently desperate to break out of a fundamental institution building dilemma in which to raise more domestic funds, they need increased infrastructural capacity to extract tax; without increased infrastructural capacity to extract more tax, they are unable to build sufficient institutional capacity. This very desperation typically leads to environments in which state builders will grasp at any shred of minimal effectiveness through increased revenue streams, without the luxury of being able to consider either fairness in assessing the collection of the revenue or efficiency in the transmission of the revenue to higher levels of the state.

Historically there have been a few, quite unusual, tax organizations in developing countries that have managed to break out of the typical negative feedback loop, in which state institutional weakness breeds ineffective and inefficient tax collection, thus furthering institutional weakness and another cycle of ineffective and inefficient tax collection. The Sino-Foreign Salt Inspectorate was established in China in 1913–14, was formally taken over by the Nationalist government in 1928–29, and, under different names, continued to exist as a recognizable entity until the Nationalist government's loss of the mainland in 1949. The ways in which the organization pursued its goals not only enabled it to separate itself from the patrimonialism, privilege, corruption and weak central tax institutions of its own time. Even today it stands as an example of how organizations can create and expand institutional effectiveness under extraordinarily adverse conditions. The strategy used by the leaders of the Inspectorate was notable in its simplicity: insistence on bureaucratization and rule boundedness. Through the formalization and consistent use of rules for both internal personnel policies and the actual business of levying the salt tax, the Sino-Foreign Salt Inspectorate was able to simultaneously pursue two main objectives: 1) near total organizational insulation from a hostile, patronage riven surrounding environment, and 2) a depersonalized and rule bound method of goal achievement, which in this context meant the effective *and* efficient collection of the salt tax. Because it was able to outperform almost all other tax collecting organizations in China at the time, the Salt Inspectorate's results made it possible for the organization to quite literally *buy* its continued existence and de facto autonomy, despite the extraordinarily unstable environment in which it operated. Between 1914 and the early 1940s, some of these challenges included: 1) marauding warlords who not infrequently robbed Inspectorate offices at gunpoint; 2) surviving its abrupt closure in the wake of the National Revolutionary Army's advance through China in 1927; 3) convincing a hostile nationalist government to revive it and put its operations under the Ministry of Finance, and 4) only closing down stations in the wake of Japanese military takeover.

The challenges that the Salt Inspectorate faced were daunting, because China in the early twentieth century was both systemically undertaxed and regressively taxed. Frequently those least able to afford it bore the worst burden. While the fiscal base of the Chinese imperial state had long been a land tax that was kept deliberately light, by the early twentieth century the demands on the state for modern militaries, modern educational, transport and communication systems had far outpaced what the state could raise domestically. The precondition for establishing a more sound land tax regime was the expertise, administrative capacity, and reach to conduct an accurate cadastral survey to determine who held what land in order to enforce a system in which rural elites paid their fair share. Unfortunately, the state's administrative capacity for conducting such a comprehensive cadastral survey was completely lacking. The most recent full investigation into land holdings had been conducted in the mid-sixteenth century under the Ming dynasty, and for the intervening four centuries the imperial state had worked in tandem with local elites through a de facto system of tax farming to ensure that at least some of the land tax was collected some of the time. From the time of the great mid-nineteenth century rebellions, a range of ad hoc local and regional taxes had sprung up and in a de facto manner had been made permanent by powerful regional viceroys who petitioned the central government to allow certain taxes to be levied in order to fund particular modernization projects in the second half of the nineteenth century. The result was the expansion of a very large informal parallel bureaucracy, often staffed by locals, in the provinces that was neither formally supervised nor audited by the regular central and provincial layers of the state (Morrisson 1959). At the same time, the growth of treaty ports and international trade created a small, but dynamic and growing, economic sector that was highly concentrated, very visible, and in theory taxable. The lower Yangzi region in the Republican period was thus characterized by the kinds of conditions present in many developing countries. The easily taxed base was new, in rapidly growing urban areas. Large newly established factories were unable to pick up and move away to escape the tax collector. Modern banks and large businesses were at least relatively easy to find and assess for tax. It was here that Republican era governments disproportionately concentrated their efforts at tax collection, while in most of the agrarian hinterland tax farmers and local toughs collected tax as they had for generations, without supervision from higher levels of the state (Rawski 1989).

The salt tax regime was therefore very different from those of commercial, excise, or stamp taxes. As salt taxes had been collected for hundreds of years in far flung rural locales with very different methods of producing salt, the salt tax regime was riven with exceptions, exemptions, privileges, and different forms of collections, ranging from lucrative concessions on transport and retailing granted by the state to salt merchants, to multiple taxes on the

50 *Julia C. Strauss*

weighing, transport, and sale. Every site for salt production works was subject to a different regime and different customary practices, which resulted in inconsistent and regressive rates. Poor areas in the interior often paid the most and wealthy commercial areas on the coast paid the least. The salt tax was also notoriously 'leaky' as it and its numerous surcharges were at best inconsistently applied and in most areas supposedly policed by paramilitary bands of 'salt police' on irregular and inadequate salaries, whose major source of de facto funds was in payoffs to turn a blind eye to the very salt smuggling that they were supposed to prevent (Adshead 1970: 20–38). Salt administration reformers astutely diagnosed these problems as early as the turn of the twentieth century, but beyond the establishment of the cosmetic and ineffective regulatory central Salt Tax Office (*Yanwu Shu*) in 1912, the institutional capacity to push through any of the obvious reforms under discussion was nil. One could scarcely imagine a taxation regime more problematic and less amenable to building strong institutions.

An anachronism in times of nationalism: the role of external influence in the inspectorate

Much of the impetus to set up a new salt tax regime in 1913–14 in China was in ways analogous to both International Monetary Fund (IMF) structural adjustment programs and institution building programs today, with organizational forms that were precursors of what are now called semi-autonomous or autonomous revenue authorities (ARAs).[2] In 1913, the then strongman of the Republic of China, Yuan Shikai, wished to contract a large loan from foreign financiers to refinance a set of debts inherited from the Qing dynasty, in order to prevent an imminent default. While he was at it, Yuan also wanted to raise a substantial advance for his central government to increase the size of the central army and put down a secessionist movement in the south. These negotiations resulted in a controversy laden deal known as The Reorganization Loan, which consolidated many of the old debts left over by the imperial government, and an additional sum of £25 million was loaned to Yuan Shikai. However, foreign bank consortiums needed a security on the loan, and the only plausible source of this guarantee had to come from the salt tax. China's Maritime Customs Administration had long been the main source of hard currency available to the central government, but it had already been mortgaged out. The collection of salt tax was at that point so plagued with corruption and 'leakiness' that without substantial reorganization it was not worth enough to guarantee the loan. The initial establishment of the Sino-Foreign Salt Inspectorate was an accident of history. It was set up at the behest of the international bank consortium in order to provide security on the loan to the Chinese government, and its first function was to ensure that China did not default on its loans by physically collecting the salt tax and then managing the transfer of funds to foreign creditors.

The reasons for setting up the Sino-Foreign Salt Inspectorate now smacks of the colonial and the bizarre:[3] the foreigner who was brought in to set up the Salt Inspectorate, Sir Richard Dane, spoke not a word of Chinese. His career had been made in the Indian Civil Service, where he had last served as the head of excise and salt. This experience served him well when he was brought in to set up the Salt Inspectorate. The location might have been different but the principles of a well-run tax organization were, to all intents and purposes, identical to those of the Indian Civil Service (and indeed, of prefectural systems anywhere): rigorous socialization into the impersonal and performance based norms of civil service, despite being thinly spread over a vast area. The Inspectorate itself had a set of far flung district offices staffed at the top by joint Chinese and foreign district inspectors with co-equal authority. This odd organizational setup, with its preponderance of foreigners in positions of actual joint administrative decision making, ran against the contemporary current of rising nationalism and anti-imperialism. But in the early twentieth century, there were ample precedents, albeit backward looking ones, for such an arrangement. The Maritime Customs Inspectorate General had had such a system of district offices and joint foreign and Chinese management since the mid-nineteenth century. Maritime Customs had in turn been modelled on the Indian Civil Service of the earlier nineteenth century. The French established Chinese postal service worked along similar lines, as did the Salt Inspectorate's direct analogues in salt administration for the two other main non-colonized states of the time, Turkey and Iran. The Sino-Foreign Salt Inspectorate was the very last of these joint-authority civil service systems to be established. Indeed, it was such a political anachronism from almost the moment that it came into existence that it is in retrospect extraordinary that it was ever institutionalized. For it to become the strong organization that provided the Nationalist government with its second largest source of tax revenues throughout the 1930s was even more incredible. Controversy and significant opposition from nationalists of all stripes and Yuan Shikai's political opponents surrounded its initial establishment in 1913, and by the early 1920s it was an increasingly politically vulnerable target for rising mass nationalism. In fact, when the revolutionary Guomindang (Nationalist) Party-state rose to power in 1927–28, among its first actions were to abolish the Sino-Foreign Salt Inspectorate, along with the Maritime Customs Administration and the French run Post Office. Despite this very hostile policy environment, the Inspectorate survived and prospered even during the most disruptive of the warlord years in the 1910s and 1920s. The fact that it was one of only two functioning agencies still remitting funds from the provinces to the central government helped the Inspectorate to successfully negotiate nearly incessant civil war from its establishment through the mid-1920s, despite the fact that its very efficiency and effectiveness made it a prime target for warlord depredation. After the demise of the warlords, the Inspectorate had to cope with the rise to power of an aggressively nationalist and hostile new government in 1927–28, which promptly abolished it before being

52   *Julia C. Strauss*

convinced to permit its revival and reincorporation within the new government, under the nominal jurisdiction of the new Nationalist Ministry of Finance. Astonishingly, even *after* absorption into the new government, it served new political masters from a new position of subordination, became the second pillar of Nationalist finance between 1929 and 1938, and even served as a model for new tax regimes in other divisions set up by reformers and rationalizers in the Nationalist Ministry of Finance in the mid-1930s. Ultimately, the organization only declined during the years of the Sino-Japanese War (1937–45), which was a period of almost universal de-institutionalization within the Nationalist government.

The sheer, unexpected organizational success of the Sino-Foreign Salt Inspectorate bears explanation, particularly given the unfavourable political and administrative circumstances in which it arose: a political anachronism from virtually its inception, its consistency in attracting hostility from nationalists both inside and outside the government, and its operation in a policy environment in which the vast majority of government organizations in general, and in tax collection in particular, were ineffective, inefficient, rent seeking, and/or corrupt. What were the secrets of this unanticipated and by any measure extraordinary success, and what, if anything, can be learned from this nearly a century on?

Bureaucratization and insulation under conditions of adversity

The two most important 'lessons' of the Salt Inspectorate experience were that it was necessary to 1) establish and preserve the organization's internal integrity, chiefly through what I call 'strategies of *insulation*' while 2) simultaneously launching externally oriented 'strategies of *goal achievement*'. Without insulation and buffering from an extremely hostile surrounding environment in which existed the pressures for accommodation with vested interests and webs of familial and ascriptive ties, the Salt Inspectorate, like many other aspiring reformist organizations in tax, would have simply failed before it had even started. But given the sheer complexity and hostility in the Salt Inspectorate's surrounding environment, internally oriented strategies of insulation could not be had for free; they could only be, quite literally, *bought*. Once the organization could demonstrate, in an objective and unquestionable way, its success in fulfilling its mission of both effectively and efficiently collecting the salt tax, it was much more likely to garner a grudging acceptance from its administrative masters and potential predators (initially the Group Banks, later aspiring warlords, and finally the Nationalist Government itself). The tables below demonstrate its success. Table 3.1 covers the years of total tax take from 1913 to 1927, which were the years in which the Inspectorate directly deposited loan servicing funds to the Group Bank consortium and then forwarded the surplus to whatever government was nominally in power in Beijing. Table 3.2 covers the years of the 'Nanjing Decade', when the Guomindang Nationalist government was making its peak efforts to

PoE: lessons from China and Taiwan 53

reintegrate the central state, before the experiment was abruptly halted by the outbreak of the Sino-Japanese War in mid-1937. When the Inspectorate was set up in 1913, absolutely no one envisioned how successful the operation was going to be; those who set it up at best imagined that the proceeds would service the debt on the Reorganization Loan. Once the system became fully operational in 1914, tax receipts leapt fivefold. Receipts climbed to a high in 1922, before beginning to fluctuate and decline in the mid-1920s, when civil war and increasingly serious warlord depredations resulted in the proceeds of entire district offices never being disbursed to the central Inspectorate office. Once the National Revolutionary Army began to win victories in 1926–27, it simply closed down any Inspectorate office in its path. Table 3.2 illustrates just how successful, measured by effectiveness *and* efficiency, the Inspectorate continued to be after its initial abolishment and then reconstitution under the Nationalist Ministry of Finance. In the Nanjing Decade, tax receipts again continued their climb upward. This is particularly impressive as these successes came with a severely diminished taxable base, as the most efficient, most easily taxable of the salt works in the three northeast provinces of Manchuria were lost when Japan invaded and established a client state of Manchukuo in 1931–32. Pressure from the central government to raise tax rates accounted for some of these gains, but so did administrative consolidation, evening out of tariffs, and administrative leanness in what are now called efficiency gains. The Inspectorate's administrative costs were never high, but when political masters in the Ministry of Finance demanded that costs be cut in the early 1930s, the Inspectorate grudgingly complied (Strauss 1998: 90).

It is a far from straightforward matter to wake up one day and implement a consistent and effective set of strategies for internal insulation linked to successful external goal achievement, and the question remains how the Salt Inspectorate managed in an environment littered with failure. The literature on contemporary ARAs suggests that insufficient insulation of staff or organizational autonomy is a recipe for ineffectiveness, inefficiency, and corruption. What is often less appreciated is that organizational insulation is not

Table 3.1 Salt Inspectorate net tax receipts, 1913–1927 (in standard silver dollars)

Year	Net tax receipts	Year (cont.)	Net tax receipts (cont.)
1913	11,471,000	1921	77,988,000
1914	60,410,000	1922	85,789,000
1915	69,278,000	1923	79,545,000
1916	72,441,000	1924	70,544,000
1917	70,627,000	1925	73,634,000
1918	80,607,000	1926	64,287,000
1919	80,607,000	1927	57,905,000
1920	79,064,000		

Note: All amounts are in standard silver dollars.
Source: Chen (1936: 1298).

54 *Julia C. Strauss*

Table 3.2 Salt Inspectorate collections under the National Government, 1928–1937

Year	Piculs collected	Tax collected
1928	53,484,000	137,045,000
1929	60,898,000	143,366,000
1930	42,109,000	147,207,000
1931	43,994,000	154,145,000
1932	47,630,000	157,752,000
1933	47,062,000	160,693,000
1934	45,041,000	177,461,000
1935	52,672,000	185,416,000
1936	48,672,000	217,817,000
1937	42,663,000	217,905,000

Notes: A 'picul' is a traditional Asian unit of weight and is as much as a man can carry on a shoulder carrying pole. The taxes are in standard silver dollars.
Source: Ding and Foding (1990: 218–219).

merely accomplished by high performance in external and measurable goal achievement. Political leaders outside the organization also need to value whatever the organization is accomplishing enough that they adopt and maintain a hands-off position, thus allowing insulation and in-house socialization to become institutionalized within the organization. De facto separate administrations, particularly those with higher pay scales than the norm, attract attention and resentment from elsewhere in the bureaucracy. By definition, nationalists are hostile to their very existence. They raise serious questions about loyalty to governments, political accountability to electorates, and neo-colonialism, particularly if a Western technocratic and advisor presence is visible. If unable to demonstrate effectiveness through ever larger amounts of tax revenue coming in, efficiency through cutting administrative costs, and relative efficiency and effectiveness compared to other tax organizations operating in the same arena, an organization like the Inspectorate in the early twentieth century or an ARA now is likely to be politically very vulnerable. This brings us back to the question of mechanics: given the necessity of simultaneously insulating the organization and demonstrating its effectiveness in goal achievement, what were the component parts of the Inspectorate's strategies of insulation and goal achievement, and how were they achieved in the exceptionally difficult policy space of Republican China?

The simple answer to both of these questions is: through a coherent and simplifying logic of bureaucratization, which applied equally to strategies of internal insulation and external goal achievement. In practice this meant: depersonalization of administration, simplification and standardization of procedures for tax collection, and wherever possible, rationalization of tax rates through a free market and an administratively straightforward policy of one point taxation called 'taxation at the yard and free trade thereafter' (*jiuchang zhengshui*). This rule bound, simplifying logic of organizational mission, structure, and program was made possible in the first instance because of the exceptional vision and administrative leadership of the founding Chief Inspector for the Salt Inspectorate Sir Richard Dane. Although Dane was initially approached by a representative from the Group Banks, both the Yuan Shikai government and the creditor Group Banks concurred in Dane's appointment. In many respects he was the obvious choice. In 1913, Dane had only just retired from a long career in the Indian Civil Service, capped by his appointment as the first Inspector-General of Excise and Salt in 1909. He had strong ideas about how to go about constructing a viable and non-corrupt prefectural service for the salt tax. And he was also willing to play bureaucratic hardball with both the Chinese government and the Group Banks. When the Inspectorate was first formed and Dane called in, most of the bureaucratic details had not yet been worked out and there was a great deal of room for manoeuvre. For example, before the organization's second year of operation, no one ever considered the possibility that the Inspectorate would work so well that there would be a surplus beyond the annual repayments to service the Reorganization Loan. Dane astutely negotiated these functions for the Inspectorate and quickly established the principle that after servicing the Reorganization Loan debt and meeting its own administrative costs, any surplus on the salt tax collection would be forwarded to the Chinese central government.

This early bureaucratic entrepreneurialism had two direct consequences. It first gave the young Inspectorate the means by which to insulate itself with a much higher rate of remuneration and benefits than was typical for regular government organizations at the time. Although it was brought into existence by the Group Banks in order to service a foreign loan, the Inspectorate was organizationally separate from the Group Banks. By insisting on transferring the excess funds after deducting operating costs to the Chinese government, it could plausibly claim to be a politically neutral and technocratic organization that served all interests – both the Group Banks and the Chinese government – in a disinterested way. It was also Dane who laid the foundation of the Inspectorate ethos in a list that later became known as the 'Fourteen Principles', which included the total separation and insulation of the organization around a norm of civil service, the drive to replace a host of customary arrangements by cajoling, undercutting and taking over assorted government and salt merchant monopolies on salt production. The Fourteen Principles also trumpeted uniformity and simplification of the salt tax. In Dane's original vision, salt sale and transport ought to be assessed by one centralized organization, with one standard and (lower) tax levied on site where the salt was produced. At all times the Inspectorate presented itself to the outside as an effective, efficient piece of administrative machinery that could get the job done. The ambiguity regarding for whom it worked – the Group Banks or the Chinese government – was both a curse and a blessing. It made the Inspectorate unpopular with two generations of Chinese nationalists and a prime target for attack. But its willingness, ability, and lengthy record in providing a core service to the Chinese central government that the Chinese central government could not itself undertake also bought it grudging legitimacy and no small amount

56 *Julia C. Strauss*

of reliance (Strauss 1998: 75–78). The Chinese central government at the time was so weak that its writ seldom, if ever, extended to the locations in which the salt tax was being levied.

The sheer force of Dane's personality and policy preferences loomed large in the first critical years after the Inspectorate's establishment. A weak central government Salt Office attempted to block much of what the Inspectorate wished to do, but without the independent financing and strong organization of the Inspectorate, they were side-lined. Local officials throughout China who were in practice operating independently also resisted. But it is equally important to note that after this early stage of institutional setup and consolidation, strong leadership at the top was not a significant factor in the Inspectorate's later successes. Dane was only with the Inspectorate for its first four years, and he was succeeded by a series of faceless and unimpressive Chief Directors. It was Dane's particular gift to insist on a clearly defined and minimalist program for both internal insulation and external goal orientation that, once internalized within organizational culture, could long outlast him and any number of less than competent leaders. The core of the organization's mission and ideology was its complete insistence on de-personalization, rationalization and impersonally applied rules and procedures in internal personnel systems and external tax collection. This fundamental overarching principle served the Inspectorate extremely well until far into the Sino-Japanese War.

Bureaucratization was not a source of alienation for those who worked for the Inspectorate. On the contrary, it was a highly motivating and positively charged set of norms that was actively aspired to. Individuals strongly identified with the Inspectorate, gave it years of service under extremely trying conditions, and recited its praises for years thereafter. This extraordinary loyalty for decades of work under difficult conditions was a function of what Dane and others consistently referred to as the Inspectorate's 'strong civil service traditions'. The core of the Inspectorate's institutional integrity, and the linchpin of its insulation and goal achievement was the creation and then preservation of the Inspectorate's own independent civil service system, complete with its own rankings, grades, entry and promotion criteria, buttressed by a salary scale and generous benefits that were far in excess of anything else (save Maritime Customs) on offer in the government service of the time. First establishing, then maintaining the impartiality and incorruptibility of Inspectorate personnel was at the very heart of all Salt Inspectorate policy: from Dane's insistence on high salaries and an independent civil service system in 1913 until well into the 1930s. In the fraught days of 1927–28, when the Inspectorate was summarily abolished and then reconstituted as a semi-autonomous organization under the Guomindang Ministry of Finance, the then Minister of Finance, T.V. Soong, agreed to maintain the original terms and conditions of the organization's internal organization and salary structure, while insisting that the final administrative transfer of funds to pay the Group Banks was undertaken by the Ministry of Finance itself rather than the Inspectorate directly. We do not know the specifics of what was said at the meetings between Soong and the top inspectors of the Inspectorate in 1928, but it is clear that Soong admired the efficiency of the Inspectorate. The government's insatiable demand for revenue in the late 1920s and early 1930s made him loathe to interfere too much in the internal procedures of a system that worked so well given the constraints of the times. By the mid-1930s, a new Minister of Finance, H.H. Kung, wanted to put the Inspectorate on a tighter leash, and as part of a wider reorganization of the organizations under the Ministry of Finance, changed the name of the Inspectorate to the 'Directorate General of Salt Tax' (Yanwu Zongju), and removed the old stipulation that all orders be co-signed by both Chinese and Western district inspectors of the same rank, and demoted the formal position of the foreign district inspectors to merely 'advising'. As might be expected, this prompted the foreign district inspectors to near hysteria with worry over the 'dilution' of the Inspectorate's 'strong civil service traditions' in general and the decline of their own positions in particular.[4] Even fifty years later, informants in Taiwan, who had joined the organization through the open examination at the district level in the mid 1930s in their teens and early 20s at the very bottom of the civil service system, waxed nostalgic over what an inherently good thing the Inspectorate civil service and personnel system was, how well it worked in comparison to anything else at the time, and how enlightened it was in view of what came later.[5]

Civil service: positively charged norm and delivering the goods

The Inspectorate's independent civil service system offered an entire career and way of life in prefectural district administration, and everything about the way it was set up reified its separation from the regular government. It encouraged stability and low turnover by rewarding seniority. Salary scales, particularly at the middle ranks, were extremely high in comparison to regular government salaries, with many different points on the pay scale. Inspectorate staff could look forward to regular salary increases and at least semi-regular promotions if they remained in service. Since one could not parachute in to the Inspectorate, it could turn away all pressure for favours in appointment and promotion. In the short run, Chinese central governments were not strong enough to interfere with it; later in the 1930s, the Inspectorate could cite its own 'strong civil service traditions' as integral to its effectiveness and efficiency in providing such a stable source of income to the central government. There was only one way into the Inspectorate for Chinese staff, and that was at or near the bottom, through a general civil service examination. After the entrance examination, successful examinees were offered a three month training course in salt administration, followed by another placement examination, and then an offer of a post in one of the lowest three grades as they became available. There were also in house examinations to progress through the lowest three grades, and after that, the promotion rate slowed

58   *Julia C. Strauss*

considerably, as promotion was a function of particular posts coming open. Skipping steps on the personnel ladder was forbidden. Since a robust annual review ensured a basic uniformity of competence throughout the organization, seniority was the critical variable for promotion. The small number of foreigners who came into the organization did so at higher levels than the bottom three grades, but even they were expected to put in years of service and rise slowly. Both Chinese and foreign staff tended to stay with the Inspectorate for their entire careers. The Inspectorate's deliberate engineering of stability and continuity had a downside: it was undoubtedly frustrating for the most capable and ambitious to have to wait for so long for promotion, and it was recognized even at the time that the Inspectorate lacked 'a forward looking spirit' (Strauss 1998: 70–72).

Stodginess was compensated for by a generous system of benefits including a sabbatical year of 'long leave' for every seven years of service, home leave, and extremely generous sick leave and pensions. The Inspectorate, like prefectural organizations the world over, was concerned about corruption and 'going native'. It therefore worked on a principle of frequent rotation: middle and higher level staff was not permitted to remain in the same district office for more than five years, and even clerical and support staff was fairly frequently rotated between different local offices within the same district. Upside positive incentives were also matched with strictly imposed negative ones. The Inspectorate's core strategies of internal organizational insulation were for a purpose: to provide an environment in which officials could reasonably be expected to work hard, implement regulations, and refrain from corruption. This was an organization that took its own principles and regulations extremely seriously. Even a hint of peculation, being subject to undue influence, or favouritism in the performance of duties resulted in immediate and severe sanctions: administrative warnings and demerits for mistakes. If corruption was discovered, the penalty was immediate dismissal, even for those who had reached high ranks.[6] Frustrating as such a conservative, seniority based organization might have been for the most fiery and ambitious, enough clearly committed and capable people remained, and remained for the long run, through years of civil war and foreign invasion.

Cultural resonance also contributed to the Inspectorate's success. Although the Inspectorate's model of a 'strong civil service' was directly descended from the Indian Civil service, and more distantly nineteenth century European notions of civil service reform grounded on putatively universal principles of fairness and efficiency, it was implemented in a host environment in which the educated and the upwardly mobile were exceptionally predisposed to these ideals. The trope of the 'career open to talent', the notion of fairness of access guaranteed by open civil service examination, and the ideal of the honest and upright official were all solidly legitimating norms that had been components of Chinese political culture and statecraft. They were indeed so deeply legitimating that they had served to bind (elite) society to the imperial state for hundreds of years (see Elman 2000 and 1991). In the institutionally and

PoE: lessons from China and Taiwan   59

politically fractured environment of early twentieth century China, these norms had lost none of their relevance. Reformers and modernizers in China had long dearly wished to create strong, effective, and meritocratic state institutions. What was lacking for most state organizations was the substantive means by which to make these aspirations a reality. The Inspectorate's emphasis on neutral civil service systems was based on a universalizing set of principles, but it surely did not hurt to have a set of norms at the organization's core that resonated so powerfully in both the society from which staff were drawn as well as among the political elites with whom accommodation would have to be reached after 1927. The organization's near fetishization of its own uniquely righteous neutral civil service overlapped substantially with a wider set of extant political and cultural norms that similarly reified civil service as both a reflection and implementer of positive norms for state action. Given the depth of nationalist hostility to the very existence of the Inspectorate, a rhetoric of civil service, and the reality of high performance that depended on maintenance of depersonalized civil service systems, were probably among the factors that ensured the organization's later survival and influence in the post-1927 world.

The other pillar of Salt Inspectorate success was that it delivered the goods. In the 1910s and early 1920s, it more than satisfied the Group Banks because it adequately serviced its loan without fuss. It provided a succession of desperately weak, nominally national Chinese governments with an annual injection of otherwise unexpected funds, and even survived and prospered when put on a much shorter leash under the Nationalist Government in the 1930s. Part of the reason for this success lies in the remarkably serviceable, but minimalist set of tasks and orientations built into the Inspectorate's core in the Dane years through the elaboration of the Fourteen Principles. Another part of the reason lies in the fortunate fit between the organization's sheer, dogged insistence on depersonalized bureaucracy in all things and the way in which the divisible, objectively knowable and measurable components of the salt tax lent itself to bureaucratic strategies of rationalization. Tax of a commodity like salt is, by definition, amenable to standardized units of measure (in this case, weight and money). Accounting is relatively straightforward. Results are clear, as one either has more or less tax that has been collected in a given annual period, and the reasons for unsatisfactory results are usually fairly easy to diagnose. Nonetheless, the Inspectorate's limited set of core tasks was never easy to accomplish. There was resistance, foot dragging, and lack of political support – not to mention the persistent danger for Inspectors of being robbed at gunpoint in remote and uncongenial locales. But the corollaries of the basics, extension of control over the salt tax environment, shoving out competitors like salt merchants and other salt tax collection regimes, and rationalization and simplification of tax collection procedures and rates had the virtue of being easy to monitor. Eventually, there were Inspectorate stations at all of China's taxed salt works. Successful projects could be readily monitored, and, circumstances permitting, rapidly

60   *Julia C. Strauss*

introduced in other districts. The predations of an individual warlord or even the loss of a whole region (as the entire northeast was lost in 1931) could be contained because of the high degree of divisibility, measurability, and specificity of the organization's key technologies. Divisibility and measurability lent themselves to the kinds of impersonal rule making at the core of bureaucratization. It was not only that norms of impersonal bureaucracy suited both internal processes of organizational insulation and external processes of goal achievement: the external goals were themselves inherently achievable through processes of centralization, standardization, and rule application.

In 1927, the Salt Inspectorate was temporarily felled by a blow that could easily have permanently ended its existence: it was abolished by a new, aggressively nationalist government. What is so surprising about the years between 1928 and roughly 1938 is how not only did the Inspectorate revive almost immediately under the Nationalist government, but by some lights it can be seen to actually have expanded its influence, despite the changed circumstances of its operation. Unsurprisingly, the Inspectorate along with Maritime Customs, the other substantive independent tax collecting agency of the time, now had to directly serve the Chinese government by being formally put under its jurisdiction. It became part of the Ministry of Finance, but with an odd formal status of semi-autonomy that is reminiscent of contemporary examples of ARAs.[7] Crucially, it was permitted to retain its separate civil service core with its separate personnel grades, entry examinations, and higher salary scales, as well as the initial preservation of the co-equal status of Chinese and foreign district inspectors. The Ministry of Finance took over the actual repayment of the Reorganization Loan.

The political position of the Inspectorate became even more fraught with a nationalist government in power. Nationalist legislators in the Guomindang's normally rubber stamp parliament, the Legislative Yuan and members of the auditing body for the government in the Control Yuan, found the heavy foreign element reminiscent of imperialism and regularly launched campaigns to abolish its special status. Groups of bureaucratic rationalizers elsewhere in the government, notably in the Examination Yuan, were offended by the Inspectorate's bureaucratic resistance to its own attempts to impose a standard system of bureaucratic classification and grades across the government as a whole. The attitude of the organization's new direct bosses in the Ministry of Finance was ambivalent, as they 'veered from wanting to use the Inspectorate and control it' (Strauss 1998: 93). T.V. Soong, the most important figure in Nationalist China's finance and the Minister of Finance in the early 1930s, genuinely admired what the Salt Inspectorate had managed to accomplish against long odds. It was well understood by all concerned with government finance that the Inspectorate and Maritime Customs provided a welcome and necessary stream of income that could not be supplied by the government's more conventional tax collecting organizations. At the same time, there was also substantial resentment over the foreigners with co-equal administrative authority to Chinese, and the higher salaries commanded by foreign personnel with the same bureaucratic status as Chinese were deemed to be particularly obnoxious features of the system. The upshot of this ambivalence was a de facto informal power sharing underneath the façade of formal government authority throughout the 1930s. The Ministry of Finance formally took over the administration of the Reorganization loan repayment, but Inspectorate staff collected the tax, kept the necessary accounts, and wrote up the required reports for the Ministry of Finance's use. After 1936, when the Inspectorate's name was changed to the Directorate General of Salt Tax and the position of foreign district inspectors slightly downgraded, the new Minister of Finance, H.H. Kung, chose the Chinese Chief Inspector. This arrangement was not without stresses: the old Inspectorate staff heartily disliked the new Chief Chinese Inspector, who was the lone political appointee in the new regime. But in the most important respects, the key features of the Inspectorate cum Directorate that made it such a success in the first place were kept in place until the war induced stresses of the early 1940s became overwhelming. The organization continued to be shielded from attacks elsewhere in the government by its superiors in the Ministry of Finance. It was permitted to retain its separate civil service system and higher salaries. At all times the Inspectorate maintained that it was nothing more than an impersonal, disinterested part of the state machinery, willing and able to do the bidding of its political masters.

From skeleton to flesh: diffusion and limits of the inspectorate model

Despite the political attacks, the Inspectorate actually *increased* in influence under the Nationalist Ministry of Finance after 1929. It convinced the Ministry of Finance to allow it to subsume the two other major players in salt tax. The first one was an old, more or less defunct artefact of the pre-1927 warlord governments, a central salt tax organization called the Yanwu Shu. It was formally absorbed into the Inspectorate in 1931. Another organization, the paramilitary Salt Police followed suit in 1932–33. More importantly, the Inspectorate attracted enough admiration from tax reformers and institution builders that its principles were incorporated into new organizations then being set up by the Ministry of Finance. The Ministry of Finance's new Consolidated Tax Administration was directly modelled on the Inspectorate minus, of course, the heavy foreign presence at the top.[8] The Consolidated Tax was an indirect commercial levy on a range of factory produced commodities. It began as a fairly simple tax applied to only machine rolled and flue cured tobacco. But it proved so successful that it expanded to include flour, cement, matches, and cotton yarn. The Consolidated Tax mantra of 'one item, one tax' levied at the site of production sounded suspiciously like the Inspectorate slogan of 'taxation at the yard and free trade thereafter'. The Consolidated Tax regime also established policies of rigorous central control, amalgamation of older and weaker tax organizations operating in the same sphere, and standardization of rules and rates. In organizational form, it also

62 *Julia C. Strauss*

replicated the Inspectorate prefectural model of highly paid experts that were frequently rotated among district offices. Consolidated Tax stands as one of the key arenas of National Government institution building during the Nanjing Decade, gradually expanding in both absolute and relative terms to comprise roughly 20 per cent of the government's tax revenue by 1937 (from roughly 12 per cent in 1929).

The reasons for the relative success of Consolidated Tax were not only its imitation of the Inspectorate's organizational form and core ideology, but that it operated in a tax domain that was strikingly similar to that of the Inspectorate. Both had at their core a single tax on easily measured and divisible products produced in concentrated and controllable geographical space. Consolidated Tax expanded outward from both its geographical core around Shanghai and in terms of the commodities it sought to tax. It did so in an incremental way, in which its reasonable administrative capacity in trained personnel to go out and assess the tax could roughly keep pace with the factories producing the goods. Other, more far reaching taxes fared much less well. In 1936, the Ministry of Finance established a new Direct Tax Administration that was also modelled on that of the Inspectorate, but this project never achieved the results of the Inspectorate or Consolidated Tax (see Strauss 1998: 133–39). Ambitious programs for direct income tax, inheritance, savings, property, and windfall profits were simply beyond the technical and manpower capacity of even the most objectively selected, highly qualified young technocrats in 1936; the outbreak of the Sino-Japanese War and the subsequent loss of the Guomindang's military, political, economic, and social base in east China in the next year put such ambitious programs even further out of reach.

On the whole, the Inspectorate's incorporation into the Ministry of Finance worked well in the 1930s for two reasons. First, it continued to produce the goods so necessary to the still infrastructurally weak and highly militarized National Government. On more than one occasion in both the pre and post 1927 political environments, the Inspectorate quite literally had to *buy* its autonomy. No less a state builder than Jean-Baptiste Colbert suggested that 'The art of taxation consists in so plucking the goose as to obtain the largest possible amount of feathers with the smallest possible amount of hissing'. In China in the second quarter of the 20th century, neither warlord governments nor the Guomindang could afford to kill a goose as productive as the Inspectorate, which bowed to political authority so readily and turned over the tax receipts with so little fuss. Less obviously but no less important was the way in which the rhetoric and core ideology of the Inspectorate made it possible for it to take a kind of refuge in its own administrative de-personalization and bureaucratization. In its insistent self-representation as an administrative machine, willing and able to bow to the will of political masters, it ensured its own organizational survival as well as quite unexpected post-1927 influence with the new regime. The Inspectorate staff disapproved of pressures from above from Guomindang party masters to continuously

PoE: lessons from China and Taiwan 63

raise tax rates, but responded to properly constituted authority in the only appropriate way for a civil service: with compliance. Despite pressures and agitation from elsewhere in the government, the Inspectorate's immediate post 1928 political masters in the Guomindang Ministry of Finance usually let the organization alone to get on with the job. It even used the Inspectorate as a model when the occasion arose that called for a new tax regime to be set up, although the extremely high performance of the Inspectorate was not nearly as replicable to other, more diffuse areas of tax as the technocrats in the Ministry of Finance had hoped for.

In conclusion, the Salt Inspectorate of Republican China worked as well as anything could have in such a hostile and fraught policy environment, even managing to survive its abolishment and revival under a new and suspicious government: it even became a model that also worked tolerably well where the tax regime conditions were broadly similar. What undid the Nationalist regime in Republican China wasn't poor performance at its job: it was being overwhelmed by war, losing its economic, social, and political base in east China and then losing control over the economy during the War. The Salt Inspectorate is an example of how oddly and surprisingly 'bureaucracy' (impersonal rules, standardization, and central control) can be extremely effective even under very unfavourable conditions, and how impersonal bureaucracy can be built from relatively little. The history of the Inspectorate also illustrates the limits of technocratic bureaucracy, particularly those of a semi-autonomous nature. The influence of technocrats comes from their expertise in speaking truth to power and submitting to political power. In the long run, speaking truth to power (or maintaining a semi-autonomous tax administration) depends on political leaders who are willing, or able, to 'hear' what is being said and act accordingly. Strictly bureaucratic and impersonal forms of administration require the means for administrative insulation, an ethic of socialization into the norms of impersonal bureaucracy, and producing enough effectiveness and efficiency that political masters will continue to listen. Bureaucratic and impersonal institutions are vulnerable to overreach in trying to achieve a set of targets for which they have neither the sufficiently socialized personnel nor the administrative capacity to fulfil. External shocks such as wartime emergencies can also affect them negatively: the Inspectorate only declined when it was subjected to the wartime demand to expand four to fivefold in a matter of two years. Under traumatic wartime conditions, it was unable to suddenly scale up in size of operations and type of tasks while retaining the bureaucratic rule bound impersonalism in its internal and external operations that made it such a success.

Before the early 1940s, however, the Sino-Foreign Salt Inspectorate was successful against all the odds for a number of reasons: its insistence on internal and external bureaucratization worked well to socialize members into the norms of the organization, and were equally effective in actually doing a job that Republican era governments desperately needed. Producing the goods and handing over the tax surplus convinced political leaders to allow the

64　*Julia C. Strauss*

Inspectorate a good deal of functional autonomy until nearly the end of the 1930s, because it provided a service that was absolutely essential to the state's continued functioning. Although geographically far flung, the Inspectorate only tried to do one, very necessary thing very well: rationalize and collect the salt tax. It never moved into other spheres. It never attempted to expand its mandate, and only once in its history attempted to absorb other state organizations not directly related to the salt tax. The single exception to this rule was its incorporation of the paramilitary Salt Police. The Salt Police were only taken over because Inspectorate officials firmly believed that the continued existence of a paramilitary organization that was notoriously ill paid and corrupt within the wider salt tax regime could only be brought to heel if formally taken over and gradually won over to the Inspectorate's norms of civil service and formal rule implementation. By and large, if other tax organizations in Republican China imitated the Inspectorate, it was out of admiration and mimicry rather than the direct expansion of the Salt Inspectorate into new areas of tax.

From bones to circulatory system: the evolution of the Joint Commission on Rural Reconstruction (JCRR)

From the 1910s through the 1930s, stable supplies of tax such as those offered by the Inspectorate were necessary, but hardly sufficient for matters of governance and legitimacy in Republican China. By the late 1940s, as the Nationalist government was losing the civil war, an extraordinary coalition arose between those in (or close to) the government who agreed that the Nationalist government had long neglected the majority of the rural population, and American government advisors, often trained in what we would now call development or agricultural economics, most of whom were profoundly sympathetic to New Deal principles of equity and social justice. After lobbying by both respected Chinese academics who had studied in the United States and Americans familiar with a China-US Agricultural mission in 1946, the US Congress passed a law in 1948 which provided for the establishment of a Joint Commission of Rural Reconstruction (JCRR). This new organization was to be funded by a provision that stipulated that 10 per cent of the aid to China be earmarked for rural reconstruction (an umbrella term that had been in use for the previous 20 years, largely in a context of integrated rural development communities of designated county 'experiments') (Fippin 1953). The first thing to be dropped from JCRR's core agenda was the notion of integrated experimental rural communities. Instead the JCRR became a conduit for project based US agricultural aid. The core principles of the organization were joint operations between the Chinese and Americans, project funding on a wide variety of felt needs of rural people, working through extant organizations rather than setting up new ones, and assisting with institutional capacity for self-help. In practice, this meant that projects were determined on the basis of felt needs, fair distribution, the willingness of a sponsoring agency

PoE: lessons from China and Taiwan   65

to come forward (and offer matching funds), a demonstration of feasibility and frequent field inspections by JCRR experts to follow up (ibid.: 7–10).

Although the JCRR did expand its staff over time, it was conceived as a development organization to funnel agricultural aid and offer technical assistance to promote equitable rural development, and to work through existing organizations rather than create new ones. With 'U.S. rural and agricultural expertise integrated *on the line* ... JCRR has always been a small organization compared to the complex of institutions it has influenced, moved, and assisted.' (Hough 1968: 7). It was also intended from the outset to have a limited life span – when the level of rural development in Taiwan was such that its services did not provide value added, it was expected to be wound down, as indeed was the case some 30 odd years later in 1979, when its functions were taken over by the government's Council on Agriculture. From the beginning, the JCRR's remit of rural reconstruction was far broader than that of the Salt Inspectorate, but equally its organizational reach was less direct. By the early 1950s divisions dealing with Plant Industry, Land Reform, Farmer's Associations, Animal Husbandry, Irrigation, Rural Health, Grain and Fertilizer, Forestry, and Rural Economics had been set up. At the same time the organization never took full operational control of any of its projects. Rather it facilitated, supplied funds, provided technical assistance and training, and also, critically, frequently followed up with on-site inspections and reports. In this respect it was more akin to a constantly flowing circulatory system, refreshing, replenishing, and carrying antibodies and hormone to improve and regulate systems (ibid.: 47).

The leadership at the top of the organization was collective but also small, initially with only three Chinese and two Americans as commissioners. There was no need to introduce into the organization the norms of civil service and technocracy, because the members of the Commission had for the most part already been well socialized into the agricultural development norms of the time by going to the same MA and PhD programs in the United States. This socializing role of Cornell University's postgraduate programs in what was then called agronomy was critical. The majority of the commissioners in the late 1940s and early 1950s had passed through the Cornell Agronomy Department and so spoke the same New Deal, agricultural and technocratic language, and the Cornell connection loomed large with subsequent generations in the JCRR (Lee Denghui, later to become the first Taiwanese president of Taiwan, attended Cornell and made the earlier part of his career with the JCRR). All of the early Chinese commissioners were highly respected within the government. Each of them had held high positions in either education (Jiang Menglin, the Chief Commissioner had served, among other things, as Chancellor of Beijing University), or in rural reconstruction (Qian Tianhe in the Ministry of Agriculture and the Central Agricultural Institute). James YC Yan had been the Deputy Director of the Central Agricultural Research Station, as well as a member of the original Joint China-US Agricultural Mission in the early 1940s. There was also a long historical association

66 *Julia C. Strauss*

with Cornell through a Cornell University-Nanjing Project that went back to the 1920s. After James Yan left the Commission to pursue his vision of integrated rural development in the Philippines in 1950, the three Chinese commissioners who were in place by 1951 continued to serve until the end of their careers. The American commissioners had less lengthy tenures, but with few exceptions had years of experience in rural development within China and/or high rank in the US Department of Agriculture (Raymond Moyer, William Fippin), or had high position in the rural affairs division of the Occupation of Japan (Raymond Davis).[9]

The JCRR in Taiwan worked well for a number of reasons. First, the leaders of the organization had been pre-socialized into a remarkably common set of developmental-cum-New Deal norms that stressed technical expertise, application of then current scientific methods to agricultural and social problems, self-help by going to the grass roots, and social justice in relative equality of results. Second, the JCRR benefitted from a remarkably stable income stream and a political environment, which at a minimum gave the JCRR a fair amount of autonomy and at a maximum was unusually supportive. The early years in Taiwan coincided with the Truman Administration in Washington, which was both socially progressive and internationally deeply concerned about the spread of Communism. These preoccupations in Washington played to the JCRR's strengths, as it could (and did) style itself as progressive, developmental and results focussed, and through sheer effectiveness, a bulwark against the spread of Communism by attending to the felt needs of the rural population. On the Chinese side, there was also a good deal of active support for the goals and programs of the JCRR. The Taiwan Provincial Governor, a reformer by the name of Chen Cheng, was immensely interested in and supportive of the kinds of technically based but socially progressive programs that were at the JCRR's core. The best known of these was the three phased land reform program of the early 1950s. Since many of the sub-components of land reform programs from cadastral resurveying to the convening of elected land reform committees were actually implemented by local offices of the provincial Land Bureau, in conjunction with large numbers of ad hoc staff trained by the JCRR, good working relations between the JCRR and the Provincial Land Bureau were imperative for success. Land reform was perhaps the JCRR's most important program and signature success in its early years in Taiwan. There were many other projects that ranged from forestry (from planting shelterbelts to combat erosion to narrow technical projects designed to raise the profitability of wood products), irrigation, public health, and the revival of local farmer's associations. These all directly involved the active cooperation of Taiwan provincial bodies such as the provincial Food Bureau, the Agricultural and Forestry Bureau and the Water Conservancy Bureau, as well as a large range of local stakeholders. Taiwan, unlike China, was relatively compact and already accustomed to statist developmentalism. In 1949 Taiwan had undergone nearly 50 years of top down Japanese colonial development, and therefore had a degree of basic administrative and organizational infrastructure that most of China did not have, such as complete cadastral records and state organized farmer's associations. While it is true that the JCRR had a great deal of work to do, as over the 1940s cadastral records had become outdated and the farmers' associations established in the earlier Japanese colonial period had collapsed, it is equally the case that the JCRR had a substantial base upon which to build. Correcting cadastral survey records and reviving farmers' associations were much more straightforward propositions than were conducting cadastral surveys with no prior baseline of knowledge, or establishing farmers' associations from the ground up. In addition, there is some evidence that the kinds of programs promoted by the JCRR were pushing at an opening door. In the early 1950s Taiwan was already approaching industrial transition, with only just over 50 per cent of the population classified as engaged in agriculture. While much was made of the JCRR's successful implementation of rent reduction and a land to the tiller program in the early to mid-1950s, of the 50 per cent of the population classified as engaged in agriculture, only 38.5 per cent of that 50 per cent fell into the category of tenants in need of land reform (see Tang 1954: 12–14).[10] Small scale and external support by no means guarantees either effectiveness or efficiency in development programs, and the favourable conditions under which the JCRR was operating in Taiwan in no way diminishes the organization's successes after 1949. But it is clear that the local political and administrative environment in Taiwan was uniquely favourable. The country's small scale, the strong political support for technocratic solutions to rural development in both Washington and Taiwan, and solid pre-existing administrative and transport infrastructure, meant that the JCRR had an unusually hospitable environment in which to work; one that was not easily replicable.

Lessons learned amid catastrophic defeat: 1948–1949

When we turn to the earliest months of the JCRR's operations *before* its retreat to Taiwan, a very different picture emerges. Unlike the Inspectorate, which was established and institutionalized in the context of a weak central government that could do little other than acquiesce to its existence, the JCRR had the great misfortune of coming into existence just as the government with which it worked was decisively losing a bitter civil war. The incoming Communists were on the cusp of establishing a very strong state, one whose ideas about how to conduct rural policy could not have been more opposed to the gradualist and technocratic principles of the JCRR. The most immediately pressing issue for the JCRR was that of continued operation, as 'the rapid advances of the Communist armies' made the activities of the JCRR extraordinarily fraught – with frequent rushes to complete projects just ahead of the loss of the territory in which the given project was being implemented. Within months of its establishment in 1948, the JCRR's most serious questions did not have to do with bureaucratic wrangling or the carving out

68   *Julia C. Strauss*

of policy space, but 'if and for how long the Nationalist government could hold on to how much territory in south and southwest China' and 'whether the Communists would permit any part of the JCRR programs to continue' (Yager 1988: 28–29). Given that in many cases JCRR staff was literally only one or two steps ahead of the advancing People's Liberation Army, that the hyperinflation of the late 1940s wreaked havoc with any ability to plan or disburse funds, and that its core goals mandated working in partnership with local government organizations, it is a wonder that the JCRR even stayed together, much less attempted to launch projects at all in the military and social chaos that typified circumstances in China in late 1948 and 1949. Remarkably, the JCRR held together in this early period, and seems to have encountered almost no infighting or serious differences of opinion amongst its staff. More remarkably still, after a 'Phase A' strategy in late 1948 and early 1949 that concentrated on projects that were already well organized and well underway, a big push 'Phase B' program was launched specifically to combat the large, serious, and hitherto intractable problems of the countryside, particularly in land reform, the reinvigoration of farmer's associations and credit cooperatives, technically based programs for irrigation, veterinary services and the dissemination of better seeds (Joint Commission on Rural Reconstruction 1950: 10).

In practice, the Phase B program concentrated on two policy areas with very different technologies and methods of implementation: irrigation and land reform. Major projects were launched in dike repair (Hunan and Guangdong), and constructing irrigation canals (Sichuan). The JCRR's own evidence from Sichuan indicates that until nearly the very time that the Communist armies arrived, the Cornell trained JCRR engineers worked extraordinarily well with the Sichuan Water Conservancy Bureau and local leaders whose support was 'both genuine and gratifying' and resulted in local farmers 'who ... willingly assessed themselves in newly threshed rice to help provide 25 per cent of the total cost of the work' (Joint Commission on Rural Reconstruction 1950: 55). In the end 'military changes' forced the abandonment of the program in Sichuan in late November 1949, nearly two months after Mao Zedong proclaimed the establishment of the People's Republic of China in Beijing.

Land reform was the JCRR's signature program and key success on Taiwan in the 1950s, but land reform was also pursued with a surprising degree of vigour as part of the Phase B 'Big Push'. Land reform was both ambitious and dangerous, in that it was generally believed that the advancing Communists were ready to execute anyone who subscribed to any version of land reform not controlled by the Communists themselves. For this most important of demonstration projects, the JCRR concentrated its power in two very different areas at two very different scales of operation: 1) Longyan County, Fujian and 2) the large interior province of Sichuan. In 1949 Longyan was the immediate beneficiary of several interrelated JCRR irrigation and rural credit projects. It was chosen for several reasons. Longyan had experienced extraordinary political and military instability throughout the previous nearly 20 years. The Communists took control of it in the late 1920s and a rebellious Guomindang army in the early 1930s, and at the time of the JCRR's involvement the county had already undergone no less than three earlier versions of land reform. The last of these three land reform initiatives had been in the fairly recent past in 1943, and had actually succeeded in redistributing a fair amount of land to some, but by no means all, tenants. The comprehensive JCRR land reform program developed for Longyan was slotted to be implemented in conjunction with the county magistrate and prefectural directors. It aimed to provide technical assistance in assessment of land to complete the work of the 1943 reform; poor families who otherwise would have had to mortgage their land were aided by JCRR establishment of rural credit cooperatives for seed and fertilizer. If enthusiastic uptake is a reasonable measure of success, then the JCRR program for Longyan had to count as such. The credit project sponsored by the JCRR was run through the Farmer's Bank of China, which received some 10,000 applications from 52 newly established farmers' cooperatives within only a few months in 1949. But here as well forces far beyond the remit of the JCRR were at work: when the military situation deteriorated to the point that 'fence sitters thought it most opportune to change sides', there was little that the JCRR could do, other than to try to complete the already underway Longyan irrigation project as quickly as possible (Joint Commission on Rural Reconstruction 1950: 67).

The limits of the JCRR's capacities were on display in the Sichuan land reform program as well. Sichuan was an important site by virtue of its enormous size, agricultural capacity, and until a very late date its position as the most militarily secure province in China for the Nationalists. Nationalist administrators were themselves moved to attempt a 'big push' in land reform in China's most populous province as the rest of the country was being definitively lost to the Communists in 1949. In order to make a desperate last attempt to shore up their legitimacy, Guomindang administrators pushed through a sweeping, province wide campaign for rent reduction. Land reform in Sichuan was therefore dramatically scaled up from anything attempted in Longyan County or, for that matter, on Taiwan only several years later. Not surprisingly, what the JCRR could manage to contribute to such a large, hastily convened campaign was very small. The JCRR's own program evaluation suggested that it was only able to directly aid some 2249 people of a total target agrarian population of around 17,500,000. In short, what the JCRR could do in Sichuan in 1949 was only a drop in the bucket.

These JCRR activities in the organization's first, doomed year of operations need to be assessed in the context of the social, geographical and military situation of 1949, and offers a prime example by which to think through a larger question of how to assess effectiveness, efficiency and failure. Was the JCRR 'effective' at a macro level before China was taken over in full by the Communists? At the most general level at which its activities were pitched – to demonstrate that a serious reformist set of government institutions and programs could

70 *Julia C. Strauss*

make a real difference to the livelihood of poor farmers in an impoverished and war torn country and to forestall Communist victory – the answer has to be no. There is no evidence that JCRR programs slowed down the Communist military advance at all. But virtually all other similar efforts on the part of well meaning, technocratically inclined Americans had run into identical failures throughout the course of the civil war. If no less an effective administrator than George T. Marshall (of the later Marshall plan to rebuild Europe) departed China in December 1946 with a famous 'a plague on both your houses' speech after a frustrating year of trying to negotiate an end to the civil war in China, then the JCRR was hardly unique in its inability to staunch the tide of civil war and military defeat. If, on the other hand, we think in terms of the micro stories told in the official reports of the JCRR itself some 60 years after these events, then a different picture emerges. These narratives yield substantial evidence of project effectiveness, a high level of commitment from JCRR staff, the enthusiastic support, even welcome given to the JCRR by reformist administrators within the Nationalist government, and even local willingness on the part of local farmers to contribute to JCRR projects. That there was this degree of positive activity under conditions of such extraordinary military insecurity is astonishing. JCRR technocracy and aid could not solve the problems of the civil war. But the 'lessons' learned in the most trying and militarized of circumstances in places like Longyan and the interior of Sichuan, and the ways in which their modest successes were understood within the JCRR even after the forced retreat to Taiwan became part of the organization's folklore and repertoire. On Taiwan, under conditions of smaller scale, sympathetic governments, unified personnel, and, most of all, military security, these presets for action were then deployed to much greater effect.

Conclusion: mixing metaphors of effectiveness, efficiency, and performance

Tolstoy had it wrong: happy families are not all alike, and many unhappy families are unhappy in strikingly similar ways. In parallel fashion, the ways in which strong and effective development organizations emerge and are consolidated are varied, and the ways in which ineffective and non-performing organizations fail to operate well are often depressingly similar. All highly successful organizations need to have personnel so committed to the organization and its goals that they are willing to work incredibly hard in very challenging environments, and therefore all need to be socialized into the organizations core goals and values. All organizations also require buffering and insulation from the wider environments in which they operate, despite often considerable demands on the organization for favours, patronage, and special consideration.

The two cases presented here suggest that there is no one universally applicable recipe to either generating these kinds of commitments from staff or establishing the means of necessary insulation and buffering. The

PoE: lessons from China and Taiwan 71

differences between the 'backbone' prefectural administration of the Salt Inspectorate and the 'circulatory' project based workings of the JCRR could not be more stark. The former built up a bureaucratic and rule bound organization that was dramatic in its insistence on insulation from the rest of society, while the JCRR spent most of its time observing, advising, and making connections with rural society and the organizations thereof. Both had highly committed and well socialized personnel in hybrid organizations staffed by both Chinese and foreigners. The Salt Inspectorate accomplished this feat through its bureaucratic strategies of insulation and civil service, and the JCRR managed it by recruiting those already pre-socialized into a commonly held set of norms through postgraduate study at the Cornell School of Agronomy. Both were quasi-autonomous, but they maintained their autonomy and buttressed their political capital in very different ways. The Salt Inspectorate's only defence in the face of political interference was to style itself a loyal and responsive technocracy while reminding political leaders of its effectiveness and efficiency, and pointing out the importance of its separate civil service organization to that success. Until several years into the Sino-Japanese War this usually worked well enough; although when political leaders truly wanted something that the Inspectorate did not, the Inspectorate had no choice but to bow to the inevitable. The leaders of the JCRR built up political capital in also demonstrating quantifiable successes, but it did so in a way that directly involved political actors at all levels of the government, astutely assessing the conditions under which projects would be likely to be successful, and giving those organizations and actors a stake in those successes. Over time, the JCRR gradually lost its 'joint' character, as more of the technical and advisory roles were taken on by Chinese, and in the very end, the remains of the JCRR folded seamlessly into the Nationalist Council on Agriculture. These examples from the opposite chronological ends of Republican era China suggest that cases of high effectiveness, efficiency, and performance in hostile surrounding environments need not be clustered in geographical or policy space as pockets, but nor are they necessarily skeletal backbones of state capacity widely dispersed over a large geographical area (the Salt Inspectorate), or teams of experts rapidly circulating and augmenting local capacity (the JCRR). Each of these organizational models, be they defined pockets or clusters, prefectural backbones, or a circulatory system of roving advisors, has the potential to become a site of high performance and productivity. But each successful case appears to demonstrate some combination of committed leadership, effective socialization of staff, sufficient funding to maintain the integrity of the organization as it pursues its defined tasks, and, perhaps most importantly, concrete demonstration to stakeholders and sources of political support of high performance in a policy area that is understood to be of crucial importance.

Equally, the varied histories of tax systems in developing countries, aid and development projects, and reformist organizations, is littered with examples of organizations that either did not survive the departure of its original visionary

72 *Julia C. Strauss*

leadership, gradually became sites of political spoils and patrimonialism, and/ or did not survive attempted transplantation of a successful organizational model to a different social and political environment. In this, the role of the surrounding political and social environment is likely to prove necessary, if not sufficient, for continued high performance. The most extreme example of this was of course the JCRR. It could not reverse the tide of war that was its undoing on the mainland of China in 1949. But it did rely on a plurality of politicians and technocrats within the government for support and as partners to work with, and it was quite successful in so doing for several decades after its forced relocation to the smaller scale and more militarily secure environment of Taiwan. There were any number of attempts in the 1960s to 'export' and replicate the successes of the JCRR model to other parts of Southeast Asia, to the Philippines and South Vietnam in particular. These worked infinitely less well because of the lack of political and social support for the model's core goals. Although it was of a relatively small scale and the recipient of masses of US aid, South Vietnam was subject to exactly the same problem that had so plagued the JCRR in China: hyper militarization and massive military insecurity. In most policy environments, organizations will only be conferred the necessary working autonomy to promote programs and go about their business insofar as the relevant political leadership sees that it is in its interests to allow the organization to continue without political pressure and interference. The curious cases of the Sino-Foreign Salt Inspectorate and the JCRR offer examples of how surrounding political environments can be benign, hostile, and radically change from one to the other; and as such suggest parameters for the consolidation and extension of high performing state organizations elsewhere in the developing world.

Notes

1 The information in this section is a significant reworking of material first published in Strauss (1998) and then condensed and recast in Strauss (2008).
2 On semi-autonomous or autonomous revenue authorities (SARAs or ARAs) and their benefits see Talierco, Jr. (2004); for a more balanced view on these sorts of revenue collecting organizations, see Moore and Schneider (2004: especially 22–26).
3 During the initial writing of this article in February 2012, a 'troika' of self-appointed guardians of the euro had just insisted that they be let in to Greece to oversee the implementation of its austerity program; the insults to nationalism and notions of sovereignty indeed have a lineage that goes way back.
4 See report by J.D. Croome (n.d.), hereafter cited as 'Croome Report'.
5 Interviews with Chen Guisheng (January 16, 1989, Taipei), Lin Jiyong (January 24, 1989, Tainan), Zhong Liangzhe (January 20, 1989, Taipei), and Zhou Weiliang (January 23, 1989, Tainan).
6 In the sample of 185 for which I had full access to personnel records between 1914 and the mid-1930s, there were 14 cases of dismissal. Most of these were low level staff engaged in corruption at the stage of 'weighment', when bags of salt were weighed and the tax assessed. But one of the dismissed had reached the rank of Assistant District Inspector, ten had worked for the organization for ten years or more, and one had even garnered a previous commendation for distinguished service (see Strauss 1998: 72–73 and footnote 30 for further details).

7 This was even formally designated in the title of the Inspectorate under the Nationalists. 'Regular' divisions under the Ministry of Finance were called *si*; semi-autonomous entities like Maritime Customs and the Salt Inspectorate were allowed to retain their own personnel systems and salary scales, and were formally designatied *shu*, which carried the connotations of substantial autonomy. The Sino-foreign Salt Inspectorate (*Yanwu Jihe Zongsuo*) became the Salt Inspectorate Special Division (*Yanji Shu*) under the Ministry of Finance in 1928, and then as part of the wider reorganization of the Ministry of Finance, again changed name to the Directorate-General of Salt (*Yanwu Zongju*) in 1936; now formally absorbing what remained of the Inspectorate's old rivals in the Salt Division (*Yanwu Si*).
8 This discussion is drawn from Strauss (1998: 126–33).
9 This biographical information is compiled from Yager (1988: 13–14 and 62–63); see also Shen (1970: 14–15).
10 In Tang (1954), see the 'table showing the total population and agricultural population of Taiwan province, 1940–52' (ibid.: 12), 'table showing different kinds of farming families in Taiwan province, 1940–52' (ibid.: 13), and 'table showing the areas of owner-cultivated and non-owner cultivated land in Taiwan province, 1939–52' (ibid.: 14).

Interviews

Chen Guisheng, Taipei, 16 January 1989: Chen grew up in the Inspectorate, as his father had worked for the organization for many years. Chen took the entry level examination in 1939 and started off as an entry level clerk. He settled in to a lifetime of work with the organization, working mostly in the personnel division, where he ended his career in the 1980s as Division Chief.

Lin Jiyong, Tainan, 24 January 1989: like Chen Guisheng, Lin took the entry level examination in 1939. His career was largely in the general affairs and transportation department, only retiring in the mid-1980s. At the time of the interview he was still active in retirement, writing histories of the Salt Inspectorate.

Zhong Liangzhe, Taipei, 20 January 1989: Zhong took the entry level examination in 1941 in Fujian. He began his career in the personnel department, and then moved into salt production and transport. He reached the top of the organization as an inspector, only retiring in 1984.

Zhou Weiliang, Tainan, 23 January 1989: like Chen Guisheng, Zhou's father had worked for the inspectorate in its early days in the 1910s and 1920s. After university the younger Zhou took the exam in 1933, and was appointed to his first post shortly thereafter. Zhou spent his entire life with the inspectorate: first as a child, then as a professional, and even in retirement, he continued to do research and write on the organization.

4 An enduring pocket of effectiveness
The case of the National Development Bank of Brazil (BNDE)

Eliza J. Willis

Introduction

'Without an effective state,' Scott Mainwaring and Timothy Scully (2008: 116) remind us, 'neither democracy nor development will flourish'. Following two decades of neoliberal reforms primarily aimed at dismantling government agencies in developing countries, scholars and practitioners of development have refocused attention on enhancing state performance. The concept of 'pockets of effectiveness' (PoE) makes an essential contribution to this revitalized discourse on the state. Moreover, the existence of PoE within even the most corrupt and incapable states gives us reasons for optimism about the ongoing project of state building.

This chapter offers a case study of the National Bank for Economic Development (Banco Nacional de Desenvolvimento Econômico or BNDE), which has been an enduring PoE within the Brazilian state for nearly 60 years. Founded in 1952, the BNDE has provided an array of financial services critical to promoting Brazilian economic development. Originally founded to finance basic infrastructure to support industrial development, the Bank has continually altered its lending practices in keeping with evolving strategies of national development. While its centrality to development policymaking has waxed and waned, the Bank's reputation as an autonomous and effective institution has remained constant through multiple transitions in governments and regimes.

This chapter argues that the BNDE's remarkable record of persistence as a PoE in a changing Brazilian state can be traced to several factors evident in its creation and first decade of existence (1952–62). These factors, which I first articulated in an in-depth study (Willis 1986), parallel closely those identified by prominent scholars of bureaucracy (especially Grindle 1997; Tendler 1997; Leonard 2008) and crystallized in the framework proposed in this volume. Specifically, the BNDE's organizational success emerged from a combination of a relatively supportive political environment, unusually committed and qualified administrative leadership and staff, and responsibility for performing the essential function of providing financial resources for national development. Together, these attributes allowed the Bank to weather early challenges and become established as one of Brazil's most respected and effective government institutions.

This chapter is divided into six parts. First, following a brief review of the BNDE's changing role, I discuss several qualitative and quantitative indicators that confirm the Bank's status as a 'pocket of effectiveness'. I then provide a more in-depth account of the Bank's creation and early history, followed by an analysis of the key factors that contributed to its emergence as a PoE within Brazil's patrimonial state during the 1950s. In the next sections of the chapter I identify key turning points in the Bank's early history, as well as its response to some challenges to its effectiveness from political interventions by two Brazilian presidents. I then discuss means through which the BNDE has had an institutional 'triggering effect' on other entities within the Brazilian state. I conclude with a summary of the most important findings and conclusions suggested by the case study.

The BNDE: creation and expansion as a premier pocket of effectiveness

Since its creation in the early 1950s, the National Bank for Economic Development (Banco Nacional de Desenvolvimento Econômico or BNDE) has been the single most important government entity offering long-term loans and technical expertise for development projects in Brazil. Through 60 years of operations, the Bank, which had the word 'social' added to its name in 1982, has evolved and expanded its loan portfolio in many new directions.[1] From its original charge of financing a handful of public infrastructure projects, the Bank has grown into a complex organization characterized by multiple programs, providing support to public and private (small, medium and large) sector borrowers in activities as diverse as cattle raising, environmental services, energy, pulp and paper, cinema, and tradable goods. Now larger than the World Bank and second only to the China Development Bank, the BNDE doubled its disbursements to a record US$230 billion between 2007 and 2010 (Financial Times 22 June 2011).

The BNDE easily meets two of the criteria – impact and longevity – associated with PoE (see Roll, chapter 2). Every major infrastructure project in energy and transportation of the past 60 years has relied on low cost financing from the Bank. It has also played a significant role in financing the development of Brazil's industrial base through low interest loans with long amortization periods. In 2011, 40 per cent of loans went to infrastructure, 32 per cent to industry, 21 per cent to trade and services, and 7 per cent to the agriculture and cattle-raising sector (BNDES 2012: 7). In recent years, the Bank has been responsible for anywhere between one-fifth and one-fourth of total investments in the Brazilian economy (Reuters 15 February 2011). Among its many contributions to national development are the creation and expansion of Brazilian capital markets, the transformation of numerous infant industries (e.g., petrochemicals and pulp and paper) into vigorous international competitors, the implementation of a successful privatization program, and, more recently, the quick improvement in GDP growth during the 2008–9 financial crisis (The Guardian 29 March 2011).

76   *Eliza J. Willis*

While impressive, size of impact and longevity alone cannot be considered definitive evidence of institutional effectiveness. However, there is ample evidence that the BNDE fulfils several other qualifications of a PoE. Bank personnel have been guided by a strong sense of mission to promote national economic development. As explained in more detail below, the creation of a cohesive *esprit de corps* in pursuit of a clearly stated mission has been the bedrock of the Bank's continuing effectiveness as a state institution.

But other criteria are also compelling. First, the diversity and complexity of lending activities over the decades reflect the confidence governmental authorities have had in the Bank's capacity and flexibility. Frequently, when faced with a change in development strategy or a particularly difficult economic challenge, higher authorities have sought the Bank's expertise in finding a solution. For example, during an intensive period of neoliberal reforms, it was given responsibility for overseeing the privatization of several publicly owned firms. In response to the international financial crisis in 2008, the government of then President Luiz Inácio Lula da Silva introduced several anti-cyclical measures. The centrality of the BNDE in this strategy was illustrated by an infusion of 100 billion reis, the reduction of the long-term interest rate, and the creation of two new lending programs designed to sustain private investment. According to the annual report (2009, 12), 'from September 2008 to December 2009, the BNDES was responsible for 37 per cent of the increase in credit in the Brazilian economy.' While not sustainable over the long term, these loans contributed to Brazil's quick recovery from the credit crunch. These examples of the Bank's status as the 'lender of first resort' and remarkable ability to adapt to new demands provide solid evidence of its effectiveness.

The BNDE's long and consistent history of financial solvency offers a further test of its capacity and effectiveness as an organization. The Bank is not wholly self-financed and remains dependent on the national government for some of its funding, yet it has never had to declare bankruptcy, nor has it required vast or controversial infusions of government funding to close a gap between loan commitments and disbursements. While the Bank has often been faced with loan requests that greatly exceed available funds, it has generally followed conservative lending policies that favour investment grade clients. As result, the percentage of defaults has remained remarkably low (0.15 to 0.20 per cent) even in the most difficult years.[2] Bank managers have sought to diversify sources of funding through various channels including bond issues in foreign currency. The confidence of international financial markets in the BNDE's credit quality (and in Brazil debt in general) is well demonstrated by upgrades Moody's gave to Bank-issued bonds in 2011 (BNDES 2011).

Other measures of the BNDE's standing as a premier PoE are more qualitative in character. Despite allocating billions of dollars in loans over nearly six decades, the Bank has rarely been the focus of scandal or accusations of corruption. Perhaps the most serious hint of scandal occurred in 1998 when illegal wire taps on the phones of various officials, including the president of

An enduring PoE: the case of the BNDE   77

the BNDE, revealed possible improprieties in the privatization of a telephone company. Although the Bank president and others were forced to resign from their positions, the Brazilian Supreme Court later found them not guilty of any charges. Moreover, as noted by Mauricio Font (2003: 30) this event did not 'cast an aura of suspicion over the privatization program as whole, which was conducted (by the BNDE) in quite a transparent way'. No other Brazilian government entity has a stronger or better-deserved reputation for incorruptibility and honest administration than the BNDE.

The BNDE has not entirely escaped close scrutiny or energetic criticism from its detractors. Critics question the Bank's strategy of supporting 'national champions', which has led to market concentration in a few large groups to the detriment of smaller producers and Brazilian consumers (The Economist 7 July 2011). Some argue that criteria applied to loans made to large corporations are not sufficiently transparent. Bank managers have attempted to respond to these criticisms by instituting a program to respond to citizen questions and complaints, subjecting its loans to scrutiny by outside accounting firms, and providing detailed reports of its activities to the national congress. Valid questions have been raised about the large influence the Brazilian government, through agencies like the BNDE, continues to wield over the economy despite decades of market-based reforms. However, these public attacks on the Bank arise from ideological debates about the proper role of the state in the economy and not from accusations of patronage politics or corruption.

So how can we account for the creation and institutionalization of the BNDE as one of Brazil's premier pockets of effectiveness? This chapter will argue that the Bank's evolution as a PoE can be traced to factors involved in its creation and early lending operations. Some of these factors—the creation of a cohesive *esprit de corps*, commitment to merit-based hiring and emphasis on technical decision-making—were internal to the Bank and its leadership. Other factors were more external, including guidance and funding from international entities and limited interference from higher political authorities in internal operations. Finally, the Bank's evolution as a PoE can be attributed to its essential function as the principal source of long-term lending for development, and to the combination of vagueness and specificity in the legislation defining its essential function as a development bank.

Creation of the Banco Nacional de Desenvolvimento Econômico

The BNDE was a by-product of the Joint Brazil-United States Economic Development Commission, established in the early 1950s to formulate an investment program in basic infrastructure, to be financed by the World Bank and the Brazilian government. The Joint Commission provided detailed analysis of the economy and studies of infrastructural bottlenecks in energy, transportation, mining and agriculture. It also introduced a new, more technical approach to the making of development policy. After two years of

78   *Eliza J. Willis*

intensive work, the Joint Commission recommended the implementation of 41 projects calling for a total investment of 387.3 million dollars. These projects became the blueprint for the Brazilian government's investment priorities for the following decade, and set forth a clear function for the soon to be created development bank.

While the Joint Commission recommended making a government agency responsible for carrying out the investment plan, deciding the exact form this agency should take was left entirely to the Brazilian authorities. Then-president Getúlio Vargas (1951–54) considered several proposals before settling on the creation of a new development bank. He explicitly rejected a recommendation making the Bank of Brazil responsible for financing infrastructure projects, because he believed it was too vulnerable to pressures from the Brazilian Congress (Willis 1995: 633). He also dismissed a proposal to create four different banks, each specializing in one sector and placed under the control of regional or local governments. Vargas preferred a more centralized institution put squarely under federal governmental control. Finally, Vargas chose a purely state-owned entity instead of a proposed mixed enterprise in which private firms would own 49 per cent. Vargas wanted an agency that would be relatively free of pressures from the private sector and the Congress and firmly under the control of the executive branch.

Legislation proposing the BNDE was presented to the Brazilian Congress in 1952. One of the laws gave the Bank the legal status of an *autarquia*, which was intended to give it a measure of administrative autonomy and a source of independent funding. However, the law also placed the Bank under the authority of the Minister of Finance and, by implication, the nation's president. According to the legislation, the Directorate and the Administrative Council would be made up of presidential appointees who would govern the BNDE. The Administrative Council had the power to: set internal rules and norms (with the final approval of the Minister of Finance); study loan operations; fix interest rates; create and eliminate staff positions; examine annual accounts; support or oppose the vetoes by the BNDE's president, and delegate powers within the Bank. The Directorate, which consisted of the President, Supervising Director, Economic Director and Technical Director, was expected to run operations on the ground. Although the law gave the BNDE president veto power within the Directorate, the Supervising Director was granted substantial control over the hiring and firing of personnel and the coordination of daily work routines. Although BNDE presidents eventually became dominant, the Supervising Director wielded the greatest power over internal affairs during the 1950s.

The Bank's legal status and ministerial placement proved to be important factors in determining its independence and effectiveness as an institution. Like most *autarquias*, the BNDE was converted to a public enterprise in the 1970s. Instead of functioning as the government's agent in financing development projects, the Bank began to operate more like a private corporation with considerable autonomous control over its internal administration and

An enduring PoE: the case of the BNDE 79

financial resources. However, Brazilian presidents retained their power to appoint top administrators and control the Bank's access to sources of domestic financing. Presidents also determined under which government ministry the BNDE would be formally placed. The relative power of the ministry within the government would either enhance or undermine the Bank's effectiveness as a development agency (Willis 1986). The BNDE's initial placement in the Ministry of Finance entailed an immediate boost to its status within the Vargas government.

In addition to the law establishing the new *autarquia*, the Vargas government offered laws permitting the Treasury to guarantee foreign credits up to 500 million dollars and created a new fund, the Fund for Economic Rehabilitation (Fundo de Reaparelhamento Econômico or FRE), to finance the local currency costs of Joint Commission projects to be implemented by the BNDE. Both of the latter pieces of legislation were necessary to meet requirements for World Bank loans.

The FRE and the right to guarantee loans were originally intended to shield Bank administrators from congressional interference in lending decisions, as they would not have to face a yearly congressional budget process or seek legislative approval when borrowing abroad. According to the enabling legislation, the FRE would fund BNDE operations through a dedicated compulsory tax. However, in fact, several provisions in the legislation threatened to undermine the Bank's access to these funds. The tax was temporary and subject to legislative review. Of greater concern was a provision granting the Treasury the power to collect and distribute the FRE and other revenues on behalf of the BNDE. This arrangement made the Bank wholly dependent on the goodwill of Treasury officials in the Ministry of Finance. Many of these revenues were never collected and others were diverted to unsanctioned uses such as covering deficits in other accounts (BNDE 1955). Despite these challenges, the FRE became the major domestic source of funding for the BNDE during its early years of operation. Without it, none of the Joint Commission projects would have been undertaken.

The government met strong resistance from some legislators who opposed the creation of a new tax to fund the FRE, foreign involvement in guiding infrastructural projects and the loss of congressional control over economic policy making to the president. After considerable debate, the Vargas government was able to overcome this opposition to secure passage of all three laws without amendments.

The legislation establishing the BNDE, funding its operations, and empowering its core function of financial intermediary, insulated the Bank from the political influence of the Congress and the private sector but did not completely protect it from politically motivated interference from the executive branch. The president, for example, had complete discretion to appoint the Bank's top managers and the Minister of Finance controlled the disbursement of the FRE. Also, the law failed to limit the scope of lending activities to specific sectors; the BNDE was permitted to act like a commercial bank

80 *Eliza J. Willis*

although it could not accept deposits from the private sector. Clearly, if the president wished to undermine the effectiveness of the Bank by turning it into a sinecure or patronage machine similar to other agencies in Brazil's patrimonial state, he had the power and the means to do so.

The BNDE could easily have been turned into another source of patronage within Brazil's patrimonial state. Instead, the Bank evolved into a PoE led by technocrats and primarily guided by technical, financial, and economic criteria. What accounts for this improbable outcome? In keeping with the PoE framework proposed in this book, the explanation is found in the mix of external, internal, and functional factors that shaped the BNDE as an organization during the early years of its operation.

Becoming a PoE: the function of development financing

The law that created the BNDE endowed the executive branch with significant discretion in defining the scope and funding of the Bank's operations. Brazilian presidents had the power to commit Bank funds to pet projects, to withhold FRE revenues, appoint political cronies to the management and staff, and to fire recalcitrant and uncooperative managers. There was nothing in the enabling law to prevent presidents from turning the Bank into another source of patronage within Brazil's patrimonial state. Part of the explanation for why the Bank instead became a PoE is found in the critical function it was expected to perform in promoting national economic development.

From its inception, the BNDE's primary mission was defined as providing long-term finance for the public and private investments necessary for promoting Brazil's industrial development. At the time, no other entity within the Brazilian state had the technical expertise or resources to offer low interest loans with long amortization periods. The BNDE occupied a niche within the bureaucracy that did not put it in direct competition with other, more established government agencies. By the 1950s, the role of the state in providing development finance through government banks or other credit agencies was becoming well recognized within the international development community. As discussed further on, the governments of both Getúlio Vargas and Juscelino Kubitschek (1956–61) embraced this new public function as part of the post-war strategy of state-led development.

The particular combination of vagueness and specificity in the enabling law enhanced the Bank's effectiveness in fulfilling its financing function. While vagueness in the law has allowed the BNDE to expand the scope of lending activities over the past 60 years, specific provisions granted the Bank substantial control over management of its internal operations.

The general and imprecise language in the legislation establishing BNDE's mandate, while increasing the Bank's vulnerability to presidential pressures, also made possible the expansion in the scope of lending activities during the 1950s and later on. As constitutional scholars frequently note, there can be a virtue to vagueness because it permits modern interpretations to override outmoded ones as the needs and attitudes of populations change. Vagueness lends flexibility and dynamism to constitutions or ordinary laws and increases the likelihood they will remain relevant and endure through challenging times. Two examples of vagueness have proved especially important to the Bank's effectiveness as a development bank over time. The law delegated broad powers to the Bank to fulfil its purpose as the government's agent in financial operations relevant to the re-equipment and development of the national economy (Willis 1986: 92). The original law failed to specify which types of production were encompassed in 'basic industries'. Succeeding administrations and BNDE managers used this clause to push for BNDE expansion into a variety of sectors beyond basic infrastructure (Willis 1986: 178). The first notable expansion in the scope of lending occurred between 1956 and 1961, when President Kubitschek tapped the BNDE as the principal source of finance and expertise for his ambitious Targets Plan for economic development. The enabling law, along with legislation passed in 1956 explicitly acknowledging the prerogative of Bank managers to adjust lending priorities as they saw fit (Willis 1986: 93), allowed the expansion of lending into a wide variety of activities and sectors of the Brazilian economy.

While the vagueness of the enabling legislation no doubt contributed to the flexibility and dynamism in the Bank's functions, specific provisions conceded broad control to managers over internal rules and norms, selecting projects, fixing interest rates (within legally designated limits), and hiring and firing regular staff. In addition, the inability to accept short-term deposits made clear that the Bank's primary function was to provide long-term loans. This provision provided managers with a strong rationale for rejecting requests from short-term borrowers who expected to use their political connections to secure loans (Willis 1986). As discussed below, Bank bureaucrats were very successful in denying requests for such short-term loans.

The critical importance of the Bank's function as the main source of long-term development financing within the Brazilian state helps explain its emergence as a PoE. No other government agency in the 1950s had the resources or expertise to perform this function, which allowed the Bank to occupy a privileged position within the Brazilian bureaucracy. However, the BNDE's effectiveness in carrying out this function also depended on supportive factors in its external and internal environments.

Becoming a PoE: a (mostly) favourable external environment

The focus on development within key international and national arenas during the 1950s proved conducive for the BNDE's transformation into a PoE. Following the end of World War II, influential international actors such as the US government and the World Bank advocated state-sponsored finance and international aid as means for promoting economic recovery in Europe and Japan and economic development in poor countries. This approach dovetailed well with an ideology of development in Brazil that championed

82   *Eliza J. Willis*

making the state responsible for guiding the development process and recognized the value of shielding state bureaucrats from external political influence (Willis 1986; Sikkink 1991).

The Joint Commission exemplified the new post-war approach to international cooperation that entailed promises of low interest loans for basic infrastructural projects. By requiring governments to meet certain technical and financial criteria prior to receiving a loan, the international members on the Joint Commission strengthened the influence and effectiveness of future BNDE bureaucrats within the Brazilian state. The Joint Commission's charge went well beyond merely promising World Bank financing. It also had the duty to recommend how to 'remove deterrents to and otherwise encourage the introduction, local development and application of technical skills, and the creation and effective utilization of capital both foreign and domestic' (Joint Commission Report 1954: 251). The American advisors placed special importance on enhancing the technical skills of Brazilian bureaucrats.

As a result of their close association with foreign technical advisers from the World Bank and the US government, future BNDE bureaucrats learned new techniques of project evaluation that revolutionized the planning and budgeting process in both public and private investments. Roberto Campos, one of the Bank's most influential managers during the 1950s, later noted that '(t)he old tradition of budget allocations for public works unsupported by detailed project studies gave way gradually to cost-benefit and marginal-social productivity studies, leading to a rapid development of the techniques of project formulation and appraisal' (Campos 1969: 79). The BNDE's effectiveness as a development institution was in no small part due to its role in providing the technical analysis the World Bank and other international lenders required of all loan projects.

Vargas and Kubitschek both saw the legitimacy of their respective governments as tied to the development and growth of the national economy. They also embraced the development strategy of 'import-substitution industrialization', which entailed building high priority national industries through state-guided investments financed by domestic and foreign sources. The idea of actively employing state resources to promote industrial expansion became known as 'developmentalism'. Although this ideology reached its fullest expression during Kubtischek's presidency, Vargas's embryonic support for its main tenets were evident in his embrace of the Joint Commission's recommendations and his decision to establish the BNDE. Both presidents offered formal plans for guiding public investment, although Kubitschek's Targets Plan was far more ambitious and elaborated than was Vargas's public investment program (popularly known as the Lafer Plan), which was solely based on the Joint Commission's report. But both plans showed considerable presidential support for a more technically based approach to state investment.

The BNDE bureaucrats benefitted from Vargas's and Kubitschek's adherence to an approach to development that gave a large role to the state and recognized the value of insulating some bureaucrats from patronage politics.

As discussed in more detail below, both presidents tried to influence specific lending decisions but such interventions were rare. For the most part, Vargas and Kubitschek governments followed the recommendations of Bank managers regarding loan requests. BNDE bureaucrats played a particularly significant role in the design and implementation of projects associated with the Targets Plan. This ambitious plan gave a major boost to Brazilian industrialization, including the development of its automobile industry. Many studies have attributed the success of this investment plan to the BNDE's standing as a PoE (Lafer 1975; Geddes 1990a; Sikkink 1991).

While the Vargas and Kubitschek administrations generally deferred to the technical judgment of the BNDE on specific loans, they curtailed the Bank's effectiveness by failing to provide adequate funds for its operations. The Bank had no independent sources of domestic funding and was completely dependent on receiving special revenues collected by the Ministry of Finance. Although the law mandated the transfer of these revenues to the Bank, the Ministry consistently diverted some portion of them to other uses. Managers registered their complaints about the diversion of funds in meeting minutes. While the record shows that the Bank was very effective in carrying out its essential function throughout the 1950s, the funding issue was a serious constraint on the scope of its impact.

In sum, several aspects of the external context in which the BNDE began operating contributed to its development as a PoE. The World Bank's requirement that foreign loan requests conform to a certain technical standard had a direct impact on increasing the BNDE's effectiveness. The linkages formed between the Brazilian members of the Joint Commission, several of whom became the BNDE's first managers, and the American members also enhanced the Bank's effectiveness in indirect, but significant ways. Strong presidential support for state-sponsored planning and investment in development helped insulate Bank lending decisions from patronage politics. The diversion of legislatively mandated funds to other uses narrowed the scope of effective Bank action but did not adversely affect completed loans.

Becoming a PoE: internal factors

Both external and functional factors contributed to the BNDE's emergence as a PoE. But we must look inside the Bank to gain a full understanding of its evolution into an enduring PoE within the Brazilian state. Key sources of effectiveness – merit-based hiring, a cohesive *esprit de corps* and technically informed loan decisions – became embedded within the BNDE's culture early in its history due to the efforts of managers and staff. These innovative technocrats or *técnicos* undertook specific measures to maintain the Bank's independence and ensure its effectiveness, even in the context of uncertain funding and irregular support from the chief executive (Willis 1995: 626).

The value Vargas initially placed on technical expertise was evident in his decision to appoint Brazilians with advanced technical training – especially

84   *Eliza J. Willis*

Roberto Campos, Glycon de Paiva Teixeira and Ari Torres – who had participated in the Joint Commission to the Bank's first board of directors. Campos, an economist who had taken graduate courses in economics at George Washington University and Columbia University, and Paiva Teixeira and Torres, both engineers trained in Brazil, had prior experience in development projects. All three men served in top posts at the Bank, including as president, though Torres left within a few months of his appointment. Roberto Campos, who later became one of Brazil's best known public figures, was the principal author of the Joint Commission's final report, which explicitly criticized political influence in economic policymaking and recommended the creation of 'effective, independent and non-political' agencies to carry out public investments and coordinate credit policies (Joint Commission 1954; Willis 1995: 633). Campos proved an important proponent of merit-based hiring and the application of technical criteria to loan decisions during his years as a BNDE administrator. Vargas and later Kubitschek generally appointed individuals with technical expertise to manage Bank affairs. These administrators, especially Campos, were responsible for embedding the practice of hiring qualified individuals for the technical staff.

Although Vargas appointed technocrats to important positions within the Bank's first administration, he reserved the powerful post of Supervising Director for his personal friend and confidante José Maciel Filho. Maciel Filho had no technical training in economics, law, or engineering (Willis 1995: 636). His personalist and political preferences for hiring staff clashed with the technical criteria advocated by Campos, Torres and Paiva. Maciel Filho opposed introducing competitive examinations that would lead to the hiring of 'ugly women and communists' (Willis 1995: 637). Though he accepted filling 80 per cent of the staff positions through a competitive exam, Maciel Filho insisted on reserving 20 per cent for patronage appointments (Campos 1994: 194; Willis 1995: 637). His direct access to Vargas ensured he would prevail in disputes over personnel decisions.

Campos and his colleagues could not accept the introduction of patronage practices in the BNDE and set about figuring out ways to circumvent Maciel Filho in hiring staff. Their efforts were facilitated by two indirect enabling factors. First, they possessed superior knowledge of the technical aspects of the Joint Commission's proposed projects. Maciel Filho was forced to rely on their expertise since he had very little understanding of development banking. Second, technically trained individuals preferred careers in the public sector where the most important development initiatives were concentrated and where they could command the highest salaries (Willis 1995: 638). Campos and Paiva Teixeira could count on having a strong pool of qualified applicants.

Campos and Paiva Teixeira succeeded in staffing the Bank with technically trained experts by adopting two recruitment strategies. They focused on recruiting individuals they believed would respect technical norms but whose adherence to a nationalist development ideology would make them acceptable to Maciel Filho, an avowed nationalist. Campos and Paiva Teixeira also turned to other state agencies, especially Brazil's Ministry of Foreign Affairs and the Brazilian Institute of Geography and Statistics, with established reputations for technical achievement. Through these strategies, they managed to hire an outstanding group of technocrats (Campos 1994: 195). Campos sought to deepen the technical abilities of these recruits by sending many abroad to US- and UN-sponsored professional training programmes and as Bank representatives to international conferences, where they could interact with experts from other developing countries. He and Paiva Teixeira also helped establish a joint study group between the BNDE and the UN Economic Commission on Latin America (ECLA), that played an instrumental role in building the technical capacity of Bank personnel for over a decade. The Joint Study Group provided a generation of Bank technocrats with a level of expertise on economic development that was not widely available in other public and private institutions in Brazil during the 1950s and 1960s.

Due to a conflict over a loan backed by Maciel Filho and President Vargas, Campos and Paiva Teixeira left the Bank in 1953 but returned in 1954 after Vargas's suicide and Maciel Filho's subsequent resignation. Campos became Supervising Director and Paiva Teixeira was appointed President. Now occupying the most powerful posts in the Bank, they worked to introduce competitive exams (*concursos*) for choosing the permanent staff. Campos was instrumental in making certain a *concurso* was held in 1956 for both the administrative and technical staff. To ensure that the entire staff was similarly qualified, all existing Bank employees were required to take and pass these exams to keep their jobs. As a demonstration of the professional level already achieved, most of the previously hired technical staff easily passed the exam. The common experience of the rigorous merit examination created strong personal and professional bonds among Bank technocrats, especially those who formed part of the same cohort. Statistics from the first *concurso* reveal just how competitive these exams were: only 19 of 231 who took the engineering exam and 8 of 71 who took the economics exam passed and were hired.

The bonds among those in the first and subsequent cohorts were strengthened further by the organization of work routines. During this period the BNDE was organized around six big departments, each dedicated to one essential function: economic, technical, financial, legal, accounting and administration. The Economics and Technical departments concentrated the most technical capacity and wielded the greatest influence through their respective analyses of specific projects. Early on, Campos created small working groups consisting of economists, engineers and lawyers, responsible for issuing technical opinions and recommendations on loan requests. These working groups reinforced the application of technical criteria and led to strong personal connections among personnel that endured throughout their careers at BNDE, many of which lasted for several decades. Moreover, this *esprit de corps* was not restricted to the staff alone but also had a powerful co-optative effect on those appointed to top managerial posts.

86 *Eliza J. Willis*

The introduction of competitive examinations, the organization of working groups, and training and educational experiences led to the development of a highly committed, coherent *esprit de corps* among the Bank's technical personnel. They shared a common sense of institutional mission and strong adherence to the application of technical norms to lending decisions. This *esprit de corps* was unique in the Brazilian bureaucracy during this period and it gave the BNDE a special identity within a largely patrimonial state. Although Campos and Paiva Teixeira had a hand in fostering this unique spirit, it has been carried forward by succeeding generations of Bank employees, though perhaps with less intensity.

The keys to the Bank's effectiveness have been the high control exercised over lending decisions and the rigorous analysis applied to every loan. Beginning with the first loans granted in the 1950s until today, Bank technocrats have wielded enormous influence over the norms and procedures that govern loans to both private and public sector borrowers. This achievement was impressive especially in the 1950s, when leaders within Brazil's patrimonial state frequently diverted funds for patronage purposes. Despite legislative provisions giving the Minister of Finance and the President of the Republic authority over specific lending decisions, Bank bureaucrats were very successful in ensuring that loans were decided according to technical, not political, criteria.

Two indirect factors reinforced the application of technical norms to the Bank's earliest loans. The investment projects already formulated by the Joint Commission were incorporated in a government plan that guided BNDE lending between 1952 and 1956. These ready-made projects acted as buffers against politically motivated requests because they made lending priorities explicit and transparent. The Bank's role in financing projects in Kubitschek's Target Plan between 1956 and 1961 had a similar insulating effect. As previously discussed, vagueness in the original enabling legislation also proved instrumental because it allowed Bank managers to develop criteria for project selection, work routines and rules governing interactions with clients.

The *diretoria* (directorate), under the stewardship of Campos and Paiva Teixeira, sought to raise the technical level of investment decisions in public and private sector firms. In their view, Brazilian development had been hampered by the allocation of government funds based on personal and political grounds. They evaluated each loan request according to three decision rules (Willis 1995: 642–43). First, loan projects that conformed most closely to government development plans and goals received the highest priority. In the 1950s, the Bank prioritized projects designed to overcome infrastructural bottlenecks impeding industrial expansion. Loan projects in industry and agriculture were considered only if they involved 'a product capable of stimulating the growth of new favourable or essential initiatives for economic development' (BNDE 1954: 71).

A second decision rule grew from the Bank's specialization as a long-term lender, favouring loans requiring large capital outlays, lengthy amortization periods and low returns. Following the Joint Commission's recommendation that public sector investment should complement, not displace, private investment, the *diretoria* usually rejected loan requests for the production of consumption goods. Finally, in an effort to protect the financial viability of the Bank itself, managers favoured projects that required a smaller percentage of government funds as a proportion of total financing. This rule gained more currency when it became apparent that the Bank would not receive all the funds mandated by the enabling legislation. To ensure solvency, managers introduced an unprecedented level of vigilance over borrowers. They would sometimes intervene in the internal operations of firms, insist on appointing members to the firm's board of directors, and require states provide guarantees for loans to public sector firms. These interventions had the positive spillover effect of improving the level of technical decision-making in the borrowing firms.

Much of the BNDE's effectiveness as a development agency can be traced to the rigorous adherence to norms of technical decision-making. The '*opinão do técnico*' (technical evaluation) has been the sine qua non for almost every loan granted over the past 60 years. With very few exceptions, Bank directorates have deferred to project evaluations carried out by the technical staff. The precise steps through which loan requests must pass grew out of the interactions between BNDE technocrats and international organizations such as the World Bank and ECLA in the 1950s. Although the process has been streamlined over the years, the basic steps for analysing projects and making recommendations have remained the same.[3] The emphasis on technical analysis has enhanced the power of Bank bureaucrats over clients and has contributed to an unusually strong *esprit de corps*.

Turning points on the path to becoming a PoE

The Bank experienced two important turning points during the 1950s that firmly established its standing as a preeminent PoE by the decade's end. A first turning point occurred when Roberto Campos and Glycan de Paiva Teixeira returned to the BNDE in 1955 after their abrupt departure a year earlier. The second took place when the Kubitschek government gave the BNDE a central role in the formulation and implementation of public investments under the Targets Plan.

Campos and Paiva Teixeira provided strong leadership in pushing the goal of building a technically competent staff within the BNDE. During their first terms on the Directorate they were unsuccessful in requiring competitive examinations for hiring 100 per cent of personnel. Although they had managed to hire many qualified individuals, it was not until their return to the Bank in 1955 that they managed to introduce this practice. This proved an important turning point because it firmly embedded merit-based hiring as an unwavering principle, although competitive examinations were held inconsistently until the 1980s.

88   *Eliza J. Willis*

As a result of the introduction of competitive examinations, the Bank's staff became largely insulated from patrimonial pressures and quickly emerged as a unique repository of technical expertise on development within the Brazilian state during the 1950s and early 1960s. Unlike those appointed as president or director who were constantly changing, the *técnicos* were long-term employees whose superior knowledge of the Bank's inner workings made the higher administration dependent on their cooperation (Willis 1986: 125). Over time the technical staff developed a strongly held institutional identity that made them willing to stand together when they felt established norms were violated. Many directors came from within the staff and others, who were appointed for their expertise, adapted easily to technically informed decision-making. Even the most politically oriented appointees would eventually 'vestir a camisa' (wear the Bank's colours) and become ardent defenders of the BNDE's technical approach to lending (Willis 1986: 126–27). Although adherence to technical norms has remained strong throughout the Bank's history, the cohesive *esprit de corps* evident in the 1950s and early 1960s was somewhat weakened by the failure to hold competitive exams in some years, accompanied by a very rapid expansion in the size of the staff beginning in the 1970s (Willis 1986: 102–7). In the 1980s, competitive examinations were reintroduced for permanent technical positions. Bank officials have rarely been accused of making loans for purely political reasons. When controversies have arisen, they have usually been in response to government development *policies* rather than to Bank *lending procedures*.

An even more important turning point occurred in 1956 when Kubitschek chose to make the BNDE a central player in the formulation and implementation of his major development initiative. The Targets Plan consisted of 41 targets or production objectives in basic infrastructure, basic industries, education, foodstuffs and the construction of a new capital city, Brasília (Lafer 1975). An industrial investment plan was the product of technical experts led by Lucas Lopes and Roberto Campos, then President and Supervising Director of the BNDE, respectively. The Targets Plan relied on a mixture of existing and newly created institutions and laws. The Bank was one of the main institutional pillars that provided the expertise and financial resources, both foreign and domestic, needed to make the plan successful.

The centrality of its role in the Targets Plan proved an important turning point for the BNDE in several respects. The fact that Kubitschek selected the Bank to guide much of the Targets Plan showed that its reputation as a PoE within the Brazilian state had already been recognized. A significant increase in funding allowed the Bank to offer more loans and new types of financial products including direct stock purchases. The BNDE's lending portfolio also underwent a dramatic change as a result of the Targets Plan. Prior to 1956, nearly all its loans went to basic infrastructure projects. After 1956 the majority of new loans were targeted toward basic industries and the energy sector, with basic industries absorbing 43 per cent of all loans in domestic currency. Because most basic industries were privately owned, the Target Plan led the Bank to become the principal source of long-term finance for both the public and private sectors. In some cases, especially in the steel and electricity sectors, the BNDE became the majority shareholder of foreign-owned companies, thereby effectively nationalizing ownership of these firms.

Finally, the Bank provided invaluable technical advice and training to managers of public and private firms involved in the Targets Plan. Through training programs like a course on development economics co-sponsored with the Economic Commission on Latin America (ECLA) and the careful instruction of all loan recipients, the Bank's technical approach to project analysis and budgeting got widely disseminated within both the public and private sectors. In its efforts to improve productivity in basic industries, the Bank introduced modern managerial and production techniques in Brazilian companies that were still dominated by traditional managerial practices.

The expansion of the BNDE under Kubitschek's presidency revolutionized the Bank's role as an effective promoter of national economic development. Its place as one of the most important and reliable 'pockets of effectiveness' within the Brazilian state became well established. While the Bank never again reached the same level of influence over development policy that it enjoyed during this period, its reputation for effective action has remained strong over the past five decades.

Challenges to effectiveness

The factors described above help explain how the BNDE evolved into a PoE during the 1950s. This transformation was not without challenges, however. Although Bank bureaucrats generally enjoyed insulation from external political interference, they were not completely immune to such pressures. Their response to these challenges showed how aggressively they asserted (with varying degrees of success) their prerogatives over lending decisions. Lack of control over funding sources constituted the second major challenge to the BNDE's effectiveness as a development agency. Throughout the 1950s, the Bank faced chronic resource shortages due to the diversion of its legislatively mandated revenues to other uses. This resource problem curtailed the scope of the BNDE's effectiveness during this period and has remained a challenge throughout the Bank's history.

Direct interference from the nation's president in loan decisions was rare, but did occur. Most directors saw their role as lobbying the BNDE's president on behalf of maintaining the *técnicos* autonomy from political pressures that challenged technical norms of decision-making. This dynamic is well illustrated by the directors' response to Vargas's request for a government-sponsored program supporting the installation of small-scale sanitary and water projects in an impoverished region (BNDE 1956). The program conflicted with the Bank's decision rule giving priority to infrastructural projects that contributed to national industrial development. Under pressure, the directors agreed to offer a small loan but insisted that the projects be subjected to the

90 Eliza J. Willis

same technical evaluation and conditions applied to higher priority projects. The Bank stopped supporting these projects after Vargas's suicide in 1954.

We have evidence of only one other direct request from Vargas. He sent a presidential directive instructing the BNDE to consider proposals from foreign companies interested in producing diesel locomotives in Brazil (Willis 1995: 645). Vargas wanted the BNDE to give preference to two German firms (IFRA and Krupp) that proposed allowing two-thirds of their production to occur in Brazil. Campos and Paiva Teixeira opposed the loan because, they argued, the national market for locomotives was too small, the project too costly, and the requirement that the Bank purchase the locomotives too risky (Campos 1994: 207). They also noted that no Brazilian firms had the technical or financial capacity to carry out such a large investment. Vargas sided with those directors and BNDE President Maciel Filho who supported making the loan. Campos attributed his and Paiva Teixeira's decision to resign their positions to Vargas's support for the loan. Despite presidential approval, funding limitations delayed implementation. As in the case of the sanitation projects, this loan project was terminated after Vargas's death.

While these presidential interventions generated controversy within the Bank, they did not significantly impact its effectiveness during this period. Internal meeting minutes of the *diretoria* confirm that BNDE officials remained committed to the function of financing infrastructural projects: by December 1954, over 81.6 per cent of total financing had gone to projects recommended by the Joint Commission. The remaining funds, with few exceptions, were allocated to projects that fit Bank criteria and that managers reasoned supported national development goals. Any deviation from the normal decision rules led to hours of intense discussion among the directors, and any exception required strong justification. No project, whether private or public, received financing without prior technical analysis and Bank technocrats often returned proposals that were not sufficiently elaborated. They were determined to educate clients (and politicians!) on the differences between a BNDE loan and traditional patronage. Even when pressured by the nation's president, Bank bureaucrats were successful in maintaining their technical standards.

Their nearly exclusive focus on public infrastructure loans during the Vargas years made it easy to reject loan requests from private firms engaged in manufacturing. However, the Bank's client base changed considerably with the introduction of the Targets Plan during Kubitschek's presidency: its lending portfolio now included manufacturers of capital goods, durable consumer goods, and basic inputs. A shift in focus toward the private sector made the Bank more vulnerable to external interventions, as spurned firms resorted to political pressure to reverse unfavourable decisions.

Two major controversies linked to private borrowers erupted during the late 1950s. The first did not concern a loan per se but a Bank opinion on the granting of Brazilian-owned concessions to companies for oil exploration in Bolivia. Following principles set forth by an interministerial commission set up by the Kubitschek government, BNDE bureaucrats evaluated the technical and financial capabilities of five petroleum firms for developing the Bolivian reserves. In a technical opinion, the directorate rejected two nationally owned firms as unfit, technically and financially, to undertake these projects. In response, the firms accused the Bank of favouring firms with greater access to foreign capital and technology. Denunciations in the press and the recommendation of a special inquiry in the Brazilian congress put pressure on the government to ignore the Bank's opinion and restrict concessions to wholly Brazilian owned firms. The Kubitschek administration succumbed to these nationalist pressures and granted concessions to three Brazilian firms. Just as Bank bureaucrats had predicted, all three failed to fulfil their concessions as a result of inadequate technical and financial capacity.

A second major controversy during Kubitschek's presidency threatened to introduce patronage politics into Bank lending decisions. In 1957 SANBRA, an Argentine food products company, requested a loan to build a factory in Brazil to produce margarine. The project had a strong advocate in Augusto Frederico Schmidt, who was Kubitschek's close personal friend and trusted adviser. The technical review found fault with two aspects of the project and recommended rejecting it. Foodstuffs were not identified as a lending priority under the Targets Plan and, thus, would constitute a major departure from past practice. Also, the *técnicos* argued that the negligible amount of Brazilian ownership in the company meant that the project did not fit in the exceptional category of 'production in the national interest.'

The negative opinion received the unanimous support at each level of decision-making in the Bank's hierarchy until it reached the directorate. A heated debate broke out between President Campos and Ewaldo Corrêia Lima, one of the directors. Campos favoured granting the loan because he disagreed with the *opinão do técnico*, arguing that the project met the BNDE's technical criteria and presented no risk to capital. Corrêia Lima favoured denying the loan on nationalist grounds. Kubitschek's personal support for the project weighed heavily in the directorate's final vote, which split 3 to 2 in favour of granting the loan.

The SANBRA loan was the most direct exercise of personal influence by a president on behalf of a private company during the 1950s. Although the loan met certain technical criteria and posed no financial risk to the Bank, it represented a significant departure from the usual lending priorities. Of the three controversial decisions discussed here, the SANBRA loan posed the greatest challenge to the Bank's insulation from patronage politics but did not seriously undermine its effectiveness. Seen in the larger context of Bank lending during this period, it was a relatively minor departure from the norm. Both the Roboré and SANBRA controversies were more significant for what they revealed about the ideological divide within the BNDE between the nationalists and the internationalists. This ideological difference did politicize discussions over some lending decisions, although the record shows that the

92   *Eliza J. Willis*

Bank managers reached consensus on the vast majority of loans. A review of every loan granted between 1953 and 1961 showed that, with the single exception of the SANBRA case, the directorate always followed the recommendation of the technical staff. A high degree of adherence to technical norms was equally true under Vargas and Kubitschek. The Bank's status as a PoE owes much to this common commitment to technically informed decisions backed by a remarkably strong *esprit de corps.*

The lack of control over its own financial resources has placed the greatest limitation on the BNDE's impact as a PoE throughout much of its history. It has had very little capacity to generate its own sources of funding but has depended on various financing mechanisms (e.g., special taxes, pension funds, foreign loans and so on) created by the legislature or executive branch. The challenge presented by lack of resource control manifested from the moment the BNDE started operating in 1953. While the flow of resources improved under Kubitschek in line with the Bank's central role in the Targets Plan, Bank lending fell short of professed goals due to inadequate funds. Throughout this period, directors lobbied hard – with varying degrees of success – to free the funds from congressional and ministerial control.

The lack of automatic access to domestic revenues, combined with high rates of inflation and the failure of some promised international loans to materialize, left Bank finances in dire straits during the Vargas government. In 1954, the Bank received no significant funds from domestic sources. The situation was so grim that a congressional investigative committee concluded that 'the failure to provide adequate funding was seriously undermining the completion of the National Program for Economic Reequipment' (Baer and Villela 1980: 427).

While the Kubitschek administration is generally credited with expanding access to resources after 1956, the improved situation was largely a result of Bank managers circumventing the executive in a bid to increase their control over resources. Led by Campos, the Bank successfully lobbied key legislators for a ten-year renewal of the FRE. Apparently, these legislators were convinced by arguments emphasizing the centrality of the Targets Plan to advancing the goal of national development. Although they were unsuccessful in persuading the Congress to arrange for an automatic transfer, the 1956 law instructed the Treasury to release a minimum of one billion *cruzeiros* per year to the BNDE. Campos proposed two additional changes to the new law, that could have helped reduce the eroding effects of inflation that frequently exceeded the amount of interest the Bank was allowed to charge. One of these provisions would have allowed the Bank to exchange loans for equity shares in the borrowing firm. The other would have introduced a form of monetary correction on loans. Neither of these provisions was implemented and so inflation remained a constant threat to the Bank's financial capacity. Campos also pushed for a new law that would have allowed the BNDE to build its own capital by issuing inflation-adjusted industrial development bonds, but Congress never voted on this proposal.

An enduring PoE: the case of the BNDE   93

Perhaps in response to the new FRE law, which Kubitschek readily signed, the nation's improved fiscal situation, and the advent of the Targets Plan, the BNDE did benefit from a dramatic increase in resources between 1956 and 1961. With more funds in hand, the Bank's impact increased. Lending capacity increased from 59 projects in the four years before 1956 to over 200 projects between 1956 and 1960. The Bank's contribution to gross capital formation rose from three per cent before 1956 to 16.4 per cent in 1957 (d'Avila Viana 1981: 106). Nevertheless, demand for loans continued to outstrip supply: between 1952 and 1958 the Bank received 91 billion *cruzeiros* in loan requests but financed only 39 billion cruzeiros' worth of projects, largely due to lack of financing. Even under the new law, the Treasury continued to redirect only 20 per cent of the funds collected for the FRE. Without its own sources of funding, Campos bitingly noted, the BNDE remained a '"gigolo" of the federal budget' (Willis 1995: 658). Clearly, lack of control over financial resources placed a significant constraint on the scope of the Bank's effective action.

Triggering effects

Over the course of its long history, the Bank can be credited with having a 'triggering effect' on improving the effectiveness of other institutions within the Brazilian state. The BNDE has helped to build the capacity of other state institutions through multiple paths. During the 1950s BNDE leaders contributed their expertise to improving development planning within the Ministry of Finance. For example, during his first stint with the Bank, Roberto Campos forged agreements with the Instituto Brasileiro de Economia da Fundação Getúlio Vargas and, as discussed earlier, the Economic Commission for Latin America (Maria da Conceição Tavares et al 2010: 25). The former provided the government with more comprehensive and sophisticated economic statistics, while the latter introduced new planning techniques in its work with the BNDE and other government agencies.

Through its lending practices, the Bank also modernized the administrative and technical capacities of numerous state-owned enterprises. The introduction of project analysis revolutionized the way these firms conducted business. Requests for financing had to be supported by rigorous analysis of all aspects of the proposed project, backed by extensive documentation. In order to meet these new requirements, firms had to hire more qualified staff and give greater weight to the their technical departments. The BNDE's influence was particularly strongly felt in the electric energy and steel sectors, where it provided the lion's share of financing but it had an impact on dozens of state-owned firms over the years (Schneider 1991).

The borrowing from and lending of staff to other state entities allowed the Bank to disseminate its technical norms throughout the Brazilian bureaucracy. Permanent members of staff have often spent years on loan to state-owned enterprises in which the Bank had a major stake. Over the decades

94   *Eliza J. Willis*

many *técnicos* with appointments in other state agencies have spent months and even years in temporary posts within the BNDE. While sharing their expertise, these temporary staff have also taken what they have learned back to their home institutions.

Finally, the BNDE has triggered the establishment of other regional and state-level development banks throughout Brazil. While adopting organizational charts and formal norms similar to the original, these development banks have had a mixed record as pockets of effectiveness. During the 1990s, several state-level development banks required enormous bailouts due to excessive lending to state governments, much of it strictly political with no development value. Many states resorted to borrowing from these development banks as a means to circumvent hard budget constraints, thus contributing to the Brazilian fiscal crisis of the 1990s (Bevilaqua and Garcia 2002). Others, however, have played important roles in supporting development within a region or state. The Banco de Desenvolvimento de Minas Gerais, which has maintained a close working relationship with the BNDE since 1962, is one prominent success case.

Conclusion

This chapter has sought to explain how the BNDE evolved into a 'pocket of effectiveness' within Brazil's patrimonial state during the 1950s. Although the centrality of the Bank to development policy has waxed and waned along with changes in regime and presidential administrations, its reputation as a premier PoE has not wavered over the past 60 years. Some of the same factors that account for the Bank's relative independence from political interference and capacity for effective action in the 1950s also explain its persistence as a PoE.

A case study of the early years of the BNDE illustrates that both the internal and external contexts in which government agencies carry out their designated function are as important as the function itself in determining organizational effectiveness. By acting as the government's principal source of long-term credit, the Bank fulfilled an essential function in promoting state-led development in Brazil. However, function alone cannot explain effectiveness. We have many examples of development banks that function as piggy banks for profligate state governments or cash machines for political clients. The BNDE was saved from such an ignoble fate by factors present in its external (international and domestic) and internal environments.

Key aspects of the international context in which the Bank was created and began to operate were the technical expectations the World Bank placed on borrowing nations, the Joint Commission's pre-formulated investment projects and the linkages formed between the Americans and Brazilians serving on the Joint Commission. These factors provided vital support for the technically oriented approach to lending decisions. In terms of the domestic political context, the pro-development ideology shared by Vargas and Kubitschek made both presidents less likely to influence lending decisions in pursuit of

An enduring PoE: the case of the BNDE 95

narrow political goals. The Bank also benefitted from the fact that no other government agency could rival its expertise in development planning, a fact that Kubitschek readily recognized when he made the BNDE a principal participant in the Targets Plan.

While the external environment was helpful, the most crucial factors accounting for the evolution of the Bank into a PoE were internal. Under the leadership of Roberto Campos and others the BNDE developed an unusually strong *esprit de corps,* guided by a clear sense of mission. The commitment to technically based decision-making and the practice of hiring through competitive exams, both of which became embedded early on, were crucial. As we have seen, the sense of cohesiveness and dedication to technical norms led to effective action, even in the face of occasional political pressures and the chronic lack of funds. The institutionalization of these norms and attitudes in its organizational culture has allowed the BNDE to remain highly effective even when external conditions have turned less favourable, as they have at various moments in the Bank's history (Willis 1986).

Given the importance of the BNDE's culture to its effectiveness, the expanding scope of its activities and the growing size of its staff have posed significant challenges to its continuing status as a PoE. The first major growth spurt occurred in the 1970s, when the Bank took on more functions and established several subsidiaries that required expanding the staff from 600 in 1972 to 1500 in 1975 (Willis 1986: 104). It was also moved from the powerful Ministry of Planning to the far less influential Ministry of Industry and Commerce. After several years of declining influence within the Brazilian development bureaucracy, the Bank began to regain its former status when given the task of supervising the privatization of several state-owned enterprises. Its flexibility in providing technical support for privatizing companies (some of which it had helped create) revealed its recognized status as a pocket of effectiveness. As discussed at the beginning of this chapter, the BNDES has re-emerged as the major source of development financing in Brazil, and has even become an important player in the global economy. While most loans are still allocated to projects in public infrastructure and heavy industry, the Bank has also become involved in a wide-ranging set of activities, including sustainable development of the Amazon, education, health care, export promotion, cultural production, capital market development and so on. Moreover, these expanded areas of activities are more politically sensitive, and have exposed the Bank to new criticisms and external pressures that challenge the application of strictly technical norms. For example, some have suggested that, although loans have not been used to bailout the private sector, firms with political connections are more likely to receive more capital (Lazzarini et al 2011). Bank managers have attempted to respond to these criticisms by instituting more accountability and transparency measures. The Bank has also been criticized by human rights and environmental organizations for its decision to finance controversial projects such as the Belo Monte Dam in the Amazon. In response to these pressures, the Bank has moved to incorporate

96   *Eliza J. Willis*

more social and environmental norms into its lending decisions (Renzler 2012). Rather than undermining its status as a pocket of effectiveness, the incorporation of social norms may lead the BNDES to become a 'pocket of responsiveness and corporate responsibility'.

The increase in the size of the staff (over 24 per cent since 2008) presents a challenge to preserving the same *esprit de corps* and sense of mission that has always been the Bank's most critical resource. In response to the challenges posed to the cohesive culture by a much larger staff and numerous retirements, current managers have introduced new training programs aimed at accelerating the 'integration of newly hired collaborators into work processes' and providing 'an overview of the BNDES, expanding the institutional vision and transmitting the organizational culture' (Banco Nacional de Desenvolvimento Econômicoe Social 2009). Whether these programs, which unite older employees with new ones, will be successful in passing on the Bank's unique organizational culture remains to be seen.

Notes

1 With the addition of social investment to its portfolio, the Bank changed its name to National Bank for Economic and Social Development or BNDES. The present chapter, which focuses on the Bank's early history, uses its original name.
2 These figures come from a review of BNDE Annual Reports from the past five years.
3 For more detail on the exact process followed, see Willis (1986: 112–23).

5 Turning Nigeria's drug sector around

The National Agency for Food and Drug Administration and Control (NAFDAC)

A. Irene Pogoson and Michael Roll[1]

Introduction

The failure of public institutions in Nigeria has for a long time engaged the attention of scholars and has given rise to a plethora of work (Adamolekun 1986; Akindele, Ajisafe and Olaopa 2001; Olaoye, 2005). What runs through most of these studies is the unanimity of sweeping condemnation of these public organizations as ineffective and corruption-ridden, and as obstacles to the socio-political development of Nigeria. What is yet to be noticed, and streamlined into the body of literature on the public sector in Nigeria, are stories of exceptional organizations that have broken the odds in terms of performance. There is evidence of some public organizations that could be regarded as effective in the discharge of the public mandates assigned to them. Within the corpus of these exceptional organizations is the National Agency for Food and Drug Administration and Control (NAFDAC). This chapter analyses why NAFDAC can be considered a 'pocket of effectiveness' (PoE) and how it became such an exceptional public organization in a country in which corruption is rife and the failure of the public sector endemic.

While NAFDAC is responsible for the regulation and control of drugs, food, cosmetics and other goods, the focus of our analysis is on the drug sector since it was there where the challenges were particularly daunting. This case study is based on both primary and secondary data analysis. Primary data were derived from semi-structured interviews conducted with individual members of NAFDAC staff, as well as groups of NAFDAC staff, other public sector organizations, experts and journalists, and informed members of the public. Interviews were conducted in Lagos, Abuja, Kaduna, Ibadan, Ado Ekiti and Owerri. Overall, three categories of interviewees can be distinguished. The first category includes the leadership, including Dora Akunyili, NAFDAC's former Director General and Paul Orhii, her successor, as well as several of NAFDAC's directors who were considered critical to the success of the organization.

The second category of interviewees includes other members of staff like the organization's National Public Relations Officer, the NAFDAC Directors based in Lagos and Abuja, as well as the North-West Zonal Coordinator in Kaduna, the Kaduna State Coordinator and staff of the Owerri Zonal Office at the time. The third category comprises members of staff of critical stakeholder organizations who are also unusually well-informed observers or customers of NAFDAC, such as the National Drug Law Enforcement Agency (NDLEA), the Standards Organization of Nigeria (SON), the Federal Ministry of Health, the Association of Pharmaceutical Importers of Nigeria (APIN), the Nigerian Medical Association (NMA), as well as patent medicine sellers, sachet water sellers, confectionary and bread bakers and others. During the interviews, either extensive notes were taken or the interviews were recorded and later transcribed. These texts were then coded and analysed, while taking the secondary data into consideration.

Secondary data were sourced from brochures, magazines and newsletters published by NAFDAC, as well as from newspapers and magazines, both online and in paper. The secondary data were included for contextualising and complementing the primary data, as well as for cross-checking internal consistency and validity of the data (triangulation).

The establishment and organization of NAFDAC

In Nigeria, the task of regulating the production and sale of food, drugs, cosmetics and medical devices falls within the Ministry of Health's responsibility. The Food and Drugs Decree from 1974 established the Directorate of Food and Drug Administration and Control (FDAC) within the Ministry to enforce this legislation. However, over time FDAC was rendered ineffective by the lack of effective laws against fake drugs, by civil service bureaucracy, political instability and corruption.

The National Agency for Food and Drug Administration and Control (NAFDAC) was then set up in 1993, but established in 1994 by the then Nigerian Head of State and military ruler General Ibrahim Badamasi Babangida, through the National Agency for Food and Drug Administration and Control Decree No. 15. NAFDAC was established as a parastatal of the Ministry of Health 'to regulate and control the manufacturing, importation, exportation, distribution, advertisement, sale and use of food, drugs, cosmetics, chemicals, medical devices and packaged water' (NAFDAC n.d. a). This includes carrying out inspections, product registration and quality control of products. Gabriel Osunde was NAFDAC's pioneer Director General. Dora Akunyili, who is commonly credited with having transformed the agency into an effective organization was NAFDAC's Director General from 2001 until 2008. She was then appointed Nigeria's Minister of Information and Communications, and Paul B. Orhii became NAFDAC's third Director General in early 2009.[2]

The Director General reports to the organization's Governing Council.[3] The Governing Council has to approve or reject all decisions with regard to appointment, promotion and discipline of employees. All internal policy changes and regulations suggested by NAFDAC also have to be approved by the Council as well as the Minister of Health. The organization became autonomous in key areas of recruitment, promotions, financing and political control from its parent ministry, the Ministry of Health, shortly after Dora Akunyili's appointment in 2001. The agency then adopted a revised tariff structure for product registration, sanctions and penalties, and has since been able to raise and keep more than two thirds of its annual income since 2003 on its own.[4]

NAFDAC maintains offices in all 36 federal states, six zonal offices for the geo-political zones of the country, three Special Inspectorate Offices in cities with the largest drug markets (Aba, Onitsha, Kano), and headquarters in Abuja. The organization employs more than 3,000 pharmacists, technicians, enforcement and administrative staff.

Nigeria swamped with counterfeit drugs and products in the 1990s

Following political instability, ineffective drugs and products regulation and control, as well as the growth of domestic and international counterfeit drugs and products networks, Nigeria was increasingly swamped with counterfeit and sub-standard drugs and other products in the 1990s. Large-scale imports and the outright dumping of counterfeit drugs in Nigeria from many countries, especially India and China, accelerated. In 1990, over 200 children in Nigeria died after taking a Paracetamol syrup which included a toxic Diethylene glycol solvent. Apart from such major scandals, many other drugs either had no active ingredients or not enough, had different ingredients, were expired, or were otherwise substandard. While representative statistical data on deaths resulting from taking counterfeit drugs in Nigeria are not available for this period, such tragedies were reported frequently in the media throughout the 1990s. It is highly likely that they are only the tip of a massive iceberg of deaths that have not been recorded or even linked to counterfeit drugs and products.

In 2001 about 80 per cent of medications sold in Nigeria were considered deficient in one way or another, many of them dangerous for the patient's health and often life-threatening (Lemonick 2005).[5] The situation was so serious that some West African countries like Ghana and Sierra Leone banned drugs made in Nigeria completely. Together with unfair competition through large-scale imports of cheap counterfeit drugs from other countries, these bans drove many domestic drug manufacturers out of business. Moreover, international pharmaceutical companies such as Boehringer Ingelheim, Sandoz, Merck, Aventis and Pfizer, withdrew from producing in or investing in drug manufacturing in Nigeria in the 1990s.

NAFDAC as a pocket of effectiveness: perceptions and indicators[6]

The incidence of counterfeit drugs and goods in Nigeria in the 1990s shows that the new NAFDAC, established to replace the defunct FDAC in 1993, was not effective. However, apart from its own organizational shortcomings it operated in an extremely difficult environment of political instability and military dictatorship, which placed many constraints on the activities of the agency such as lack of political support, inadequate funding and the overall dominance of political and military objectives. Furthermore, largely uncontrolled borders allowed counterfeit drugs to flow into the country on a massive scale.

With Nigeria's return to democratic and civilian rule in 1999,[7] the appointment of Dora Akunyili as NAFDAC's new Director General in 2001 and the reforms she implemented, this situation changed dramatically. Her mission for NAFDAC was to safeguard public health by eradicating counterfeit drugs and substandard products in Nigeria.[8] A series of representative nation-wide surveys on government agencies in Nigeria from 2007 to 2009 revealed that NAFDAC was consistently perceived as the most effective government agency in the country (74 per cent agreement in 2009) (NOI Polls 2009: 11, 19). With 79 per cent agreement (2007), people also had far more confidence in the agency than in any other government institution, 13 per cent ahead of the agency in second place (NOI Polls 2009: 6).[9] The emergence of NAFDAC from seeming obscurity to national and even international limelight within just a few years easily passes as one of the most important developments in the past decades of the history of the public sector in Nigeria.

This public perception that has been mirrored in numerous journalistic accounts is supported by significant achievements. A 2006 survey report found that the incidence of counterfeit drugs in circulation in Nigeria had dropped from about 41 per cent of all drugs sold in 2001 to 16.7 per cent in 2006 (Barriaux 2007), or even less than 10 per cent in the country if the area around the biggest fake drugs market in Onitsha is excluded (Akunyili 2010: 128). The percentage of unregistered drugs was also reduced from 68 to 19 per cent during the same period (Nduwugwe 2008). The sanitization of bottled and sachet water production had greatly reduced cholera and other water-borne disease outbreaks, which used to be rampant in the country. In 2007, Nigeria also became the first country in Africa to achieve universal salt iodization, based on a programme that NAFDAC managed and enforced (UNICEF 2007). Moreover, according to the agency, it destroyed substandard products valued at over $200 million between 2001 and 2009, achieved 45 convictions related to counterfeit drugs, had 60 more cases pending at the time of research in 2009 and a steadily increasing number of sanctions against manufacturers.

The enforcement of NAFDAC's standards and mandate are also reflected in the organization's annually increasing internally generated revenue (see below). The revival and growth of Nigeria's domestic pharmaceutical industry is another indicator for the agency's effectiveness. By reducing the high volume of imported counterfeit or unregistered drugs, local companies as well as international companies producing in Nigeria won back market shares. Turnover and profits of these companies increased and their share prices on the Nigerian Stock Exchange rose (Akunyili 2010: 251–52). To satisfy growing demand, the number of pharmaceutical companies in Nigeria rose from

70 in 2001 to 150 in 2008. International pharmaceutical companies returned to the country. Collectively, they produced more than 40 per cent of the country's drugs domestically in 2007, compared to under 25 per cent in 2001 (ibid.: 252).

Both producers and consumers have come to appreciate NAFDAC's work and value its seal of approval. This success and the newly gained trust furthermore led the West African countries that had previously imposed bans on drugs made in Nigeria to lift them again in 2002. This opened new markets for exporting Nigeria-produced drugs which contributed to the revival of the Nigerian pharmaceutical industry.

These impressive figures earned the organization, and particularly its then Director General, national and international recognition. NAFDAC became a model for other African countries, while Dora Akunyili became a frequent speaker at international conferences and Nigeria's probably most award-decorated public sector executive, earning recognition from leading international organizations such as the World Health Organization (WHO), the European Union (EU) and Transparency International (TI). As early as 2003 Akunyili received Transparency International's Integrity Award and went on to win the *Time Magazine* Award in 2006 – to mention just two of the hundreds of awards presented to her.[10]

Perhaps the best indicators of NAFDAC's effectiveness since 2001 are the reactions of the counterfeit drug production and importation cartels. Several NAFDAC laboratories and offices were vandalized and set on fire, and inspectors were threatened and assaulted. Akunyili's youngest son was almost kidnapped and in 2008 her younger brother was kidnapped but later rescued by the police, all by people related to the counterfeit drug business. Moreover, there were several attempts to bribe and even assassinate Akunyili.[11] When policing a sector dominated by criminal cartels making huge profits, this, it appears, is the price of effectiveness.

How and why did NAFDAC become a PoE?

Several categories of factors explain NAFDAC's emergence and persistence as a Pocket of Effectiveness. The following presentation is based on the qualitative analysis of our empirical data, largely based on the framework developed in this book. After we had carried out our analysis, Dora Akunyili's book on her experience at NAFDAC, *The War Against Counterfeit Medicine. My Story,* appeared in Nigeria in 2010, and we used it to complement and expand our study.[12] In her book, the former Director General presents information that previously had either not been available at all or not in an organized and confirmed way, and complements them with 'inside-story' aspects covering the period of her leadership.

After our analysis we arrived at five categories of factors that explain NAFDAC's exceptional performance. We present each of them in turn and

102   A. Irene Pogoson and Michael Roll

discuss the individual factors that they contain below (see table 5.1 below for an overview).

Organizational factors

This category of factors includes those factors that are 'internal' in the sense that they deal with the leadership and management of the organization. They cover a wide variety of factors such as recruitment, training, anti-corruption, commitment and others. These factors have been studied extensively and have been found to contribute strongly to the emergence of effective public organizations in challenging environments (Grindle 1997; Hilderbrand and Grindle 1997). Our findings confirm many of these results. In our interview with the then NAFDAC Director for Establishment Inspection, she even referred to what was achieved through the measures analysed in this section as an 'organizational cultural revolution' (NAFDAC Director, Establishment Inspection, interview, 2009).

For people familiar with the Nigerian public sector, Akunyili's description of the state that NAFDAC was in when she assumed office is not surprising. At that time, the head office in Abuja was located in a 'rented, dilapidated two-story building comprising six small flats' (Akunyili 2010: 31). Modern office equipment was lacking, employees were qualified but poorly trained, not motivated and many were overtly involved in corruption and other forms of misconduct (ibid.). The factors described in this first category changed this desperate state of affairs.

Table 5.1 Categories and factors explaining NAFDAC as a PoE

1. Organizational factors	Functional restructuring Merit-, integrity- and commitment-based recruitment Anti-corruption regime Training and performance regime Inclusive leadership Public service commitment
2. Operational factors	Strategic decisions Registration and control regime Embedded technology Institutionalization of procedures
3. Political factors	Political interest Political management
4. Institutional factors	Autonomy Focussed powers
5. Outreach and cooperation	Public communication Domestic cooperation International cooperation

Functional restructuring

The functional restructuring was essential for the agency to be able to carry out its mandate. Apart from more procedural reforms that we discuss in the second category of factors below, the most important structural reforms were the following. First, in 2001 two new directorates were created in addition to the six existing ones: the Ports Inspection Directorate and the Enforcement Directorate. After five years of absence from the ports, which are major gateways for the importation of counterfeit and genuine drugs, NAFDAC was allowed to return to the ports in 2001 (more on this below). The separate Ports Inspection Directorate ensured NAFDAC's effective work at the ports. An Enforcement Directorate also had not existed at NAFDAC before, which had hampered the effectiveness of enforcement activities.

The second part of the functional restructuring of NAFDAC was the expansion of the agency's field office network. By opening 12 new state offices, NAFDAC was now represented in all the 36 federal states and in Abuja. In addition, the laboratories were upgraded to international standards, with some of them having later been accredited by the World Health Organization (WHO) and the European Union (EU). Moreover, six Zonal Offices were established to coordinate the work of the state offices in the respective zones,[13] and three Special Inspectorate Offices in the cities of Aba, Onitsha, and Kano, which have large drug markets, were opened. Together with narcotics offices, land border and port offices, its own warehouses and a new headquarters NAFDAC's infrastructure increasingly allowed it to work more effectively.

The third and probably most important element of functional restructuring was the way positions were allocated to staff. Previously, this had been done in a rather arbitrary or random manner. In the process of making NAFDAC more functional, employees were redeployed based on their competence and area of specialization, with the support of consultants. In combination with training this might have been one of the most important steps, since Hilderbrand and Grindle found that 'human resource constraints are more likely to derive from the failure to provide people with meaningful jobs and to utilize their skills effectively than from problems related to training per se' (Hilderbrand and Grindle 1997: 34).

Merit-, integrity- and commitment-based recruitment[14]

Other studies of exceptionally well performing organizations in hostile environments have identified merit-based recruitment as an explanatory factor (see Owusu 2006a). The NAFDAC case study confirms this but goes beyond it. For her management team, Akunyili selected two directors from within the agency and brought in others from the private sector and an international organization. However, in addition to merit, proven integrity and commitment to the NAFDAC mission were also important. While these include more personal and not strictly merit-based elements, they complement and do not compromise professional standards.

104   *A. Irene Pogoson and Michael Roll*

For rank and file positions, NAFDAC contracted a recruitment company to invite applications, shortlist candidates, administer an aptitude test and interview candidates with the organization's participation before job offers were made (NAFDAC Director, Planning, Research and Statistics, interview, 2009).[15] According to Akunyili and the then Director for Planning, Research and Statistics, such an assessment centre based on qualifications and merit 'was unprecedented for a government agency [in Nigeria, A.I.P. and M.R.] where tribalism, nepotism and political leanings are the order of the day' (ibid.; Akunyili 2010: 47).

Anti-corruption regime

In addition to the about five per cent of staff that were dismissed on grounds of corruption, among other reasons, the new NAFDAC management team built a strong anti-corruption regime. Apart from the fact that corruption was widespread in the 'old' NAFDAC, this was necessary because the agency works in a field in which the profits for criminal cartels are high and where vested interests are strong. It is therefore a field in which inspectors trying to enforce regulation and control have to be particularly resistant to bribery and other forms of corrupt behaviour. At NAFDAC, internal whistle blowing is explicitly encouraged and rewarded if the case is confirmed. Apart from internal cooperation and collegiality this introduced an element of social control, since most of the work was carried out in teams. Members of staff that were found to have engaged in corrupt practices were dismissed.

In addition to this sanctioning regime, the management team and Akunyili emphasized their 'leadership by example' in practising transparency and integrity at the executive level. Dora Akunyili sent out a powerful signal to confirm that in 2002, when she dismissed her husband's brother who had been a member of staff. A company owner had informed the agency that he had allegedly collected a bribe and then asked for more. The NAFDAC investigation confirmed the case and Cyril Akunyili was dismissed (Akunyili 2010: 48). Other persons who had known Akunyili before she became Director General or were related to her or her husband tried to use this relationship for skipping NAFDAC procedures but were rejected (ibid.: 180–81). Since nepotism is widespread in Nigeria and personal bonds are usually regarded to be more important than abiding by the law, these were highly unusual and widely publicized occurrences.

In 2008 NAFDAC formally established an internal Anti-Corruption and Transparency Unit (ACTU) to further strengthen its anti-corruption regime (ibid.: 50).

Training and performance regime

Shortly after assuming office, Akunyili and her management team dismissed about five per cent of NAFDAC staff, since they found them to be corrupt, redundant or not open to organizational change (Akunyili 2010: 46). For those who remained on board and were redeployed within the agency, an extensive training and retraining programme was established. This included in-house training as well as international training, which was offered at no cost to NAFDAC staff by various international organizations and companies.[16]

Such international training opportunities and the participation in collaborative missions were employed in a strategic manner by the leadership to reward performance and as performance incentives for other members of staff. The responses of members of staff who participated in them as well as in foreign factory inspections which were later introduced, show that they returned highly motivated, equipped with new knowledge and networks. Especially lower rank staff, who had never expected to be participate in such programmes or activities overseas, were grateful for this opportunity which in turn strengthened their loyalty to the organization (several of our interviews with NAFDAC staff; Olamuyiwa 2010 and Kine 2010, both quoted in Akunyili 2010: 273, 284). NAFDAC's training programme was therefore an inherent part of establishing an internal culture of performance.

As a semi-autonomous organization, NAFDAC did not use the regular civil service pay scale. NAFDAC staff earned higher salaries than regular public servants, and they enjoyed much more generous welfare packages and health benefits that were continued and expanded after Akunyili had become the agency's Director General. This added to NAFDAC's attractiveness as an employer for highly skilled professionals.

At the same time, the agency ensured that all the necessary equipment and resources were available for employees to carry out their duties. This included functional offices, mobile phones, cars, generators, diesel for operating them, computers and internet access, and many other things which are often lacking in other public organizations in Nigeria. Compared to the run down state of affairs of NAFDAC in 2001 this was a major change, and for the first time really enabled the workers to carry out their tasks as requested.

Akunyili and her management team provided an enabling environment, training and good salaries and benefits for their staff but they also expected strong performance from them in return. Staff performance evaluations were introduced and expectations were made clear. For example, documents were not allowed to be delayed for more than 48 hours or a query could be issued (Akunyili 2010: 48–49). In our interviews, members of staff reported that they were expected to be fully committed to the organization's mission and to work longer hours, or be transferred if necessary. However, while they said that working in the new NAFDAC under Akunyili was tough, they all appreciated having been part of this organizational 'revolution', as some of them called it.

Inclusive leadership

We use the term 'inclusive leadership' to describe a leadership style in which the leader is accessible to the members of staff, invites and pays attention to criticism, ideas and suggestions, communicates clearly and cares for its staff in

106 *A. Irene Pogoson and Michael Roll*

terms of defending them and providing above-average benefits. Based on this definition, Dora Akunyili did practice inclusive leadership at NAFDAC.

Within certain limits, the Director General was accessible to both NAFDAC staff at all levels, but also to NAFDAC customers who could contact her with problems, suggestions and complaints. While delegation of duties and empowerment of staff were emphasized, Akunyili made sure that she was accessible also to junior staff and that senior staff were accountable. She introduced the rule that if junior staff had reported a case to a senior officer and this person had not taken action within one week, the junior staff were encouraged to contact the Director General (Akunyili 2010: 48).

Akunyili communicated her understanding of NAFDAC's mission extensively both inside and outside of the agency. She clearly had strong ideas and was very firm in executing them. However, while this may not sound particularly participatory, she invited and valued new ideas and suggestions from staff and external experts. Instead of the 'power of the hierarchy' she promoted the 'power of the better argument' (Ejiofor 2010 and Osakwe 2010, both quoted in Akunyili 2010: 278).

NAFDAC's Director General did also care for its members of staff. For the organization as a whole she pushed through better working conditions, salary increases and welfare packages. On a more personal level, she visited offices and inspectors throughout the country which had come under attack or pressure from drug counterfeiters (Adamu 2010, quoted in Akunyili 2010: 283). She could even be approached by staff with serious private problems and helped out, for example by paying school fees for the child of a member of staff whose husband had died unexpectedly (Osakwe 2010 and Keri 2010, both quoted in Akunyili 2010: 279, 275).

Due to this caring, communicative and inclusive leadership style in combination with her professional qualification and vision, Akunyili earned widespread respect, authority and loyalty from her staff. This, in turn, motivated staff to copy her working style and reinforced their commitment to NAFDAC as an organization and its mission.

Public service commitment

A strong public service commitment is both the result of the improvement of organizational performance as it is a contributing factor. We discuss public service commitment here at two levels: first, the public service commitment of the leader and second, the public service commitment of members of staff of the organization at large.

Dora Akunyili had at least three sources of public service commitment that made her determined to succeed in her job as NAFDAC's Director General. The first source is very personal. In 1988 her sister Vivian Edemobi, who had diabetes, died from an injection of false insulin at the age of 23: 'Not only was it fake and did not contain the insulin she was supposed to take, but it was also contaminated and gave her abscesses. She did not respond to antibiotics, and we just watched helplessly until she died' (Akunyili in Barriaux 2007).

In her book she wrote that this traumatic experience 'continued to be the driving force in my work' (Akunyili 2010: 42). Such a personal connection to or experience in the field one is working in appears to reinforce both personal and professional commitment in a way that is particularly strong and long-lasting.

Two other sources of commitment for Akunyili were to give something back to her country and finally to prove all those wrong who had fiercely opposed her appointment as NAFDAC's Director General by the then-President Olusegun Obasanjo.

How does one ignite public service commitment among the 95 per cent of staff retained from the 'old' NAFDAC plus those who were newly recruited? In order for commitment to become a strong motivating factor for staff across the board, leadership at all levels must nurture and communicate it. Public service commitment can be ignited and maintained through inclusive and motivating leadership, management and support as outlined above. While this commitment existed in the management team, our interviews indicate that the lower ranks also became increasingly committed to the organization's mission. NAFDAC's mission became a kind of self-fulfilment or personal mission for many of them, and an opportunity to contribute to their own country's and people's development.

Due to NAFDAC's turn-around within a short period of time, its successes and the growing public recognition, members of staff developed a strong esprit de corps and a pride of working for this organization (several interviews with NAFDAC staff, 2009). Positive feedback from the media, citizens, even politicians and international observers further strengthened this feeling of being part of something special. By fighting criminal fake drugs cartels and doing this in a political and administrative context like Nigeria, such pride and commitment may be especially effective in boosting staff morale and motivation, since the members of staff perceive themselves as the 'chosen few' (or 'Davids'), who are successfully fighting and defying two much larger systems (or 'Goliaths') that had previously been thought of as untouchable and invincible.[17]

Operational factors

The category of operational factors includes factors concerned with those essential strategies and procedures through which NAFDAC managed to carry out its tasks more effectively, as well as the internally generated revenue used to finance their implementation. Certain technologies have helped NAFDAC to become more effective, but they would not have done so independently of the organizational improvements analysed above and the operational changes described below. Therefore, while technological means can help to boost organizational effectiveness, the degree to which they can do so depends on their embeddedness in the organization's overall work and procedures. The contribution of technology is discussed in this context below.

108 *A. Irene Pogoson and Michael Roll*

Strategic decisions

In order to be able to successfully control and regulate the drug and food sectors, certain strategic decisions had to be taken at the political level. While Akunyili confesses that in the beginning she 'had no clear-cut ideas or strategies on how to fight the war [against counterfeit, unregistered and substandard drugs and food items, A.I.P. and M.R.]' (Akunyili 2010: 43) she gradually saw what needed to be done. For changing the laws and pushing such decisions through, Akunyili needed the political support and protection from the then-President Olusegun Obasanjo and the government which she received (see next section for more on this).

In the same year that Akunyili had been appointed, the Federal Government approved three policies that enabled NAFDAC to carry out its task, especially with regard to drug imports, much more effectively than before. These policies included the prohibition to import drugs and other regulated products through land borders from 2001, the designation of the seaports in Calabar and Lagos and the airports in Lagos and Kano as exclusive ports of entry for imported drugs and pharmaceutical raw material, and finally the release of cargo and shipped items by the Nigerian Ports Authority, Customs, shipping lines and airlines to NAFDAC inspectors (Akunyili 2010: 75–76). By law, NAFDAC inspectors had been banned from the ports in 1996 due to accusations of corruption. Since then, drugs and other items could be imported into the country without any control by a qualified regulatory authority. Without these new policies approved by the government, NAFDAC's attempts to control imported drugs and goods more effectively would have been much more difficult, if not outright impossible.[18]

Registration and control regime

Achieving legislative change and government approval is difficult and often time-consuming. The new NAFDAC management team therefore prioritized some of the strategically most important changes to lobby the government for approval (see above). However, given that Nigeria's laws on drugs and food were outdated, often overlapping or even conflicting, and that NAFDAC was expected to operate within these laws, a solution to this dilemma had to be found. Since the NAFDAC decree empowered the organization to enact its own regulations, these regulations were used as pragmatic solutions.

Existing regulations were reviewed together with other stakeholders, old regulations were abandoned or revised, and new ones were enacted. In 2009, close to 50 regulations had either been enacted or were drafted and ready for approval by the Minister of Health. Through these regulations, together with new guidelines and Standard Operating Procedures (SOPs) that are discussed below, NAFDAC made its registration and inspection regime much more rigorous. NAFDAC registration numbers, for example, had been compulsory for all products under the agency's control before then, but this had not been enforced. The organization now widely publicized the fact that these registration numbers were required by law and began to monitor whether they had been obtained. Another example is the registration process itself. Before then, it was sufficient to present only samples of food or beverages to the agency, together with the necessary documents, to get the product registered as meeting the required standards. In 2002 this procedure was changed, and a physical inspection of all production facilities by NAFDAC inspectors was made compulsory. Moreover since then, all drug registrations have to be renewed every five years or the registration expires. Another new regulation stipulated that after ten years of importing a drug that is not classified as an 'orphan drug' for rare diseases, NAFDAC would not allow a renewal of the import approval. This should encourage importers to start producing these drugs in Nigeria.

While NAFDAC is authorized to draft its own regulations and get them approved by the Minister of Health, the regulations have to some degree become functional substitutes for missing or conflicting legislation. This is confirmed by Akunyili when she writes that because of flawed legislation 'we have *in the interim* created regulations within the laws to enable us operate effectively' (Akunyili 2010: 56; our emphasis, A.I.P. and M.R.).

Embedded technology

In order to be able to carry out systematic investigations, evaluations and registrations, NAFDAC needed to completely overhaul its infrastructure. Laboratories were re-equipped to meet international standards, and many of them were subsequently internationally accredited by the WHO, other United Nations organizations, the European Union and others. The computerization and automation of laboratory procedures reduced the time needed for laboratory analysis. Members of staff at all levels were also trained to use computers effectively in order to use forms, write and distribute reports, etc. Computer literacy was made a requirement for promotion from 2001 onwards. This computer literacy was also necessary for using the newly established NAFDAC Regulated Products Automated Database (NARPAD), and the comparatively advanced website where regulations, guidelines and other documents are digitally available.

In 2009, NAFDAC further improved its effectiveness and efficiency in detecting counterfeit drugs. It was arguably the first country in the world to introduce handheld spectrometers for drug inspection. The inspectors can take these devices to remote markets and analyse whether drugs are genuine or substandard in a matter of seconds, instead of first having to take them to their laboratories.

Another technical innovation that NAFDAC introduced was a Mobile Authentication Service for drugs. From 2013, all anti-malaria and antibiotic drugs have to come with scratch cards attached to them. Customers can then scratch these cards, send the code as a text message to a toll-free NAFDAC line, and receive an instant response whether the drug is genuine or not. These are just some examples of how technology was and is employed to improve NAFDAC's effectiveness.

110   A. Irene Pogoson and Michael Roll

Institutionalization of procedures

In order to provide a new legal and operational framework for its activities and for institutionalizing procedures, NAFDAC acted at three levels: at the highest level it lobbied for new legislation, at a lower level it drafted its own regulations, and for its own operations the agency developed new guidelines and Standard Operating Procedures (SOPs). Akunyili writes that when she arrived at NAFDAC, there were 'no procedures and guidelines for the performance of our duties, decisions were subjective, and members of staff did not have a clear-cut understanding of their roles' (Akunyili 2010: 221). NAFDAC's regulation regime was therefore unpredictable, decisions were often arbitrary and prone to corruption and all sorts of interference. Together with the organizational changes discussed above, the agency has over the years developed numerous guidelines and SOPs for all kinds of procedures the organization performs.[19]

The NAFDAC guidelines and SOP state every step that a member of staff has to perform when carrying out a certain procedure. They also contain information about the fines and sanctions. Through extensive training, working in teams and communicating these procedures to the public through the media, NAFDAC procedures became increasingly standardized. Over time, drug importers and producers learned that in strong contrast to the 'old' NAFDAC, these procedures were non-negotiable and would actually be implemented. Two results of this increase in predictability and effectiveness were the decrease of unregistered and counterfeit drugs in circulation and the increasing number of product registrations (see ibid.: 250–59). Another result was that drug importers adapted to NAFDAC's increased effectiveness by developing new strategies for smuggling counterfeit drugs into the country, for example by using passenger planes and concealing the drugs in other consignments in ways that were more difficult to detect for the inspectors (ibid.: 255).

While the guidelines and SOPs standardized procedures and ensured external predictability, they also allowed the agency a high degree of flexibility. Since the agency developed and enacted these guidelines and SOPs, it could afford to keep them 'dynamic' (Akunyili 2010: 221), in the sense of adapting them whenever it deemed it necessary to do so. One example where this was done was for reducing the magnitude of imported unregistered drugs. When it took charge of NAFDAC, the new management team first requested importers of unregistered drugs to pay a fine plus the costs of the laboratory analysis. A few years later the agency realized that this sanction was not bringing down the magnitude of imported and unregistered drugs as fast as they wanted. The procedure was therefore changed and imported unregistered drugs were now seized and destroyed, abolishing the option of paying a fine and receiving the drugs. Such changes in procedures were communicated through the media.

What increased NAFDAC's effectiveness was therefore not a simple standardization of procedures, but the combination of standardization and actual enforcement, which created external predictability plus continuous learning and adaptation. The fact that the agency could draft its own regulations and enact its own far-reaching SOPs provided it with the flexibility to do that.

Political factors

Many of the organizational and procedural factors presented above sound familiar. That in itself is interesting. Apparently, some organizational and procedural features that characterize effective organizations in the OECD (Organization for Economic Co-operation and Development) world can be implemented in a much more challenging context as well. However, as we have seen, there are limits to that, since some factors also work in ways that are different from what would be expected and there are certain preconditions for their effectiveness. It is these preconditions that we turn to now in this section on political factors.

Public administration in OECD countries is to a large degree based on formalized procedures (see Luhmann 1983). This extends to the interaction between politics and public administration. In developing countries with a history of political instability, weak party systems, endemic corruption, patrimonialism and political interference, this is not the case, although formal rules and procedures do also exist. There, the public sector and its interaction with politics tends to be much more personalized, relationship-based and prone to political interferences and sudden changes. Such a context requires adequate strategies from public sector executives for enabling organizations to transform into PoE. We discuss these under the heading 'political management' below. We start with another factor that helps to understand why potentially effective organizations emerge in such political environments in the first place.

Political interest

Without the political protection from the then president Olusegun Obasanjo, Dora Akunyili would have never become the Director General of NAFDAC. He appointed her single-handedly against strong opposition. At that time, she was not even a member of the ruling party. Some thought she was too young for this position, others argued she did not have enough experience for it and still others simply ruled her out as a woman. Another concern was about her ethnicity, since she is Igbo while the then Health Minister and most drug counterfeiters were Igbo as well.[20] Why did Obasanjo take these people on and pushed Akunyili's appointment through? The general answer is: because he developed a strong interest that this particular public organization performs its mandate effectively, and he saw Akunyili as uniquely capable of making that happen.

After Obasanjo had been elected president in 1999, he became increasingly aware of the frequent counterfeit drug scandals and the deaths caused by them.[21] At that time Nigeria was considered to be a global dump for fake drugs. As a founding member and former chairman of the advisory council of the anti-corruption agency Transparency International, and with a wide international network, Obasanjo was very much aware of Nigeria's disastrous international image at that time. The organization placed Nigeria at the bottom of its corruption-perception ranking in 2000, making it unofficially the 'most corrupt country in the world'. Given Obasanjo's passionate and at times almost religious patriotism (Iliffe 2011: 2, 168, 185, 253, 258) he was determined to improve Nigeria's reputation abroad (ibid.: 217) and at the same time confirm and further boost his personal prestige as an international statesman (Gillies 2007; Iliffe 2011: 230). Apart from that, the Nigerian government was seeking a debt relief deal with the 'Paris Club', a group of 19 lenders, which was completed in 2006 (Iliffe 2011: 270; Okonjo-Iweala 2012: chapter 6).

This interest in cleaning up the drug and food sector in Nigeria is only part of the story. While other presidents also may develop such interests they are often not able to follow them through, since party members or other politicians need to be rewarded. In the case of NAFDAC, Obasanjo did not do this. Instead, he began to look for the right person to turn NAFDAC around.

At that time, Dora Akunyili worked as the Zonal Secretary for the Petroleum Trust Fund, a governmental social infrastructure provision agency.[22] When she was diagnosed with potentially serious health problems, she travelled to London for medical treatment and was given £17,000 to pay her medical bills, possibly including surgery. However, it was discovered that she did not need surgery and most of the money was returned to her. On her return, Akunyili wrote a letter to the Executive Chairman of her employer, the former Nigerian Head of State and military ruler Muhammadu Buhari, thanking him for the assistance and returned the money. Buhari's hand-written memo on this letter, directed to the Petroleum Trust Fund's financial department reads: 'See above report from PTF Zonal Secretary Zone I. You see that there are still Nigerians with personal integrity. Please take action in line with the financial regulations' (Buhari 1999, reprinted in: Akunyili 2010: 320).

Buhari told this unusual story of a member of staff of a government organization returning money to her employer to his friend Onalapo Soleye, a former minister of finance, who in turn was a close friend of and advisor to the then president. By accident, Akunyili later met Soleye in the Petroleum Trust Fund's headquarters when visiting a friend. Soleye told her that the president was looking for somebody to head NAFDAC and that, as a pharmacist, she was qualified. He requested her CV and took it to the president. The president later called her and asked her to come to see him. At that meeting he 'asked about the money that I returned, and other general questions' (Akunyili 2010: xxxviii) and subsequently appointed her as the new Director General of NAFDAC. While she was a pharmacist, Obasanjo's key criterion on which she stood out was her proven integrity and incorruptibility. Since she did not bring any of the 'qualifications' to the table that are usually required for such a position in Nigeria, such as being a member of the ruling party and the political elite networks, it is safe to say that without Obasanjo's special interest in appointing somebody with proven integrity, and perhaps somebody from outside of the usual elite circles, Akunyili would have never become the head of NAFDAC. The strong political opposition against her appointment attests to this.

This story shows how important the political context but also the personality of the president is for understanding why PoE emerge. Political and personal interests seem to go hand in hand here. Without Obasanjo's attention to the fake drugs tragedies, his interest in improving the country's international reputation and his decision to take the risk and appoint somebody from the lower ranks of the public sector but with proven integrity, most likely the NAFDAC miracle would have never occurred.

Political management

The term 'political management' refers to the lobbying for political support and influencing decisions that enable the organization to improve its effectiveness. It can be carried out by different actors, including media and civil society but in our understanding it is usually the public sector executive of the organization who does this. In political systems with formally and informally powerful presidents, direct access to him[23] and other top politicians is indispensable. However, access is only a precondition for being able to use political management as a strategy. Even if this access exists, the political support and protection has to be continuously 'earned' through exceptional performance and positive media coverage. Otherwise, the president and other politicians, who initially have an interest in this organization's effectiveness but have to deal with lots of other issues, might lose interest in responding to lobbying by the organization's executive.

Political management itself is rather unspectacular. It happens through meetings, dinners, side-meetings at cabinet meetings, conferences or foreign trips, as well as through telephone calls. With regard to state governors, field trips to these states or the inauguration of new offices or equipment are often used for such purposes. For convincing politicians from the ruling party at all levels of government to support a PoE, the intensity of political management that is required is often rather low, since for many of them it is sufficient to see that a public sector executive is close to and supported by the president.

Akunyili's political management was fairly successful. While she was not a member of the Nigerian elite political networks when she assumed office, she had the then president Obasanjo's explicit support. At the same time, she quickly began to make her own contacts and establish networks. Cordial relationships with the Minister of Health and the members of NAFDAC's Governing Council were particularly crucial, since they had to approve each of the agency's organizational decisions such as appointments, promotions or salary decisions, as well as proposed regulations and guidelines. Although sometimes the Director General had to fight hard to push suggestions through (Ekweogwu 2010, quoted in Akunyili 2010: 274), in general this worked fairly well (Akunyili, interview, 2009). While some of this support NAFDAC received was according to formal procedures, much of it was the result of interactions with politicians and other public sector executives, as well as semi-formal and ad-hoc requests.

One example for successful political management was the quick passing of new legislation that made the land import of drugs illegal and singled out selected air- and seaports for drug import (see above). Another critical piece of legislation was the return of NAFDAC to the ports. In all these cases, Akunyili and her management team convinced the president and legislators that in order to be effective, these pieces of legislation would have to be passed quickly. In many cases, the agency received the requested support and the legislation was passed. Regarding the ports, NAFDAC returned with a stronger mandate, following a presidential directive in 2001 (Akunyili, interview, 2009). Apart from the president, Akunyili also successfully lobbied legislators and many state governors. In addition to changes in NAFDAC-relevant legislation, legislators approved rising budget votes for the organization (see table 5.2) while state governors provided premises or buildings for offices when the organization was rebuilding its infrastructure.

Apart from legislative and operational support that enables the organization to be more effective, plain political protection of the executive leader is sometimes necessary, and is therefore one of the most important functions of political management. However, like political management more generally, it can never be entirely relied on. Since effective public organizations often interfere in sectors in which politicians have their own stakes, there is never a shortage of enemies. Organizational failures, the reshuffling of political positions or plain rumours are sometimes sufficient for chief executives to be removed from their positions. In such a context, political protection is key.

Institutional factors

Autonomy

In this paragraph, we discuss the autonomy of public organizations in terms of key procedures, such as staff recruitment and promotion, remuneration and welfare as well as finances. Moreover, some degree of autonomy from politics is essential in an environment in which political interference in public organizations and their use for employing political clients and supporters is the rule.[24] While the NAFDAC act which was tailored to the needs and functions of the organization did play a role in ensuring this autonomy, political protection and the continued enforcement of the act were essential, since laws can be overruled in an environment dominated by political interference and informal power.

The laws governing the agency vested the power of appointments, promotion and discipline in its Governing Council. They also allowed NAFDAC to create its own salary scale and welfare scheme and move away from the general public service scheme (NAFDAC Director of Finance, interview, 2009). The organization used this autonomy to hire, promote and discipline according to its internal effectiveness and performance objectives. It did not allow personal relationships or political interference to interfere with internal matters.

Formally, as a parastatal, NAFDAC is supposed to be fully financed by the government. Through extensive political lobbying and the organization's impressive performance record, Akunyili convinced the president and legislators year after year to increase NAFDAC's budget vote. However, a provision also allows the agency to keep the internal revenue it generates and reinvest it in its work. NAFDAC's management team realized that they would need more money than they received from the government for rebuilding their infrastructure, and that acquiring this money through internally generated revenue would make them more independent of the notoriously volatile government allocations. Therefore, they asked consultants to review NAFDAC's tariffs, including registration fees and penalties in 2001. All fees were raised, especially those for penalties, which boosted the agency's internal revenue over the coming years. Table 5.2 shows that since 2003, NAFDAC's internally generated revenue contributed between 65 and 88 per cent to its overall annual income. In addition to its massive infrastructural expenses, this allowed the organization to pay for its new headquarters building in Abuja in 2003 entirely from internally generated funds. Eventually, the agency even generated enough internal revenue to cover its capital budget, excluding personnel costs (NAFDAC Director of Finance, interview, 2009; Akunyili 2010: 260).

Apart from these two sources, government allocations and internal revenue, international donor organizations and private companies supported

Table 5.2 Income, sources of income and expenditure of NAFDAC, 2000–2007

Year	Income		Expenditure	Surplus/deficit
	Government (%)	*Internally generated revenue (%)*		
2000	317,713 (60.10)	210,893 (39.89)	542,318	-13,712
2001	369,490 (55.77)	293,038 (44.23)	847,093	-184,565
2003	544,684 (16.94)	2,671,337 (83.06)	2,042,785	1,173,236
2004	426,141 (11.74)	3,203,620 (88.26)	2,689,164	940,597
2005	679,437 (20.18)	2,687,620 (79.82)	3,262,375	104,682
2006	1,390,839 (32.04)	2,950,020 (67.96)	3,646,080	694,779
2007	1,657,428 (34.22)	3,186,607 (65.78)	4,229,970	614,065
2000–2007	5,385,732 (26.16)	15,203,135 (73.84)	17,259,785	3,329,082

Notes: All values are in million Naira. The data for 2002 were omitted since they were incoherent.
Source: NAFDAC, Department of Finance and Accounts (2009).

NAFDAC with money, laboratory equipment and free services. Overall, the agency's strong autonomy with regard to finances is an important factor for explaining how NAFDAC managed to become so much more effective within such a short period of time.

Focussed powers

The term 'focussed powers' is used to refer to the fact that an organization like NAFDAC, which was set up through an organization-specific decree, has comprehensive legal powers with regard to its mandate. As we have seen, it is empowered to draft – and later adapt – the regulations and guidelines which then govern its own procedures. Although the way NAFDAC used these two instruments might have stretched legal principles, it earned them a large degree of flexibility, independence and effectiveness.

Another important factor is that NAFDAC is a regulatory agency with executive powers including enforcement and prosecution. This makes the organization both more powerful and more independent. It makes it more powerful because the agency can actually enforce its own regulations. The fact that it does not rely on other government agencies to do so makes it more independent. Especially in a fragmented administrative system like the Nigerian one, this leads to a dramatic reduction of transaction costs. The establishment of a separate enforcement directorate as part of the agency's restructuring has allowed NAFDAC's to make full use of its executive powers and improve its overall effectiveness.

Outreach and cooperation

The factors that enabled NAFDAC to become a strong organization in the Nigerian context have been outlined above. They also partly explain the agency's effectiveness. However, factors related to outreach and cooperation are crucial for understanding how NAFDAC could achieve its success in a country of more than two and a half times the size of Germany, a population of approximately 170 million people, a poor quality infrastructure and widespread circulation of counterfeit drugs in such a short time. The three factors that our analysis showed to be most important in this regard are public communication, domestic cooperation and international cooperation.

Public communication

In the 1990s the level of awareness about counterfeit drugs in Nigeria was minimal. Since the regulator did not work properly and was not trusted, just like most other government organizations, no credible information about fake drugs and their risks were available. The fact that they costed far less than genuine drugs was sufficient to convince Nigerians to buy them. By the end of the 1990s most Nigerians would not have known that a government organization by the name of NAFDAC existed. Only a few years later, not only did most of them know the agency but 79 per cent also had confidence in it (NOI Polls 2009: 6). The most important reason for this dramatic change is the strategic and extensive use of public communication by NAFDAC. An interview with the Director of Finance and Accounts revealed that publicity takes a lion share of NAFDAC's liabilities, comparable only to the expenses of laboratory, chemicals and consumables (NAFDAC Director, Finance and Accounts, interview, 2009). At the end of her term, Akunyili concluded that 'The most effective strategy in the war against fake/ counterfeit drugs is public enlightenment which sensitizes the public on the evils of counterfeit medicines and the necessity to eradicate them.' (Akunyili 2010: 302).

One of the public communication strategies that NAFDAC used throughout the whole country were 'public enlightenment campaigns'. For these campaigns, the agency usually invited particular producer or trader groups, such as water producers, market drug traders or drug importers for interactive workshops, informed them about current regulations and discussed problems and possible solutions with them. As we discuss further below in the section on 'domestic cooperation', many of these groups began to cooperate with NAFDAC after this initial contact.

The agency also used the media like newspapers, radio, TV, electronic media as well as leaflets, posters and grassroots campaigns in various languages, to communicate new laws, regulations or alerts to producers, traders and customers. In addition to these direct messages, the dynamic Nigerian press covered NAFDAC's emerging and increasingly successful struggle against fake drugs and the cartels and individuals involved. The organization knew how to organize events in a way that would make them attractive to the media and would give them publicity, for example by publicly burning or otherwise destroying large amounts of counterfeit drugs or by exposing perpetrators. As a person who was accessible to the media and very skilful in dealing with them, Dora Akunyili became the symbol of this struggle for the media and the wider public. In this process, she was nicknamed 'Lady Teflon' due to her uncompromising determination despite all kinds of challenges and dangers. She called the press an important support factor for NAFDAC's work and its 'town crier' (Akunyili 2010: 266).

While some observers noted that the agency was being overly 'hyped' by the media, this publicity would not have worked and created the public attention it did, had there been no real achievements. As many of our interviews as well as newspaper articles and cartoons show, NAFDAC has been successful in creating public awareness about counterfeit drugs and the risks involved in taking them. Even in remote areas, Nigerians learned that they should check the label and expect to find an expiry date and NAFDAC registration number on drugs and other regulated products.[25] Since the introduction of the agency's Mobile Authentication Service, customers can even check the genuineness of their drugs instantly.

118   A. Irene Pogoson and Michael Roll

Domestic cooperation

'Domestic cooperation' is probably the single most important factor that multiplied NAFDAC's effectiveness as an organization. In this section, we single out two groups of domestic actors that cooperated with NAFDAC and that have been key to its success: government agencies and drug producers. Our focus in the section on 'political management' above was on the strategies that public sector executives employed to earn political protection and support. In this section, we have already covered the 'cooperation' between NAFDAC and politicians and political bodies.

Cooperation among public agencies is rare in Nigeria. To establish cooperation with some of the agencies working in related fields was not a straightforward process for NAFDAC either. Some public organizations did not want to work with the agency. Even in cases where presidential directives to do so were given, they were sometimes ignored. It then took the intervention of the executive of these organizations, such as the Head of Customs Services or in one case the military police, having received written complaints from the NAFDAC Director General, to make sure that their staff on ground did comply with these regulations (Akunyili 2010: 97–98, 167–68). In some cases, this was done only reluctantly and not without trying to 'work around' the agency.

After NAFDAC's return to the ports, for example, containers were often released without NAFDAC's prior consent, as the presidential directive required. The Nigerian Customs Service did also continue to auction consignments that had been abandoned and that included products that fell under NAFDAC's regulatory control, without informing the organization (ibid.: 215). In 2002 NAFDAC even started tracking containers with imported fake drugs that were illegally transferred through government warehouses (ibid.: 216). Such conflicts reveal the glaring difference between the standard mode of how public sector organizations in many developing countries like Nigeria work, and the way a PoE operates. They also demonstrate that, even if there is political support for a specific organization from above, the broader system remains hostile and actually fights attempts to increase public sector effectiveness.

In such conflicts, even existing legislation concerning its operations needed to be enforced by NAFDAC, through both official administrative channels and political and informal pressure. Over time, public organizations such as the police, the National Ports Authority and the Customs Service did cooperate with NAFDAC, although to varying degrees.

The second group that we discuss here are the drug and regulated goods producers. NAFDAC's new management team's assumption was that especially small domestic producers often did not act out of criminal motives but simply did not understand the implications of what they are doing (Akunyili 2010: 43). Their approach of working with domestic producers was also informed by the high level of general unemployment in Nigeria, and the awareness that since most counterfeit drugs were imported, building a strong domestic pharmaceutical industry would be a powerful instrument for fighting the prevalence of fake drugs. NAFDAC's strategy for the local industry was therefore not one of strict prosecution but rather of interaction, communication, information, education and assistance.[26] During this period, the agency was a proactive social worker rather than a police officer.

Through the 'public enlightenment campaigns', that included workshops, publications, sensitization campaigns, consultative meetings with stakeholders and public communication (Akunyili 2010: 77), NAFDAC gave producers the opportunity and time to upgrade their facilities and procedures to meet the expected quality standards. This approach proved to be very successful in turning many of these producers from actual perpetrators into allies of NAFDAC in the fight against counterfeit drugs. Once they had upgraded their facilities, they developed a strong interest that unregistered drugs would no longer be available as cheap alternatives to their own registered products for customers.

Given the massive size of the country and the number of persons involved in fake drug production and trade, while NAFDAC could reach out and mobilize these groups to cooperate and comply with the standards it would have been extremely difficult and expensive to police this comprehensively. While the agency *did* police markets and factories and carried out random inspections and tests, it also established two systems of public and self-control. The first strategy was to create incentives and opportunities for those who would benefit from a fake drug-free Nigeria to report cases of misconduct to the agency. This large group included concerned citizens who came across counterfeit drugs, as well as drug producers who had upgraded their facilities and wanted to sell their registered and more expensive drugs. Via telephone, personal communication and reports, NAFDAC received important information and tip-offs that it would not have been able to get without the cooperation of concerned stakeholders.

The second strategy was that after it had trained producers, traders and retailers, the agency encouraged and supported them to either establish or use existing associations to perform self-regulation (Akunyili 2010: 63).[27] As a result, in addition to NAFDAC policing the compliance with drug laws and regulations, these associations also did that. While this strategy can never ensure a 100 per cent success rate, it seems to have worked well and probably much better than any government-organized large scale policing initiative would have. This 'associational policing' is based on social and informal control and pressure. If a conflict arises, NAFDAC or other government agencies can be brought in, but many cases are prevented and resolved without official involvement. This observation mirrors the importance of informal processes either complementing or substituting formal and official ones, as discussed above in the sections on 'political management' and cooperation with politicians.

For going beyond scratching at the surface of counterfeit drug production and trade in Nigeria, NAFDAC used the networks of cooperating groups to

120 *A. Irene Pogoson and Michael Roll*

identify and arrest the 'bosses' behind the business. This approach is also reflected in differential treatment for distributors, retailers and importers in the Standard Operating Procedures. While the first two have to pay a fine and have their shops or warehouses closed for some time, they are usually released thereafter while the latter is prosecuted (Akunyili 2010: 221–22). At the same time, the agency's approach of dealing with the local pharmaceutical sector cannot be called 'soft', since NAFDAC did indeed crack down hard on those responsible for the production or importation of counterfeit drugs or those who did not cooperate and maintain the standards.[28]

Through its proactive, supportive and pragmatic approach, over time NAFDAC managed to overcome many important domestic groups' suspicion towards collaborating with a government organization. The agency won their trust and turned many perpetrators into allies in the fight against counterfeit drugs and products in Nigeria. This allowed the agency to get to the roots of counterfeit drug production, importation and trade in the country in a number of cases instead of just arresting 'small fry'.

International cooperation

International cooperation with NAFDAC took different forms. Here we only discuss training for members of staff and cooperation with countries that exported drugs to Nigeria. NAFDAC interacted with several government and private business organizations in Europe, the United States, Asia and Africa (see Akunyili 2010: 101; 266–67). Apart from exchanging information and receiving offers of technical support, these organizations regularly invited NAFDAC staff for free training or internships overseas. As we discussed above, these international training opportunities, as well as the introduced mandatory overseas factory inspections, were used in a systematic manner by the NAFDAC leadership to reward good performance, which not only improved the participants' expertise but also their motivation and loyalty to the organization.

Shortly after Akunyili's appointment in 2001 and together with the House of Representatives' Committee on Health, NAFDAC organized meetings with the High Commissioners or Ambassadors of countries that exported large amounts of counterfeit drugs to Nigeria at that time, especially India and China. Together with the Indian High Commissioner to Nigeria and several Indian companies operating in Nigeria the Indian Pharmaceutical Manufacturers and Importers in Nigeria (IPMIN) association was established (Akunyili 2010: 101). In several meetings IPMIN advised and informed NAFDAC about challenges and potential perpetrators. During a meeting with the Commissioner of India's Food and Drug Administration in the same year, Akunyili suggested introducing independent pre-shipment analyses of drugs for export from India to Nigeria, for which the exporters would have to pay. The Commissioner did not object to this suggestion, and the first of several independent foreign pre-shipment analysis companies was appointed (ibid.: 103–4). Other pre-shipment analysis agreements have since been finalized with companies in China and Egypt (Akunyili, interview, 2009).

In addition to ensuring that foreign drugs would be analysed for genuineness before being shipped to Nigeria, Akunyili also used Nigeria's new reputation as a country fighting counterfeit drugs to invite pharmaceutical companies to invest and produce in Nigeria (Akunyili 2010: 106). It is noteworthy that international training for NAFDAC staff and pre-shipment analyses – both very powerful instruments for enhanced effectiveness – were organized in such a way that they did not cost NAFDAC any money.

Conclusion

In order to arrive at a parsimonious and potentially generalizable model for explaining why and how PoE emerge in hostile environments, we do the following below. First, where it makes sense, we combine some of the explanatory factors we identified. Second, and based on the analytical framework introduced in this book, we distinguish between factors that are more important for the *emergence* and others that are more important for the *persistence* of PoE. Finally, we offer preliminary models, exclusively based on the NAFDAC case study, that suggest why and how PoE emerge and persist in more general terms.

We reduce the individual factors that we arrived at from our analysis by combining all organizational factors into the factor '(performance-oriented) organizational culture'. We justify this by referring to Merilee Grindle's work (Grindle 1997; Hilderbrand and Grindle 1997), which identified similar individual factors, and used the term 'organizational culture' (Grindle 1997) to refer to them.[29] We do so too below, keeping the individual factors that emerged from our analysis of NAFDAC in mind.

We also conflate 'autonomy' and 'focussed powers' from the category 'institutional factors' into 'autonomous power', since both factors are closely related. Finally, we combine 'public communication' and 'domestic cooperation' from the category 'outreach and cooperation' into 'domestic cooperation', since the former can be regarded as an element of the latter, in which we are more interested (see table 5.3 for an overview).

The framework of this book suggests distinguishing between factors that explain the emergence and others that explain the persistence of organizations as PoE. While there is certainly a degree of overlap between these factors, we agree that for analytical reasons it is useful to distinguish between them.

What does our conclusion of how PoE emerge look like, based on the NAFDAC case study? Building on our qualitative analysis we singled out those of the above factors that we identified as essential in the case of NAFDAC, those without which the agency would not have been able to emerge as a PoE (see table 5.3). We therefore disregarded others which have contributed but without which NAFDAC would still have been able to

122 *A. Irene Pogoson and Michael Roll*

Table 5.3 New categorization of factors

Old categories and factors	New factors
1. Organizational factors Functional restructuring Merit-, integrity- and commitment-based recruitment Anti-corruption regime Training and performance regime Inclusive leadership Public service commitment	A. (Performance-oriented) organizational culture
2. Operational factors Strategic decisions Registration and control regime Embedded technology Institutionalization of procedures	B. Strategic decisions C. Registration and control regime D. Embedded technology E. Institutionalization of procedures
3. Political factors Political interest Political management	F. Political interest G. Political management
4. Institutional factors Autonomy Focussed powers	H. Autonomous powers
5. Outreach and cooperation Public communication Domestic cooperation International cooperation	I. Domestic cooperation J. International cooperation

emerge as a PoE, although perhaps with a somewhat lower degree of effectiveness or at a later point in time.

Figure 5.1 summarizes our model for explaining how PoE emerge. The arrows do not signify causal relationships. They rather show that the factor before the arrow was the precondition for the one after it. The model is furthermore stylized in the sense that it does not reflect a strict temporal order – quite the opposite: in most cases factors that are shown as following one another in reality were at work at the same time. However, a certain degree of, for example, performance-oriented organizational culture had to be established and some strategic decisions taken before a meaningful registration and control regime could be established.

In our model for how PoE emerge (see figure 5.1), everything starts with 'political interest'. If a top politician, in our case the president, with significant powers, develops an interest in a particular public service being provided effectively, he appoints an executive who he thinks will be able to achieve this. This person in turn employs various strategies of 'political management' to establish and constantly renew political protection and support from the necessary groups of actors in the given context.[30] Based on this support, a performance-oriented organizational culture with the elements outlined above is built up by this executive and the management team, and strategic decisions are taken and approved. The registration and control regime – a rather NAFDAC-specific factor – is then reviewed and rebuilt, while other actors are being sensitized and mobilized to cooperate with the organization. 'Autonomous powers' is an enabling factor which determines how fast and to which degree progress in terms of the other factors can be achieved.

How do we model the persistence of PoE in hostile environments, based on the NAFDAC case study? Only those factors are included that we regard as essential and that, compared to the model of the emergence of PoE, continue to change constantly. Political interest, organizational culture, registration and control regime and autonomous powers continue to be important and can change every now and then, but they have been established during the emergence phase and can therefore be taken as a given for the purpose of this model. Political management and domestic cooperation on the other hand, which appear in both models, continue to be dynamic and are likely to change very often during the persistence phase. The model (see figure 5.2) shows that constant political management is a precondition for the other three factors. Based on that, domestic cooperation is being expanded and

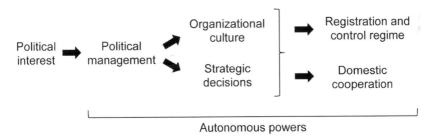

Figure 5.1 Model for how pockets of effectiveness emerge

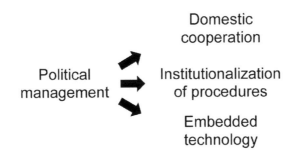

Figure 5.2 Model for how pockets of effectiveness persist

124 *A. Irene Pogoson and Michael Roll*

consolidated, procedures are being increasingly institutionalized and embedded technology is employed to boost organizational effectiveness.[31]

'Political management' appears as a particularly important factor in both models. This is hardly surprising, given the fact that we are talking about countries where the environment for effective public service provision is hostile and where, in practice, politicians have the power to ignore or even overrule laws or formal agreements. Nevertheless, in the literature on PoE this factor has not yet received the attention it deserves.[32] Moreover, as our models indicate, even in such unfavourable contexts, once PoE have been successfully established, are working and receive support and recognition both domestically and internationally, this provides a certain degree of protection against political arbitrariness. Politicians who do not want this particular public service to be provided can still reduce or even destroy the organization's effectiveness, but the costs for doing so are now higher than before. Citizens who have started to cherish this public service and international organizations could at least turn into an inconvenience for this politician during his time in government, and it would seriously damage his legacy.

Based on our analysis of the NAFDAC case study, we have offered models for the emergence and persistence phase of a PoE that emphasize the interaction of various factors and the special importance of 'political management'. We hope that, together with the other case studies presented in this book, this case study contributes to a more generalizable model for explaining the emergence and persistence of PoE in developing countries.

Notes

1 Research for this case study was conducted from 2009 to 2010 by Irene Pogoson, Suraj Mudasiru and Azeez Olaniyan. It was one of the case studies of the 'Pockets of Effectiveness in Nigeria' project, initiated and coordinated by the Friedrich-Ebert-Stiftung (FES), Nigeria Office. While this case study was funded by FES Nigeria, the views expressed in this chapter are those of the authors and should not be attributed to the FES. We thank Suraj Mudasiru and Azeez Olaniyan for excellent research assistance.

2 Due to the timing of our research, the focus of this case study is on the period of Dora Akunyili's leadership of NAFDAC.

3 NAFDAC's Governing Council is comprised of representatives of the Federal Ministry of Health, the Standards Organisation of Nigeria (SON), the National Institute for Pharmaceutical Research and Development (NIPRD), the National Drug Law Enforcement Agency (NDLEA), the Pharmaceutical Council of Nigeria (PCN), the Pharmaceutical Group and the Food and Beverages Group of the Manufactures Association of Nigeria (MAN), and three members representing the interest of the general public. The council meets at least once every quarter.

4 For more on this, including data, see below.

5 The few studies that cover this period look at different samples of drugs but largely support the impression that counterfeit and substandard drugs were a major problem in the 1990s in Nigeria. In her book about her experience at NAFDAC, Akunyili refers to four different studies: Poole (1989) found that 25 per cent of the drug samples were fake, 25 per cent genuine and 50 per cent inconclusive, while

Ochekpe *et al.* (1993) reported that 41.4 per cent of their drugs did not contain the specified percentage of active ingredients, and Taylor *et al.* (2001) establish that 48 per cent of the drugs tested were substandard (all studies quoted in Akunyili 2010: 33–34). According to Akunyili, NAFDAC's own study in 2002 revealed that about 68 per cent of the drugs in Nigeria were unregistered, and almost all drugs had been counterfeited (Akunyili 2010: 34).

6 Data and information in this section were first obtained from the records of the Director of NAFDAC's Planning, Research and Statistics Directorate (2009). They were later complemented and validated with the sources quoted in the text.

7 For an analysis and discussion of whether Nigeria can be considered a 'democracy' or not, and what has changed in various domains of policy more than ten years after the return to (formal) democracy and civilian rule, see Olurode (2010) and Adejumobi (2011).

8 NAFDAC's official mission statement reads: 'To safeguard public health by ensuring that only the right quality drugs, food and other regulated products are manufactured, imported, exported, advertised, distributed, sold and used.' (NAFDAC n.d. b)

9 The questions that NOI Polls asked in these surveys differed slightly. While they asked for the confidence people had in a selected group of government agencies in 2007, they asked for their effectiveness in 2008 and 2009. In 2007, 79 per cent said that they have confidence in NAFDAC, with the anti-corruption agency Economic and Financial Crimes Commission (EFCC) coming second with 66 per cent (NOI Polls 2009: 6). In 2007 and 2008 70 and 74 per cent agreed that NAFDAC is an effective government agency, again followed by the EFCC with 58 and 57 per cent agreement respectively (NOI Polls 2009: 11, 19).

10 For a detailed overview of some of the more than 500 domestic and international awards and recognitions presented to her, see appendix 24 of her book (Akunyili 2010: 389–410).

11 For a detailed overview of these attacks, see Akunyili (2010: 183–99).

12 Due to the obvious risk of a biased presentation of her work at NAFDAC, we used the book just like we used all other kinds of empirical data. The analysis always included systematic cross-checking to make sure the facts were correct, as well as triangulation which allowed us to put data into context and therefore assess their validity, consistency and relevance. For another important reference, see Ovadje and Utomi (2009).

13 These zonal offices in the six geo-political zones of the country are located in Ibadan (South West), Port Harcourt (South South), Enugu (South East), Jos (North Central), Kano (North West) and Maiduguri (North East).

14 Some of these factors were identified during an earlier analysis of case studies of NAFDAC and the Nigerian National Agency for the Prohibition of Traffic in Persons and Other Related Matters (NAPTIP) (see Simbine's chapter 6 in this volume), and some of these terms are used here (Roll forthcoming).

15 As we describe in more detail below, together with its Governing Council, NAFDAC is autonomous in terms of personnel appointment, promotion and sanction.

16 According to Akunyili, as many as 15 members of staff were on training with international organizations in the first few years (Akunyili 2010: 46). In total, between 2002 and October 2008, 349 members of staff attended international training programmes (ibid.: 260), which does not include international investigations or the inspection of foreign factories.

17 It should be noted that there are strong similarities between this analysis and the findings reported by Tendler (1997), and those about a positive 'organizational culture' or 'organizational mystique' by Grindle (1997).

18 However, as we will see in the discussion of the fifth category of factors below, in a context like Nigeria a government-approved policy does not automatically lead to compliance of the agencies involved on the ground.

126 *A. Irene Pogoson and Michael Roll*

19 For an overview and examples of guidelines and SOPs, see Akunyili (2010: 221–32 and 361–86) or NAFDAC's website www.nafdac.gov.ng.

20 The Igbo are the third largest ethnic group in Nigeria. They live predominantly in the southeast of the country.

21 In a speech that the then president Obasanjo gave when Dora Akunyili was honoured with the Order of the Federal Republic of Nigeria (OFR) in 2003, he said: 'When we came into government, one of the things that worried me tremendously was the issue of counterfeit medicines. I know not one, not two people who should not have died, but have died because of counterfeit medicines.' (Obasanjo 2003, quoted in Akunyili 2010: 268).

22 This story has been reported in many Nigerian newspapers and journals. We used these sources and later validated them with Akunyili's own account that she gave us during the interview (Akunyili, interview, 2009) and in her book (Akunyili 2010: xxxvii-xxxviii).

23 Since the Nigerian president at that time was male, we continue to use the male form only in this chapter. All arguments do of course also apply to female presidents and politicians.

24 In the context of administrative reform strategies in OECD countries, the model of the semi-autonomous executive agency has emerged in the last decades. NAFDAC reflects some of the characteristics of such agencies, even if – as far as we know – its establishment was not informed by this model. The focus of the 'agencification' literature is still largely on OECD countries, but case studies from developing countries are sometimes included. For more information, see van Donge (2002), Pollitt and Talbot (2004), Ayee (2008: 134–37) and Moynihan (2006).

25 See also a sample of cartoons about NAFDAC reproduced in Akunyili (2010: 288–89).

26 See Akunyili (2010) for examples of NAFDAC working with various groups such as water producers (ibid.: 78–80), patent and proprietary medicine dealers (ibid.: 81–83), pharmacists (ibid.: 85–86), traditional medicine practitioners (ibid.: 86–88) and bakers (ibid.: 90–92).

27 With regard to the water producers, NAFDAC worked with the National Association of Table Water Producers (Akunyili 2010: 80–81), the patent and proprietary medicine dealers established a self-regulating association (ibid.: 83) while the National Association of Road Transport Owners already existed (ibid.: 84). Traditional medicine practitioners were encouraged to join self-regulating professional associations (ibid.: 87), and caretaker committees of markets where counterfeit drugs were pervasive were instructed to support NAFDAC in identifying people involved in the fake drug trade (ibid.: 130–31). In response to the agency's initial success, Nigerian drug importers and increasingly also producers established the Association of Pharmaceutical Importers of Nigeria (APIN) in 2004, to regulate themselves and thereby assist NAFDAC and promote their own business interests as importers and producers of genuine drugs (APIN President, interview, 2009).

28 Evidence for this is provided by the closure of several markets which traded counterfeit drugs in particularly large amounts. Together with hundreds of police officers and soldiers, NAFDAC closed the notorious Onitsha Bridge Head Market for more than three months in 2007. From this market most counterfeit drugs were distributed throughout the country. NAFDAC only allowed the market to re-open after certain conditions had been met. The same happened with other markets where market committees declined to fully cooperate with NAFDAC (Akunyili 2010: 127–32).

29 Some of the individual factors that Grindle's concept of 'organizational culture' comprises are: commitment to organizational goals, professionalism, elitism, hard work, a sense of mission, effective managerial practice, high employee performance expectations, and job-relevant training (Grindle 1997: 489–90).

30 Political 'support' does not necessarily mean active support as long as no major conflicts arise. 'Benign neglect' in the sense of the absence of political interference may be enough for a PoE to emerge if finances are available.
31 The only factor from our new categorization of factors that does not appear in both of our models is 'international cooperation'. While we think that international cooperation boosted NAFDAC's effectiveness in many ways, we arrived at the conclusion that while its level of effectiveness would have been lower or it would have increased more slowly without it, the agency would still have been able to become and persist as a PoE.
32 While Tendler's work (1997) touches upon political management phenomena, to date Leonard (1991) has been most explicit in analysing this.

Interviews

APIN (Association of Pharmaceutical Importers of Nigeria) President, Lagos, 28 May 2009.
Dora Akunyili, former NAFDAC Director General and at the time of interview Minister for Information and Culture of the Federal Republic of Nigeria, Abuja, 24 September 2009.
NAFDAC Director, Establishments Inspection, Abuja, 20 July 2009.
NAFDAC Director, Finance and Accounts, Abuja, 20 and 21 July 2009.
NAFDAC Director, Planning, Research and Statistics, Abuja, 20 July 2009.

6 Taming the menace of human trafficking

Nigeria's National Agency for the Prohibition of Traffic in Persons and Other Related Matters (NAPTIP)

Antonia T. Simbine[1] with Franca C. Attoh and Abubakar Oladeji

Introduction

Globally, trafficking in human beings, especially women and girls, is not a new phenomenon. While the United Nations estimates a figure close to 4 million as a total for internationally and internally trafficked people, the United Nations Children's Fund (UNICEF) estimates that 1,200,000 children were trafficked globally in 2000 (UNICEF 2005). Human trafficking has become multi-faceted, involving multiple stakeholders at institutional and commercial levels. It is a demand-driven global business, with a huge market for cheap labour and commercial sex confronting often insufficient or unexercised policy frameworks or trained personnel to prevent it (ibid.).

Human trafficking is a clear and blatant violation of the rights of its victims. It remains an abhorrent act of modern day slavery and denotes that people are forced, tricked or threatened into situations in which they are exploited sexually, financially and/or through forced labour. In human trafficking, human beings, often reduced to 'commodities' for sale by traffickers, are not only deprived of their free will, but equally denied the opportunity to develop the life-skills and competences that enable them to make meaningful contributions to society. This is not to deny the fact that some people go into the practice deliberately and knowingly.

What is or constitutes trafficking? According to an internationally agreed definition of trafficking, human trafficking is

> the recruitment, transportation, transfer, harbouring or receipt of persons, by means of the threat or use of force or other forms of coercion, of abduction, of fraud, of deception, of the abuse of power or of a position of vulnerability or of the giving or receiving of payments or benefits to achieve the consent of a person having control over another person, for the purpose of exploitation.
>
> (UNODC 2004: 42)

Human trafficking can take two forms. The first is internal or within the country, where children and women are moved from either rural to urban centres or from one part of the city to another, for the purpose of labour or sexual exploitation or both. The second is external or trans-border, where people are trafficked from Nigeria to other African countries, Europe, or to other parts of the world, mostly for prostitution. This corroborates the conclusion reached by the United Nations African Institute for the Prevention of Crime and the Treatment of Offenders (UNAFRI) (UNAFRI 2003) that human trafficking is a trans-border problem and that organized criminal cartels are the major engines of this terrible business.

The phenomenon of human trafficking is universal and has been practiced in different forms in different parts of the world. Okogie et al. (2004, quoted in Maicibi et al. 2007: 3) observe that the phenomenon is a multi-billion dollar business for the criminal gangs involved. It has also been assessed to be the fastest growing category of organized crime and the third largest profit making business outside of drugs and arms deals (African News Services 2002, quoted in UNAFRI 2007: 3). Maicibi (2005: 50) holds the view that human trafficking is second only to illicit drug dealing. Indeed, there are millions of women and children who are victims of human trafficking, working as either prostitutes or labourers in different parts of the world.

Being such a profitable and large business, even countries in Europe or international organizations are finding it hard to effectively fight it. It is therefore surprising that a public agency in a country that is known for its public sector ineffectiveness and corruption has made significant inroads in fighting human trafficking in recent years, Nigeria's National Agency for the Prohibition of Traffic in Persons and Other Related Matters (NAPTIP). This is all the more true as Nigeria is considered a 'source' country from where people are being trafficked. This implies that several criminal human trafficking syndicates exist in the country, which makes fighting them all the more challenging.

The data on which this chapter is based were generated through a combination of interviews, including expert interviews, key informant interviews, focus group discussions, non-participant observation and document analysis. Most of the research was conducted between 4 May and 8 June 2009. Several follow-up discussions, telephone and e-mail contacts with NAPTIP officials for additional answers and clarifications took place until 2011. In total, 19 formal interviews were conducted with high level NAPTIP staff, representatives of international and domestic NGOs working in the field, as well as a diplomat and a representative of an international organization. We also conducted focus group discussions with a total of 29 junior level and medium level NAPTIP officers. In addition to headquarters in the capital Abuja, two of the agency's zonal offices were visited. We chose Benin City and Lagos, based on the fact that trafficking is most prevalent in these cities. Three shelters for victims of trafficking that the agency runs were also visited, observations made and informal discussions held, including with one (suspected former) trafficker. Mostly through informal discussions and conversations, some members of the public were included to ascertain their perception of the agency. Throughout the research, academic literature, NAPTIP documents, newspaper reports and other kinds of publications were reviewed and included in the analysis.

In analysing how NAPTIP has become and remained a 'pocket of effectiveness' (PoE) we will proceed as follows in this chapter. In the next section we give an overview of human trafficking in Nigeria. We then introduce NAPTIP in more detail, focussing on its establishment, organization and operations. Before analysing the organization's route to effectiveness, we present evidence that it can actually be considered a PoE in line with the definition and framework employed in this book. The following section presents our findings of why and how NAPTIP emerged and managed to persist as a PoE in a hostile environment. In the final section we draw some conclusions.

Human trafficking in Nigeria

Nigeria's commitment to fighting the scourge of trafficking is partly because over the past few years, the country has acquired a reputation for being one of the leading African countries in cross-border and internal trafficking (UNESCO 2006). Teriba (2001) observes that of the 500,000 Africans trafficked annually to Europe, Nigerians account for 67 per cent. Similarly, Germono (2001) has shown that there are about 10,000 Nigerian prostitutes in Italy alone. Many other studies conducted by local and international NGOs have demonstrated the widespread manifestation of the problem of human trafficking in Nigeria (Ebigbo 2000; Women's Consortium of Nigeria 2000; Nwogu, 2005; NAPTIP 2005a).

The origin of the menace of human trafficking in the country has often been traced to the oil boom of the 1970s, which created opportunities for migration both inside and outside of the country, and which provided avenues for exploitation, for international trafficking in women and children, for forced labour and for prostitution (UNESCO 2006).

With regard to international human trafficking, Nigeria is a transit country as well as a country of origin and destination. Destinations for trafficked Nigerians include neighbouring West African countries (Côte d'Ivoire, Mali, Benin, Equatorial Guinea, Cameroon, Gabon and Guinea), European countries (particularly Italy, Belgium, Spain, the Netherlands, Germany and the United Kingdom), North Africa (Libya, Algeria and Morocco) and Middle Eastern countries (especially Saudi Arabia). Recently, South America, particularly Venezuela, has also become a point of destination for trafficked persons.

Apart from trans-border trafficking, there is also strong evidence of internal trafficking as minors are moved from one part of the country, often rural areas, to other, often urban centres, for the purposes of serving as domestic aids in middle and high class homes and/or as child prostitutes in brothels run by criminal syndicates. In the last two decades, there has been an increase in internal trafficking of Nigerian women and children from rural communities in the South-West (Oyo, Osun and Ogun), in the South-South (Akwa-Ibom, Cross River and Bayelsa), in the South-East (Ebonyi and Imo) and in the Middle Belt (Benue, Niger and Kwara) to cities such as Lagos, Abeokuta, Ibadan, Kano, Kaduna, Calabar and Port Harcourt (UNESCO 2006). Trafficking to these cities is predominantly for exploitative domestic work, farm labour, mineral exploitation and prostitution, with incidents of human trafficking and forced labour particularly prevalent in Lagos. It is primarily women and girls but also boys that are trafficked for purposes of sexual exploitation, forced labour and organ harvesting (UNESCO 2006). It is in the area around Benin City in Edo state that human trafficking is most prevalent in Nigeria.[2]

The pattern of human trafficking in Nigeria fits within the category of organized crime, although family and relatives networks play an important role. At the head of the trafficking networks is the baron also known as the 'boss' or 'madam', who is usually a large-scale financier responsible for recruitment, transportation, importation and reception of victims. This mode of operation is syndicated in nature, where there are identified networks (Ojomo 2001 and Teriba 2001, both quoted in Maicibi et al. 2007: 4). 'Recruitment centres' and contact persons exist, mainly in urban centres, where young girls between the ages of 15 and 26 are deceived with promises of school enrolment or well-paid jobs in cities or outside Nigeria. A crucial link in the chain is what Joseph (2005, in NAPTIP 2005b: 18–20) calls the 'head-pimp'. He or she coordinates the recruitment, movement and exportation of the victims (UNICRI 2004; UNESCO 2006).

Several studies have been carried out on the root causes of the phenomenon of human trafficking. It is attributed to poverty, unemployment, illiteracy (see, for instance, Joseph 2005, in NAPTIP 2005b: 18–20).[3] According to NAPTIP's founding Executive Secretary, poverty is essentially the principal driving force behind this trade, with other factors being illiteracy, ignorance, greed, and the glorification of the West (former NAPTIP Executive Secretary, interview, 2009). A report by the International Labour Organization's International Programme on the Elimination of Child Labour (ILO/IPEC) found that 40 per cent of Nigerian street children and hawkers are trafficked persons (ILO/IPEC 2000: 13), and confirms poverty as the most visible cause of the vulnerability of women and children to trafficking in Nigeria. Other factors responsible for human trafficking include defective socialization patterns in homes and peer groups, ignorance of risk of involvement on the part of parents and victims, high demand for trafficked persons in destination centres both within and outside Nigeria, and strong social pressure from families or relatives networks. Maicibi (2006) has stressed the need to shift from the push to the pull factors which, according to him, have more explanatory weight than the push factors that make youths ready to submit themselves to traffickers.

Despite the high prevalence of human trafficking in some parts of Nigeria, it was not until the 1990s that the phenomenon began to receive broader public attention. One of the most popular Nigerian films at that time that caused a lot of public debate was 'Glamour Girls II: The Italian Connection', depicting the prostitution of a Nigerian woman in Italy. The print media also

132 *Antonia T. Simbine*

increasingly covered the topic and local non-governmental organizations (NGOs) started to work on it in the 1990s.

The International Reproductive Rights Research Action Group (IRRRAG), an action research welfare organization that works on women reproductive and sexuality issues in Benin City, claims to have first started raising the awareness of the phenomenon in the area. According to the coordinator of IRRRAG, the Group first noticed that trafficking was going on and started to raise awareness of it in 1996, which earned them many threats from traffickers (Coordinator, International Reproductive Rights Research Action Group, interview, 2009).

Prior to the establishment of NAPTIP, there was no formal organization in Nigeria to address the problem of human trafficking, and though it was a common phenomenon, people were not alert to the problem and it was not perceived in criminal terms. As awareness grew, NGOs were in the vanguard of the campaign against human trafficking. Among them were the Women Trafficking and Child Labour Eradication Foundation (WOTCLEF) and Idia Renaissance, along with some law enforcement agencies, especially the Immigration Services and the Police, which had anti-trafficking units that primarily exist to deal with the problem of trafficking in persons. For them, however, a major constraint was the absence of specific laws to deal with human trafficking. Similarly, existing international conventions such as the Geneva Convention for the Suppression of Trafficking in Women and Children, that had been signed back in 1921, did not sufficiently address Nigeria's worsening profile in trafficking. For instance, these NGOs and law enforcement groups could apprehend traffickers, but they could not enforce prosecution (NAPTIP 2009a: 11). The establishment of NAPTIP was meant to fill this gap.

NAPTIP's establishment and structure

In August of 2003, Nigeria enacted a comprehensive law, the first of its kind in West Africa, on the prohibition of trafficking in persons, and created NAPTIP to execute this law.[4] Officially, the organization came into being on 26 August 2003, with the appointment of its founding Executive Secretary and chief executive Mrs Carol Ndaguba.[5] At that time, Ndaguba was already a seasoned lawyer, former head and director of legal services at the Federal Ministry of Justice, and director of public prosecution.

The establishment of NAPITP was made possible by the strong interest of the then Vice-President's wife Amina Titi Abubakar in fighting human trafficking in Nigeria. As a response to the increasing public attention this phenomenon received in the late 1990s, she had founded the NGO 'Women Trafficking and Child Labour Eradication Foundation' (WOTCLEF) in 1999. In Nigeria, the wives of senior politicians, often referred to as 'first ladies', enjoy an unusually strong position and are sometimes involved in policy-making. They also tend to have their 'pet projects'. Most of these projects, such as the 'Better Life Programme' by Mariam Babangida or the 'Child

Care Trust' by Stella Obasanjo, die soon after their husband's tenures have ended. This time it was different. WOTCLEF led a civil society committee which, with the support of experienced international organizations, drafted an anti-human trafficking bill. As the wife of the Vice-President and with support from civil society organizations, Abubakar ensured that there was top-level political support for the bill, which was enacted in 2003.

The birth of NAPTIP is also a fulfilment of Nigeria's international obligation under the 2000 United Nations Convention against Transnational Organized Crime, and the Protocol to Prevent, Suppress and Punish Trafficking in Persons, Especially Women and Children ('Palermo protocol') that it contains (UNODC 2004). Nigeria had ratified the anti-trafficking protocol in 2001. Article 5 of the trafficking protocol enjoins state parties to criminalize practices and conducts that subject human beings to all forms of exploitation which includes, at the minimum, sexual and labour exploitation.

The NAPTIP law seeks to address human trafficking with its associated problems by creating a multi-disciplinary crime fighting agency. To effectively tackle the problem associated with trafficking, section 4 of the law, inter alia, vests in NAPTIP the following functions: coordinating all laws on trafficking; enforcing those laws through investigation and prosecution; enhancing the effectiveness of law enforcement to suppress trafficking; establishing and maintaining communication among agencies, and coordinating and supervising the rehabilitation of trafficked persons. In response to NAPTIP's founding Executive Secretary's request, this law was reviewed and amended only two years after it had been passed. The new amendments assigned NAPTIP more comprehensive powers to prosecute offenders, allowing them to access the federal high court, criminalized the trafficking of children as house helps, regulated the seizure of assets from traffickers and established the Victims Trust Fund (NAPTIP 2009a: 15). These amendments allowed NAPTIP to address major issues of concern and enhanced the organization's effectiveness significantly.

With regard to its structure, the agency is under the office of the Attorney-General of the Federation. NAPTIP enjoys a semi-autonomous status, which means that it can carry out staff recruitment, promotion and dismissal independently. Its salary scale is also different from the regular civil service salary scale. The organization has six main departments, two units and seven zonal offices. The structure and operation of NAPTIP reflects a hierarchical order in which the Executive Secretary serves as the administrative head. The Executive Secretary is expected to report to a Board that had not been put in place at the time of research.[7] The Executive Secretary is assisted by the Director of Administration and Finance and the Director of Planning, Research and Programming. Zonal offices are headed by Zonal Directors, who report directly to the Executive Secretary on a monthly and quarterly basis as required.

At headquarters, NAPTIP has four main departments whose functions are presented below.

Investigation and Monitoring Department: This department deals with investigations and the coordination of all cases of human trafficking, child labour and arrest of suspected traffickers. In the seven zones created by the agency, the operational unit of the zones is headed by an investigation officer, who co-ordinates all investigation activities in collaboration with the Head of Investigation and Monitoring at the headquarters in Abuja. Since its responsibilities include the rescuing of victims, the arrest and detention of violators of the Act, the preparation of reports for the prosecution unit and – together with other security agencies – the protection of witnesses, this department can be said to be the brain box of this model approach to criminal justice system, called the 'one stop centre', which NAPTIP has become. Beginning from investigation, on to prosecution and even counselling and rehabilitation, all processes are carried out in-house. This model eliminates the delay and frustration inherent in the conventional system of Nigerian criminal justice, where different law enforcement agencies are saddled with different functions and communication and cooperation is often lacking. This model has completely eliminated delays in the prosecution of offenders, resulting in 57 convictions since its inception at the time of research in 2009.

Legal and Prosecution Department: This department addresses human trafficking and other related offences by way of prosecution of offenders. The law which governs its responsibilities was amended in 2005, and its powers were increased and specified.

Public Enlightenment Department: The mandate of the Public Enlightenment Department of NAPTIP includes the organization and execution of awareness/sensitization programmes, in virtually all the states of the country in collaboration with NAPTIP's seven zonal offices. Together with ministries and other organizations, the department is responsible for campaigns, seminars and workshops aimed at educating the public on the problem of trafficking.

Counselling and Rehabilitation Department: As its name says, this department is responsible for counselling and rehabilitating victims of human trafficking. The department collaborates with relevant government ministries, agencies and departments, NGOs and developmental partners for realizing its objectives.

Is NAPTIP a PoE?

Until mid-2009, NAPTIP had rescued more than 3,500 victims (see table 6.1), sheltered them and rehabilitated a good part of them. From its inception until then it had achieved 57 (see table 6.1) convictions with more pending. This may not sound much, but has to be put into context. For the whole of Africa, the annual number of trafficking convictions rose from only 10 in 2003 to 90 in 2008 (U.S. Department of State 2009: 51). Furthermore, securing convictions for human traffickers is particularly difficult, since the victims have to provide evidence against them which, in many cases, they do not want to give, since due to the density of social networks and possible revenge of the traffickers, this could be very dangerous for the victim.

NAPTIP's achievements have been acknowledged internationally, and the agency has been invited by foreign law enforcement agencies to cooperate

Table 6.1 Number of convictions and rescued trafficking victims achieved by NAPTIP

Year	2004	2005	2006	2007	2008	2009 (June)	Total
Convictions	1	4	4	7	23	18	57
Victims rescued	332	75	924	339	867	1,004	3,541

Source: NAPTIP (2009).

with them for investigating and cracking international human trafficking syndicates. One of these collaborative secret investigations was 'Operation Koolvis'. In 2007 and 2008, NAPTIP collaborated with government organizations from seven European countries in an operation led by the Netherlands Dutch Crime Squad to crack an international human trafficking ring, which transferred women from Nigeria to the Netherlands and from there onward to other European countries.[8] The success of the operation earned NAPTIP profound respect, as that particular operation was not compromised in any form and led to the arrests of international traffickers and the rescue of many victims across Europe and Nigeria (NAPTIP 2009b: 42).

A representative of an international NGO working in the field of human trafficking in Nigeria confirmed NAPTIP's good work, especially in the difficult environment it is in, because 'it is not heavy bureaucratically, is responsive and has a different culture [compared to other Nigerian public sector organizations; A.T.S.]' (Terre des Hommes Head of Mission in Nigeria, interview, 2009). He also confirmed that through its effectiveness, NAPTIP had shown the world that Nigeria is serious about fighting human trafficking, and that the government would lose a lot of international credibility if it withdrew its support for NAPTIP.

A diplomat in the Netherlands embassy in Nigeria at the time of research confirmed this: 'There are many other things in this country which are not going very well but NAPTIP is not actually one of them. NAPTIP is one of those few state organizations that are functioning very well.' (Second Secretary, Embassy of the Netherlands, interview, 2009).

Another more indirect pointer to NAPTIP's effectiveness was the armed raid on the organization's headquarters in May 2006. In what was apparently a deliberate attempt to render anti-trafficking data unusable, armed men destroyed computers, documents and archives. This shows that the trafficking networks are taking NAPTIP seriously and that they regard the agency as a real threat to their business.

Perhaps the most convincing evidence that NAPTIP actually is a PoE comes from the United States Department of State. In its 'Trafficking in Persons Report 2009', it upgraded Nigeria from tier two to tier one. This means that the government complies with the U.S. Trafficking Victims Protection Act's minimum standards for the elimination of trafficking (U.S. Department of State 2009: 225–27).[9] Together with the island state Mauritius with only little more than a million people, Nigeria is the only African country to be placed in tier one: 'Nigeria's strengthened anti-trafficking record over the last years

136   *Antonia T. Simbine*

reflects the cumulative impact of progressively increasing efforts made by NAPTIP over the last several years.' (U.S. Department of State 2009: 226).[10]

NAPTIP as a PoE

Why did NAPTIP emerge as a PoE?

The political factors that explain why NAPTIP emerged as a PoE can be distilled from the information above. In the 1990s human trafficking had become a publicly recognized and discussed problem in Nigeria. Soon after the country's transition to civilian and democratic leadership in 1999, it ratified international frameworks that required the development of domestic laws against trafficking. The problem was thus on the political agenda, particularly because as an important 'source' country of human trafficking, it damaged Nigeria's international reputation. One of the then President Olusegun Obasanjo's missions was to improve this reputation. However, while all these factors created a favourable context for action they did not bring about the NAPTIP legislation, the organization and its effectiveness.

The driving force behind this was the then Vice-President's wife Amina T. Abubakar. She took a strong interest in the problem of human trafficking in Nigeria and has promoted the fight against it with her own NGO WOTCLEF since 1999. Many people we spoke to confirmed that behind the scenes, she had apparently lobbied senior politicians to support her cause and pass the law in 2003, which established NAPTIP as an organization with far-reaching powers and responsibilities. These comprehensive powers, that were even extended two years later, combined with a semi-autonomous status with regard to things such as the recruitment of staff, salaries and benefits, enabled NAPTIP to become an exceptionally effective public organization in the Nigerian context. The last crucial factor is the agency's founding Executive Director. She actively used the powers and autonomy that the organization had been granted to build an exceptionally effective organization. We analyse how this happened in the following section.

How did NAPTIP emerge and persist as a PoE?

Based on the analysis of our data, we can single out five groups of factors that were instrumental in making NAPTIP a PoE and helping it to remain effective in the Nigerian context. These groups of factors are leadership and management, operational power and independence, staff, external collaboration and international support (see figure 6.1).[11] We now look into each of this group of factors and illustrate their importance with empirical material from our case study.

Leadership and management

Leadership: Most respondents attributed NAPTIP's achievements to the leadership executed by the founding Executive Secretary Carol Ndaguba.

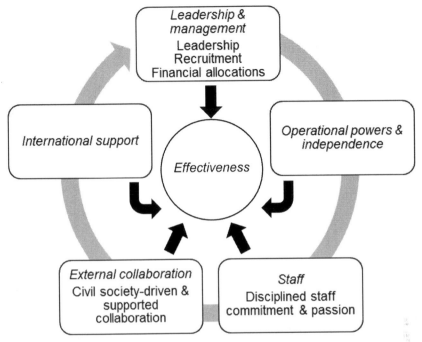

Figure 6.1 Factors explaining how NAPTIP emerged and persisted as a PoE

According to them, it was her commitment, her management qualities, her ability to interpret her job, to recruit the right people and ensure that financial allocation from the government were forthcoming and growing that made the agency a success.

Discussions and interviews with NAPTIP staff at various levels revealed that leadership in the agency was not exercised in terms of 'the leader as a strong man' but rather as 'distributed leadership', which means that the vision of the leader is shared among members of the top management of the organization. According to many accounts, the nucleus of the management team was committed, focused and highly motivated to succeed. They bought into the initial vision and were encouraged by the Executive Secretary to drive their various departments to achieve the mandate of the organization. According to the directors and other top level managers, there was room for personal initiative and even dissent, provided the final outcome would improve the organization's performance.

Staff described Ndaguba's leadership style as caring for staff when they had concerns or problems, responsive, constructive, making people buy in into her mission and motivating them by acknowledging achievements and taking them into account when taking decisions about training or promotion. Some additional characteristics of her management style given by staff as well as practices put in place were: 'introduction of an attendance register', 'cross-zonal office relations', 'no delayed replies/quick response', 'encourages team-work', 'brings out the hidden capacity to perform', 'regular at work even after long trips', 'open door policy', 'humaneness', 'humility', 'followed rules', 'faithful', 'trustworthy', 'active' and 'encouraged research'. Right from the beginning of the existence of NAPTIP as an organization, it seems, together with her management team, Ndaguba set up a performance-oriented organizational structure and culture that differs vastly from what exists in other Nigerian public sector organizations.

International observers in the country referred to Ndaguba's 'extremely strong commitment' (UNODC Representative in Nigeria, interview, 2009) to reduce human trafficking in the country (Second Secretary, Embassy of the Netherlands, interview, 2009). How can this special commitment be explained? In our interview with Ndaguba, she referred to the particular nature and importance of the work they were doing at NAPTIP and the challenge of making an impact in this field with the new organization:

> ... it was the biggest challenge of my life, you know, if you are given something to start from the scratch ... and for me, I became extremely involved emotionally and I put in everything I have into NAPTIP ... And I must confess that the success of NAPTIP is not my success alone. I have honest, real, dedicated Nigerians. Maybe it's because of the nature of what we have been trying to do. They got emotionally involved and quite bitter against the abuse that is meted out to Nigerian girls, children and women.
>
> (Former NAPTIP Executive Secretary, interview, 2009)[12]

Recruitment: Especially in the very beginning, building a strong management team that shared Ndaguba's vision and approach for the organization was crucial. Most of the founding directors were recruited from various ministries and parastatals and a few from NGOs or the private sector. Apart from focusing on qualifications and integrity, due to her long career in the public sector Ndaguba knew many of these people personally, and therefore was familiar with their working style and attitude. Based on this careful selection of the members of the management team, Ndaguba knew she could trust them and they would share her vision and mission. On the other hand, since they were selected, they were also committed to the organization's mandate. This created a degree of trust and common mission within the leadership of the organization that is highly unusual in Nigeria's public sector.

NAPTIP's example shows that some features of the Nigerian public sector system alone do not explain the pervasive failure of effective public service provision. One such feature that, in one form or the other, the country shares with other developing countries is the so-called 'federal character' principle (see Adamolekun, Erero and Oshionebo 1991; Mustapha 2007). This principle, which has been part of the Nigerian constitution since 1979, tries to ensure that appointments in the public sector reflect the country's diversity.

The application of this principle over time has varied, but most often a quota system based on the federal states of origin of applications is in place. This is also the case within NAPTIP. However, due to its attractive working conditions (see below) and an active attempt to find the most qualified and committed candidates, the agency has been able to follow the federal character principle without letting this compromise its attention to merit.

Due to its semi-autonomous status, NAPTIP could offer higher salaries and better welfare packages than most other public sector organizations, which allowed the agency to recruit and retain qualified staff. Those recruited are given basic training on security and human rights. Thereafter, they are continuously trained in their areas of specialization to ensure that they continue to add value to the organization. Such training programmes are offered both within the organization and outside of it, sometimes also by international organizations outside the country.

Financial allocations: We include this discussion under 'leadership and management' because we think that the two are closely linked. Government commitment to an organization in Nigeria only translates into consistent financial allocations if both the executive and the legislative agree that the organization works on an issue that is of crucial importance to the country. The commitment of government and the National Assembly are also based on the previous performance of that very organization. In that sense NAPTIP has been extraordinarily successful, since its budget allocations between 2004 and 2009 (June) have increased most of the time, often quite dramatically (see table 6.2).[13]

One event that illustrates the link between leadership, performance and increased budget allocations was the visit of national assembly members to NAPTIP's shelter in Lagos in 2004. The then Director of Administration and Finance argued that the members of the national assembly were shocked when they saw the trafficked persons in the shelter, heard their stories and learned about the magnitude of the problem. At the same time, they were impressed with the then newly established agency's work so far and the prudent use of the resources allocated to them since inception (NAPTIP Director of Administration and Finance, interview, 2009). According to him, their recommendation of an upward review of the agency's budget allocation was crucial for the almost fivefold increase in funds that NAPTIP received the following year (ibid.; see table 6.2). Government funding was complemented with funding and contributions from various domestic and international organizations and companies (see table 6.2). For the latter source of funding, Ndaguba's leadership and the performance of the organization from the very beginning were also crucial. This and other forms of international support are discussed below.

Operational powers and independence

For NAPTIP to be able to execute its mandate effectively, the comprehensive legal powers it was given in 2003 and amended in 2005 were crucial. Being

140 *Antonia T. Simbine*

Table 6.2 Budget allocations and international and domestic development partners' contributions to NAPTIP, 2004–2009 (June), in million Naira

Year	Budget allocation	Development partners	Two highest-paying dev. partners (amount)	Dev. partners' contributions in % of budget allocation
2004	149	21	UNICEF (7) NDDC[a] (7)	14.09
2005	742	123	Italian govt. (94) UNICEF (22)	16.58
2006	688	32	UNICEF (18) UNAFRI (6)	4.65
2007	1,063	16	UNICEF (9) ILO (2)	1.51
2008	1,366	42	UNICEF (11) French embassy (9)	3.07
2009 (June)	1,301	97	IOM[b] (35) Italian govt. (28)	7.46

Notes:[a] Niger Delta Development Commission.
[b] International Organization for Migration. All amounts are adjusted upward or downward to the next full million in Naira. Some amounts include fixed assets or free services valued at market rates at that time.
Source: NAPTIP (2009).

able to investigate and prosecute traffickers in-house with only a minimal amount of collaboration with external security or other agencies, avoided delays, coordination problems and political or organizational interference. This made the organization independent of the public sector environment in which it was operating, and therefore also independent of the practices and problems prevailing there. While these powers and independence do not at all guarantee that an organization becomes a PoE, in the case of NAPTIP these enabling conditions were combined with a performance-oriented organizational culture by the founding management, as outlined above.

Staff

Any sign of a member of staff being involved in corrupt practices leads to an investigation and, if confirmed, immediate dismissal. However, as the NAPTIP Director of Investigation and Monitoring told us, the agency is aware that staff are working in a high-risk environment with regard to corruption, which is why they are trying to discourage such practices as much as possible through four measures: first, they are paid a comparatively high salary; second, they are provided the support and funds that they need for carrying out their duties; third, suspects are always handled by teams instead of individual officers; and fourth, members of staff are dismissed when found guilty (NAPTIP Director of Investigation and Monitoring, interview, 2009).

In general, the response from international and domestic organizations working with NAPTIP was that their staff are very 'disciplined' in the sense that corrupt practices rarely occur, and that they stick to the formal rules and procedures when carrying out their work. From our experience and observations during fieldwork we can confirm that NAPTIP staff had a very professional approach and attitude.

However, this cannot be said about all the staff. Compared to the experiences at headquarters and at the Lagos zonal office, and the accounts about other NAPTIP field offices, the level of professionalism and enthusiasm with which the job was being exercised in the zonal office in Benin City was low. This point is critical, given the fact that Benin City is the area where human trafficking is most pervasive in Nigeria. While an analysis of why that particular office seems to perform less well, compared to the others, would be crucial both for analysing the sources of the success elsewhere and for understanding NAPTIP in its environment better, this analysis would require a separate case study. One factor for which we received some accounts certainly is that in this particular area, trafficking networks are fighting back harder than anywhere else with both violence and bribery.

Apart from discipline, commitment and passion for the organization's mission and the work at NAPTIP were frequently mentioned by staff at all levels. The higher salaries and better welfare packages than in the rest of the civil service are a key factor that make this commitment possible but, alone, do not generate it. Based on our data, the commitment and passion of staff has two sources: first, the experience of what trafficking victims go through and, based on that, the motivation to do something against these traffickers and second, the perception of being a member of a an 'elite' organization that is fighting a fight that is of national importance. However, as they noted in interviews and discussions, this commitment and passion had been nurtured by the leadership of the organization, particularly its Executive Secretary.

A participant of a focus group discussion of NAPTIP officers said that through his interaction with victims and suspects on a regular basis he had developed a strong passion for the job, with determination to contribute what he can to see an end to the scourge of human trafficking. He believes that it is only passion that can explain the persistence of staff in a job as dangerous as with NAPTIP:

> Most times we don't look at the financial aspect because the money you are given sometimes may not be enough for you to work ... but when there is genuine interest, when there is passion for victims of human trafficking you will go any mile to make sure you track them down.
>
> (NAPTIP middle-level officer, focus group discussion, 2009)

Similar statements were given by many other members of NAPTIP staff at various levels. This confirms the former Executive Secretary's observation that

142 *Antonia T. Simbine*

many of her staff got 'emotionally involved' (former NAPTIP Executive Secretary, interview, 2009). It is also supported by the fact that staff sometimes go beyond their call of duty and take risks when they chase suspected traffickers, or when they use their own funds for undertaking official assignments. During our research several cases of such incidences were reported.[14] In one case, for an example, official cars were not available but trafficking victims had to be taken to hospital for emergency treatment. In such and other cases, staff used their private vehicles to carry out official duties. This attests to their personal commitment to NAPTIP's mission.

While the commitment of NAPTIP staff primarily derives from the leadership of the organization, they also encounter encouragement and appreciation for their job from the media, domestic civil society organizations, sometimes former trafficking victims and their families and also from international organizations.

External collaboration

From the very beginning, the attempt to create an organization like NAPTIP has been supported by civil society organizations in Nigeria, with the NGO WOTCLEF only being one of the most prominent of them. Especially in the early years, NAPTIP also worked with local NGOs, which had sprung up in the areas in which human trafficking had been realized to be a serious problem. The agency depended on the information these organizations provided.

NAPTIP also worked together with the previously established local anti-trafficking units in police divisions and immigration offices. Especially in states where the agency does not have own offices or staff, it collaborates with these units and they therefore expand its investigative capacity. Beyond that, they collaborated with the State Security Services, the National Intelligence agency, the National Union of Road Transport Workers and other public or private organizations that had been working on human trafficking before or could make a contribution to this work.

The founding Executive Secretary's successor, Simon Egede, a former lawyer and government attorney who took over in early 2009, told us that more partnerships and collaborations are planned for the future for extending NAPTIP's public sensitization programme:

> We are also collaborating with the Nigeria Television Authority (NTA) to bring into being some drama series to highlight the danger of human trafficking. We are working on programmes and a drama series because I know that Nigerians watch a lot of television ... We are working with Wale Adenuga's production to get out a drama series that will be watched by millions of Nigerians. This, we think will further enlighten and bring to the fore what we are doing and how to watch out for trafficking.
>
> (NAPTIP Executive Secretary, interview, 2009)[15]

International support

When NAPTIP emerged, human trafficking was high on the agenda of international development organizations. After the first positive signs of organizational effectiveness, donor organizations and government of countries which were concerned about the level of human trafficking from Nigeria (especially Italy) were eager to support the agency's work (see table 6.2). Under the umbrella of a 'Joint Programme Sponsorship', various organizations, most of them international, supported NAPTIP with funding, material assistance and training programmes for staff. In terms of funding, the international donor's contributions were particularly helpful in the first two years of NAPTIP's existence (2004 and 2005), when their financial support constituted 14 and more than 16 per cent, respectively, of what they received through budget allocations at that time. In many interviews, members of staff refer to international training programmes and the exchange with international organizations working in the same field as very instructive and motivating, especially in the early phase of NAPTIP.

In contrast to most other Nigerian public sector organizations, NAPTIP enjoys a good reputation with international organizations, foreign governmental anti-trafficking units and law enforcement organizations. This degree of trust makes collaboration and common investigations like in the 'Operation Koolvis' (see above) much easier, which in turn enhances the effectiveness of both sides.

Conclusion

Human trafficking still is a big business in Nigeria. NAPTIP also faces challenges such as funding for its expensive and expansive operations, cooperation with courts due to the slow judicial process and especially re-trafficking of previously rescued victims.[16] Nevertheless, since its establishment in 2004, NAPTIP has made significant inroads with regard to curbing human trafficking in Nigeria.

NAPTIP was established in a way that allowed the organization to become effective because of three major factors: an enabling international environment in which frameworks against human trafficking were being developed; a Nigerian who, first through her NGO and then through her political network as the Vice-President's wife, ensured that a legislation was drafted and an organization set up; and finally an appointed founding Executive Secretary, who was very committed and qualified to build an effective public organization.

In terms of how NAPTIP emerged as a PoE and persisted as an exceptionally effective organization, we have identified five groups of factors which, in combination with each other, were at work. Since she was familiar with the public sector in Nigeria, the founding Executive Secretary hand-picked people from other departments whom she knew shared her work ethic and integrity. Together with them she created an environment in which a performance-

144 *Antonia T. Simbine*

oriented and professional organizational culture could flourish. In order to be able to do so on a permanent basis, she convinced government and the National Assembly to increase the budget allocations to the agency.

The pioneer Executive Secretary also used the extensive operational powers that had been granted to the agency in a proactive way, which allowed the organization to work with minimal delay and dependence on other public organizations. She even lobbied successfully for an extension of powers, which were then written in to law in 2005.

The management team also managed to instil a sense of passion and commitment into NAPTIP staff which, through their own experiences with victims, the trafficking business and the media's and international organization's positive reactions to their work, was further strengthened. While good salaries and welfare packages allowed the organization to hire the people it needed, the specific function that NAPTIP performed and its organizational culture apparently made them truly committed to their job. Clear internal rules about how to go about the job and not to get involved in corrupt practices were also set up and enforced.

Especially in the beginning, NAPTIP worked closely with existing anti-trafficking NGOs. It then also established working relationships with other relevant public sector organizations and began to collaborate with them, which allowed the agency to work more effectively. International organizations and embassies were particularly important partners. Not only did they provide significant funding and material support for NAPTIP, they also provided joint investigations, training programmes and encouragement.

It is encouraging that a PoE could emerge and persist in a field dominated by criminal syndicates which make huge profits, and in a context in which most public sector organizations are dormant or simply hollowed out by political or private interests. NAPTIP and the other surprisingly successful public organizations studied in this book provide justified hope (and maybe some guidance) that even in the least developed of countries, public institutions will one day provide adequate public goods and services.

Notes

1 Research for this case study was conducted from 2009 to 2010 by Antonia T. Simbine, Franca C. Attoh and Abubakar O. Oladeji. It was one of the case studies of the 'Pockets of Effectiveness in Nigeria' project, initiated and coordinated by the Friedrich-Ebert-Stiftung (FES), Nigeria Office. While this case study was funded by FES Nigeria, the views expressed in this chapter are those of the authors and should not be attributed to the FES. I thank Franca C. Attoh and Abubakar O. Oladeji for valuable research assistance.

2 There is a special historical relationship between Benin City (Edo state) and Italy. There have been business transactions between some natives from Edo state with Italians when the Nigerian economy was more robust. These Nigerians visited Italy to buy gold, shoes and clothing to sell in Nigeria. When the Nigerian economy began to dwindle, some of these businessmen and women stayed longer to pick potatoes for quick returns before returning home. As the economic situation in

Nigeria worsened and the business of picking potatoes was taken over by immigrants from Eastern Europe, the growing sex industry in Italy became more lucrative for these Nigerians. Hence, it is believed that they started the human trafficking activities, using their relatives, friends and community members as 'commodities'. Being a clandestine criminal activity, the gang members feel safer recruiting from trusted family members. According to unofficial estimates, over 80 per cent of trafficked persons for prostitution in Europe, especially Italy, are from Edo State.

3 Dagmar Thomas, at the time of research the Resident Representative of the United Nations Office on Drugs and Crime (UNODC) in Nigeria, was also of the view that as poverty is deepening, new endemic areas are being discovered in the country, especially as regards internal trafficking (UNODC Representative in Nigeria, interview, 2009).

4 The full name of the act is 'Trafficking in Persons (Prohibition) Law Enforcement and Administration Act' (2003), hereinafter referred to as 'the Act'.

5 NAPTIP leadership has changed two times since the organization's establishment. Carol Ndaguba was in office from 2003 until 2009, when Chuzi Egede took over (2009-July 2011). At the time of writing, NAPTIP is headed by Beatrice Jedy-Agba (since 2011).

6 As a law-enforcement agency and with its particular semi-autonomous status, salaries at NAPIP are generally higher than those in the regular civil service, and the welfare packages are also better.

7 According to the founding Executive Secretary, the non-existence of a Board was perhaps helpful in making her achieve as much as she did. However, she holds the view that the agency needs a Board that is composed of people who are knowledgeable about the phenomenon of human trafficking, so that they can aid rather than be a hindrance to the work of the agency (former NAPTIP Executive Secretary, interview, 2009).

8 'Operation Koolvis' was about dismantling organized criminal human trafficking syndicates. It targeted girls who arrive in the Netherlands from Lagos, Abuja and Kano, seeking political asylum. Once in the asylum centre, they disappear two or three weeks later with the help of traffickers, who keep them in the Netherlands or move them to other parts of Europe such as Italy and Spain to work as prostitutes.

9 Tier two includes countries 'whose government do not fully comply with the Trafficking Victims Protection Act's minimum standards but are making significant efforts to bring themselves into compliance with those standards' (U.S. Department of State 2009: 49).

10 However, after having been placed in tier one for three years from 2009 until 2011, the 'Trafficking in Persons Report 2012' downgraded Nigeria to tier two again (U. S. Department of State 2012: 271). It states that Nigeria's government 'does not fully comply with the minimum standards for the elimination of trafficking' (ibid.: 270), mainly due to weak law enforcement, since the number of convictions was low and the penalties for traffickers were too moderate.

11 The order in which the groups of factors are presented does not imply any judgement about their relative importance.

12 The fact that, with Ndaguba, a woman was heading a prominent public sector organization, also came up during our research. While this is still unusual in Nigeria, many respondents referred to her qualities as a 'mother' of being both 'caring' and 'strict'. She herself said that 'because I am a woman, I wanted to prove that I can do it [setting up and leading the agency, A.T.S.]' (former NAPTIP Executive Secretary, interview, 2009). However, since our evidence is inconclusive, we decided not to include gender here.

13 It is important to note that in Nigeria, budget allocations do not necessarily translate into actual releases of funds. However, our fieldwork shows that NAPTIP did not face problems with the release of funds.

146 *Antonia T. Simbine*

14 This point was also made by the NAPTIP Director of Administration and Finance (interview, 2009).
15 The drama series *Itohan: A Call to Action*, produced by Nigerian film and series producer Wale Adenuga in his popular *Superstory* soap opera series, screened in 2012 and 2013. It features the story of a young Nigerian women caught up in international human trafficking, and was the outcome of the cooperation with NAPTIP.
16 On the latter, one woman interviewed for this study said that: 'NAPTIP is trying but we are helpless. The 'madams' want their money back with profit and our families cannot pay back. Refusal to go back could result in death or disability' (rescued trafficking victim, interview, 2009). Former trafficked women or other members of their families are sometimes killed or seriously injured in car accidents or other incidents.

Interviews and focus group discussions

This list only includes those interviews and focus group discussions quoted from or referred to in this chapter.
Former NAPTIP Executive Secretary Carol Ndaguba, Abuja, 8 June 2009.
International Reproductive Rights Research Group Coordinator, Benin, 4 May 2009.
NAPTIP Director of Administration and Finance, Abuja, 5 May 2009.NAPTIP Director of Investigation and Monitoring, Abuja, 6 May 2009.
NAPTIP Executive Secretary Simon C. Egede, Abuja, 21 May 2009.
NAPTIP focus group discussion, middle level officers, Abuja, 6 May 2009.Rescued trafficking victim, Benin, 4 May 2009.
Second Secretary, Political Affairs and ECOWAS, Embassy of the Netherlands, Abuja, 8 June 2009.
Terre des Hommes Head of Mission in Nigeria, Abeokuta, 27 May 2009.
UNODC (United Nations Office on Drugs and Crime) Representative in Nigeria, Abuja, 20 May 2009.

7 'Confidence in our own abilities'

Suriname's State Oil Company as a pocket of effectiveness[1]

Wil Hout

Introduction

At the end of 2010, the State Oil Company of Suriname (or *Staatsolie*, as it is usually referred to) celebrated its thirtieth anniversary. This event was organized by the much-heralded oil company under circumstances that seemed to signal a change of attitude vis-à-vis the firm among the Surinamese political elite. President Desiré Delano Bouterse, who had been elected into office in July 2010, as well as all members of his government, allegedly refused to attend the anniversary because they were not given a prominent role during the festivities (De Ware Tijd, 15 December 2010). Bouterse, founder and leader of the National Democratic Party (NDP) and previously leader of the military regime that ruled the country between 1980 and 1987 (Chin & Buddingh' 1987: 36–67), was reported to have been irritated by the company's decision, which was taken as a sign of neglect of the role that the military had played in the establishment of *Staatsolie* in 1980.

The apparent disagreement between the President and *Staatsolie's* leadership seemed be more than an isolated incident. The tensions showed up against the background of the earlier decision of the government, which is the company's single shareholder, to replace three of the five members of *Staatsolie's* Board of Supervisors by government supporters and amid uncertainties about the succession of the firm's long-serving Financial and Managing Directors (Staatsolie Nieuws, December 2010: 3; De Ware Tijd, 12 March 2011; Starnieuws, 21 March 2011). Further, various members of the NDP-led coalition, among whom was Minister of Natural Resources Jim Hok, had been calling repeatedly for an increase of *Staatsolie's* oil production (De Ware Tijd, 24 July 2010; Starnieuws, 16 and 22 March 2011).

The tensions between the government and *Staatsolie's* management around the firm's thirtieth anniversary led observers to draw a parallel with the previous NDP-led government under President Jules Wijdenbosch (1996–2000), which had dismissed *Staatsolie's* Board of Supervisors in March 1998 and had attempted to discharge then Managing Director Eddy Jharap (De Ware Tijd, 31 December 2010; De West, 26 March, 28 March, 17 June and 23 September 1998). In the light of increasing budget deficits, the Wijdenbosch

148 *Wil Hout*

government had made various attempts to extract more money from *Staatsolie* to cover its expenditures. Among other things, the government tried to force the company to increase its oil production from 9,500 to 20,000 barrels per day, sell off its major oil field in Tambaredjo and initiate a joint venture between Staatsolie and foreign oil companies (De Ware Tijd, 6 June and 12 September 1997 and 18 March 1998).

Despite pressures from the political environment, *Staatsolie* has managed to flourish and develop into a major pocket of effectiveness in Suriname's public sector. The oil company was set up as a state-owned enterprise with the legal status of a public limited company, in which the role of the government was restricted to the nomination of members of the Board of Directors. At various moments in its existence, the company's board of directors has managed to play out its independent role vis-à-vis the state.

Well-informed observers of the Surinamese economy agree that *Staatsolie* is one of the best-run state-owned enterprises in the country and, in important respects, a model for the management of commercial firms (interviews, March/April 2004).[2] With over 800 employees, an annual production of approximately 6 million barrels of crude oil, an annual turnover around US\$800 million and a contribution to gross domestic product around 10 per cent, the company has become one of the engines of the Surinamese economy (State Oil Company of Suriname 2012a: 15–16; 2012b). In recognition of its achievements, *Staatsolie* was selected as 2008 International Company of the Year by the International Management Development Association (IMDA) at the Seventeenth Annual World Business Congress in Paramaribo, Suriname (De Ware Tijd, 28 June 2008).

Contrary to the predictions of the theses of the rentier state and political underdevelopment (Ross 1999; Moore 2001), and contrary to the experience of other state-owned enterprises in the country, the revenues earned by *Staatsolie's* oil sales have not been siphoned off and used as rents by the political elites. Threats that could have led to such misuse of funds were countered successfully. The company's financial transfers to the state have taken place on the basis of generally accepted norms. The company has been paying a normal dividend to its shareholder, set at 50 per cent of net profit in the past several years. The rest of the company's net profit was typically added to the general reserve, and used for investment purposes.

In addition to its achievements in the public domain, *Staatsolie* has been very active in upgrading its corporate performance. An important sign of this was the obtainment and implementation of externally assessed quality control certificates for its operations. In 2001, the Marketing and Sales Division and the *Staatsolie* laboratory received ISO certification status (State Oil Company of Suriname 2006). This first step was followed by the ISO9001:2000 certification of the refinery operations at Tout Lui Faut in March 2004 and of the whole of *Staatsolie's* operations in March 2006 (Staatsolie Nieuws, March 2004: 12–13; State Oil Company of Suriname 2006). Finally, the company obtained ISO 9001:2008 certification for its quality management system (State Oil Company of Suriname 2009: 8).

The success of *Staatsolie* is paradoxical in several important respects. First, *Staatsolie's* achievements are remarkable because Suriname's political system has traditionally had important characteristics of a patrimonial state. Secondly, the company's success is noteworthy because Suriname, as one of the world's best-endowed reservoirs of natural resources (most notably, but not limited to, bauxite, gold, oil and timber), has been a prime example of a primary commodity producing and exporting country. Against the background of these characteristics of the country's political system and economic structure, the argument of this chapter is that *Staatsolie's* accomplishments need to be understood in relation to a set of internal and external factors. The internal characteristics relate, in particular, to its effective leadership and management, coupled with a clear vision focussing on the strengthening of home-grown technological and managerial skills, while the most notable external variables are the company's strategy to steer clear of political influences and the playing out of the firm's formal-legal position in the petroleum sector. In addition to these two main sets of factors, which were the core of the first two hypotheses on pockets of effectiveness developed in the introduction to this volume, function- and task-related elements have also contributed to *Staatsolie's* success, as the company has consciously invested in its workforce and provided staff with material and immaterial incentives to give their best to their work.

This case study has been prompted by several explicitly theoretical considerations. The literature on patrimonial and rentier states tends to focus on the macro, or state, level, and on the impact of rent-seeking, patronage and clientelism on social processes and economic performance (cf. Schneider 1987: 217–18). As a result of this focus, actors at the meso and micro level have received far less exposure; studies that included such actors generally used them to illustrate general patrimonialist or rent-seeking hypotheses. The present study zeroes in on *Staatsolie* because the analysis of the company's attempt to be a development agent provides good insights into the scope and limits of the patrimonial state. In light of this, the analysis of Staatsolie as a pocket of effectiveness emphasizes 'agency' and leadership as explanatory factors of development strategies. As noted by Leftwich (2010: 93), structural and institutional explanations of development problems often fail to see 'the important success stories which run against the general patterns of institutional failure or corruption'.

Connected to these considerations, the focus of this study on *Staatsolie* as a state-owned oil company adds to the literature on the impact of economic sectors on the role of the state in development and, in particular, to the analysis of the so-called mining state and the petro-state (Shafer 1994; Karl 1997). The Surinamese experience is, on the one hand, in accordance with the findings of previous studies that the presence and export of minerals, in this case bauxite, have an important influence on policy-making and governance of developing countries and lead to a focus on the rents resulting from mineral exports. On the other hand, however, the case of *Staatsolie*

150 *Wil Hout*

demonstrates that state-owned firms may be capable of escaping from the prevailing rent-oriented behaviour and actually follow a relatively independent course, aimed at developing technological and management skills. The conditions under which these independent activities proved possible are the subject of this chapter, and the analysis of these conditions aims to contribute to the more general theorising about pockets of effectiveness that all contributions to this book focus on.

Staatsolie has been able to develop into a pocket of effectiveness largely because of the recognition of the company's management that the features specific to the petroleum sector in Suriname would enable them to establish a relatively independent enterprise. The conditions present in Suriname were quite different from those in other developing countries where oil had been discovered, such as Venezuela, Iran, Nigeria and Algeria (Karl 1997: 197–208). One important factor in this was the perception, held until the late 1990s, that oil production was quite marginal to Suriname's economy. The dominance of other sources of rent (most notably, bauxite and aid flows from the Netherlands) no doubt contributed greatly to this outlook of the political elite. All of the above mentioned factors contributed to *Staatsolie's* relatively independent functioning and enabled the company to build a corporate culture and create public support that, eventually, sustained the company's claim to autonomy. Importantly, the 1997–98 clash with the government led to a victory for *Staatsolie,* as a result of successful popular mobilization supportive of home-grown economic activity and resistant to a corrupt and rent-seeking elite.

Staatsolie can usefully be seen as a pocket of effectiveness in an otherwise inefficient and rent-oriented public sector. The company is different from some other pockets of efficiency that were set up by politicians as a tool for modernising the state apparatus, such as the Brazilian National Development Bank founded in the 1960s (Evans 1989: 577; Willis, this volume). *Staatsolie* does, however, have certain features in common with the Brazilian petrochemical sector, where the development of industrial capacity in the 1970s resulted from the activities of a relatively independent state enterprise, *Petroquisa.* According to Evans (1989: 580), the 'ties ... to private capital, both domestic and transnational' proved important conditions for the success of Brazil's petrochemical sector. As Schneider (1987: 228) has noted, the desire to consolidate the company's market position and to diversify production resulted in *Petroquisa's* pressure on the Brazilian government to loosen the ties with the company and move towards a different form of government intervention in the sector. The greater reliance on private capital seemed to stimulate a change of government policy, as 'some investors prefer market uncertainty to the strategic uncertainty for political products' (Barzelay, quoted by Schneider 1987: 229).

Staatsolie, which is part of the Surinamese public sector, has achieved a high degree of managerial and technological excellence, due to a large extent to the skilful way in which the company's management dealt with the political dynamics in the country. Largely as a result of their understanding of the political environment, the company proved able to carve out a relatively autonomous place in the public sphere, from where it could operate without being subjected directly to political considerations. The gradual diversification of *Staatsolie's* portfolio (to, among others, refinery activities and its evolving role in the national electricity sector), and its cooperation with foreign firms in the off-shore exploration of oil resources, may induce the kind of changes in government policies that Evans and Schneider alluded to in relation to Brazil. Such policy changes may have positive effects on *Staatsolie's* autonomy.

This chapter is structured as follows. The second section contains a discussion of Suriname's political economy from the perspective of recent scholarship on the role of the state in development, thus providing an argument why *Staatsolie's* role as a development agent is paradoxical. The third section discusses the expansion of *Staatsolie's* operations since 1980 and briefly analyses the company's contribution to Suriname's economy and society. The fourth section analyses the double strategy that *Staatsolie* adopted to effectuate its developmental role. The fifth section contains some concluding observations.

Suriname's political economy

Staatsolie's paradoxical success needs to be understood against the background of Suriname's political economy. Placed in the context of theorising on the role of the state in development this section illustrates that, with the exception of a short interlude of military rule, Suriname has been a democratic, non-developmental mining state, where the public sector has typically been a source of patronage and clientelism.

The state in development

Recent scholarship shows various approaches to theorising the role of the state in development. Two sets of approaches, in particular, seem to be pertinent to the case of Suriname. The first relevant set of approaches relates variations in state structure and state-society relations to variations in developmental performance. The second group of approaches focuses on the impact of sectoral characteristics on state features and developmental outcomes.

Of the scholars taking the first approach, Peter Evans has had great influence. He juxtaposed several ideal types of states, notably the 'predatory' and the 'developmental' forms. Predatory states 'extract such large amounts of otherwise investable surplus while providing so little in the way of 'collective goods' in return that they do indeed impede economic transformation', while developmental states 'foster long-term entrepreneurial perspectives among private elites by increasing incentives to engage in transformative investments and lowering the risks' (Evans 1995: 44). Evans has conceptualized the developmental state in terms of 'embedded autonomy', in an attempt to highlight the combination of an insulated bureaucracy, organized on the basis of Weberian rational-legal principles, and close relations between the state and social (market) institutions. Most developing countries should, according to Evans, be placed in an 'intermediate' category, with states ranking somewhere between these two ideal types and combining predatory and developmental features (Evans 1989: 563; Evans 1995: 60).

Evans' ideal types have been criticized, among others, by Hutchcroft (1998: 57), who argued that 'Evans has overlooked important elements of variation among patrimonial polities. In particular, by presenting Zaire as his archetypal example of a state that fails to promote development, he does not consider other cases that would also be patrimonial but be properly placed elsewhere according to the relative strength of state apparatuses and business interests'. Among the more patrimonial states, Hutchcroft (1998: 20, 45–55) differentiates between patrimonial administrative and patrimonial oligarchic states. The former type, also labelled 'bureaucratic capitalism', found in Thailand and Indonesia, is dominated by a bureaucratic elite that extracts rents from the business sector. The latter type, also referred to as 'booty capitalism', is characterized by the existence of a powerful business class that exploits an incoherent bureaucracy. This form has been dominant in the Philippines.

Leftwich has put forward a classification of democratic non-developmental states on the basis of the relative importance of class-oriented or patronage-oriented political parties. 'Class-compromise' non-developmental states, with Venezuela and South Africa as examples, are built on the awareness of major political forces that certain radical changes that could be beneficial from a developmental or social justice point of view, are not feasible because of the opposition, with possibly non-democratic means, of others (Leftwich 2002: 70). 'Party-alternation' non-developmental states, such as Jamaica and Costa Rica, are characterized by the existence of rival 'cross-class' parties, 'each (when in power) dispensing clientelist patronage to its followers and supporters, and each differentiated from the other mainly by a combination of historical association, personal loyalties, anticipation of patronage prospects, and – at times – ideological-policy orientations' (Leftwich 2002: 74).

The failure of many developing countries to transform into developmental states can usefully be understood within the framework of 'political underdevelopment' or the 'rentier state' (Ross 1999; Moore 2001, 2002). This framework implies 'that when governments gain most of their revenues from external sources, such as resource rents or foreign assistance, they are freed from the need to levy domestic taxes and become less accountable to the societies they govern' (Ross 1999: 312). Following the same logic, states that are based on rent-seeking are expected to be weaker and less effective, since they have less incentive 'to reduce the influence of patrimonial principles and personal linkages when recruiting and managing the public service' (Moore 2002: 106).

The second set of approaches to the state in development that was outlined above has related the dominance of certain economic sectors, such as mining, to development outcomes and features of the state in developing countries.

According to several authors working in this tradition, certain types of economic sectors are particularly conducive to rent-seeking practices. Shafer (1994: 10, 23–24) has drawn attention to the prevalence of rent-seeking in so-called mining states. Because the mining sector is highly capital intensive and shows high economies of scale, and production and the employment of production factors are very inflexible, the sector is characterized by monopoly rents that are 'easily tapped by the state' (Shafer 1994: 35). The economic dependence on a single resource, produced by an enclave-like industrial sector that is dominated by foreign capital, generates extraordinary rents. These rents are almost unrelated to the productive processes of the domestic economy and are almost exclusively channelled to the state (Karl 1997: 47–48). Petro-states take a special place among mining states, because of the sheer magnitude and duration of the extraordinary rents that result from oil production and export (Karl 1997: 49).

Suriname's state and economy

Based on the above, Suriname would most aptly be characterized as a party-alternating, democratic, non-developmental mining state.[3] In addition to this, its post-World War II history shows that the country has many features of a patrimonial administrative state, as described by Hutchcroft, in which the state apparatus has dominated the economy and has been a major source of rents for office holders and their clients (Schalkwijk, interview, 2004).

Since its independence in November 1975, Suriname's per capita gross domestic product has not experienced substantial growth, despite the fact that, since World War II, Suriname has been one of the world's major bauxite exporters and the country ranks among the world's best-endowed countries in terms of natural resources. The Inter-American Development Bank (2001: 5) concluded that the '[e]xploitation of Suriname's large bauxite reserves has generated rents that are large in relation to the economy'. Van Dijck (2001: 57) has calculated that bauxite mining and processing generated between 30 and 33 per cent of Suriname's GDP in the 1945–75 period and, despite a decline in relative importance, still accounted for an important 15 per cent of GDP at the end of the twentieth century.

In constant 2000 prices, Suriname's GDP per capita peaked at US$2,860 in 1978, fell to a low of US$1,808 in 1987 and had reached a level of US$2,737 by 2010 (World Bank 2012b). The share of manufacturing in Suriname's gross domestic product fell from 18.6 to 9.0 per cent between 1980 and 2000, and increased to 22.7 per cent in 2010 (World Bank 2012b). As Martin (2001: 52–76) has indicated, Suriname's economic situation was highly volatile during the 1990s, with clear boom-bust cycles mainly as a result of fluctuations in alumina prices.

In addition to natural resources, aid has been another major source of rents. Aid is estimated to have accounted for more than three-quarters of the

154   *Wil Hout*

Surinamese government budget in the period between 1956 and 1975, and to have amounted to more than 1 billion Dutch guilders (equivalent to over € 450 million) in this twenty-year period (Oostindie and Klinkers 2001: 133–34). At the eve of independence in 1975, the Dutch government provided Suriname with a development fund of approximately € 1.95 billion. In per capita terms, Suriname received roughly four to five times the median aid amount transferred to other lower-middle income countries during the 1990s (Van Dijck 2004: 43–45). There is widespread agreement that the development fund has been spent largely on prestige projects that have produced relatively little value added in terms of the development of the country; as one critical observer of Surinamese politics put it: 'foreign aid to Suriname has not proven to be an economic lever. In Suriname, the money has disappeared into a black hole' (Silos 2002: 4). Foreign aid has also enabled Suriname to maintain its oversized public sector, referred to as the 'principal vehicle for sharing the rents' (Inter-American Development Bank 2001: 41). Data reported by the Inter-American Development Bank (2001: 39) show that, in 1998, the government provided employment for 43.7 per cent of the total labour force.

With a brief interval of military rule between 1980 and 1987, Suriname's political system has been relatively democratic ever since the Statute of the Kingdom of the Netherlands (1954) gave the Surinamese *Staten* (Parliament) more powers. With the exception of the military era, Freedom House has rated the Surinamese political system as free or partly free during its post-independence period (Freedom House 2012).

The post-war political system of Suriname has been characterized by the existence of multiple political parties. Analysts agree that these parties are an expression of the ethnic diversity of the country and that they have played an important role in the emancipation of various ethnic groups, notably the Creole (black) working class, the Hindustanis (East Indians) and Javanese (e.g. Ramsoedh 2001: 95–96).[4]

One of the most persistent elements of the Surinamese political system has been the attempt by political forces to exercise power in order to serve the interests of a particular ethnic group, rather than to achieve ideologically defined objectives (Schalkwijk, interview, 2004). Class relations have been of marginal importance only in post-World War II Surinamese politics. As Menke (1991: 63) has put it, 'the state was an instrument of class formation through political patronage by giving facilities and resources (e.g. land) to members of the own political party or ethnic group'.

Patrimonial features of Surinamese politics and the state find expression, *inter alia*, in the attempt of political parties to assure their hold of particular ministries. To an important degree, government employment has served as an instrument of clientelism, where support for political parties was built on their ability to create jobs (referred to as *regelen*, 'arrange') in the ministries (Sedney 1997: 27–28; Menke 1991: 63; Derveld 1999: 5, 15). The continuing dominance of Suriname's public sector employment in the total labour force (see above) is an important sign of the persistence of the 'pervasiveness of patron-client networks' (Inter-American Development Bank 2001: 40) in the country's political system.

The creation of state-owned enterprises (or 'parastatals') has been an equally important tool of patronage, witness the formation of 76 such enterprises in the 1948–87 period, more than 60 per cent of which were in the tertiary sector (Menke 1991: 60). Despite the numerical importance of state-owned enterprises in the Surinamese economy, the assessment of their performance by the Inter-American Development Bank (2001: 76) has been very negative: 'They have generally been inefficient and have produced inferior quality goods and services. ... As a result, subsidies to state enterprises have represented a considerable drain on the treasury'.

The defeat of the electoral alliance, *Front for Democracy and Development*, which brought together the 'old' ethnic parties of Creoles, Hindustanis and Javanese, in the 1996 parliamentary elections and the subsequent election of Jules Wijdenbosch to the Presidency, were the beginning of a period in which the patrimonial features of Surinamese politics came to the fore with renewed vigour. Wijdenbosch was the representative of the NDP, the political party that was founded by the former military leaders. The NDP was built on a class of *nouveaux riches,* that had benefited from corruption, drug trafficking, gold mining and other illegal activities in the military period (Buddingh' 2000: 364). The 1996–2000 period is widely regarded as a time of intensifying corruption in politics and society and of a fast growing informal sector. The appointment of political allies to 'strategic positions' in the public sector and in state-owned enterprises, as well as economic favouritism of companies that supported the NDP government and the misuse of public funds became the order of the day (Buddingh' 2000: 372–80; Derveld 1999: 15). The government's economic policies led to a massive increase in public spending, resulted in a rapid depreciation of the Surinamese guilder and plunged Suriname into crisis (Buddingh' 2000: 402–8). According to Buddingh' (2000: 375), the Wijdenbosch regime showed much resemblance to the 'military-civilian oligarchy' of Suharto's Indonesia.

The return to power of the NDP, as part of the so-called Megacombinatie (Mega Combination) that was the main winner in the 2010 elections, can be seen as an expression of the dissatisfaction with the New Front among large parts of the electorate, which had gradually built up during their latest period in office. The current government, headed by NDP Chairman Bouterse, is supported by the Megacombinatie (a coalition of NDP with the Javanese KTPI and the Progressive Workers' and Farmers' Union, PALU) and two other electoral coalitions: the A Combination, led by Maroon leader and former Bouterse opponent Ronnie Brunswijk, and the Volksalliantie (People's Alliance), dominated by Javanese Pertjajah Lahur, which broke away from the New Front before the 2010 elections.

The Bouterse government is a coalition that brings together three main ethnic groups: the mainly urban-based Creoles, the jungle-based Maroons and the Javanese. The largest and wealthiest ethnic group, that of the Hindustanis, is represented only marginally in the coalition.[5] Since the formation of the Bouterse government in August 2010, the most senior civil servants at eight of the 17 Ministries have been replaced by allies of the ruling coalition (De Ware Tijd and Starnieuws, various editions). Moreover, the directors of a host of state-owned enterprises and other parastatal organizations have been dismissed.[6]

The Bouterse coalition government seems subject to various political-economic cross-pressures that may have serious impacts on the public sector of Suriname, including companies such as *Staatsolie* (see further in the fourth section below). The policy statement delivered by the new President on 1 October 2010 placed much emphasis on curbing the government deficit that had resulted from the increase of government expenditure, coupled with the fallout from the 2007–8 worldwide financial crisis (President of the Republic of Suriname 2010: 22–25). The policy statement made clear that the Bouterse government is intent on reducing the expenditure level – for example by delaying the introduction of a new payment scheme for employees in the public sector – while also attempting to find new sources of income. In line with this, Vice-President Robert Ameerali emphasized that he is committed to making a break with the past and reducing the size of the state apparatus. In light of this, the Vice-President indicated that he is not willing to give in to pressures from ministers to appoint their supporters to the bureaucracy (De Ware Tijd, 28 March 2011).

The conclusion is that Suriname's society and economy has been dominated by the state apparatus, which has been serving as a prime instrument of patronage and clientelism. This has resulted in the amassing and redistribution of rents derived from the country's rich natural resources and substantial inflows of aid. The country has thus been a prime example of a non-developmental or *rentier* state.

Staatsolie as a pocket of effectiveness

Staatsolie has developed, in the context of post-independence Suriname, into a pocket of effectiveness, the performance of which stands in sharp contrast to other state-owned enterprises. *Staatsolie* has gradually come to occupy an important economic role in Suriname, and is generally acknowledged as a well-managed and meritocratic organization. Before moving to an interpretation of *Staatsolie's* role as a development agent (in section 4), this section provides some data on the company's main achievements.

Staatsolie was founded on 13 December 1980 on the advice of the Oil Commission of Suriname. Its original assignment was to enter into a production-sharing service contract[7] with the former U.S. oil company Gulf Oil for the exploration of petroleum in the Tambaredjo field in the central coastal area of Suriname, where oil reserves had been anticipated ever since the 1920s. The Head of the Surinamese Mining Office, Eddy Jharap, was appointed as the first director of the State Oil Company of Suriname by the military authorities that had taken over power in a *coup d'état* in February

1980 (Jharap 1998: 15–17). As a reflection of its specific mandate, *Staatsolie* was created as a public limited company.

Next to its role as oil company, *Staatsolie* has also been acting as 'agent of the state' in matters of oil exploration and exploitation. Decree E-8B of 1981 had granted *Staatsolie* the concession on oil exploration and exploitation in Surinamese soil, as well as the exclusive right to negotiate with foreign investors (Staatsolie Nieuws, June 1998: 16). In addition to this, the Petroleum Act 1990 specified certain conditions regarding the exploration and exploitation of hydrocarbons. In particular, the new act ruled that the state's share of oil revenues (the 'take') should be maximized, and that operations should lead to technology transfer and the training of Surinamese employees (Staatsolie Nieuws, June 1998: 15–16).

The government, initially represented by the Minister for Natural Resources and the President of the Surinamese Planning Agency and currently by the Vice-President, possesses all of *Staatsolie's* shares, but does not have direct influence on the company's day-to-day management. The Board of Directors is the company's main management body, in charge of all internal management decisions. The Board of Directors is accountable to the annual shareholders' meeting, which is also responsible for the appointment of *Staatsolie's* management team, as well as the dismissal of management team members. *Staatsolie* has had two Managing Directors during its existence. Eddy Jharap served as Managing Director until the company's twenty-fifth anniversary in 2005, when he was succeeded by erstwhile Refining and Marketing Director, Marc Waaldijk.

The production of oil in Suriname started officially on independence day (25 November) in 1982 in the Catharina Sophia area in Tambaredjo. Since 1982, *Staatsolie* has identified petroleum reserves of 152 million barrels in the oil fields of Tambaredjo, Calcutta and Tambaredjo North-West (the latter two in exploitation since, respectively, 2004 and 2010), and produced approximately 73 million barrels of crude oil until the end of 2010. Annual production was close to 6 million barrels between 2008 and 2010 (Moensi-Sokowikromo, interview, 2011).

Next to petroleum exploitation, *Staatsolie* has gradually diversified its activities. After the completion of a pipeline between the Catharina Sophia area and Tout Lui Faut on the Suriname River in 1992, a refinery was built, financed with a loan from ABN AMRO Bank and ABB-EFAG (De West, 1 March 1994). As of 2010, annual refining capacity has been approximately 2.8 million barrels (State Oil Company of Suriname 2010b: 12). In addition to this, a pipeline was built in 2000 to cover all energy needs of the Suralco alumina plant in Paranam. Since 2006, the Staatsolie Power Company Suriname (SPCS) has been producing electricity. Its capacity was increased to 28 megawatts in June 2010. SPCS has had a power purchase agreement with the Suriname Energy Company, EBS, for the supply of at least 14 megawatts of electricity (Murli, interview, 2011). As part of its 'Vision 2020', *Staatsolie* has made plans for diversifying into the production of other sources of energy,

158   *Wil Hout*

most notably hydropower and biofuels from sugarcane. The TapaJai project aims at generating hydroelectricity by constructing dams in the Tapanahony River and Jai Creek. The production of biofuels has started with a pilot project, which aims at ultimately producing 1 million tonnes of sugarcane and 70 million litres of ethanol annually. Ethanol would be used for electricity generation and as a replacement for the imported octane booster that is used in the oil refinery process (Murli, interview, 2011).

Over the years, *Staatsolie* has been expanding its range of products. In 2001, it was reported that *Staatsolie's* production of crude oil was sufficient to cover the energy needs of Suriname, expressed in barrels (Staatsolie Nieuws, March 2001: 11–12). Over time, *Staatsolie* has developed into an important supplier of fuel oil and gas oil to the region: in 2011, the company exported 45 per cent of its total sales (or 3.2 million barrels), mainly to neighbouring countries as Guyana, Curaçao, Barbados and Trinidad (State Oil Company of Suriname 2012a: 20). Moreover, the company was an important exporter of bitumen to French Guyana, Guyana, Montserrat, St. Vincent and St. Lucia, with total export reaching 5,200 barrels in 2009 (State Oil Company of Suriname 2010a: 11). Since the company is not yet able to produce all required end-products (such as diesel oil, petrol and kerosene), Suriname still has to import part of its energy products. As part of its Vision 2020, *Staatsolie* aims to increase its refinery capacity from 8,000 to 15,000 barrels per day by 2013 and further diversify its production, eventually also producing high-quality diesel and gasoline for the local market (State Oil Company of Suriname 2010b).

In May 2010, the company announced an investment of approximately US $1 billion, 60 per cent of which was meant for expansion of the refinery, with the remainder to finance exploration activities, expansion of onshore oil production, increased power generation and renewable energy projects. Around 70 per cent of the investments were covered from the company's internal cash flow, while the rest was financed with US$235 million in loans from Credit Suisse and ING Bank and US$55 million from a major bond issue for the local market in Suriname. This way of financing the largest investment during *Staatsolie's* existence was generally perceived as a major expression of confidence by the international financial sector in the company's operations (De Ware Tijd, 24 May 2010; Moensi-Sokowikromo, interview, 2011).

The expectation that the mainland coastal area as well as the continental shelf off the Suriname coast contain significant petroleum reserves has resulted, over the years, in major exploration activities. Staatsolie organized various 'international bidding rounds' for foreign exploration firms, most recently between January and July 2013 (State Oil Company of Suriname 2012d). In the past decade, *Staatsolie* has signed production-sharing agreements aimed at offshore oil exploration with companies such as Spanish-Argentinean Repsol-YPF, Danish Maersk Oil and U.S. Occidental Petroleum Corporation (Brunings, interview, 2004). At the end of 2012, offshore exploration activities were being undertaken by Chevron Global Energy,

Inpex Group, Kosmos Oil, Murphy Oil and Tullow Oil (State Oil Company of Suriname 2012c and 2012d).

The macro-economic importance of *Staatsolie's* activities for Suriname in the last two decades (1990–2010) can be illustrated with the data presented in figure 7.1 and table 7.1. Figure 7.1 shows that Staatsolie's revenues from oil sales quadrupled in the 1990–2000 period, and increased almost sixfold between 2000 and 2010. By 2010, profits had risen to US$182 million, after having reached an all-time high of US$230 million in 2008. Average investment, despite fluctuations, increased to an annual US$98 million in the five most recent years. Shareholder's equity – representing the 'value' of *Staatsolie* to Suriname's government and the Surinamese Planning Agency – has steadily increased, to peak at more than US$611 million at the end of 2011 (State Oil Company of Suriname 2012a: 43).

Table 7.1 presents data related to two indicators that shed light on *Staatsolie's* contribution to the Surinamese economy. Figures in the second column of the table indicate, for the 1990–2010 period for which data are available, that oil revenues have constituted an important source of Suriname's gross domestic product. Since the turn of the century the oil sector has contributed annually, on average, almost 10 per cent to the country's GDP. Stockholders' equity has represented more than 10 per cent of GDP since 2000, and reached a peak of 12.1 per cent in 2010. Data on corporate and income taxes and dividends paid by *Staatsolie* to the state show that the company's payments represented a significant, and increasing, share of total government consumption expenditure. Over the years for which data are

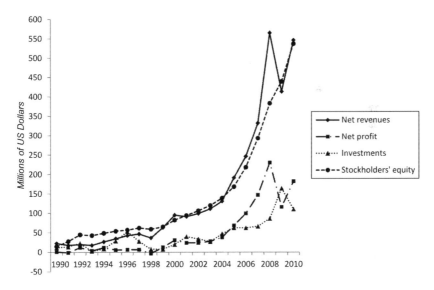

Figure 7.1 Staatsolie's financial results, 1990–2010
Source: State Oil Company of Suriname, Financial Department.

160   *Wil Hout*

Table 7.1 Staatsolie's contribution to the Surinamese economy, 1990-2010

Year	Oil revenues as percentage of Surinamese GDP	Shareholder's equity as percentage of Surinamese GDP
1990	5.8	3.8
1991	4.1	6.4
1992	4.9	11.1
1993	4.1	9.9
1994	4.5	8.2
1995	6.0	7.8
1996	5.7	6.7
1997	6.0	6.7
1998	4.7	6.3
1999	7.9	7.5
2000	11.2	9.1
2001	12.5	12.2
2002	9.7	9.8
2003	9.0	9.4
2004	7.9	9.4
2005	9.7	9.4
2006	9.2	8.3
2007	10.6	9.7
2008	12.3	10.8
2009	8.0	11.4
2010	9.8	12.1

Sources: State Oil Company of Suriname, Financial Department (1990-1994), Annual Reports (1994–2010); World Bank (2010).

available the percentage increased from 10.7 (2000) to 13.1 (2003) and 19.1 (2005). *Staatsolie* is known as one of the few Surinamese firms that brought foreign exchange into the country (Tuur, interview, 2004), with the company's foreign earnings amounting to approximately US$250 million in 2010.[8]

Staatsolie's performance can be illustrated also on the basis of a commonly used financial indicator. In figure 7.2, data are given on the company's return on investment (the ratio of a company's net income and its total investment) from 1990 to 2010. The graph presented in figure 7.2 indicates that *Staatsolie* has achieved a noteworthy level of efficiency in its use of resources. Despite some fluctuation over time, due to variations in the price of crude oil, *Staatsolie* has been able to secure a rate of return on investment of over 36 per cent over the 2000–2010 period (and even 51.3 per cent over the last five years), which compares favourably with the performance of other oil companies.[9]

The data presented in this section have demonstrated that *Staatsolie*, over the past three decades, has become a true pocket of effectiveness in patrimonial Suriname. Figures show that the activities of *Staatsolie* have expanded considerably, leading to a notable diversification of the company's activities. Moreover, the company has been contributing significantly to the overall economic wealth of the country. The next section will attempt to contribute towards the explanation of the company's role.

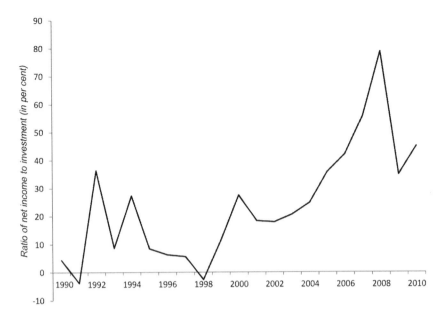

Figure 7.2 Return on investment, *Staatsolie*, 1990–2010
Source: State Oil Company of Suriname, Financial Department.

'Confidence in our own abilities': **Staatsolie's double strategy**

State-owned enterprises are a common phenomenon across the developing world, where they have often been set up to 'rapidly lift the entire economy to a level of self-sustaining industrial growth' (Waterbury, quoted in Evans 1995: 79). Typical explanations of the generally weak performance of state-owned enterprises in non-developmental or *rentier* states tend to focus on the fact that such enterprises have little autonomy from the state, and thus are easy instruments for pursuing political objectives. The emphasis of such explanations is often on the rent-seeking attitude of management, who have themselves been appointed as part of clientelist schemes, and on the political instrumentalization of the enterprises' activities (cf. Schneider 1999).

This section serves to analyse the conditions under which *Staatsolie* developed into and maintained its status as a pocket of effectiveness. The discussion focuses, in particular, on the double strategy that was developed by *Staatsolie* to become a successful medium-size oil company. The internal part of this strategy, derived from the management vision and ideological commitment of the company's leadership, was aimed at developing technological and management skills. The external part of the strategy was aimed at steering away from political influences on the company and politically deploying the formal-legal position of the firm in Suriname's petroleum sector.

162   *Wil Hout*

It was noted above that *Staatsolie* was established at the beginning of the period of military rule in Suriname. In the immediate aftermath of the *coup d'état*, the military's role in Surinamese politics was generally regarded as legitimate, as its intervention reflected a general discontent with the 'old order', an order founded on pernicious practices of patronage and clientelism on the basis of ethnicity (Menke, interview, 2004).

Staatsolie's inception in the military era was important, because the military rulers originally embraced a nationalist economic agenda and saw the possible expansion of the oil sector as a step towards self-reliant development. Oil was being regarded as a strategic mineral resource, the exploration and production of which would best be done under control of the state. In order to enhance the effectiveness of the state's presence in the oil sector, the state would need to have a specialized instrument, in the form of a state oil company (De Ware Tijd, Kompas, 9 December 2000; interviews: Sedney, 2004, and Jharap, 2004; Jharap 2006: 6).

The economic agenda of the military ran parallel with the ideas propounded by the Surinamese *Volkspartij* (People's Party), a Marxist party that was very much in favour of achieving self-reliance for Suriname (Jharap, interview, 2004; Lotens 2004: 73–75; Hira 2007: 111–19). During the 1970s, Eddy Jharap had been a very active member of the *Volkspartij*, which was dismantled, as were all existing political parties, after the military coup.[10] Jharap's background in the *Volkspartij* seems to have played a role in his appointment to the chair of the Oil Commission and, later, to the directorship of *Staatsolie*. According to Jharap (2006: 6; Hira 2007: 134), then Minister for Reconstruction, Herman Adhin,[11] selected him with a view to his left-wing orientation, as this would make him a 'useful counterweight' in negotiations with foreign oil companies. Adhin argued that Jharap would not give in to the demands of multinational corporations, in contrast with negotiators in the bauxite sector, who had agreed too easily to profitable concessions given out to foreign firms.

The creation of *Staatsolie*, made necessary because there was a need for a legal entity to enter into a production-sharing service contract with Gulf Oil, was in line with the political commitment of Jharap, who left the *Volkspartij* after the coup. In his role as managing director of *Staatsolie*, Jharap saw himself as expert *and* ideologue. Looking back, he argued that the challenges for the oil company were to use Suriname's wealth for the benefit of the country's population and to undertake resource exploration and exploitation with the company's own, not foreign-dominated, means (Lotens 2004: 77).

In its official publications, *Staatsolie* has been using two slogans to underline its vision that the creation and further development of Suriname's oil sector have been important not only to contributing to the country's level of wealth, but also to signalling the endogenous capacity of the Surinamese to build a modern enterprise (Jharap 1998: 19). The slogans 'Confidence in our own Abilities' and 'Building on our own Abilities' – the latter adopted in 2001 to reflect the company's offensive nature in a more prominent way, but dropped again in the post-Jharap period (Waaldijk, interview, 2011) – are attempts to express *Staatsolie's* corporate 'ideology' in words. On the basis of his analysis of the operations of major oil companies, Jharap came to see the challenges of the oil industry less in terms of technical than management skills. Trained as a geologist in The Netherlands, Jharap used the experience of Norway and its government-owned private oil company *Statoil* to argue that the Surinamese state oil company should operate as much as possible as a commercial firm, aiming at the development of expertise that is required to manage the inputs of consultants, subcontractors and in-house experts. Apart from this, the company would need to develop the infrastructure that would enable it to do business with foreign oil firms as an equal partner (Jharap 2006: 8).

During the first few years of its existence, *Staatsolie* acquired its technological and managerial know-how by working closely with foreign consultants, most notably from Gulf Oil's division Geoman[12] (Hira 2007: 145–52). According to Jharap, the establishment of master-apprentice relationships was very important in this respect, as the main problem of the transfer of technology and management skills appeared to lie in the absorptive capacity at the receiving end. In Jharap's view, a master would, in general, be willing to transfer knowledge and expertise, provided that the apprentice displayed an appropriate attitude. In the relationship between the master and apprentice, a certain degree of submission would be required, as the master would only then stop seeing the apprentice as a possible threat and instead perceive him or her as somebody who can be trusted with the knowledge and expertise (Jharap, interview, 2004). Jharap applied this philosophy both within *Staatsolie* and in relation to its international partners. In the early years of the company, Jharap organized weekly motivation and mobilization meetings with staff in order to discuss the company's objectives, implementation and results. Moreover, Jharap was known to work in the field with his staff in order to share experiences and enhance motivation (Jharap 2010a: 9–10). Externally, *Staatsolie* made extensive use of Gulf Oil's training facilities, and staff were encouraged to 'learn the tricks' from foreign consultants when these were visiting Suriname (Jharap 2010b: 18–19).

In addition to the acquisition of technological and managerial expertise by *Staatsolie* staff, the spreading of know-how about aspects of the oil industry throughout the Surinamese economy was considered to be important. The construction of the first oil plant in Catharina Sophia, in 1982, was undertaken with local contractors and constructors. *Staatsolie's* first oil drill was purchased second-hand in Canada and overhauled by local staff. Drilling staff were trained by Geoman consultants (Jharap 1998: 37).

In later years, *Staatsolie* has placed much emphasis on the need to maintain well-defined standards for its operations (Hira 2007: 324, 329–30). Apart from the company's adoption of external quality control mechanisms (in particular, the ISO certifications that were mentioned above), *Staatsolie* has instituted an internal safety award and certificate for divisions and staff members that contribute to

164 *Wil Hout*

enhancing company safety and completing operations without accidents (Staatsolie Nieuws, March 2004: 20–21).

In contrast to prevalent practices of patronage and clientelism, *Staatsolie* adopted meritocratic principles in its human resource policy. From the outset, background and ethnicity were considered irrelevant as criteria for appointment and promotion within the company (Essed, interview, 2004; Jharap 2010a: 13–14). In order to upgrade the quality of its staff, *Staatsolie* has instituted a sizeable training programme, the budget of which is currently in the order of US$1 million annually, as well as a management development programme. Much attention is paid to enhance the attractiveness of *Staatsolie* to well-qualified applicants. Secondary labour conditions, such as a holiday allowance, a profit-sharing scheme, a company car for senior staff and health care and pension facilities, serve to make the company competitive *vis-à-vis* the foreign-dominated bauxite sector (interviews: Essed, 2004, and Waaldijk, 2011).

Staatsolie's history demonstrates that the company's management has consistently kept an eye on developments in the Surinamese political system. A lack of trust in Suriname's political leaders – and particularly the fear that *Staatsolie* could become an instrument of patronage, should the company become too dependent on political decision-making – resulted in the desire of the company's leadership to keep politics at a distance (Jharap 2010a: 17–18). The inclination on the part of Jharap, later shared by other *Staatsolie* staff, was related to his political engagement with the *Volkspartij* and its ideology. The *Volkspartij* rejected traditional Surinamese political practices and profiled itself as a national party, unaffected by ethnic biases. In order to build a successful company that would contribute to the wealth and capacities of the Surinamese people, Jharap felt he should not depend on political favours.

Jharap was engaged in a balancing act with the military regime. On the one hand, he knew that he could count on the support from the National Military Council, which had been set up by the leaders of the coup, because they shared Jharap's vision regarding the setting up of a national oil industry. On the other hand, Jharap tried to distance himself and the company – literally as well as figuratively – from the military regime, because he realized how harmful their interference with *Staatsolie* could turn out to be. Jharap purposefully made *Staatsolie* into an 'island' during its early years. As the company's operations were centred on the oil fields, at quite a distance from the capital, Paramaribo, they were out of sight for most people (Jharap, interview, 2004).

The military rulers, who were mainly sergeants in their early thirties and inexperienced in governing, were preoccupied with running the country, and did not pay much attention to *Staatsolie*. Nevertheless, Jharap made sure to provide information about the company and organize company visits for the government and the National Military Council, in order 'to keep channels open'. In an attempt to strengthen *Staatsolie's* reputation, Jharap continued to emphasize that 'the production of our own oil would greatly benefit the image of the "revolution"' (Jharap 2010a: 9, translated from Dutch).[13]

Attempts by military from the lower ranks to use *Staatsolie* as a source of jobs for relatives and friends were averted, by pointing out that such requests would be discussed with the military leadership. As the latter's credo, according to Jharap (2006: 21–22; Hira 2007: 180), was that *Staatsolie* should be autonomous, no interventions of the military took place in the company's employment policies. Occasional pressures on the company from within the military government were also warded off after intervention by the National Military Council. One of those incidents was Deputy Prime Minister Haakmat's unsuccessful attempt to intervene in the agreement between Suriname and Gulf Oil in late 1980, based on his assessment that the benefits for the country were too meagre (Jharap 2006: 21).

Staatsolie's resolve to stay clear of politics was also reflected in its search for capital. Except for a relatively small advance that was received from the Ministry of Finance, most of the risk capital needed in *Staatsolie's* early days was received from Gulf Oil (Jharap 1998: 25; Hira 2007: 146, 259–60). Other amounts, required for the financing of exploration activities and the purchase of oil production facilities respectively, were obtained from the Surinaamsche Bank, with a bank guarantee from the Central Bank of Suriname (Sedney, interview, 2004), and from a consortium of six banks in Suriname (Jharap 1998: 33).

Staatsolie preferred not to draw on the aid funds provided by The Netherlands, partly because of the bureaucratic procedures involved and partly because of the company's desire to maintain a business-like, non-political relationship with its financiers (Jharap 1998: 35; Sedney, interview, 2004). The only exception to the rule was the guarantee from Dutch Treaty funds sought – and received – by *Staatsolie* as collateral for its major investments in the refinery, which itself were financed with private bank credit (De Ware Tijd, 19 March 1993; Hira 2007: 188–89).

After 1985, the main sources of finance were a revolving credit and long-term loans obtained from international banks, with ABN AMRO taking an important position among these (Kortram, interview, 2004). The revolving credit arrangement with ABN AMRO was only partly inspired by financial considerations: it also served to enhance *Staatsolie's* financial independence. In response to the deterioration of the country's financial situation since 1983 – primarily because Dutch development assistance had been cut off in response to the military-led '8 December killings' of 15 opponents – the government had decided that all exporting firms in Suriname should deposit their hard currency in the Central Bank, in exchange for steadily depreciating Surinamese guilders. *Staatsolie* had been able to free itself from this requirement as part of the revolving credit arrangement. The company had agreed with ABN AMRO that its earnings on exports, which ultimately served as collateral, had to be deposited at the bank's Houston branch. As a result of the deal, *Staatsolie* managed to retain control over its foreign earnings, which it needed for reinvestment purposes, and could influence the amount of foreign currency that was handed over to the Central Bank of Suriname (Jharap 2006: 18).

166   *Wil Hout*

Staatsolie's legal position as 'agent of the state' has been used consistently by the company as a powerful tool to pursue the objectives of building an independent oil company and upgrading the technological and management expertise present in Suriname. As a result of its legal position, *Staatsolie* has been the 'spider in the web' when it comes to bidding rounds for exploration projects in the offshore blocks of the Suriname-Guyana basin, where significant oil and gas reserves are expected to be uncovered.

Staatsolie has consistently tried to live up to the requirements set by the Petroleum Act 1990 relating to the maximization of the government 'take'. Notwithstanding occasional complaints by politicians that the company has not been contributing sufficiently to the government budget, *Staatsolie's* timely transfer of all profits, apart from a share needed for investment, to the state, has produced great confidence among many politicians in the reliability of management. This, in turn, produced support for the policies adopted by the company's Board of Directors. This assessment was the basis of Managing Director Waaldijk's observation that the Bouterse government, since it assumed office in July 2010, has paid much attention to the company. Waaldijk felt that the importance of *Staatsolie's* contribution to government revenue demands prudent decision making on the part of the Board of Directors, for which government support needs to be ensured. (Waaldijk, interview, 2011).

Staatsolie's attempt to stay clear of political interference was successful, ultimately, because of the quality of the company's internal operations and its resulting ability to act as a role model. The absence of patronage and ethnically-based appointments within the company underline *Staatsolie's* commitment to maintain quality standards (Menke, interview, 2004). The confrontation with the Wijdenbosch government in 1997 and 1998 was the clearest demonstration to date of *Staatsolie's* standing as a role model and an example for other firms. During this period, Jharap and the staff at Staatsolie were able to ward off the pressure from leading politicians to appropriate *Staatsolie's* resources for political means.

The main conflict between the Wijdenbosch government and *Staatsolie* derived from various attempts by the government to extract more money from the company to finance its increasing deficits. Among other things, the government tried to force *Staatsolie* to increase its oil production from 9,500 to 20,000 barrels per day, sell off the Tambaredjo oil field and initiate a joint venture between Staatsolie and foreign oil companies (De Ware Tijd, 6 June 1997, 12 September 1997 and 18 March 1998). The ensuing dismissal of the Board of Supervisors in March 1998 (De West, 26 and 28 March 1998) and the double attempt to dismiss Jharap should be seen as efforts to bring *Staatsolie* under direct government control. *Staatsolie's* management mobilized legal advisors, who emphasized that the role of the state was limited to the appointment and dismissal of the Board of Supervisors. Jharap successfully challenged the decision of the General Meeting of Shareholders to fire members of the Board of Directors. He did so with reference to the non-compliance with government policy (De West, 17 June 1998 and 23 September 1998).

Jharap's successful recourse to the available legal means and the massive protests, first of the *Staatsolie* trade union (the *Staatsolie Werknemers Organisatie Suriname* or SWOS) and later of the joint political opposition and labour unions, warded off the government's bid for power in the oil sector. An important factor spurring popular resistance against the government on the issue of *Staatsolie* was the widespread feeling that the oil company, as one of the most successful firms in the country, should be protected against political machinations. The resistance became particularly fierce because of the involvement of politicians, such as NDP President Wijdenbosch and Central Bank President Goedschalk, who were suspected of placing their personal interest in the sale of oil rights above the national interest, and whose financial-economic policies were felt to be leading the country to disaster (De Ware Tijd, 4 June 1998; Read, interview, 2004).

The 1997–98 protest movement fed into broader popular protest against the Wijdenbosch government, which ultimately led to earlier elections. During the two governments led by President Ronald Venetiaan between 2000 and 2010, *Staatsolie's* position beyond the reach of politicians was secured. The smooth transition of the company's leadership to the long-serving Director of Refining and Marketing, Marc Waaldijk, after Jharap's retirement in December 2005, as well as the reorganization of the company's leadership structure in March 2007 (Staatsolie Nieuws, June 2007: 3), underlined *Staatsolie's* autonomy from politics. Both the leadership transition and the reorganization were induced and implemented according to *Staatsolie's* own management priorities.

During recent years, *Staatsolie* has been faced with changes in its external environment. The political uncertainty emanating from the election of NDP leader Bouterse to the Presidency is an important factor for *Staatsolie*. The company appears to have demonstrated its continued capacity to limit political interference in the conflict over the appointment of a new Finance Director in early 2011. With the retirement of long-serving Director Iwan Kortram, it was assumed widely that the second person in the Finance Directorate, Deputy Director Agnes Moensi-Sokowikromo, would be the successor. Mrs Moensi had been groomed in the company for a long time and was seen as the most desired internal candidate. Deliberations within the Board of Supervisors led to the proposal to nominate economist Iwan Poerschke, an active member of the Progressive Workers' and Farmers' Union (PALU) and member of the Board of Supervisors since October 2010, to the post of Financial Director. Commentators argued that the Board of Supervisors had given in to political pressure to reward the PALU, the party of Natural Resources Minister Jim Hok and a much-needed supporter of the Bouterse government (De Ware Tijd, 17 March 2011). After a period of confrontation between the Board of Supervisors and labour union SWOS, Poerschke's tenure as Financial Director was limited to three years. According to Starnieuws (17 and 21 March 2011), *Staatsolie's* management had compromised

168 *Wil Hout*

on Poerschke's appointment in exchange for the appointment of home-grown Deputy Director Moensi upon the retirement of the new Director in 2014.

The announcement, in December 2012, of the appointment of John Sew A Tjon as Director Productions and Development and successor to Managing Director Waaldijk upon his retirement in October 2013, is the latest challenge to *Staatsolie*. The professional background of Sew A Tjon, who was trained as a mining engineer and was the last Managing Director of BHP Billiton's bauxite operations in Suriname (Starnieuws, 19 December 2012), seems to indicate that the company has succeeded in placing expertise above political allegiance, but the long-term outcome of this change of guard remains to be seen.

Another element in the external environment concerns the changing political economy of Suriname, which was alluded to already above. The steady (and growing) stream of income from *Staatsolie's* operations, coupled with the impact of the financial crisis and the increasing government deficit, has led to an increased awareness of the company's importance for Suriname's economic well-being. According to Managing Director, Marc Waaldijk, it is 'only normal' that the government's interest in *Staatsolie* has increased over the years, as the company has transformed from a 'US$100 million into a US $500 million firm' and thus has become a strategic economic player, particularly since the company's income transfer to the state is amounting to approximately 25 per cent of total government income (Waaldijk, interview, 2010). The company has been feeling the pressure from the government – exemplified, for instance, by statements made by the Minister of Natural Resources (see section 1 above) – to increase its oil production in order to generate more income for the state. *Staatsolie's* management have so far been hesitant about such suggestions, because they feel that Suriname does not possess the 'proper institutions' to manage the wealth that would derive from sharply rising income flows (De Ware Tijd, 1 October 2010; Waaldijk, interview, 2011).

In general, company management seem to prefer an initial public offering of *Staatsolie* shares in international stock exchanges, as an alternative to the current situation in which the Surinamese state is the sole shareholder. They feel that the growth of the firm may be hampered in due course by its legal status, as uncertainties persist about the exact influence of the government on company policies. It is argued that the company's market value would greatly exceed its current book value, and that public trading of *Staatsolie* shares would expand the company's business opportunities. The experience of Petrobras, which is a publicly traded corporation with the government of Brazil as majority shareholder, is seen as an example of the way in which the Surinamese government could safeguard the interests of the state as well as guarantee the corporate performance of *Staatsolie* (Waaldijk, interview, 2011).

Conclusions

The literature about patrimonialism and rentier states has focused traditionally on macro-level institutions (primarily, the state) and on the influence that

Suriname's State Oil Company as a PoE   169

rent-seeking, patronage and clientelism exert in society and the economy. The theoretical argument that this chapter has made is that it is necessary to look beyond such macro-level institutions, and include actors at the meso and micro level, to 'unpack' the argument about the patrimonial or rentier state. Only if attention is focused on meso- and micro-level actors, is it possible to gauge the political and social dynamics in particular sectors of the economy. The study of sectoral dynamics may help analysts to avoid all too crude generalizations about the impact of patrimonialism, in particular, in the form of rent-seeking, patronage and clientelism.

More specifically, the current analysis has demonstrated how and under which conditions concrete development activities can take place in a seemingly hostile environment. This chapter has focused on a typical 'hard case' – the oil sector in a country that has traditionally been characterized by patronage and clientelist politics – where the patrimonial/rentier state argument would predict rent-seeking to prevail. The case of the Surinamese State Oil Company indicates that sectoral development under committed leadership is possible against all odds.

The analysis of *Staatsolie* contributes to the argument about so-called pockets of effectiveness sketched in the introduction to this volume. The current analysis shows that the creation of a pocket of effectiveness within the public sector need not signal an overall improvement in the functioning of the state bureaucracy. More particularly, the Surinamese case supports Evans' (1989: 578) observation that a successful state-owned enterprise can coexist alongside inefficient parastatals and a government bureaucracy infested with practices of patronage and clientelism. At the same time, however, the case of *Staatsolie* illustrates how the dynamics within a pocket of effectiveness – in particular, the need to consolidate the market position and diversify production – lead to changing preferences about the relations with the state. Current discussions about the public offering of *Staatsolie* in international markets may produce a legal *volte-face* in the relationship between *Staatsolie* and the Surinamese government, as that would lead to de facto privatization (interviews: Gemerts, 2004, and Waaldijk, 2011).

The theoretical significance of *Staatsolie's* case is that it brings out clearly how a company could be set up that is committed to the acquisition and further development of technological and managerial expertise, despite its insertion into a patrimonial environment. The discussion of the conditions for *Staatsolie's* role as a development agent (in the previous section) attributed the company's success to its double strategy, built on the management vision and ideological commitment of the company's leadership, and the ability on the part of management to steer away from political influences and to play out, politically, the formal-legal position of the firm in the petroleum sector. It is important to realize that these were, at most, necessary, and clearly not sufficient conditions for *Staatsolie's* success. In particular, the fact that the company started as a marginal enterprise in 1980 and remained in the shadow of major rent-producing activities – such as, in

170 *Wil Hout*

particular, the bauxite sector and Dutch development assistance – until the mid-1990s produced the conditions under which *Staatsolie's* skills could be developed without much interference from those who, as shareholder, could have pulled the strings.

Despite the fact that most people in Suriname now seem to respect *Staatsolie* and its leadership for what has been achieved over the past 30 years, it has to be realized that the immediate external environment for the oil company is not without threats. The major challenges for the company, and for its desire to maintain its role as a development agent in the years ahead, seem to be related to the same factors that contributed to *Staatsolie's* achievements. Since the smooth succession of Jharap by someone with a comparable vision and commitment, *Staatsolie's* resolve to continue building on its own abilities seems to be guaranteed. The most important threat to the future success of the oil company is, therefore, to be found in the interaction between *Staatsolie* and the Surinamese government, and particularly in the willingness of the shareholder to grant *Staatsolie* a substantial degree of autonomy. Such autonomy will be required in the light of major decisions on off-shore exploration and exploitation and the further diversification of its activities, for all of which the company will undoubtedly need to attract more private capital than was secured in the US$1 billion investment programme for the 2008–12 period.

Fundamentally, the discussion about *Staatsolie's* future touches upon the nature of Suriname's politics and, more broadly, its governance structure. As demonstrated by, among others, the Inter-American Development Bank (2001: 4–5), the creation of wealth and other public goods in Suriname is seriously hampered by the pervasive nature of patronage and clientelism, which support rent-seeking rather than productive initiatives. The flowering of initiatives such as *Staatsolie*, aimed at the acquisition of technology and management expertise, is heavily dependent on the capacity and will of the political leadership to curtail patrimonial practices. In this perspective, a major step forward in the securement of *Staatsolie's* legacy would lie in the establishment of more reliable governance structures, and the ensuing institutionalization of mechanisms of effective self-restraint among those working in the Surinamese public sector.

Notes

1 Research for this chapter was done in two phases. Initial research, including interviews and data collection in *Staatsolie's* documentation centre, was done with financial support from WOTRO Science for Global Development in April 2004. The results of this first phase were published in Hout (2007). Follow-up research was done in February 2011.
2 See the list of interviewees in the appendix to this chapter.
3 Suriname does not have all the characteristics of a 'petro-state' as described by Karl (1997). Although its reserves per capita (roughly 0.3 billion barrels per million persons) and the share of oil production in GDP (over 11 per cent between 2000

and 2002) would place the country in Karl's category of capital-deficient oil producers, the share of oil in total exports (approximately 2 per cent in 2003) falls far short of the 40 per cent threshold used by the World Bank (Karl 1997: 17). In addition to this, Suriname's oil reserves and the country's share of world oil production render the country insignificant by international standards.

4 In 1998, the population of Suriname counted roughly 431,000 people, and consisted of 27 per cent Creoles, 40 per cent Hindustanis, 16 per cent Javanese, 12 per cent Maroons (former slaves who escaped to the interior of Suriname), 3 per cent Amerindian and 2 per cent others (St-Hilaire 2001: 1002).

5 The Bouterse government that took office in 2010 contained only two office-holders of Hindustani background. Both were 'technocrats' with little or no previous political experience: Vice-President Robert Ameerali, former Chairman of the Surinamese Chamber of Commerce, and Minister of Finance Wonnie Boedhoe, former Director of the Surinamese National Development Bank and President of the Association of Economists. Among the other 16 Ministers were five Creoles, five Javanese and six Maroons.

6 These include at least the Central Office of Population Affairs (Centraal Bureau Burgerzaken), the Internal Revenue Service (Belastingdienst), the Telecommunications Authority, the Surinamese Energy Company (Energiebedrijven Suriname, EBS), the National Transport Company (Nationaal Vervoersbedrijf), Airport Management Ltd. (NV Luchthavenbeheer), the Civil Aviation Safety Authority Suriname (CASAS) and Surinam Airways (De Ware Tijd and Starnieuws, various editions).

7 A production-sharing service contract is a contract between a state and a foreign oil company, under which the state retains the property rights of all oil that is produced as well as the jurisdiction over the exploitation. Payment of the foreign company for an agreed set of activities (such as a minimum level of exploration and production) takes place through the granting by the state of a fixed share of the annual oil production to the company (Jharap 1998: 15).

8 Data on *Staatsolie's* payments to the government were provided by Staatsolie's Financial Department; data on general government final consumption expenditure were taken from World Bank (2010). Overall, it has appeared to be difficult to gather reliable data on the Suriname economy. As documented by a former President of the Surinamese Audit Office, there is systematic underreporting of data related to government spending (Prade 1999).

9 Differences in the size and nature of operations of oil companies as well as in the financial data provided by these companies make comparisons difficult. A comparison of the financial results reported by *Staatsolie* and by David Wood, President and Chief Executive Officer at Murphy Oil, a firm that is active in exploration off the Suriname coast, shows that Murphy Oil's average rate of return on investments (24 per cent in the 2005–9 period) was significantly lower than *Staatsolie's* (Wood 2010: 34).

10 The *Volkspartij* split over the issue of cooperation with the military. A fraction of the party allied with the military regime under the name *Revolutionaire Volkspartij* (Revolutionary People's Party).

11 Adhin was a minister in the government headed by Henk Chin A Sen, which was appointed by civilian president Ferrier after the military coup of February 1980. Chin A Sen and most of his ministers were recruited from the non-traditional parties, in order to signal a break with the past. Some of the ministers, including Adhin, had a clearly leftist profile, but most of them can be considered to have been 'technocrats' (Buddingh' 2000: 324).

12 Gulf Geoman was an affiliate of Gulf that was set up to provide technical assistance to oil countries. It had concluded a Technical Assistance Agreement with *Staatsolie* for offshore exploration and drilling in 1981 (Jharap 2010b: 15).

172　*Wil Hout*

13 Jharap used the term 'revolution' in accordance with the way in which the military coup of 1980 was (and still is) generally addressed.

Surinamese news media (in Dutch)

De Ware Tijd, daily newspaper (online available HTTP: http://www.dwtonline.com/ archief).
De West, daily newspaper.
Starnieuws, daily news website (online available HTTP: http://www.starnieuws.com).
Staatsolie Nieuws, quarterly news bulletin published by the State Oil Company of Suriname.

Interviews

Leon Brunings, Treasurer, State Oil Company Suriname, 5 April 2004.
Vincent Essed, Manager Human Resources, State Oil Company Suriname, 6 April 2004.
Glenn Gemerts, Deputy-Director for Mining, Ministry of Natural Resources, 7 April 2004.
Dr. Eddy Jharap, Managing Director, State Oil Company Suriname, 5 April 2004.
Niermala Hindori-Badrising, Advisor in the Cabinet of the President of Suriname, 31 March 2004.
Iwan Kortram, Financial Director, State Oil Company Suriname, 6 April 2004.
Jack Menke, researcher, affiliated with the Anton de Kom University of Suriname, 2 April 2004.
Agnes K. Moensi-Sokowikromo, Deputy Director Finance, State Oil Company Suriname, 8 February 2011.
Sam Murli, Deputy Director Refining and Marketing, State Oil Company Suriname, 8 February 2011.
Lloyd Read, Chairman, State Oil Company Employees' Organisation Suriname (SWOS), 6 April 2004.
Marten Schalkwijk, Director, Nikos (NGO Institute for Training and Research), 2 April 2004.
Jules Sedney, Advisor to the Minister of Trade and Industry and former Prime-Minister of Suriname, 1 April 2004.
Mauro R.L. Tuur, Permanent Secretary of the Ministry of Trade and Industry, 1 April 2004.
Marc Waaldijk, Managing Director, State Oil Company Suriname. 17 February 2011.

8 Defying the resource curse

Explaining successful state-owned enterprises in rentier states[1]

Steffen Hertog

Introduction

This chapter focuses on one particular pocket of effectiveness in a particular type of country: state-owned enterprises (SOEs) in oil-rich states. It explains how several Gulf rentier monarchies have managed to create highly profitable and well-managed SOEs, confounding expectations of general SOE ineffectiveness and inefficiency as well as the particularly bad quality of rentier public sectors. The selection of cases might appear quite specific, but in many regards they constitute 'least likely' cases in which according to conventional wisdom(s) pockets of effectiveness are least expected to emerge. Although some development challenges of oil-rich states are quite specific, the reasons for the emergence of effective institutions in them are potentially relevant beyond the rentier and SOE realm.[2]

As the chapter deals with profit-oriented and often internationalized entities, the focus is not on public services, strictly speaking, as in much of the rest of this book, but the main explanandum is effectiveness. The former and the latter do in fact appear to be in tension in some of the cases under study, an unfortunate but important finding. The following paragraphs will outline the argument of the chapter in summary fashion, which is then spelled out in detail and in the same order in the subsequent sections.

Although SOEs in the oil monarchies of the Gulf Cooperation Council (GCC) have been subsidized in various ways, and often enjoyed local monopolies or duopolies, several of them are increasingly proving themselves competitive, both in a liberalized domestic setting and in international markets. Both older players like Saudi Arabia's Basic Industries Corporation (SABIC), and newer actors like Industries Qatar, Dubai logistics giant DP World and UAE telecoms conglomerate Etisalat, have produced impressive returns and acquired a reputation for capable management. Most of the new Gulf SOEs have so far survived the global economic crisis rather well.

As they enjoy certain strategic advantages, it is difficult to compare the success of these SOEs with 'conventional', private multinational enterprises. The Gulf SOEs' track record does, however, stand in stark contrast to that of public companies in other resource-rich states: the economic histories of

174 *Steffen Hertog*

Algeria, Indonesia, Iran, Libya, Nigeria and Venezuela are cluttered with monumental white elephants. SOE performance has been lacklustre at best; public industry in these countries is usually politicized, stagnant and, at the best of times, slated for partial sell-offs.

What explains this relative success of Gulf SOEs? The deck, it seems, was in many ways stacked against them: Gulf monarchies have weaker pre-oil traditions of statehood, administration and economic development, and are ruled in a patrimonial fashion by extended kinship groups. None of this seems to augur well for rational-bureaucratic development.

When can resource riches be turned into efficient, state-controlled enterprises that deliver both added value in production and a net fiscal contribution? I will argue that the immediate cause is a profit- and market-oriented management that is *autonomous* in its daily operations, hence insulated against political and bureaucratic predation, and receives *clear incentives* from a strictly limited, *coherent group of high-level principals* in the political regime.

This answer however begs a deeper question: why is such a set-up possible in some, but not in other places? Based on a cross-sectional and, in parts, longitudinal comparison of 11 cases, I find two underlying necessary factors making profit-oriented, insulated rentier SOEs possible: first, the *absence of a populist-mobilizational history of economic development*, and secondly, *substantial decisional autonomy of the regime leadership* from interest groups within state and society.

The chapter seeks to contribute to both the debate about public companies and the debates about rentier states, and the developmental state more broadly. I will show that there are very different types of rentier states, and that some provide political conditions in which the oil *can* be 'sowed' productively through public investment. I will also show that the building of pockets of effectiveness in an otherwise bloated state apparatus can be a politically viable second-best development strategy, if wholesale administrative and public sector reform is not feasible or not desirable politically.

In the framework of the book, the chapter hence addresses specifically the 'why' question about pockets of effectiveness. Although it focuses to some extent on the corporate governance, institutional culture and 'defence mechanisms' of Gulf SOEs in explaining their successes, it sees these factors as critically enabled (although not exhaustively determined) by the larger political economy environment. It therefore corroborates hypothesis 2 from the framework chapter, which places special emphasis on the larger political economy context as influencing effective institutional outcomes – a context that regrettably is hard to change through purposive policy decisions.

The cases: 'traditional' rentier SOEs

The cases included in this chapter are Algeria, Bahrain, Indonesia, Iran, Kuwait, Libya, Nigeria, Qatar, Saudi Arabia, United Arab Emirates, and Venezuela.[3] The list includes *all resource-dependent developing countries that have at some point engaged in ambitious SOE-based industrialization* and diversification drives beyond infrastructure and utility investment.[4] In all cases, only companies with at least majority state ownership are included. The research is largely kept within the rentier universe, not only because the puzzle of successful SOEs is the most striking there. As important, the politics of development in rentier states is arguably subject to somewhat different challenges than in other developing countries: There is an acute imbalance between fiscal and administrative resources and development tends to unfold much more rapidly.

In oil exporters outside of the Gulf, strategies of SOE-based heavy industrialization and import substitution have without exception lived up to the low expectations we would expect on the basis of conventional literature on SOEs (Aharoni 1986; Alessi 1969; Lawson 1994; Kornai 1979; Lin, Cai and Li 1998; Boycko, Shleifer and Vishny 1996; Vernon 1984; Waterbury 1993): In all 6 non-GCC cases SOEs are unprofitable, overstaffed, suffer from corruption, lack managerial autonomy, are politicized, carry huge social overhead, and often cannot set their prices freely.[5]

Very low or – at least as frequently – negative returns are documented for all cases. In the most extreme case of Algeria, net financial flows from government to the SOEs have at times amounted to almost a quarter of GDP.[6] Indonesia is by many measures the 'least bad' non-GCC case, yet in 2006, the total profit of its 139 SOEs was a paltry US$1.56 billion on total assets of US $147 billion (Inusantara Networks 2007).

In all cases, large SOEs have operated under 'soft budget constraints', receiving subsidies throughout decades of deficit. In Iran, some two thirds of the national budget is allocated to SOEs and religious foundations ('bonyads') that command large enterprises. Ambitious attempts to boost non-oil exports through SOEs have faltered without exception. Under public management, Iranian heavy industry capacity has shrunken to the degree that Iran, endowed with the world's second largest hydrocarbon reserves, has to import refined petrol.

Overstaffing and use of SOEs as 'employers of last resort' (Ugorji 1995: 540) is widespread. At the same time, capacity is often underutilized; Algeria used only 35 per cent of its public industrial capacity in the late 1990s (Ruppert 1999: 156). Corruption, both by external principals and management, is rampant and well-documented. While perhaps less surprising in unstable and/ or authoritarian cases like Nigeria, Iran and Algeria, it also reached high levels in democratic Venezuela, where 1970s heavy industry projects became caught up in the distributional politics and business cronyism of governing elites. The corruption scandals of Pertamina, an Indonesian heavy industry conglomerate built up in a few dizzying years in the 1970s, are legendary.

Much in line with existing literature, public sectors in the six cases have suffered from conflicting priorities among political principals, aiming to use SOEs not only as revenue-generators – be it public or private – but also as employment providers, sources of patronage and of subsidized goods. Against this background,

176　*Steffen Hertog*

SOEs – even if autonomous on paper – in fact have little control over strategic decisions. Senior bureaucrats on company boards or sectoral ministries meddle with corporate strategy, be it through price controls, employment regulations, or informal interventions of patronage and rent-seeking.

As effectiveness competes with other targets, these have often come to be represented by different political constituencies. In Libya and Algeria, technocratic and 'revolutionary' factions have squabbled over distributional, effectiveness and efficiency goals, while SOEs in Nigeria are used for competing purposes of regional and ethnic patronage.[7]

But even in the case of more unified political principals, as in Suharto's Indonesia or Chavez's Venezuela, SOEs have been used for political purposes, be it supporting Suharto's high-level crony networks or the lower-class constituencies of Chavez's 'Bolivarian revolution'. Political considerations of one kind or the other have intruded the public sector in all cases.

The majority of the non-Gulf cases are now trying to privatize parts of their public industries, often seeking foreign partners to 'fix' their SOEs. Reform attempts in many cases have come unstuck, however.

Non-Gulf SOEs display most or all of the pathologies we expected. There seems to be not a single example of a large SOE outside of the upstream sector that has consistently delivered solid returns. Taking 'traditional' rentier state public sectors as null hypothesis for our comparison with the Gulf gives us a low baseline indeed.

The cases: Gulf SOEs

Although not all GCC SOEs have been paragons of lean management, the Gulf has seen a number of SOE successes that are unrivalled in the rentier world. The examples discussed in the following section come from Saudi Arabia, Qatar, the UAE and Bahrain (see table 8.1). Kuwait is the one rich GCC country lacking successful SOEs, a fact we will address later.

Several of the large public companies in the Gulf seem to belie the received wisdom about the curse of state ownership. They offer the reverse picture of the above cases, operating under unified government principals, with great day-to-day autonomy in management, and with profit as their main strategic target. They do play a developmental role in terms of technology acquisition, infrastructure-building and, at least in some cases, support for the local private sector that goes beyond pure profit-maximization, and they employ larger shares of nationals than the respective private sectors. Yet they are not abused as corporate charities, and although corruption does occur, it is the exception rather than the rule.[8]

Saudi Arabia controls perhaps the most remarkable Gulf SOE: SABIC (see table 8.1). The company's profit outlook was rated as dim by multinational petrochemical companies when it was created in 1976 with a huge paid-up capital of US$2.7 billion (Middle East Economic Survey, 13 September 1976). It has however produced returns ever since its plants have come on

Table 8.1 The leading successful SOEs in the GCC

Country	Company	Sector, year of founding	2008 profit (in US$)
Saudi Arabia	Saudi Arabian Basic Industries (SABIC)	Heavy industry (esp. chemicals), 1976	5.9b on revenue of 40.3b
Bahrain	Aluminum Bahrain (Alba)	Heavy industry, 1971	376m
Qatar	Qatar Industries	Heavy industry, 2003	2.0b on revenue of 4.1b
Qatar	QTel	Telecoms, 1998	630m on revenue of 5.6b
Bahrain	Batelco	Telecoms, 1981	280m on revenue of 850m
UAE/federal	Etisalat	Telecoms, 1976	2.4b on revenue of 7.1b
UAE/Dubai	Emaar	Real estate, 1997	830m on revenue of 4.4b
UAE/Dubai	Emirates Airlines	Aviation, 1985	270m on revenue of 12.1b*
UAE/Dubai	DP World	Logistics, 1999	530m on revenue of 3.3b

Notes: *2008–09 fiscal year.

stream in the 1980s, remaining profitable throughout market slumps when international chemicals companies incurred losses (various annual reports of SABIC). Its operating margins are higher than those of both of its main rivals, Dow and BASF.[9] Given SABIC's local feedstock advantages, this is explicable. Yet the company is worlds apart from the loss-making heavy industry dinosaurs in resource-rich places as Algeria, Libya and Nigeria. SABIC's 2006 exports alone were about seven times larger than the *total non-oil exports* of Algeria and Nigeria combined.[10]

Drawing on cheap energy and feedstock, other Gulf countries have used their rent surpluses to emulate SABIC's heavy industry success on a smaller scale. As remarkable, several governments own telecoms SOEs that have been expanding rapidly, and profitably, into neighbouring markets and into Asia and Africa, where their home government cannot shelter them. All of them have lost their local monopolies. Dubai moreover has carved out a niche in state-owned transport, logistics and real estate services, all of which are exported across the Middle East and beyond.

Several players such as SABIC, Alba or Emirates have been profitable even during the leanest of times in the 1980s and 1990s, when OPEC went through

178 *Steffen Hertog*

a collective fiscal crisis – more than can be said about any significant rentier SOE outside of the Gulf. The graph in figure 8.1 documents SOE successes for the second half of the 1990s – a time when depressed oil prices put the Gulf economies under severe strain.[11]

The employment structure of the leading SOEs is lean, certainly compared with their non-GCC peers. In the richest GCC countries, this is perhaps explained by the high share of expatriates among workers. Payrolls however are also reasonably lean in the poorer GCC states of Bahrain and Saudi Arabia. In 2007, 85 per cent of SABIC's 17,000 employees were Saudi nationals, yet its workforce relative to its sales volume was considerably smaller than that of its international rivals.[12] SOEs are not subject to civil service regulations, but can hire freely and on a competitive basis.

Gulf SOEs often use international recruitment firms to identify top talent in local markets and have the autonomy to devise attractive packages for their smaller and more selectively recruited staffs. They pay considerably above conventional government salaries – which arguably acts as a disincentive to corruption – and promote the most promising recruits. Much of their training is done either in-house or overseas, i.e. independent of the often mediocre national educational systems of the GCC. Although usually less transparent to the outside, their corporate structures and internal governance resemble these of large, Western corporates, reflecting the GCC's close integration in the international capitalist system and its liberal use of foreign manpower and expertise.

The institutional context

The bulk of GCC bureaucracy is regarded as slow-moving and opaque.[13] What allows the leading SOEs to be so different from their environment? The most obvious and immediate cause seems to be the relationship to their

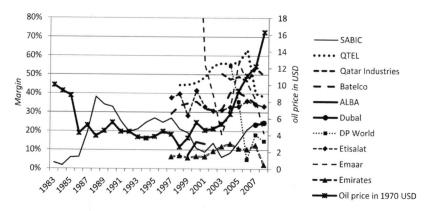

Figure 8.1 Profit margins of selected Gulf SOEs (net income/sales)
Source: Company reports, Reuters Knowledge, Markaz Financial Center.

Successful SOEs in rentier states 179

principals: large and successful SOEs enjoy the direct protection of rulers. Different from most non-GCC cases, the regular administration has little leverage to intervene in their affairs. Instead, SOE-related bodies sometimes hold explicit mandates to cut through existing bureaucracy, as has been the case with the Royal Commission for the Industrial Cities of Jubail and Yanbu in Saudi Arabia, the historical handmaiden of SABIC (interview with former RCJY advisors 2004).

SOEs are usually set up by special decree, and their managers report directly to ruler, crown prince or their close advisers. Senior managers tend to develop long-term relationships of trust with rulers, resulting in higher social status and less personnel fluctuation than in other developing countries (interviews with government advisors, chamber of commerce representatives and high-level bureaucrats in Bahrain, UAE, Qatar and Saudi Arabia, several years; Waterbury 1993: 165). Historically, they have been recruited from local universities, research institutes and the better-functioning parts of the regular civil service: in some cases, senior royals even sent out informal 'talent scouts' to report on promising young technocrats. With the increasing maturity of Gulf SOEs, however, senior managers are usually nurtured internally.

While ruling family members are often present as company chairmen, the CEOs are almost invariably commoners – which makes SOEs different from the remaining state apparatus, in which princes or sheikhs often play a large role (Gause 1994). Corporate boards exist in most cases (although not for the Emirates airline), but are often staffed with generalist bureaucrats with limited expertise and de facto limited say in the corporate affairs of the company, and therefore are often bypassed by senior management and their royal principals.

Hence, different from run-of-the-mill SOEs, Gulf public companies operate under *unified principals* and enjoy *relative managerial autonomy* from the rest of the state. With such status and backing, it has been easier for their managers to keep a consistent focus on generating profits, which is indeed the main task their sheikh principals have given them (interviews with former SABIC and Aramco functionaries and former deputy ministers, Saudi Arabia 2003–8) – different from SOEs elsewhere that are burdened with social and political tasks. Profit targets are publicly announced, as are international sales targets reflecting the outward orientation of Gulf SOEs.

With profits as core target, the leading Gulf SOEs have not only been spared over-inflated payrolls, but also excessive obligations to support local consumers. Given the distributive nature of Gulf regimes, how is this possible? The answer seems to lie in the separation of leading SOEs from the distributional structures of the state. Subsidized consumer prices in the Gulf exist, but they tend to be administered through either producer subsidies or state-supported purchase of imported goods separate from SOEs. Similarly, subsidized housing is guaranteed through special funds rather than through obliging real estate SOEs to sell at a loss.

Thanks to their privileged political status, successful SOEs are also by and large shielded from excessive rent-seeking and predation by senior bureaucrats and minor ruling family members. National oil champion Saudi Aramco and SABIC in particular are perceived as institutional 'fortresses' in a system that is otherwise shot through with rent-seeking, and whose administrative and regulatory capacities are limited. Both have been defending themselves successfully against bureaucratic encroachments and predation by minor royals (interviews with former Saudi bureaucrats and Western oil executives, several years). Their formal status, under which no government 'line agency' has direct control over their operations, contributes to this. At least as important, the chairman of SABIC is a royal with a good marital connection to the king, while the CEO of Saudi Aramco and the Minister of Petroleum and Minerals (himself an old 'Aramcon') also have direct access to the court. Attempts to interfere are referred upwards and are usually repelled by the court, following a long tradition of protecting the kingdom's top assets.

The above model first appeared in Saudi Arabia (Aramco and SABIC) and Bahrain (Alba), and has subsequently spread within countries and across the region, arguably due to demonstration effects. It has however never led to the reform of existing entities along the 'pocket of effectiveness' model, but rather to the creation of new 'pockets' through the rulers' fiat.

GCC systems are certainly not free from corruption and patronage politics. For every effective SOE, there is a white elephant. Aviation, heavy industry, and real estate all have seen monumental failures next to the above-mentioned successes. However, the main resource for large-scale patronage tends to be not public enterprise but rather the national bureaucracy, which in most GCC countries continues to employ more nationals than the private sector.[14] Moreover, large-scale rent-seeking is tolerated, and hence easier to conduct, in areas in which the SOEs usually do not operate, such as 'commercial agencies' in import trade, resale of state lands, ministerial procurement, and trade in visas for expatriate labour (interviews with businessmen in UAE, Bahrain and Saudi Arabia, several years; Field 1984; al-Naqeeb 1990; Holden and Johns 1981; Hertog 2010b). When Dubai's ruler Mohammad bin Rashed attempted to increase his stock holding in Emaar through a swap of state land against shares in 2007, this caused a lively debate among investors which led him to abandon the project lest Emaar's international reputation suffer (IHT, 27 August 2007; interviews with Dubai businessmen and government advisors several years). In the 1980s, Saudi King Fahd protected the management of newly nationalized Aramco against a takeover by the inefficient national oil bureaucracy (discussions with Ministry of Petroleum and Aramco representatives; Jaffe and Elass 2007).

GCC rentier administrations carry similar burdens and suffer from similar ailments that characterize resource-rich regimes elsewhere (Chaudhry 1997; Crystal 1990; al-Naqeeb 1990; Hertog 2010b) – but the profit-oriented bits of their public sectors are shielded from these pressures. They constitute pockets of effectiveness markedly at odds with the rest of the state, unaffected by the overstaffed and unresponsive rentier bureaucracies surrounding them. This compartmentalization seems unique to the GCC.

Unified principals and *relative managerial autonomy* seem to be the immediate causes explaining Gulf SOE successes. But if these causes are relatively easy to detect at closer inspection, why have not more rentier regimes been able to bring about these conditions? On the face of it, every ruler should be interested in profit-generating public assets. Something else must be at work. The next section will address this puzzle: what are the broader conditions that have allowed Gulf elites, but not elites in other oil-rich countries, to set up the institutional framework described above?

Explanations

In no case at hand have *all* SOEs been successful. There is unlikely to be a fully sufficient explanation of success which is not to some extent case-specific: there will always be idiographic factors leading to failure even under auspicious circumstances. Conversely, however, a significant number of rentier countries have seen no successes at all, whatever the vagaries of personality, elite rivalry and chance. Something systematic seems to be at work: it appears that these cases have lacked certain conditions which might not be sufficient, but necessary for SOE success. The following section therefore will look for enabling causes which have allowed SOE success in the Gulf, while not guaranteeing it, and whose absence has prevented SOE success in other cases.

A number of obvious candidates are quickly ruled out: levels of rent dependence are similar across successful and failed cases. Per capita rent levels are generally higher in the GCC, but have varied greatly over time, reaching lows at times of successful SOE development in the 1980s that were below rent levels witnessed in other countries with failed SOE experiments in the 1970s. All of the GCC states pursued import substitution strategies like their OPEC peers, and all countries, GCC or not, tried to leverage Western technology and advisors in the process.

Costly populism

While ISI strategies cut across all cases, there is another, more ideological facet of economic strategy that is not shared by all: economic populism, as defined by the political use of distribution in the economic development process.

Economic populism as understood here means *political use of economic resources to mobilize support from* what are perceived as previously *marginalized classes*, newly recruited as support bases for the regime. Often tied up with *rhetoric of 'social justice'* and a *distrust of elites* (domestic or foreign), it gives economic policy a strong (re)distributional component. Productive assets become part of a nation-building exercise and assume a *direct* role in redistribution; economic populism conflates production and distribution. This can mean controlled consumer prices or the provision of extensive social services, but also direct state interventions to create employment. In its more radical variants, economic populism can aim for a refashioning of class structures, but this is not necessarily the case.[15]

It bears highlighting that economic populism is more than just patronage: its use of distribution to create organized, actively mobilized lower and middle class political support, its egalitarian rhetoric, and its anti-elite bias give it particular features absent from other patronage systems, notably those of the GCC.

Whatever the rhetoric, the effect of populism on public sectors tends to be more dramatic than that on class hierarchies. The central role of distributional and (purportedly) egalitarian considerations in populist economic policy has led to the kinds of target conflicts and compromised managerial autonomy that have brought about the failure of SOEs in non-Gulf rentier states. Economic populism explains the pervasive manipulation of prices, overemployment and welfare tasks imposed on SOEs, all of which make a clear focus on profit almost impossible to maintain, and usually necessitate the relaxation of budget constraints. As another near-necessary corollary, the imposition of overarching, politically determined, system-wide distributional goals on managers of specific enterprises compromises their operational autonomy, subjecting them to the influence of bureaucratic principals (see figure 8.2).

Numerous developing countries have gone through extended phases of economic populism, among them four of the cases at hand: Algeria, Iran, Libya, and Venezuela. In all of these, the immediate causes of SOE failure are best understood as symptoms of a broader populist regime strategy.

The four cases are a very mixed bunch, including a populist Latin American state that has been democratic for most of its post-WWII history, a revolutionary Islamic theocracy, a post-colonial bureaucratic-military regime, and a highly personalized oil dictatorship with tribal accoutrements. If there is one cross-cutting theme in the political science literature on them, it is the identification of politics and regimes at critical junctures as populist, mixing redistributional strategies with 'third worldist' rhetoric.[16]

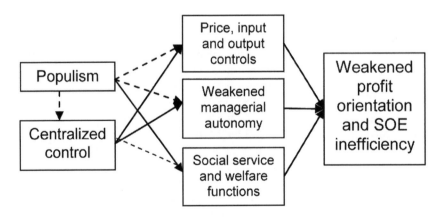

Figure 8.2 Populism and central administrative control of SOEs

Successful SOEs in rentier states 183

In all four cases, SOEs have been set up and/or operated in order to benefit populist political constituencies. State-controlled means of production have been at the core of a transformative, or at least redistributive, socio-economic strategy. In the three more radical cases of Algeria, Iran and Libya, public sectors have played an explicit role as instruments for building a new state and society, through creating and empowering new classes and social identities to transcend old elite structures. While such grand transformative visions are harder to detect in the populist clientelism of 1970s and 1980s Venezuela,[17] Chavez' populism, and use of SOEs, is closely in line with a transformative vision of state and society.

As SOEs have become tools to support specific social strata, profits in the four cases have become a secondary consideration, subordinate to redistributive concerns accompanied by a rhetoric of economic nationalism, distrust of old elites and social justice. The latter concern is used to explicitly justify both broad-based (over-) employment policies serving specific social strata – e.g. the 'oppressed' in Iran's bonyads and revolutionary veterans in Algeria's bloated industrial concerns – and price controls.

The redistributive agenda is also reflected in wages above market levels, extensive social services for employees and families, as well as egalitarian pay schemes – the latter very different from the GCC cases. Although technically empowered to do so, Algerian SOEs have not dared to deviate from the civil service pay scale (World Bank 1994: 81f.). In all cases, SOEs have at various points seen experiments with workers' self-management, prioritizing class empowerment over stable management. SOE workers are often unionized, with unions representing a powerful lobby group in line with the regimes' redistributional ideology.

Economic populism is more than mere patronage: drawing on anti-elitist rhetoric, it implies the targeted mass political mobilization of 'marginalized' classes and uses SOEs to rectify perceived social injustice. It is part of a larger ideological project. It explains not only SOE failure per se, but also accounts for a number of very specific characteristics thereof. Even when radical steps like nationalization and workers' co-management were eschewed, socially motivated employment structures, workers' politicization, price controls and welfare provision by SOEs have been a direct outcome of populist mobilization. Across the board, these structures have led to major inefficiencies, soft budget constraints, and – in the guise of imposed prices and welfare targets – strongly reduced managerial autonomy in public enterprises. It stands to reason that mixed performance aims have also widened opportunities for corruption.

Conversely, Gulf SOEs have operated in an ideological and institutional environment that in many regards is the opposite of populist. Although distribution plays a large role in the politics of the Gulf monarchies, this is paternal and conservative in nature rather than mobilizational. GCC regimes have been politically quietist, conservative on matters of class structure and openly pro-business (Luciani 2005; Henry and Springborg 2001; Niblock 2007).

184   *Steffen Hertog*

Avoiding the revolutions and military coups that most other Middle East monarchies experienced, the GCC has never gone through a phase of populist mobilization. Instead, Gulf rulers have tried to prevent the formation and organization of domestic lower classes, not least through their policy of large-scale labour imports. Unions have been prohibited in most Gulf states for most of their history, and rulers have tried to develop a paternal, Islamically coloured conservatism as a counter-model to the populist Arab nationalism that seemed to threaten their survival in the 1960s and 1970s (Holden and Johns 1981; Yizraeli 1997; Davidson 2008; al-Naqeeb 1990).

Patronage policies in the GCC have never aimed at the empowerment of subordinate classes or the deliberate refashioning of the socio-economic hierarchy, and they have been much less directly linked with the prevailing ideology of economic development. Economic strategy as reflected in regime statements and planning documents was never tied up with egalitarian rhetoric. Industry has not been a tool of political mobilization. GCC economic planning has therefore not automatically been infused with considerations of redistribution.

This explains why, instead of using all their productive assets for wholesale distributional 'empowerment' as in the populist cases, GCC regimes have often used institutions not involved in production for the provision of free jobs to nationals of all classes, as outlined above (Beblawi 1987; International Labour Organization 1994). Different from populist leaders, GCC regimes apparently were under no illusion that all good things – patronage, redistribution and productive economic development – would go together.

Gulf elites have gone to much greater lengths to keep distributional and economic policies, i.e. the administration of productive assets, separate. This anti-populist separation of state functions explains why they could give much clearer incentives for select SOEs to be profitable.

Presence or absence of populist economics seems more important in explaining sectoral successes and failures than ISI or state ownership as such. Waterbury has argued that the distributional role of developing world SOEs tends to dwarf their economic role, and that ISI has an 'inclusionist' bent (Waterbury 1993: 2, 25, 193). He seems to conflate different issues here, however. Waterbury happens to have studied four developing countries that have all gone through pronounced phases of economic populism. Moreover, as far as there was significant ideological change, SOE performance seems to have deteriorated the most during the most populist phases (Turkey and Mexico in the 1970s, and India before Indira Gandhi's state of emergency, as documented in Waterbury's own account). It is not ISI per se, but the combination of ISI and economic populism – in which distributional considerations are deeply entangled with economic development strategy – that leads to large-scale SOE failures.

Our explanation thus far seems to provide a good fit with the evidence both cross-sectionally and in terms of the internal logic of our cases. Still, it does leave a number of anomalies. First, there have been widespread SOE failures in two cases that do not have a distinctly populist history: Indonesia and

Successful SOEs in rentier states 185

Nigeria. One might explain this away with bad luck, ham-fisted leadership or other ideographic factors. Another problem is that several of the populist cases have entered 'post-populist' phases of rule, in which they have failed to convincingly reform existing SOEs or set up new, profitable structures. But perhaps populist legacies are simply too difficult to overcome.

A more serious anomaly is that one very well-endowed and non-populist GCC state has failed in all of its major SOE undertakings: Kuwait. The Kuwaiti regime is pro-capitalist and similar to the rest of the GCC in many regards. Given the availability of Kuwaiti resources, and the number of failed projects, it appears unlikely that the failure is pure coincidence. How could it be explained?

Accounting for most of the above anomalies, I will argue in the following section that there is a further necessary condition required for a successful SOE strategy to be enacted: the regime in question needs to enjoy substantial autonomy in economic decision-making.

SOEs and regime autonomy

For our purposes, autonomy is defined by a *coherent regime core that can make economic decisions independent of larger interest groups* within state and society.[18] In other words, a small number of reasonably unified leaders can set SOE-related allocative strategies reasonably freely and select teams that implement them accordingly. The section will first discuss non-GCC cases with low regime autonomy, then the GCC, then the important exception of Kuwait.

Before engaging with the anomalous cases mentioned above, it should be noted that Venezuela in its classic urban-populist phase from the 1960s to the 1980s probably combined economic populism with a lack of regime autonomy. Due to the competitive electoral nature of Venezuelan politics, 'political party and state leaders needed to accommodate the growing factions of the populist coalition' (Di John 2006: 55). Populist distribution, it seems, was not only part of the regime's economic development strategy, but also an immediate necessity of political survival. The cronyism ('amiguismo' [Karl 1997: 147]) in large cement and petrochemical projects of the 1970s seems to reflect tight informal networks of regime support that compromised regime manoeuvrability.

The authoritarian regimes in Algeria, Iran and Libya arguably were more independent of societal clienteles when they first started their ambitious SOE projects.[19] By the time the Algerian and Iranian regimes revisited their populist developmental tenets, however, their very own public sector strategies had created new vested interests constraining their policy-making manoeuvrability.[20]

Like many other Middle Eastern regimes, Algeria started revising its generous populist policies from the 1980s on, fiscally squeezed by the post-1986 oil crisis and the large deficits of its SOE sector (Ehteshami and Murphy 1996; World Bank 1994). Reform attempts, including an ambitious privatization program, however, have progressed very slowly (World Bank 1994;

Werenfels 2002). A number of interest groups seem to be responsible, all of which came into being through the regime's own public sector strategy. These have included unions – enjoying a veto over any redundancies (Ruppert 1999) – SOE management and, more important, a bureaucratic and military lobby profiting from SOE-related structures of protection and subsidization. The Algerian regime, politically fragmented by the 1990s, has lacked a clear decision-making centre and been reluctant to revoke distributional entitlements (Cheriet 1992; Werenfels 2002). Reform has progressed haltingly, as populist regime building seems to have created its own vested interests (World Bank 1994; World Bank 2003b).

Similar to Algeria, Iran has suffered from a post-populist fiscal hangover since the 1980s oil price collapse. When moderate conservative Rafsanjani became president, the government attempted to trim down SOEs and planned for privatization (Oxford Analytica, 18 May 1992). Most SOE reform attempts have been unsuccessful: bonayds have largely managed to defend their privileges, including virtually tax-free status (Oxford Analytica, 18 July 2002), and operate independently of the cabinet (Saeidi 2001). Neither Rafsanjani nor his reformist successor Khatami could exert sufficient leverage over a parastatal sector dominated by revolutionary militants catering to a large lower-class clientele. Populist-distributional SOE strategies have led to a fragmentation of interests in the Iranian state apparatus (Maloney 2000). Privatization policies have remained stuck since the 1990s (Oxford Analytica, various reports).[21]

One might argue that reform of inefficient populist SOE legacies is a different process from the creation and preservation of effective structures, which is the main subject of this article. Perhaps a more important question is therefore whether infringed state autonomy can explain the failure to *create and maintain* effective SOEs in the non-populist cases at hand, among them Nigeria and Kuwait. Nigeria is one non-Gulf rentier state without a clear record of organized economic populism (Bienen 1985; Bevan, Gunning and Collier 1999; Lewis 1992; Lewis 2007). It seems that its state structure was too underdeveloped, its society too plural and its regimes too brittle to allow for a coordinated, large-scale campaign of lower-class mobilization and inclusion.

So why have successive Nigerian regimes been incapable of converting oil surpluses into productive, insulated SOE structures? The answer seems to have much to do with the very weaknesses just outlined: with frequent coups and changes in government – 7 heads of state alone were deposed or assassinated between 1966 and 1993 – there has not been a coherent regime core that would have been sufficiently independent of various supporting groups in society to pursue a long-term development strategy.

Nigerian regimes have been deeply penetrated by social interests and, in the interest of survival, been compelled to use the SOE sector for wide-scale discretionary patronage to different bureaucratic, regional and ethnic interest groups, to the extent that very little money was left for infrastructure (Bienen

Successful SOEs in rentier states 187

1985; Ugorji 1995; Bevan, Gunning and Collier 1999). Public sector management has been inconsistent due to its deep politicization and capture by narrow interest groups (Lewis 2007; APS Review Downstream Trends, 13 August 2007). Nigeria seems to be a typical example of a kleptocratic state lacking autonomy (Evans 1995).

In contrast to the above cases, GCC oil regimes have had, and continue to have, very different relationships with the interest groups surrounding them. All the ruling families had to strike political deals with local merchant groups in the pre-oil age in return for taxes or loans. The severe underdevelopment of pre-oil societies, however, meant that large-scale oil income rapidly made the incipient oil states fiscally autonomous from local society and endowed them with unprecedented power (Chaudhry 1997; Crystal 1990; Gause 1994).

As mentioned above, conservative monarchical rule meant that classes were never politically mobilized in a top-down fashion: ruling families rather put a premium on political quiescence, working to keep society vertically divided and state-dependent (al-Naqeeb 1990; Crystal 1990; Khalaf 2003; Hertog 2010b). At the same time, basic coherence of the ruling family cores was maintained through elaborate intra-family deals, usually struck in the course of negotiations over succession (Herb 1999). These have allowed the perpetuation of a clear status hierarchy between ruling family and the rest of the bureaucracy, which is a mere functional appendix of the rulers without specific ideological legitimacy, political support bases or resources of political organization (Hertog 2010b).[22] Public sector unions are outlawed everywhere but Kuwait.

Oppositionist movements in most countries after the onset of oil, and especially since the 1970s boom, have been absent or purely ephemeral phenomena (Vitalis 2007; Davidson 2005; Gause 1994; Byman and Green 1999) while business soon became utterly state-dependent (Chaudhry 1997; Crystal 1990; Gause 1994). The Gulf has seen decades of non-politics, with hardly any formally organized interests in society.

With the exception of Bahrain, post-oil GCC history has seen no mass political movements: state and bureaucracy have dominated the scene. Even today, political life in most GCC societies remains remarkably anaemic: participation rates in elections, if any are held, usually are very low, public demonstrations are rare, and institutional reform initiatives are driven from the top, eliciting little resonance in society (Oxford Analytica, 14 August 2007; Kapiszewski 2008; Ehteshami and Wright 2007).

There are only two countries with lively civil societies that aspire to independence from the government: Bahrain and Kuwait. Bahrain has a much larger domestic working class than the other GCC states and has had a strong tradition of bottom-up labour activism since the 1930s, which has been blended with Shiite political mobilization after the 1970s. This activism has been harshly suppressed by the large police apparatus of the pro-business conservative ruling family, however, thus preserving the regime's political manoeuvrability (Lawson 1989; Khalaf 2003; Niethammer 2006). Significantly, unions are thus far only allowed in the private sector.

188   *Steffen Hertog*

The political weakness of independently organized interest groups inside and outside of the state does not mean that GCC regimes are not compelled to spend considerable resources on patronage to keep various large if disorganized strata in society happy. But how this is done is up to the leadership: there are no labour, bureaucratic or other interest groups that can exert a veto over major institutional decisions, as has been the case in Iran or Algeria. This has given the GCC regimes considerable discretion in their allocative policies during crucial phases of increasing state income, allowing the dedication of different parts of the state to very different purposes.

Waterbury describes how political coalition maintenance has damaged the productivity of developing country SOEs (Waterbury 1993: 119, 190). In the GCC, coalitions – or rather socio-economic clienteles – are managed elsewhere. Gulf SOEs are much less tied up with vested distributional interests than public enterprises in Iran, Algeria, or Nigeria, and there are no strong organized groups to lay claim to them. Instead, they are managed by small teams directly subordinate to the leadership: other bureaucratic principals have no purchase over them.

The comparative evidence for regime autonomy as a necessary condition for SOE success thus far is weaker than that for populism. We have found economic populism as a clear, recurring 'type', a constellation of factors, among otherwise very different cases. Lack of regime autonomy by contrast can have many different facets and is less easy to pin down. All of the comparisons above are imperfect: Algeria and Iran dealt with SOE rehabilitation rather than SOE creation and maintenance, and the Nigerian state suffers from many other problems in addition to low autonomy. Indeed, these cases are so different from the GCC that the comparison is weak. To really prove the point, a more similar case is needed.

This case is Kuwait. Among the five rich GCC states that have tried to engage in SOE-driven diversification, Kuwait is the one salient failure. And although as pro-capitalist as the other cases, it is the one regime that has been much less autonomous in economic decision-making. Different from all other GCC cases, the Kuwaiti leadership has been under strong pressures from electoral politics and organized bureaucratic interests, which it has not been able to contain.

Kuwait has the longest parliamentary tradition in the GCC, going back to pre-oil national assemblies in the 1920s and 1930s, and a 'primus inter pares' status of the ruling family that distinguishes it much less clearly from other local clans than is the case in the rest of the Gulf. Parliament nowadays represents a well-organized middle class, which has far greater organizational freedom than civil society in any other Gulf state (Tétreault 2000; Crystal 1990; Gause 1994; Koch 2000; Herb 2009).

Parliament can force individual ministers to resign and can veto the government's legislative initiatives. In recent decades, parliamentary politics – not directly accountable for government performance, as the cabinet is recruited by the ruler – have acquired a fiscally reckless character, forcing salary increases in the public sector and direct hand-outs to Kuwaiti citizens on the reluctant government in order to pander to the electorate (Oxford Analytica,

28 March 2008; IHT, 6 May 2008). At the same time, many of the government's economic reform initiatives, several of them related to existing or new SOEs, have come unstuck in parliament, as they seemed to threaten domestic distributional interests (see Herb 2009; Arab Times, 8 March 2008; Financial Times, 17 March 2008; Arabian Business, 26 December 2007).

The government has for years tried to get several Dubai-inspired infrastructure and logistics projects started. All of them have suffered severe delays, as issues of local participation and employment have been contentious in parliament. Project Kuwait, an attempt to get international oil companies to invest in new oil fields in partnership with Kuwait Petroleum, has been mired in parliamentary politics for about a dozen years, with MPs trying to defend employment privileges for nationals in the oil sector, and interests of local firms in upstream contracting (Oxford Analytica, 8 May 2001, 9 October 2003; Christian Science Monitor, 16 March 2006). Similarly, plans to convert Boubyan Island into a Dubai-style logistics hub have faltered over political bickering. The parliament only agreed on the privatization of Kuwait Airways, the badly loss-making national carrier, in January 2008, twelve years after the company first pleaded for a sell-off (Reuters, 9 January 2008; Arab Times, 5 June 2008).

Public sector labour has been an important coalition partner in the parliament's veto policies: employees of Kuwait Airways are unionized and have gone on strike against privatization and for higher wages (Kuwait Times, 12 November 2007, 8 May 2008). National labour in heavy industry SOEs has played a similar role in perpetuating bloated structures. Kuwaiti petrochemicals in the public sector have made losses over many years. Overemployment and lack of incentives have played an important role, as senior management find it difficult to sanction workers. The latter, again, are unionized and can complain to ministers or MPs if they feel mistreated (Tétreault 1995; interviews with Kuwaiti oil sector technocrats 2009). As in many countries in the wider Middle East, but different from its GCC neighbours, organized labour in Kuwait has been a staunch defender of ineffective SOE structures: the Kuwaiti public sector has failed to build up technocratic expertise over the years (The National [UAE], 4 June 2008).

Privatization, Project Kuwait and other initiatives have all been seen as threatening national privileges of Kuwaitis, and have therefore been fought against by parliament and public sector interest groups (AMEINFO, 4 July 2006). Different from all its oil-rich GCC neighbours, Kuwait has not managed to set up a single large-scale, profitable, publicly owned heavy industry project. The one successful, mid-size petrochemicals project ('Equate') is a joint venture with majority involvement by local and foreign businesses – thereby insulated against parliamentary and public sector politics.[23] While political principals in other GCC states have been able to act in a unified fashion thanks to their relative independence of vested interests, the administration of the Kuwaiti public sector has become caught up in infighting between government, parliament, bureaucratic interest groups and the public.

190   *Steffen Hertog*

Table 8.2 SOE successes and failures: overview

	Nonpopulist	*Autonomous*	*Successful SOEs*
GCC cases			
Bahrain	yes	yes	yes
Kuwait	yes	no	no
Qatar	yes	yes	yes
Saudi Arabia	yes	yes	yes
United Arab Emirates	yes	yes	yes
Non-GCC cases			
Algeria precrash	no	yes	no
Algeria postcrash	yes	no	no
Indonesia	yes	yes	no
Iran precrash	no	yes	no
Iran postcrash	yes	no	no
Libya	no	yes	no
Nigeria	yes	no	no
Venezuela pre-Chavez	no	no	no
Venezuela under Chavez	no	yes	no
Auxiliary cases			
Egypt precrash	no	yes	no
Egypt postcrash	yes	no	no
Syria precrash	no	yes	no
Syria postcrash	no	no	no
Mexico precrash	no	yes	no
Mexico postcrash	yes	yes	yes (divestiture)
Suriname	yes	yes	no

The combination of non-populist politics and a high degree of regime autonomy provides the best explanation for the success of GCC SOEs, and the comprehensive failures elsewhere. Moving beyond case histories, the two necessary factors provide a remarkably good cross-sectoral fit for all cases under consideration (see table 8.2).[24]

The combination of factors might not only be at work among semi-rentiers,[25] but also outside of the rentier realm, as indicated by SOE successes under cohesive, non-populist authoritarian regimes like pre-1990s Taiwan, and post-Deng China. Yet, among non-rentier systems, there appear to be alternative channels to successful SOEs, as evidenced by the Brazilian and Chilean democracies, both of which command impressive public enterprises. The tension between distributional politics and development appears to be less stark in non-rentier democracies than in participatory rentier states like Kuwait.

Conclusion

SOE politics are complicated and contingent. The stylized facts presented in this article do not allow for firm predictions of what a specific rentier SOE is going to look like. Elite agency and historical context cannot be modelled in the abstract. By the same token, however, existing literature on public sectors and rentier bureaucracies has also painted with too broad a brush in predicting universal failure.

By keeping politically motivated distribution and profit-oriented economic planning separate, non-populist rentier elites can provide space for profit-oriented management. Moreover, if they are reasonably coherent and politically autonomous from major economic interest groups, they can protect techno-crats and their mandate over time. In this sense, the politically fragmented and quiescent GCC societies have provided the ideal environment for the creation of insulated SOEs.

Gulf SOEs show that rent inflows do not automatically lead to institutional stagnation or decay, as 'resource curse' theorists have posited. Which institu-tions are built with oil money instead strongly depends on political circum-stances, and some circumstances lend themselves to a developmental strategy built on pockets of effectiveness.

GCC ruling elites appear to have adopted some features of the Asian developmental state within a broader institutional context that is decidedly non-developmental. While economically this might be a second-best strategy, it is arguably politically optimal for ruling families, allowing the parallel pur-suit of patronage and economic diversification – an option that is particularly attractive in an environment of (at least temporarily) lax resource constraints.

There are many signs that GCC states contain 'pockets of effectiveness' also outside of the SOE sector (Hertog 2010b), and it is likely that the cir-cumstances leading to their emergence are quite similar to what has been argued here. They still await systematic comparative investigation, however this book will contribute important comparative context for such endeavours.

Notes

1 This chapter is an abridged and adapted version of an article of the same title that has appeared in *World Politics* (Hertog 2010a).
2 Although the country cases under study also have non-SOE pockets of effective-ness, these are not discussed, as measurement of their institutional qualities is more difficult in a medium-n research design.
3 It is too early to judge GCC member Oman: it is on the road to heavy indus-trialization, but its large projects are only just about to come on stream.
4 Iraq, which started an ambitious industrialization strategy in the 1970s, is excluded as it has been in an almost perpetual state of war since 1980. In any case, its overstaffed and ineffective SOE sector has been and remains similar to those of its non-GCC peers. As the latter, it now seems on the way to partial sell-offs. Russia is a semi-rentier whose SOE sector is still so strongly determined by the Soviet legacy that it is a case sui generis. After recent renationalizations, the jury on its rejuvenated SOEs is still out.
5 The section draws on reports from Oxford Analytica, Economist Intelligence Unit and Oxford Business Group, international newspapers, oil and industry trade journals, and the reference work by Amuzegar (1999). Further main sources include: [Algeria] Entelis (1999); Werenfels (2002); Ruppert (1999); World Bank (1994); World Bank (2003b). [Indonesia] Bevan, Gunning, and Collier (1999);

192 Steffen Hertog

Barnes (1995); Bresnan (1993); Inusantara Networks (2007); Lewis (2007). [Iran] Karbassian (2000); Karshenas (1990); Maloney (2000); Saeidi (2001). [Libya] Naur (1986); Vandewalle (1986); Vandewalle (1998); World Bank (2006). [Nigeria] Bienen (1985); Lewis (1992); Lewis (1994); Nwokeji (2007); Onoh (1983); Ugorji (1995). [Venezuela] Di John (2006); Karl (1997); Mares and Altamirando (2007).

6 Data from World Bank Bureaucrats in Business data base.

7 It is too early to judge the future of public enterprise in post-Qaddafi Libya. Given the revolutionary state's rudimentary capacities, it is unlikely that SOEs will be quickly or easily depoliticized however.

8 The following section is based on interviews and discussions with GCC bureaucrats, businessmen and expatriates during field research stints since 2003 in the UAE, Bahrain, Qatar, Kuwait and Saudi Arabia, a daily press survey of 14 Gulf newspapers since 2003, and official company and auditors' reports.

9 Pre-tax profits and sales for 2008 are US$1.3b/57.5b (Dow), US$6.0b/62.3b (BASF) and US$6.3b/40.3b (SABIC) (annual reports).

10 Calculated from World Bank Development Indicators, SABIC reports.

11 Most of the figures here go back to the point when companies were first publicly listed. As Dubai's Dubal and Bahrain's Alba are not publicly traded, only sporadic numbers are available. Alba however reported to have been consistently profitable since its creation in 1971, and has been consistently expanding (see Project Finance International no. 263, 16 April 2003). The same is true about pre-1997 Emirates airline, where profit figures (but not turnover/margins) are available for various pre-97 years.

12 http://www.sabic.com/corporate/en/career/peopleatsabic/default.aspx (accessed in July 2008); BASF and Dow employed 95,000 and 46,000 workers respectively.

13 GCC states score significantly worse than non-oil cases with similar GDP per capita on various measures of 'governance' contained in the World Bank Governance Indicators (author's calculation).

14 This share of publicly employed nationals is far above the average of both developed and developing countries (International Labour Organization, *World Labour Report*, various issues). Resulting problems in bureaucratic performance are akin to what one might have expected for SOEs. On declining public sector productivity, see Girgis and Diwan (2002).

15 There is a wide debate about the definition of populism as a form of political rule which I cannot engage with here (Weyland 2001; Ayubi 1992; Dornbusch and Edwards 1991; Ellner 2003). My working definition here is limited to a specific and recognizable style of politically motivated economic policy.

16 In addition to sources already cited, this section draws on Cheriet (1992); Malley (1996); Hooglund (1992); Bayat (1983); Behdad (2000); Davis (1987); Hawkins (2003); Levine (1973); Karl (1986).

17 While pre-Chavez Venezuelan politics has been more bourgeois than in the other three cases, leading parties have clearly pursued populist themes of economic nationalism and have served a specific lower-to middle class clientele in the public sector. Broad-based socio-economic inclusion has been prioritized over effective management of SOEs; Di John (2006); Karl (1997).

18 The definition is inspired by Evans' discussion of the developmental state (Evans 1995). Different from him and later authors such as Chibber and Kohli, I am less interested in the state's links to business, and more interested in the corporate coherence of senior decision-makers vis-à-vis not only society, but also the rest of bureaucracy (see Chibber 2003 and Kohli 2004).

19 Both Algeria and Libya had underdeveloped class structures, and a strong military regime enjoying high levels of autonomy thanks to growing external income (Davis 1987; Henry 2004). Iran is the case on which the idea of rentier state autonomy was first developed (Mahdavy 1970).

20 For a similar argument on developmental states, see Evans (1995).

21 Different from Algeria and Iran, Libya has only very recently started to seriously contemplate economic reform. Its reforms so far have been halting.
22 While ministers from the ruling family are seldom reshuffled, technocrats are often sacked unceremoniously. In Saudi Arabia, moreover, princes in junior ranks are treated with much more deference than formally senior bureaucrats.
23 The contrast is further underlined by the fact that Kuwait has a number of very successful companies in sectors in which Dubai's SOEs have excelled, but all of which are outside of the public sector. Kuwaiti logistics company Agility is a regional leader, as is telecoms giant Zain/MTC. The latter relocated from Kuwait to Bahrain in 2007, citing the bad regulatory environment in Kuwait.
24 The table is broadly inspired by Charles Ragin's qualitative comparative methods. I have settled on crisp coding as real-world cases fit rather neatly into dichotomous categories (Ragin 2000). Note that Indonesia's failure to build successful SOEs is not at variance with the theory advanced here, which is about necessary rather than sufficient drivers of success. Contingent factors like the availability of a substantial local bourgeoisie and foreign investment might have allowed Suharto to use public industry primarily as an instrument of patronage, even if he could have chosen to build pockets of effectiveness.
25 For a more detailed discussion of the cases in table 8.2, see Hertog (2010a).

Interviews

Discussions with Ministry of Petroleum and Aramco representatives in Riyadh, 2007.
Interviews with former RCJY advisors, Riyadh and London, 2004.
Interviews with government advisors, chamber of commerce representatives and high-level bureaucrats in Bahrain, UAE, Qatar and Saudi Arabia, several years.
Interviews with former SABIC and Aramco functionaries and former deputy ministers; Saudi Arabia, 2003–8.
Interviews with former Saudi bureaucrats and Western oil executives, several places and years.
Interviews with businessmen in UAE, Bahrain and Saudi Arabia, several years.
Interviews with Dubai businessmen and government advisors, Dubai, February 2009.
Interviews with Kuwaiti oil sector technocrats, Kuwait, February 2009.

9 Comparative analysis
Deciphering pockets of effectiveness

Michael Roll

This chapter answers our four research questions. It does so based on the comparative analysis of the case studies. The focus is on the processes and mechanisms through which pockets of effectiveness (PoE) emerge and persist, as well as the necessary conditions under which they do so. By comparing our findings to results from another recent study of institutions and PoE in developing countries, we undertake a first test of their generalizability.[1] We also discuss the potential of PoE for triggering more comprehensive public sector reform, what they teach us about externally induced public sector reform programmes and finally the impact of PoE on state-society relations more generally. Since the generation of middle range theoretical concepts and explanations from which further research hypotheses can be derived is a main aim of this study, we engage in brief theoretical discussions throughout this chapter.

We reassert our methodological remarks from the introduction, that the conditions or factors we identify in this comparative analysis are *necessary*, not *sufficient* conditions. We expect our model and explanations to apply in developing countries with strong heads of state, weak public service delivery and a high degree of personalization of the politico-administrative system in which the relevance of formal rules and laws is at best uneven (see chapter 2). Furthermore, the type of PoE that we focus on is the result of deliberate and targeted top-down political decisions and actions, and does not emerge as a niche of 'subcultural bureaucracy' (see McConnell 2012) from within the administration.

Our distinctions between the various factors, as well as between the answers to our four research questions, are analytical. They are based on the qualitative coding and analysis of the data. While we argue that these distinctions are useful, in some cases they may seem abstract and artificial. If this is the case, we urge the reader to go back to the case studies where the empirical descriptions are 'thicker' than they can be in this comparative analytical chapter.

Why do pockets of effectiveness emerge?

The PoE in our sample emerged partly as the result of deliberate top-down political decisions. In light of this, a full answer to *why* PoE emerge has to include at least three elements: the motivations behind the decision to create a PoE, the decisions themselves and the conditions under which these decisions are taken. Table 9.1 summarizes the main drivers behind establishing or reforming the respective public organizations in our study, their main driving motivations and the relevance of international influence.[2] It is apparent that very different actors or groups of actors served as main drivers, and that their respective motivations were equally diverse. Moreover, the relevance and form of the international influence in each of the cases varied strongly.

Given the diversity of both the main drivers and their motivations for lobbying for or establishing the public organizations that later became PoE, we have to narrow down the first part of our answer to what all cases have in common. Abstracting from the original drivers behind PoE and their motivations, we argue that it is *the political or personal interest of the head of state in the effective execution of a particular task that allows the public organization that is mandated with executing this task to emerge as a PoE*[3]. Due to the

Table 9.1 Factors behind the establishment of pockets of effectiveness

Organization (country)	Main drivers	Motivations	International influence*
Sino-Foreign Salt Inspectorate (Republican China)	Foreign banks	Assured credit repayment	Executing
Joint Commission on Rural Reconstruction (Republican China/Taiwan)	Chinese & U.S. experts	Ending governmental neglect of rural population, promoting rural development	Instrumental & supportive
National Bank for Economic Development (Brazil)	President	Nationalist developmental ideology	Instrumental & supportive
National Agency for Food and Drug Administration and Control (Nigeria)	President	Country's and personal international reputation, improving life of citizens	Supportive & pressuring
National Agency for the Prohibition of Traffic in Persons etc. (Nigeria)	Vice president's wife	Anger about suffering caused by trafficking, country's international reputation	Supportive & pressuring
State Oil Company of Suriname (Suriname)	Oil Commission	Engage successfully with foreign companies, nationalist military development agenda	Indirect
Several (several, Middle East)	Rulers	Sustained source of income (profit on investment)	Indirect

Note: *Degrees of influence in order of decreasing importance: *executing, instrumental, supportive, pressuring, indifferent, opposed, indirect*.

196 *Michael Roll*

powerful position of the heads of state in our case studies, without their interest in the execution of the organization's task and their support, no 'driver' could have succeeded in establishing a public organization. This part of our answer refers to the interaction of the task that a public organization performs and the specific interest of the head of state at a given point in time as an explanation for why PoE emerge. Both what that task is, and why the head of state has an interest in its execution at a particular point in time, remain empirical questions that have to be examined in the respective context. While this first part of our answer is relatively abstract, we can get more specific than that. After discussing the theoretical implications of the diversity of motivations behind the establishment of PoE, we turn to the second part of our answer to the 'why' question and specify three conditions under which PoE are more likely to emerge.

While the diversity of motivations for the establishment of PoE in our sample prevents us from deriving a more precise conclusion about them, it allows us to do something that may just be as important. Political economy frameworks usually assume that political survival is the chief incentive behind most, if not all, things politicians do. Our study finds that their motivations for establishing PoE at least, are more diverse than commonly acknowledged in these frameworks. They include nationalist developmental ideologies, concerns for people's lives as well as concerns about the country's international reputation, and others (see table 9.1). While political survival may still be the chief incentive for most politicians in the medium to long term, along the way other motivations do play an important role as well. We cannot do more here than alluding to this finding, and pointing out that there is a need for more research into the diversity of motivations behind political decisions in states dominated by strong heads of state and personalized forms of governance. For PoE to emerge, this variation of motivations is crucial. Or, to quote two prominent economists: 'the motivations of the political elites are complex enough that it may be in their interest, at a particular time and place, to implement some policies that happen to be good for the poor' (Banerjee and Duflo 2011: 254).

Do international factors have any role to play in this process at all? Table 9.1 shows that the form and strength of the influence of these factors varies. While not having a direct effect, except in the cases of China and Taiwan, the interests of the respective heads of state in particular tasks being performed effectively often developed with some kind of reference to international developments. In Nigeria, this included the domestication of a previously ratified United Nations protocol on human trafficking (NAPTIP), the concern about the country's international reputation (NAFDAC, NAPTIP), in Brazil the state-led development ideology that reflected the internationally dominating development paradigm in the 1950s and 60s, and in Suriname the response to the interest of international oil companies in explorations in the country. Nevertheless, overall we found that international factors were influential but not decisive.

Comparative analyisis: deciphering PoE 197

Based on the original motivations and the interests of the heads of state, what are the specific decisions that are crucial for PoE to emerge? We argue that PoE can emerge *when the head of state breaks with the usual public sector appointment practice based on patronage rationale.* Allocating top level positions in government is among the most important sources of patronage available to a head of state. Intense lobbying in the political party or the respective elite patronage networks starts immediately, as soon as top-level positions become vacant or new positions are available. This was also common in the countries in which our case studies are located. However, often against significant political and informal opposition, in the cases which later turned out to be PoE, the heads of state turned these demands down. Instead, they used other criteria to select their candidates. While qualification and prior experience were important, the criteria varied from context to context and included technical qualifications (Taiwan, Brazil), proven leadership and management qualities (China, NAPTIP, Middle East), proven incorruptibility (NAFDAC) and nationalist ideology (Brazil, Suriname). The very fact that these heads of state broke with established appointment practices despite resistance, indicates that they had indeed a strong interest in the execution of the respective organizational tasks.

While in principle, people from within the elite networks with the necessary skills could have been appointed, that did not happen in our cases. It seems that the heads of state were acutely aware of the dangers that this would have entailed for the performance prospects of the organizations. Even if these appointees from within the network had possessed the necessary skills and qualifications they would have still been vulnerable to what could be called the 'insider's dilemma'.[4] As a member of an elite and patronage network who has attained a high position, he would now have jobs to allocate, contracts to award, money to spend and other resources under his jurisdiction.[5] To reward 'clients and friends' (Eisenstadt and Roniger 1984) for previously received support and 'investments' and consolidate his position in the networks and the party, this person would have strong incentives to use the position and the organization for patronage purposes.

However, the appointments of chief executives in our case studies were also not made through official job advertisements and formal procedures.[6] The process was still highly personalized, but there were two crucial differences. First, although personalized, this time the process was based on 'weak ties' instead of 'strong ties' (Granovetter 1973).[7] The appointees came from outside of the established political elite networks but were still connected to them through weak ties. The head of state did not usually know them but they were referred to him through other individuals in his network. Party membership was either not important at all or played a minor role compared to other criteria. This is a crucial difference and clear deviation from common practice in the politico-administrative systems of these countries. The appointees did not face the insider's dilemma but were introduced into these networks from the very top with a strong tie to the president which, at least for some time, isolated them from and protected them against demands from the elite network. The second difference to usual appointments to top level positions in the public sector was that the appointees were all administrators and technocrats and not politicians.[8] We can now put together the two elements of our answer: *PoE can emerge when the head of state breaks with the usual public sector appointment practice based on patronage rationale and appoints a person with weak ties to the political elite network and administrative experience as the chief executive of a public organization.*

Based on our analysis we can specify three conditions under which it is more likely that heads of states – given a substantive motivation – try to establish a potential PoE. The first condition is what we call the *strong head of state/low risk constellation*. The head of state's position has to be sufficiently strong and independent for him to be able to easily withstand the opposition against his unusual appointment decision.[9] At the same time the nature of the task that the newly established organization is to execute has to be relatively low risk, so that the president will not be seriously threatened by a strong opposition or groups with vested interests in the respective field. While opposition arose against the establishment of some of the PoE in our studies, it was rather short-lived. This constellation is dynamic because the stronger the president is the more opposition he can withstand, and the weaker he is the less opposition he will be able to withstand.[10]

The second condition under which it is more likely that PoE are established relates to timing. Excluding the state-owned enterprises in the Middle East, the PoE in our sample were established by the respective governments, democratic or not, soon after coming into office, and nowhere later than by mid-term in office (see table 1.1).[11] This finding is confirmed by a case study of public organizations in the Dominican Republic, which found that two of them, the civil aviation and the tax agency, were effective in a context of overall public sector ineffectiveness (Lozano 2012). Both organizations were established in 2006, two years after the presidential elections and only months after the ruling party had won the absolute majority in legislative elections and gained control in both houses of congress.[12,13] This evidence suggests that, *if* governments or heads of state are prepared to establish effective public organizations, they tend to do so *within the first two years after taking office or after beginning a new term*.[14] Another finding that is worth noting here but requires further research is that more than one PoE tends to emerge in a given context at the same time. In Brazil, for example, the then President Vargas established Brazil's state oil enterprise *Petrobras* in 1953, only one year after the National Bank for Economic Development (BNDE).[15] While this book covers only two of Nigeria's PoE in the early 2000s, even more could have been identified for that period. The case of the Dominican Republic is instructive once again, where two out of the four organizations studied turned out to be effective, relative to their public sector environment (Lozano 2012).

A third condition that is vital for understanding when the establishment of PoE is more likely is the *head of state's preference for agencies that produce quick and politically tangible results.* If they initiate change, heads of state typically want to see that change happens rapidly enough so that it can still be associated with them. That is much harder to achieve in some fields than in others. In basic education and health services, extensive networks of public organizations already exist that cannot simply be substituted. Reforming and making them perform is difficult, time-consuming and, due to the number of actors involved, highly uncertain. For other tasks such as central banking or law-enforcement in specific fields, organizations can be quickly and relatively cost-effectively established and, if given the necessary means and support, be expected to cut through the existing administrative apparatus. With the exception of NAFDAC, all organizations in our sample were newly established. Furthermore, all organizations were comparatively small in the beginning, and grew with increased effectiveness and additional tasks given to them. They also produced 'politically tangible' results, meaning material or symbolic outcomes that are useful for political legitimization and competition. Revenues from tax agencies or state oil companies, and positive media reporting based on the reduction of the prevalence of counterfeit drugs and the fight against human trafficking, serve these purposes well.

From our review of the PoE literature in chapter 2, Arturo Israel's concept of task specificity comes to mind. He claims that the more specific an organization's task is, the more likely is its good performance, independent of other factors. This sounds similar to our last point above. However, based on our analysis we reject his claim that an independent, automatic effect of the degree of specificity of a public organization's task on its performance exists.[16] Without engaging in a more detailed critical discussion of his argument here, we note that political or personal interests – or disinterests – of the head of state trump any effect that task specificity might or might not have. Second, our analysis suggests that whether a public organization receives the political support it needs to perform well in a hostile environment does not primarily depend on an 'objective' measure of task specificity, but much more simply on whether – given the political or personal interest – the head of state *believes* that an organization can deliver quick and tangible results.[17] To the degree that high specificity contributes to that belief it is important for the emergence of PoE.

In light of our findings about the conditions under which PoE are more likely to emerge, we briefly review Hertog's explanatory model for successful state-owned enterprises in rentier states (chapter 8). He argues that two factors explain this outcome: regime autonomy in (economic) policy-making, where 'regime autonomy' is defined as 'a small number of reasonably unified leaders', and the absence of a populist-mobilizational history (ibid.). In our sample only Nigeria and Suriname are rentier states in addition to Hertog's cases from the Middle East. These cases confirm his model. While regime autonomy or strong and independent heads of state are also important factors for PoE to emerge in non-rentier states, as we have seen above, the same is not true for his second factor. Economic and political populism was a dominant

200   *Michael Roll*

feature of Brazilian politics from after the Second World War until the *coup d'état* in 1964, for example. We cannot go beyond stating this finding here and noting that the link between populist mobilization and the emergence of PoE in non-rentier states merits further research.

In conclusion, we argue that the specific interest of a head of state in the execution of a particular task can lead to the emergence of a PoE if it translates into a break with the patronage appointment practice. Instead, other criteria that are at least partially merit-based are used to appoint a chief executive with prior administrative experience, who is connected to the political elite through weak ties. We argue that in the context of contemporary developing countries this is a necessary condition for PoE to emerge. With reference to the 'critical juncture' concept, we could call this the 'necessary juncture' for the emergence of a PoE in the political system.[18] However, a mechanism that would automatically lead to a PoE once this juncture is passed does not exist. But without that decision it would not be possible for one to emerge at all. This is precisely what 'necessary' means: if the necessary condition is present the outcome could or could not be present, but if it is absent the outcome will also be absent. In the next section we turn to the factors that explain *how* PoE emerge once this necessary juncture has been passed.

How do pockets of effectiveness emerge?

Based on the analysis of our case studies we now look at the other factors that are necessary for a PoE to emerge. Our particular focus is on the processes and mechanisms of *how* this happens. We distinguish three categories of factors that best explain how PoE emerge: organizational strength, organizational culture and organizational proactivity (see table 9.2). Our presentation of each of the factors contained in these categories below is deliberately selective. We go into more detail when discussing factors, mechanisms and aspects that are counterintuitive and/or have not featured prominently in the PoE literature so far. On those factors that are already well covered, we merely discuss how our findings are in line with or diverge from prior results. Before turning to the discussion of the factors we introduce a distinction between two types of organizational effectiveness, 'core' and 'scale' effectiveness, and take a look at the importance of the 'founding features' of public organizations.

Table 9.2 Categories and factors that explain how pockets of effectiveness emerge

Organizational strength	Organizational culture	Organizational proactivity
Focussed powers	Inclusive leadership	Political management
Staff deployment	Performance-orientation	Autonomy
Standardization	Organizational identity	Outreach and cooperation*

Note: *Necessary only for scale effectiveness.

Comparative analyisis: deciphering PoE 201

Core and scale effectiveness

For thinking about effective public sector organizations in hostile environments, we distinguish analytically between 'core' and 'scale effectiveness'. This distinction is useful, because the relevance of some of the 'how' factors we introduce below for each of the two kinds of organizational effectiveness differs. 'Core effectiveness' denotes the effectiveness of the centre of the organization at headquarters. 'Scale effectiveness' on the other hand refers to the capacity of an organization to deliver public goods and services across the territory it is responsible for. Due to the nature of their tasks, some organizations operate almost exclusively at headquarters without a network of field offices. Their services can be provided in a highly centralized manner and the number of clients they interact with is often small (e.g. central banks, development banks and civil aviation authorities).[19] These organizations are considered PoE as soon as they have achieved a relative degree of effectiveness at their 'core', and it is not necessary for them – although it is sometimes desirable – to go beyond building core effectiveness.

For other public organizations, those that regulate goods or provide services in more direct and frequent contact with clients and citizens all over the country, achieving scale effectiveness is key. Even if they are highly effective at headquarters, as long as they do not actually deliver their services across large parts of the country with a certain degree of effectiveness, they will still be considered ineffective. These 'scale effectiveness organizations' are often, but not always organizations responsible for tasks that Israel would have called low specificity tasks. Regulatory agencies with offices and officials all over the country, for example, are scale effectiveness organizations, while their tasks may have a relatively high degree of specificity.

Founding features

When a public organization is being established, some 'founding features' are critical for its transformation into a PoE. However, rather than strictly determining whether an organization will be able to become a PoE or not, these founding features constitute enabling and constraining conditions and provide resources that actors can employ. One of the founding features is a strong legal mandate of the organization, combined with a certain degree of autonomy. While all organizations in our sample had such a legal mandate, the legislation that underpinned the organizations' operations were often both specific in some but vague in other respects. PoE chief executives have made creative use of this vagueness to improve the organizations' performance. The vagueness of the legislation, for example, left room for the organizations to develop pragmatic internal rules for issues not covered in the legislation. This provided them with a higher degree of agency and flexibility than they would have had otherwise.

Another important founding feature is the immediate generation of a performance-oriented organizational culture. All public organizations we studied

202 *Michael Roll*

were effective pretty much from the year they were established (see table 1.1).[20] While it took some time until they could start providing the public goods and services they were responsible for, all of them did so much faster than observers would have expected. Founding chief executives started working long hours immediately after they had been officially appointed, usually together with small and close-knit management teams.[21] They began communicating their mission and goals to staff from the very beginning, and set clear expectations in terms of performance, discipline and integrity. Together with the dismissal of a small group of former staff, if applicable, and the recruitment of new staff, all this usually happened within the first few weeks or months. The transformation or generation of the new organizational culture did take some time, but it is crucial to note that it began immediately, progressed quickly and provided a strong foundation for the next steps. Taken together, while the founding features do not determine whether an organization becomes a PoE or not, they build a crucial foundation that is difficult or even impossible to establish at a later point in time. We argue that whether or not such activities directed at creating a new organizational culture occur in the first few weeks and months of a public organization's existence is a good indicator for whether or not it will become a PoE.

Organizational strength

'Organizational strength' includes factors that form the human, material and operational infrastructure of an organization (see table 9.2). We focus on the three factors we identified as necessary: focussed powers, staff deployment and standardization.

'Focussed powers' refers to the specific, and with regard to the organization's mandate comprehensive legal powers. In our case studies these powers enabled the organizations to maintain a high degree of autonomy as we will show in more detail below. In a context in which other public organizations, especially law enforcement authorities, are ineffective, not having such comprehensive powers could render any attempt at making the organization effective useless. The Nigerian regulatory agencies in our sample illustrate this point well. Their comprehensive powers allowed them to carry out almost all steps necessary for executing their tasks internally. For the most part, they did not rely on the cooperation of other public organizations. Their independent prosecutorial powers even enabled them to prosecute offenders, order them to pay fines or hand them over to the courts.

The specific and comprehensive legal powers also served as powerful frameworks for the chief executives to refer to when defending the organizations against political or other kinds of attempted interference. Apart from being specific and comprehensive with regard to the organization's task, the legal provisions were in part also vague. In many cases, this turned out to be an ideal combination. The vague aspects were interpreted in creative and pragmatic ways that helped to increase the organization's flexibility and effectiveness.

Comparative analyisis: deciphering PoE 203

The legislations therefore served operational, enabling and protective purposes, all of which were important when strategically employed by the chief executive.

'Staff deployment' is crucial for PoE. In our cases the appointed chief executives were either directly or indirectly responsible for recruiting members for their management teams. They selected staff who shared their own work ethic in terms of promoting performance and integrity. Either they knew these people personally, or they were recommended to them through friends they trusted or from credible sources outside of the dominating political and administrative elite networks, such as international organizations or private companies. Loyalty and trust were important features of these relationships, particularly during the strenuous phase of establishing the organization in the first few months. For rank and file staff, more standardized and systematic merit-based recruitment procedures were introduced, that often included interviews in which integrity and public service commitment issues were covered.[22]

All organizations in our sample paid salaries and provided welfare benefits to their staff that were considerably higher than in the regular civil service.[23] Staff were usually placed according to their qualifications and/or trained for the positions they filled, both of which were highly unusual in the civil services in these countries. In many organizations, adequate internal and external training for staff was provided on a regular basis. This included specialized training for new members of staff. Especially international trainings were often used strategically by PoE chief executives to reward outstanding performance.

The 'standardization' of operations and procedures is also a key factor for building organizational strength, but is less covered in the literature than the two previously mentioned aspects. The degree to which standardization is possible and useful depends on the nature of the organization's task. We have strong evidence that standardization was an important factor for the emergence (and persistence) of the PoE in our sample. While Brazil's BNDE standardized project appraisals and subsequent decisions on the basis of objective technical criteria, China's salt tax inspectorate and Nigeria's regulatory agencies developed and used written internal guidelines and standard operating procedures, based on what they saw as feasible, effective and efficient. When the strategies of their clients or the perpetrators they were trying to find changed, often in response to the agency's increasing effectiveness, the agencies adapted their procedures to maintain or increase their effectiveness. This involved both explicit and implicit mechanisms for evaluating the organization's performance and for learning from the findings. In these organizations, standardization is therefore the process of setting, enforcing and adapting exclusive, impartial and mandatory procedural rules.

In a political and administrative environment in which uncertainty and arbitrariness prevail, the advantages of standardization cannot be overestimated. Standardization creates internal stability and external predictability and thereby enables overall effectiveness. The successful enforcement of rules and standards eradicates parallel systems of informal rules and practices

204   *Michael Roll*

which often exist in developing countries, and which tend to contradict formal bureaucratic rules. These parallel systems turn every decision into a multidimensional process, in which it is usually rational for individual actors not to take a decision at all, or at least to delay the decision for as long as possible due to general uncertainty about preferences, rules and interests. Standardization also contributes to internal stability and effectiveness by providing criteria and guidelines for how to act, depending on the evidence or information received. For this to work, information must be reliable. This can be achieved through a process to which standardization also contributes: 'uncertainty absorption' (March and Simon 1958: 164–65). According to James G. March and Herbert A. Simon '[u]ncertainty absorption takes place when inferences are drawn from a body of evidence and the inferences, instead of the evidence itself, are then communicated' (ibid.: 164–65). Since members of staff can now routinely rely on the information they receive from their colleagues, based on the established rules, they can use these decisions or information as their input and continue to work on them without having to doubt or confirm their validity first.

Externally, standardization creates predictability after a certain period of time. When citizens or other public servants observe that the agency is following the same standards repeatedly, irrespective of the individual official and the client he or she is dealing with, they adapt their expectations accordingly over time. One of the several instances in which this happened was the case of NAFDAC. In her first weeks and months in office, Dora Akunyili had been offered numerous bribes and informal deals. After refusing them week after week, the number of offers first dropped and eventually fell to zero. Akunyili claimed that 'even if I suddenly became interested in accepting bribe from the criminals, there would be no one ready to offer one because they would suspect it to be a set-up' (Akunyili 2010: 182). NAFDAC went through this process as an organization as well. After some time most clients had not only learned what the official rules and requirements actually were but also that it was better for them to obey them. Moreover, they learned that there were now formal procedures that – unlike previously – actually *did* work for applying for registrations, for example, while the old strategy of bribing officials no longer worked. Lozano (2012) reports a similar story from the Dominican Republic's effective tax agency:

> Instead of massive fraud or evasion, powerful groups sought to reduce their tax payments via formal agreements with the authorities. The struggles between different interest groups were subsequently played out within a formal framework, through legislation and negotiations
>
> (ibid.: 119, with reference to Guzmán 2008).

Changing internal and external expectation structures is one of the most difficult, yet also most important tasks for an organization to emerge as a PoE. Standardizing procedures and decisions is essential for this.

This discussion of standardization could lead to the impression that agency officials turned into robots and simply executed prescribed administrative programmes. Nothing could be further from the truth. In contact with the clients they had to regulate or provide services for, these 'street-level bureaucrats' (Lipsky 1980) communicated and acted in a flexible and often creative manner. In these environments, clients are typically not used to officials who try to do what they are officially supposed to do and who cannot be bribed. In order to carry out their standardized procedures in ways that produce sustained results, officials have to explain, negotiate, moderate, mediate, convince, build trust and use other strategies that would normally not come to mind when one thinks about standardization and bureaucracy. The case studies of Nigeria's regulatory organizations provide the most detailed evidence of these practices. The effectiveness of a public organization rests on both components.

Furthermore, in a hostile environment, bureaucratic standardization comes at a cost. To allow internal standardized procedures to be carried out undisturbed, external protection of the organization and its procedures has to be ensured. Organizing this protection is hard work and could well count as the opposite of working along standardized procedures, as we will see below (see 'political management').

One factor that was important in many but not all our case studies should be mentioned here: technology. In the environments we are talking about, even simple technological means such as functioning computers or electronic filing systems cannot be taken for granted. Therefore, their introduction has the potential to increase administrative effectiveness. Advanced technology can also be useful as the case of NAFDAC demonstrates, where handheld spectrometers were introduced for drug inspection and a countrywide mobile phone drug authentication service was set up. The key point is that it is not the introduction of technology per se that does the trick. Technology only contributes to organizational effectiveness when it is embedded in the organization's overall procedures, operations and staff development. It can *improve* effectiveness where it already exists, but it cannot produce it where it is absent. That is why we call this non-necessary factor 'embedded technology'.

We can now conclude our discussion of the contribution of organizational strength to the process through which PoE emerge. While all three factors of organizational strength (focussed powers, staff deployment and standardization) are necessary, they are necessary *components* for PoE to emerge, rather than the factors driving or 'causing' organizational effectiveness. We now turn to this latter category of factors.

Organizational culture

On the importance of 'organizational culture' for PoE, Grindle's work is still authoritative (Grindle 1997; Hilderbrand and Grindle 1997; see also Crook 2010), and much of what we found resembles her as well as Tendler's and

206 *Michael Roll*

Leonard's analyses.[24] The factors that we identified as most important are inclusive leadership, performance orientation and organizational identity.

'Inclusive leadership' denotes a leadership style, in which the chief executive communicates his goals, mission and expectations clearly, is accessible to members of staff, invites and pays attention to new ideas and suggestions, and cares for staff. When developing this category we faced some challenges. It applied well to organizations in some countries (Nigeria, Brazil, Taiwan, Suriname) but less so in others (Republican China, Middle East) (see table 9.3). With regard to Republican China, it is obvious that in the early twentieth century, Sir Richard Dane did not employ this kind of modern leadership and management style. However, two elements that belong to this category were important at that time as well. They were also relevant in the cultural context of the Middle East where social hierarchies are particularly strong. These two elements are: internal communication of the organizational mission and expectations, as well as the leadership caring for staff in the sense of defending them against political and other attacks, if necessary. We opted to include inclusive leadership with this latter, narrower definition as a necessary factor. However, we note that our broader understanding of this factor is likely to apply in contemporary PoE and in contexts in which social hierarchies are less rigid than they are in the Middle East.

Just like introducing the standardization of procedures, introducing 'performance-orientation' is an enormous cultural change for most public organizations in developing countries. Prior logics of operation and de facto organizational value systems have to be replaced by new ones. To achieve that, a self-perpetuating process has to be set in motion, supported by a growing organizational identity, especially at the higher levels of the organization. However, if that top-down process is successful, most members of staff can perform well in this new system.

While formal performance evaluation systems existed in some of our case studies, our conclusion is that they helped to identify those who were performing below average, rather than motivating anybody to perform better than they already did. Performance in these organizations was not based on the disciplining elements of the performance framework. It was also not primarily based on formal incentives such as high salaries.[25] People did not work hard to earn a fortune or to achieve high performance scores but because they saw their jobs as meaningful and fulfilling, and because they developed a personal responsibility or even passion for doing what they did (see Tendler 1997 for a similar argument). This is in line with well-established but often ignored findings from management studies (Kovach 1987, 1995; Appelbaum and Batt 1994; Hay Group 2012).[26] It is not material incentives and formal controls that produce motivated and 'principled agents' (DiIulio, Jr. 1994).

We have evidence for all our case studies that strong 'organizational identity' provided members of staff with a sense of purpose, motivation and commitment with regard to their work that boosted and maintained performance orientation.[27] 'Organizational identity' exists when staff identify

Comparative analyisis: deciphering PoE   207

strongly with the organization's mission in a way that is backed by personally held values and convictions. 'Mission' does not refer to the mission statement here, but rather to the meaning and purpose of the organization's task in the broader context of the country's challenges and development. It is a shared, normative understanding of the special and unique importance of the task that the organization performs. Such organizational identities have to be deliberately created and nurtured by the chief executive and his management team. When selecting and appointing members of the new management team, the incoming chief executive usually chose people who had shown drive and initiative in other organizations or professional fields before, and who there-fore brought an intrinsic motivation for performance and change to the organization. Given their higher salaries and benefits, the PoE usually received much more applications than they had positions. They could therefore select the most qualified and experienced applicants at all levels.

However, as Hilderbrand and Grindle have noted, in many developing countries the problem is not so much that civil servants are not trained, but that their skills are not used effectively and that the jobs they are given are not meaningful and offer little motivation (Hilderbrand and Grindle 1997: 34). The case of NAFDAC confirms that the failure of these organizations has to do less with the people who work there and their formal qualification but with the way they are organized. NAFDAC is the only organization in our sample that was reformed instead of newly established. The 'old' NAFDAC before 2001 was not a well performing public organization.[28] Nevertheless, the incoming chief executive retained about 95 per cent of the old staff and managed to transform the organization into a clearly performance-oriented PoE within a very short period of time.

The first thing new chief executives typically did was to communicate. Especially those who practised more modern and inclusive forms of leader-ship explained their personal mission and how it connected to the organization's mission. They took the organization's mission seriously, and framed it with reference to overarching goals such as national development, protection of women and children or improvement of the country's image in the world.[29] This was the beginning of a process of instilling members of staff with a sense of meaning and purpose in their work that many of them had never experienced before. It also gave members of staff the feeling of being part of something special. This establishment or reform euphoria can quickly get lost if no steps are taken to actually implement these plans. However, the PoE chief executives and their management teams worked almost round the clock in the first few weeks and months to restructure the organization, recruit new people, find adequate positions for staff, provide training, talk to the media, renovate buildings and offices, purchase equipment and start first initiatives. All these steps confirmed that they were not just there to talk but were serious about implementing their ambitious plans. This provided significant drive to the organization and motivation for members of staff.[30]

208   *Michael Roll*

However, at the same time chief executives clearly communicated their expectations with regard to performance. Together with the reorganization of the PoE, job descriptions were developed which spelled out individual responsibilities and expectations. By working hard to put the organization's infrastructure in place, the leadership provided a role model for other members of staff. This was the expectations side of creating organizational identity. Providing support was the third element of this process. Offering extensive job-specific training was an important part of this support to members of staff, as was the accessibility of most chief executives when problems arose. Moreover, in most cases the leadership made sure that the salaries and benefits continued to rise. All this created a loyalty of staff to the leadership that was both professional and personal.

For understanding why such apparently simple changes were so forceful and provided members of staff with significant motivation, one has to keep in mind where many of the rank and file staff came from. In much of the regular patronage-based civil service, these office holders are just left to their own devices, since the leadership of the organization is busy with political networking and personal businesses and does not care about the organization's task, let alone its effectiveness. Unless the head of department or unit provides a higher degree of task-oriented leadership, individual bureaucrats can just sit out their days in the office or run their own private businesses as many of their colleagues do.[31] Especially rank and file staff, who do not even have the opportunity to draw significant rents from their bureaucratic positions, are often frustrated with their jobs. They feel that their skills are wasted, and they experience first-hand how the public sector is crumbling because political and administrative elites divert and share the money. For those who want to contribute to their country's development it is therefore easy to see how a meaningful job, clearly defined responsibilities, adequate equipment, a good salary with benefits, an organizational purpose and public recognition can act as strong motivating factors for performing well.

While all these steps are essential, the process through which organizational identity is institutionalized in the sense of being stabilized and made sustainable is an interactive one. Based on the steps described above, a group-dynamic process may be set in motion. It begins with the leadership and those staff members who are most receptive to and convinced by the new orientation of the organization and its mode of work. Those who are more sceptical are still likely to respond to the established incentives and sanctions system. In this process, the communication and interaction of members of staff becomes increasingly structured by the shared acceptance that it is now task and performance orientation that regulates their actions as members of the organization. Along with informal mutual monitoring and social control, this process of collective realignment of action frames, patterns and expectations characterized organizational change.[32]

Another important factor that has a strong effect on these internal group-dynamic processes is the relationship of the organization with its environment. In organizational terms, PoE are highly selective and exclusive organizations. Not just anybody, not even with adequate formal qualifications, can become a member of this group. Every member of staff must 'earn' his or her belonging to this group by passing highly selective exams and interviews. This process alone instils a sense of pride, elitism and organizational identity, not only in the successful applicant but also in those who are already members of staff. At the same time, those who defy internal rules and procedures or do not fulfil the performance expectations are dismissed, which reinforces the internal rules and values. Such events and procedures clearly demarcate the boundary between the organization and the rest of the public sector. While such boundaries between organizations and their environment are important everywhere, they have a special significance in the case of PoE. These organizations operate in hostile environments to which they are opposed in terms of the logic of social action. This boundary between PoE and their environments is, therefore, also a boundary between the 'order' and 'morality' within the organization and the 'chaos' and 'corruption' in the rest of the politico-administrative environment.

This suspicion towards and opposition to its environment contributes to the forging of organizational identity in a powerful way. We can draw an analogy between organizational and other kinds of identity groups such as ethnic groups here. Despite all the differences, 'boundary maintenance' (Barth 1969: 10) is a constitutive feature of both kinds of groups. Moreover, a common 'enemy' or opposition is one of the strongest known forces for establishing and maintaining a common 'we-group' (Elwert 1989) identity.[33] That is also the reason why attacks on PoE, whether from politicians who try to capture the organization or from drug counterfeiters who see their illegal income opportunities shrinking, tend to further strengthen organizational cohesion and identity instead of weakening it.[34] PoE leadership often used such events to motivate their staff to work even harder in order to successfully resist or even defeat these seemingly invincible forces. Given these hostilities and the sheer magnitude of the tasks that PoE are often requested to perform, even small initial and subsequent successes can boost organizational identity. They do so by providing staff with a sense of organizational efficacy that would previously have been considered highly improbable.

Another factor that helps to build and strengthen organizational identity is positive feedback. Many interviews with PoE officials showed that personal feedback from citizens, as well as praise from the media, civil society organizations, diplomats, international organizations and even politicians, made them feel proud of being a member of this PoE and motivated them personally to continue to work hard. As a result, for many members of staff their job became much more than a 'normal' well-paying job over time but rather a 'calling' or 'mission' that they personally identified with.[35] It is this alignment of an organization's and a group of individuals' mission that is at the heart of organizational identity. These members of staff increasingly developed a strong motivation for and commitment to the task their organization was

210   *Michael Roll*

responsible for, because they derived organizational and professional, as well as considerable personal, pride, prestige and status from it.

Other authors have also referred to this sense of mission or 'mystique' (Grindle 1997: 488–89) and (public) service commitment (Tendler 1997; Crook 2010) as important motivating factors for organizational effectiveness. Rephrased in political economy terms, this commitment reduces the principal's costs for controlling his or her agents significantly. Intrinsic motivation pushes officials to higher levels of self-discipline and performance than external evaluations and incentive systems could ever do. We argue that in the type of politico-administrative environment in which PoE exist, such commitment can only develop and become effective and enduring if it is embedded in organizational identity.

The factor 'organizational identity' integrates many of the factors that we have discussed so far. Overall, we regard organizational identity and the other organizational culture factors as those that mainly drove the remarkable increase of organizational effectiveness in PoE.

Organizational proactivity

Of the three categories of factors that explain how PoE emerge, 'organizational proactivity' is perhaps the most neglected one in the literature so far. It includes the factors political management and organizational autonomy, which are closely interrelated as well as – for scale effectiveness – outreach and cooperation.

We use the term 'political management' for referring to primarily informal activities of the leadership of PoE, which aim at influencing decisions and conditions that enable the organization to maintain or increase its effectiveness. Based on our analysis, political management is essential for the emergence and persistence of PoE (on persistence, see further below). The PoE chief executives in our case studies devoted significant amounts of time and attention to it. It is carried out with varying degrees of intensity but is a continuous activity that never goes away. A study of Brazil's bureaucracy in the 1970s confirms our finding, going so far as to characterize the national development bank BNDE not as an administrative institution but rather as a political party, due to the nature of its activities such as making alliances and propagating ideology (Martins 1985: 93, referred to in Schneider 1991: 36).

Political management may be exerted through a broad variety of methods, including casual small talk, invitations to inaugurations or other ceremonies, personal letters, praising a certain politician's contributions in public statements, the quiet mobilization of NGOs or members of the diplomatic corps or international organizations, cooperation with the media, press conferences, progress reports, technical presentations and studies, moral statements, emotional pleas and many others. The strategies that are employed and the resources that are used for this are equally varied. The framing of the organization's mission in such a way that it aligns with the broader strategic goals of the head of state or elite, as well as being able to refer to an organization's reputation for effectiveness, are two major elements. We discuss some of these strategies and the resources they require more in detail below, when we look at how PoE manage to persist.

Depending on the political context, the range of persons and organizations that have to be lobbied or negotiated with for maintaining or enhancing the conditions for a PoE's effectiveness differs. Apart from the head of state they often include relevant ministers and ministries, related government agencies, members of parliament and parliamentary committees as well as relevant and powerful politicians at the sub-national levels. For some of them, particularly those who do not have some kind of independent power over the organization, it is usually sufficient to see that the chief executive is close to the head of state. In order to please him it is then wise to support people that are close to the head of state and that he deems worthy of support. Other, more independent politicians like ministers or state governors often require more attention. In general, for being able to practice political management successfully, an organization's reputation for being effective is critical. A certain degree of public visibility through positive media reporting, civil society, diplomatic or international attention is helpful for conveying this 'performance message' to decision makers.

We distinguish three general purposes of political management, although in practice the boundaries between them are fluid. The first purpose is 'strengthening trust and interest'. In politico-administrative systems characterized by weak institutionalization and strong personalization, personal trust is crucial but it is at the same time under constant threat. Rumour and unfounded accusations are a common political and administrative weapon used against inconvenient actors. That is why in such systems it is essential for PoE chief executives to continuously build and confirm personal trust with key actors, above all the head of state. Often, but not always, building this trust through meetings, communication, public praising and other means is related to renewing the head of state's or more generally the elite's interest in the task the organization is carrying out. While the head of state has shown a strong degree of interest in this very task by establishing the organization in the first place, unless there is a particularly strong and persistent interest in this task (like in the case of revenue generation, for example) the interests of heads of states and elites in such environments tend to shift with time. Apart from shifting interests, heads of state and other top politicians are simply busy people. They have to do deal with lots of issues and could easily lose sight of what is going on in a particular organization after they have done their part and appointed a chief executive. Ensuring that the head of state and other relevant politicians do not lose interest in this particular organization's effectiveness is therefore one of the most basic responsibilities of a PoE's chief executive, with regard to political management. If he is not successful in doing that, the likeliness that political management will be successful with regard to the two other purposes we describe below is much lower. If the

212   *Michael Roll*

personal trust of a head of state in a particular chief executive is very strong, this may to some degree substitute for the need to keep the head of state interested in the task of the organization. Overall, an organization's reputation of performing well is particularly crucial for (re)activating trust and interest.

The successful reproduction of interpersonal trust and interest in the task of the PoE is the precondition for accomplishing each of the other two purposes of political management. The second purpose is 'obtaining political support and protection'. In many of our cases, heads of state issued directives or pushed bills through parliament quickly that enhanced organizational effectiveness. This happened in response to requests from the PoE's chief executives in the cases of NAPTIP, NAFDAC and Brazil's BNDE, for example. In Republican China, on the other hand, related but previously separate and to some degree rival organizations were merged. Political protection is indispensable for PoE, since these organizations often interfere in or come into conflict with activities in which other politicians or members of the elite have specific interests. That implies that the next person that would like to see a PoE chief executive removed from office is never far away. Political protection from a powerful politician, often the head of state, is an effective safeguard against such attacks.

The third purpose of political management is 'negotiating political interference'. In the type of politico-administrative system we are looking at, political and/or personal interference in public organizations is the rule rather than the exception. It may be spontaneous but is more frequently institutionalized through patronage appointments. Despite top-level political support, PoE are likely to be confronted with particularistic political or personal demands or objections at some point. This attempted interference may be exerted by members of the political elite or even the head of state himself. If other members of the political elite tried to interfere, PoE chief executives usually remained calm and did not immediately respond to such demands. They either referred to certain formal rules or procedures or promised that they would take the issue up in their next meeting with the responsible minister or the head of state, as they did in the Brazil and Suriname case studies (see more on this below under PoE persistence).

It is more complicated if the head of state himself is involved. Even then the reference to formal rules, international standards or the implications for the organization's performance can be used to fend the demand off. If that does not work, political management can be used to at least negotiate a compromise that allows the PoE leadership to restrict or control interference in a way that reduces the damage that it does to the organization's effectiveness. Our case study of Brazil's BNDE illustrates that strategy well. The directors of that organization negotiated that a programme they did not regard as a priority but that the country's president imposed on the bank was only implemented under specific conditions. The directors insisted that the same technical standards that applied to higher priority projects had to be met by the activities under that imposed programme before they could be approved.

Comparative analyisis: deciphering PoE 213

This effectively reduced the number of activities that could be realized in that programme (see chapter 4).

Another example from the same organization is a compromise that the leadership negotiated with a new director who had strong links to the president and who preferred to make patronage appointments. They agreed that he could make 20 per cent of the appointments based on political and personal connections while 80 per cent of the positions would be filled through competitive exams (ibid.).

The case of Suriname's state oil company provides another illustration. There, the organization's management agreed to accept a financial director with close links to the respective minister's party in exchange for appointing a home-grown, technically competent person as the new deputy governor (see chapter 7).

While political management is used for all three purposes, taken together it does more than organizing trust, interest, support and the negotiation of interference in an ad hoc fashion. Rather, through political management, PoE leadership proactively and constantly shape and (re)create the immediate environment the organization operates in and the conditions under which it does so. This already refers to 'organizational autonomy', the second factor in the organizational proactivity category, to which we now turn.

It may be surprising to find 'organizational autonomy' in this third category of factors instead of the first one. After all, is autonomy not something formal, legal and fixed? We argue that in the context of weakly institutionalized and strongly personalized politics and administration this is not the case. Formal institutional guarantees of independence and autonomy alone do not provide effective protection against political interference and patronage in systems in which those features are pervasive.[36] We argue that in developing countries with a low degree of administrative institutionalization, autonomy should therefore neither be regarded as an established fact nor an executable right, but essentially as a constant bargaining relationship.[37] Moreover and paradoxically, far from referring to an organization that is *isolated* from politics, in such environments actual organizational autonomy critically depends on strong political relations and successful political bargaining. Recent scholarship on historical state and public organization development in the United States confirms that bureaucratic autonomy rests on political foundations (Carpenter 2001a). Indeed, Carpenter argues more generally that 'where it prevails, *bureaucratic autonomy is explicitly political*' (ibid.: 113; emphasis in original). He adds that to a large degree it rests on the reputation that the organization has managed to build (Carpenter 2000, 2001b). While we agree that there are strong continuities between the realities and practices of administrative autonomy in OECD and developing countries, we hold that there are also qualitative differences.[38] In contexts in which legal rules and political checks and balances are much less institutionalized, a public organization's dependency on personalized political protection and support is much stronger, and its position is therefore much weaker than in the OECD world.

214　*Michael Roll*

In this kind of environment, formal rules and laws are tools and resources for negotiating autonomy, rather than inherently reliable, sustained and independent guarantees for autonomy.

The nature of organizational autonomy as a bargaining relationship can be illustrated with reference to financial autonomy, one of its most important dimensions. Financial autonomy is a key condition for an effective public organization. Yet, this is precisely a field in which 'real' autonomy does not usually exist. In our sample, no organization had a formal and legally guaranteed financial commitment from the government. Therefore, despite all their political connections, before every budget cycle these organizations could never be sure whether the allocations would remain stable, would grow or be cut. Allocations can vary dramatically from year to year in the type of developing countries we look at, depending on available funds, shifting political priorities or simply political power plays in parties, between committees or in the legislature more broadly. That is why the PoE organizations were very active in lobbying heads of state, ministers, committees and individual members of parliament. They also lined up with non-governmental organizations or the media to draw public and political attention to their work and its significance, and thereby indirectly pushed for higher allocations. Especially the chief executives were very active in doing that. This is a good example of how political management was used to maintain or enhance organizational autonomy through financial autonomy. NAFDAC is an example of a PoE that managed to go one step further and institutionalize this financial, and thereby organizational, autonomy to some degree. The organization's chief executive saw sufficient potential for raising task-related revenues, and therefore lobbied for the right to retain and reinvest this revenue at a point in time when that revenue was not high. Dora Akunyili managed to convince NAFDAC's governing council, the ministry of health and the head of state, and the organization was granted the right to retain self-generated revenues. This offered NAFDAC a significantly higher and more stable degree of financial autonomy than it had before, reduced the time and energy wasted for annual competitive budget allocation lobbying, and therefore contributed a great deal to the organization's increasing effectiveness. This is also a good example of how PoE use political management for shaping and (re)creating their environment and the conditions under which they operate in it.

We turn to the last factor in the category of organizational proactivity. This factor differs from all other factors that explain how PoE emerge in our framework, because it is not necessary for all types of public organizations. At the beginning of this section we introduced our distinction between core and scale effectiveness. We argue now that the factor 'outreach and cooperation' is a necessary factor only for the emergence of 'scale effectiveness organizations' as PoE, but not for 'core effectiveness organizations'. 'Outreach and cooperation' refers to a public organization proactively reaching out to its clients, domestic non-governmental organizations and actors and other public organizations, in order to build trust, establish relationships and eventually cooperate with each other. These interactions and subsequent cooperation cover a wide range of forms, from sporadic and temporary to systematic and sustained. We exclude international actors from this definition because, while frequently important, their contributions did not turn out to be necessary for the emergence of PoE in our case studies.

Organizations that were closer to the scope effectiveness end of the continuum in our sample, such as Taiwan's Commission on Rural Reconstruction or Nigeria's regulatory agencies, could not have become PoE without their strong proactive approaches, through which they built trust and cooperated with numerous actors. To overcome the initial scepticism that public organizations, especially new ones, naturally incur in developing countries, they did not start with implementing the laws by the book. Rather, they first listened to actors in their respective fields and tried to turn them into allies through a combination of offers of support and general rule-setting for the future. In order to be effective these PoE relied on information from clients and citizens and on their active cooperation. One of the most important aspects was that they did not implement all their policies directly, but rather taught community and business groups and organizations how to carry out certain tasks themselves (especially self-regulation and control, see chapter 5). Nigeria's regulatory agencies, for example, gradually became public education and regulation facilitation agencies in addition to law enforcement agencies. On their own and with coercive power alone they would have never been able to become so effective in such a short period of time.

Organizations that were closer to the core effectiveness end of the continuum, on the other hand, while sometimes also reaching out and cooperating with clients and other organizations, did so to a much lesser degree since they did not depend on doing that for being effective.[39] For Republican China's salt tax inspectorate and Brazil's development bank BNDE, the cooperation of their clients was a facilitating rather than a strictly necessary factor.[40] For a truth table that summarizes which of the factors were present and which were not for each of our cases, see table 9.3.

The model

We can now bring all the necessary factors together in one model (see figure 9.1). It is the result of the comparative analysis of our case studies and provides the summarized answer to the research questions of why and how PoE emerge. These are all necessary factors under the conditions that we specified above. That means that even if they are present the outcome might not be present, while without their existence the outcome is absent. In the way we have described the factors, their dimensions and interaction above, if they are present they do not normally follow upon each other in a strict sequential order as the model seems to suggest. Especially in the first months and even years after the organization has been established, many processes are going on at the same time, and many factors are at work in a parallel fashion.

Table 9.3 Truth table scores for PoE cases (Crisp set score key: *1 = Presence; 0 = Absence*)*

Organization	Factors												Outcome
	Why?		How (emergence and persistence)?										
			Organizational strength			Organizational culture			Organizational proactivity			
	Political interest in task	Break w. patronage appointment practice	Focussed powers	Staff deployment	Standardization	Inclusive leadership	Performance-orientation	Organizational identity	Political management	Autonomy	Outreach and cooperation [a]	Pocket of effectiveness
Salt tax inspectorate (Rep. China)	1[c]	1[d]	1	1	1	0	1	1	1	1	0	1
Rural reconstruction (Rep. China/Taiwan)	1	1	1	1	0	1	1	1	1	1	1	1
Development bank (Brazil)	1	1	1	1	1	1	1	1	1	1	1	1
Food and drug regulation (Nigeria)	1	1	1	1	1	1	1	1	1	1	1	1
Human trafficking control (Nigeria)	1	1	1	1	1	1	1	1	1	1	1	1
State oil company (Suriname)	1	1	1	1	1	1	1	1	1	1	1	1
State-owned enterprises (GCC)[b]	1	1	1	1	0	0	1	1	1	1	0	1

Notes: *Truth tables normally list pre-defined factors or conditions and then score whether or not they are present in each of the cases. This truth table is different in the sense that we developed the categories and factors that are listed in the table through a qualitative comparative analysis of the cases. It is therefore not surprising that most of the factors are present in most of the cases. However, for a better overview and for finding those cases in which not all of the factors are present, this truth table is useful.

[a] Necessary only for scope effectiveness.

[b] Gulf Cooperation Council: members are Bahrain, Kuwait, Oman, Qatar, Saudi Arabia and the United Arab Emirates.

[c] When the inspectorate was set up in 1913, the government's interest was only indirect, since a consortium of foreign banks had demanded a security for a large loan to the government and salt tax was the only potential source of significant and regular income.

[d] The founding chief inspector was identified and recommended by the consortium of foreign banks and then approved by the Chinese government (1913). After 1928, the Chinese government had more say.

Comparative analyisis: deciphering PoE 217

However, each factor has to be at least partially fulfilled so that the subsequent one can emerge. For example, a founding chief executive has to be appointed before staff deployment or inclusive leadership can begin. There are a variety of reasons why this process of the emergence of a PoE could break down at any one of the junctures in the model. It is likely that many public organizations exist in developing countries that satisfy this model up to a certain point, but have then failed to become full-fledged PoE.

Instead of sticking with the earlier categorization of the factors into the three categories of organizational strength, organizational culture and organizational proactivity, in the model the factors are now arranged in a stylized sequential order. When the head of state decides to break with the usual patronage appointment practice, this may lead to the appointment of a founding chief executive with only weak ties to the established political elite networks and with at least some administrative experience. Provided with focussed powers that are appropriate for the task the organization is responsible for, the chief executive may then practice inclusive leadership and introduce standardization and performance-orientation, as soon as the first round of staff deployment has been completed. This may lead to an increasingly strong organizational identity and a growing external reputation as an effective organization. Throughout this process, the chief executive is constantly involved in political management at various levels, to maintain and expand the actual autonomy of the organization and the necessary support and

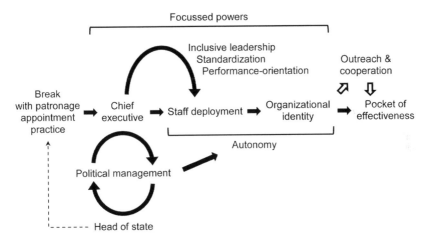

Figure 9.1 Model for the emergence of pockets of effectiveness
Notes: The filled arrows refer to modelled sequential orders. The two circular arrows refer to bargaining relationships. The narrow dotted arrow refers to a decision and the horizontal brackets symbolize more structural features that are external conditions for the other factors, although they themselves are to some degree based on bargaining processes. The unfilled arrows add an additional factor to the model that is specific to scale effectiveness.

218   *Michael Roll*

protection. If successful, the interaction of these factors leads to the emergence of a PoE.

While our three overall categories of factors do not appear in the model, they are still useful for distinguishing between the different ways in which the factors contribute towards the emergence of a PoE. The factors in the category 'organizational strength' (focussed powers, staff deployment, standardization) provide the *infrastructural and procedural components* or *'ingredients'* without which a PoE would be impossible. The 'organizational culture' factors (inclusive leadership, performance-orientation, organizational identity) are the *driving forces* that do the main work of transforming a public organization into a PoE, by changing internal structures, orientation and action. The factors in the category 'organizational proactivity' (political management, organizational autonomy, for scope effectiveness organizations: outreach and cooperation) are the necessary *facilitating factors*.

This whole process is more likely when the head of state is strong and relatively independent in the politico-administrative environment, and the task area in which the organization is working is politically low risk. It is also more likely soon after a new government has assumed office or has been re-elected, rather than later in their term. Finally, an organization is more likely to emerge a PoE when the head of state can reasonably expect it to deliver quick and politically tangible results.

Characteristics of process and approach

We have analysed and described the necessary factors and how they interact in various ways so that they may eventually lead to the emergence of a PoE. Before we continue with how PoE manage to persist, we want to highlight two general characteristics of this process and the approach that the PoE leadership employed. These characteristics were present in all our case studies, and allow us to better understand the nature of the interaction of effective public organizations with their challenging and often hostile environments. We call the first characteristic 'creative pragmatism'. Despite focussed powers and often considerable top-level political support, all PoE chief executives had to cope with imperfect context conditions. While they constantly tried to improve these conditions through political management, they also used the available room to manoeuvre in unexpected ways. NAFDAC, for example, increasingly compensated for missing or conflicting laws and time-consuming and ineffective judicial processes by introducing more encompassing internal regulations. Through them they substantially increased the fines that were payable to the agency, and extended the range of sanctions that the agency could impose (Akunyili 2010: 109–19). Except for 'very serious violations' (ibid.: 109) that were still prosecuted and handed over to the courts, NAFDAC basically internalized and resolved all remaining challenges.

To improve their effectiveness, PoE also began to carry out tasks that were outside of their official mandate. Brazil's development bank sometimes

Comparative analyisis: deciphering PoE   219

intervened in the internal operations of firms to ensure their solvency (see chapter 4). In Nigeria, NAFDAC's chief executive frequently engaged in dispute resolution between contending companies that, in the courts, would have dragged on for years (Akunyili 2010: 75).[41] While most of these activities were not strictly illegal they clearly went beyond bureaucratic routine, the official mandate and a narrow interpretation of the legal provisions of these organizations. These PoE increasingly diversified their spectrum of activities both formally and informally, in order to shape their environment in a way that allowed them to be more autonomous and more effective. We classify these phenomena under 'creative pragmatism', because the organizations (re) acted in unconventional ways to practical problems that arose and that, while not part of the organization's official mandate, would have inhibited their effectiveness. They engaged in pragmatic problem solving and prevention.

The second characteristic of these organizations is that they emerged as PoE in an incremental process rather than by implementing a predefined blueprint.[42] Sir Richard Dane is an exception to this pattern, since he had been the head of excise and salt in India's civil service before coming to China. However, while he has to some degree transferred general bureaucratic principles he also adapted them to the new context and conditions, which were quite different. By adopting this incremental approach, the organizations learned and adapted themselves to their environment and changes in this environment over time. These two general characteristics already provide us with an idea of how the PoE managed to survive in their hostile environments. It is this issue to which we turn next.

How do pockets of effectiveness persist?

In our comparative analysis we identified multiple strategies that PoE used to survive. Many of the factors that were important for the organization's emergence as a PoE (see above) were relevant here as well. However, presenting the answer to our third research question in as much detail as we did to questions one and two above would consume too much space. We therefore restrict ourselves to briefly describing one factor and three main strategies that were most frequently employed. The factor is the 'foundational legacy' and the strategies are the 'president's strategy', the 'effectiveness strategy' and the 'legitimate referencing strategy'. These strategies were often used in combination with each other.

The 'foundational legacy' is straightforward, and is linked to the founding features of PoE we discussed above. A strong legal position right when the organization is established is so important because these legal basics are difficult to change, although that also sometimes happened (e.g. the case of NAPTIP). Moreover, these legal powers cannot be easily ignored by politicians, which is also why a strong legal position is the exception rather than the rule. In more general terms, the stronger and the more clearly defined the legal position of a PoE is when it is established, the more resources the

220   *Michael Roll*

organization has available for actively protecting it against interference. Focused powers are a particularly important point in this regard. But the importance of the foundational legacy goes beyond the legal position of the organization, and includes the management team that comes on board with the chief executive, the first successes and the subsequent reputation that the organization is able or not able to establish. First impressions last long and contribute to structuring the expectations, constraints and opportunities that the organization will operate under in the future. If PoE have successfully established a reputation for non-corruptibility and effectiveness, external expectations shift and fewer attempts are made to bribe the organization. In that sense, getting things right from the very beginning builds a strong structural and symbolic legacy that provides additional resources for preventing and coping with interference in the future.[43]

Heads of state may endanger but can also protect PoE. PoE chief executives therefore often used the 'president's strategy' if lower level politicians tried to erode the autonomy of the organization. They did not usually block and protest against such attempts on the spot, but rather replied that they would take this up at a higher level or with the head of state himself. This strategy was employed in almost all of our case studies. It was used by the Surinam state oil company and even by the state-owned enterprises in the Middle East, although it was not their closeness to the head of state but rather to the royal court that allowed them to effectively fend off such attempts. This confirms our finding from above that in such political and administrative systems, autonomy from politics critically depends on political connections.

We found most evidence for the 'effectiveness strategy'. When using this strategy, PoE representatives explicitly refer to the effectiveness of the organization in carrying out a specific task, and make a case why that function is unique and essential to the interests of the head of state or the political elite. In other words, they frame the organization's mission in a way that aligns with the elite's strategic goals and interests. Depending on what the task of the organization is, they may refer to the contribution the organization is making to the budget (China), to national development (Brazil) or to regulating fields which, due to missing regulation, previously damaged the country's image (Nigeria).

While successfully demonstrated effectiveness may to some degree rest on 'objective' data, this 'effectiveness' is essentially socially constructed. It rests on a process of successful reputation building (see Carpenter 2000, 2001b, 2010; Carpenter and Krause 2011). This shows once again why and how skilful administrative entrepreneurs who employ political management strategically are so crucial. By managing to build an organization's reputation for effectiveness and then using this reputation for employing the effectiveness strategy, they may create the very conditions that then allow the organization to survive and become more effective. However, whatever the skills of a particular chief executive, all this only works as long as two conditions are

Comparative analyisis: deciphering PoE   221

fulfilled. First, the organization has to be at least minimally effective, and second its task has to be generally valued more than its potential for patronage or the tasks executed by other, related organizations.[44]

Another strategy that was widely employed is what we call the 'legitimate referencing strategy'. When using this strategy, the PoE chief executives tried to fend off political interference by referring to principles that they claimed to have general legitimacy. We observed three variants of this strategy. First, they referred to overarching ideological goals such as national development or independence from foreign oil companies (Brazil, Suriname). The second form involved the reference to legal provisions and the law more generally (Suriname, Brazil). The third referred to minimal qualification standards, especially for getting a job at one of these organizations (China, Nigeria, Brazil). The last point is confirmed by Lozano, who writes in his case study of the Dominican Republic that 'meritocracy constitutes a weapon to achieve protection against privilege' (Lozano 2012: 127). However, in none of the cases did the pure existence of some kind of law or standard *automatically* ensure the persistence of the organization as a PoE. This is the case because in these environments, abstract laws and standards did not yet have an inherent and generally acknowledged legitimacy. The PoE chief executives had to skilfully, and often carefully, argue for the acknowledgement of the legitimacy of the principles they were referring to, and then convince politicians that they applied to the organization at the given point in time for defending the PoE's continued existence.

How powerful were these persistence strategies? For answering this question we refer to two dimensions from our analytical framework (see chapter 2): the turning point and dynamic lifecycle perspective and leadership and leadership change. Since the emergence of PoE is so closely linked to a particular head of state (or ruling elite), a new person in that office could undermine the very preconditions for organizational effectiveness. Whether that happens or not depends on a number of factors that we cannot discuss here in detail. Instead, we use the case of Nigeria to briefly highlight some of them. In 2007 President Olusegun Obasanjo had completed his two terms in office and handed over to his successor Umaru Musa Yar'Adua, whom he had previously handpicked and installed as his party's candidate (see Iliffe 2011: 294–97). Therefore the party in power did not change, and many of the financiers of Yar'Adua's election campaign had previously supported Obasanjo. Nevertheless, the change in the presidency also led to changes in the leadership of both NAFDAC and NAPTIP. While NAFDAC's Dora Akunyili was appointed as Nigeria's Minister of Information and Communication in 2008, NAPTIP's Carol Ndaguba was prematurely retired in February 2009. However, despite rumour that in the case of NAPTIP this replacement aimed at rendering the organization less effective, both organizations continued to perform well and remained PoE.[45] Neither the change in the presidency nor the leadership change constituted turning points in which the performance of these organizations was seriously affected.

222 *Michael Roll*

However, the same was not true for other PoE. The case of one of Nigeria's anti-corruption agencies, the successful Economic and Financial Crimes Commission (EFCC) is telling in that regard. One year after Obasanjo, who had appointed Nuhu Ribadu as the first executive chairman of the EFCC in 2003, had handed over to Yar'Adua, Ribadu was removed from office for dubious reasons, despite strong protest from the media, civil society, the diplomatic community and foreign governments. Unlike the case of NAFDAC and NAPTIP, the EFCC under Ribadu had been increasingly perceived as a threat by a powerful group of people close to the president.[46] This shows that, while the reputational costs of removing a well-respected chief executive of a PoE are high, especially for organizations that cooperate closely with international actors and organizations, the benefit that a powerful clique close to the head of state and/or the head of state himself expect to derive from this removal might offset these costs. This case demonstrates clearly that while PoE can use various strategies to fight for survival, and might amass domestic and international reputation for organizational effectiveness and public goods and service delivery, the environment they operate in remains hostile. Persistence is, therefore, fundamentally fragile and can never be taken for granted.

Yet, how are we to explain the fact that, although the leaders that succeeded Akunyili and Ndabuga in NAFDAC and NAPTIP were much less charismatic than their predecessors, the organizations still remained effective? The two historical case studies of PoE in China and Brazil also showed that some less impressive chief executives did not significantly hurt the effectiveness and the reputation of these (see chapters 3 and 4). The short answer we suggest, based on our data, consists of three factors: the 'second guard' or 'second row' leadership, internal organizational identity and external reputation. 'Second guard' refers to those senior officials within the organization who have been members of the founding (or reform) chief executive's founding (or reform) management team. Together with him, they have built up the organization, have been involved in all the crucial steps and decisions and have become the 'faces' of this organizational change for the members of staff. They are now the 'guardians' of the organizational culture and identity, and have significant power to facilitate it as long as they are not removed from office. To varying degrees, all members of staff are now affected by and/ or represent the organizational identity, which includes mutual performance expectations, a sense of mission and task commitment, certain standardized procedures and values, as well as the social status and prestige that being a member of the organization brings with it. This organizational identity has now been institutionalized and every incoming chief executive or senior official who tries to change it is likely to either be ignored or to face stiff resistance. Indeed, given a strong organizational identity, the reverse might happen: newly appointed leadership personnel from the patronage-based elite networks may be disciplined by, and even socialized through, the PoE's organizational culture and identity. The case studies from China and Brazil provide examples for this process of the 'appointee's capture' by the organization (chapters 3 and 4). From the Dominican Republic, Lozano also reports a case in which a manager who had originally been appointed for non-meritocratic reasons came to acknowledge and adopt the organizational identity, and subsequently protected the organization and its staff from external interference (Lozano 2012: 123).

The history of Brazil's BNDE also illustrates that – irrespective of leadership – the quality and reputation of an organization as a PoE can save it when it seems that its period as a PoE is coming to an end. The bank went through such a turning point or period in the 1980s. Due to the rising number of functions it was assigned, a more than twofold increase in the number of staff in a short period of time, its subordination to a weaker ministry, macroeconomic instability and the shift from statist import substitution industrialization to a more neoliberal development strategy, by the early 1980s 'it became a huge, diluted, fragmented bureaucracy, with little of its old spirit' (Schneider 1991: 37). However, in part due to its by then somewhat outdated reputation for technocratic capacity and effectiveness, the bank was given a central role in Brazil's stabilization, privatization and export-promotion programme from 1993, and subsequently regained its status as a PoE (see Font 2003).[47]

Our conclusion on this point also qualifies our assessment of the importance of the leadership factor more generally, that we were sceptical about in our framework (see chapter 2). We argue that the founding chief executive is absolutely crucial for whether an organization becomes a PoE or not. He is the link between the critical political juncture, exemplified by the head of state's decision to break with the patronage appointment practice and organizational effectiveness. It is the founding chief executive who has to successfully exercise political management and create a performance-oriented organizational culture and identity. However, once that has been successfully done and the agency also proactively employs persistence strategies, the organization is protected by the second guard, organizational identity and its external reputation, and the importance of the chief executive is greatly reduced. He might become more relevant again whenever the organization is seriously challenged or attacked. His importance therefore depends on the extent to which this particular organization is exposed to such challenges. To conclude, in the cases we analysed, leadership was crucial during the establishment period and the first few years of the organization's existence, but its importance declined and that of other factors increased thereafter, depending on changes in the environment.

Generalizability

A thorough comparison of our results with other studies would demand far more space than we have here. Nevertheless, we take a look at whether other studies of PoE and PoE related phenomena largely confirm our analysis or contradict it. The outcome of this comparison can either strengthen or

224   *Michael Roll*

weaken our claim that the answers we provided to the research questions apply to PoE more generally.

The four studies we reviewed in chapter 2 differ from our study in many ways. Apart from Grindle's study (1997; Hilderbrand and Grindle 1997), none of these focused explicitly on public organizations. Nevertheless, there are many commonalities between their findings and ours that are worth looking at.[48] We noted in chapter 2 that most of these authors focus on research question two about how PoE emerge, but less so on the others (see table 2.1). Our comparison therefore reflects this focus.

On our first research question about why PoE emerge, we have discussed Israel's concept of specificity above, which only plays a subordinate role in our analysis. But on this first question, Leonard's concise answer to why PoE emerge is worth noting: 'The necessary conditions for the existence of a pocket of excellence appear to be political demand for its particular services and a professional group sustaining its values' (Leonard 1991: 300). While 'political demand' is similar to our concept of political or personal interest in the effective execution of the task an organization performs, a 'professional group sustaining its values' is close to what we call organizational culture and identity. Leonard's study therefore supports parts of our analysis and vice versa.

On the question of how PoE emerge, we find considerable support for our analysis. Grindle emphasizes the importance of 'organizational culture' and to some degree the 'organizational strength' factors. Strong worker dedication and a sense of calling and mission are two factors that Tendler and Leonard also highlight. All this is in line with our argument about the importance of organizational identity. Leonard's account also offers strong support for our model on this question.[49] Perhaps most interesting is his evidence for what we have called 'political management' and the ensuing relational nature of organizational autonomy. He writes that in his case studies the managers manipulated their organization's environment, that they proactively used political connections and that they were often 'risk taking' in doing that (Leonard 1991: 253, 257–59, 268–69), which is very much in line with our analysis, although the concepts differ. Overall, we did not find significant discrepancies between these authors' findings and ours but merely different emphases of factors. These studies therefore offer a fair degree of support for our analysis, especially with regard to our answer to the question of *how* PoE emerge.

While literature on PoE and related phenomena was scarce when we started the research project in Nigeria in 2009, this is slowly beginning to change. Some studies have recently been completed (Abah 2012; Barma, Huybens and Viñuela 2012; McDonnell 2012)[50] and other research projects are ongoing.[51] The three studies just mentioned provide considerable support for our analysis. However, because the final published versions of these studies were not available at the time of writing, we restrict ourselves to comparing our findings to the results of a comparative study of institutional performance in Latin America (Portes and Smith 2012a), as far as it focusses on PoE phenomena. Similar to our motivation behind this project, the researchers

Comparative analyisis: deciphering PoE   225

wanted to explore the diversity of institutional performance both within and across countries.[52] Unlike us, they did not select on the dependent variable of organizational performance and, with 23 organizations from five countries (Argentina, Chile, Colombia, Dominican Republic, Mexico), their sample is bigger than ours. Contrary to our hypothesis-generating approach theirs is more geared towards hypothesis-testing. Nevertheless, in addition to using Qualitative Comparative Analysis (QCA) with Boolean algebra for identifying necessary and sufficient conditions for their outcome variables, their study also provides detailed case studies.[53,54] Their outcome variables are 'institutional adequacy' and 'contribution to development' (Portes and Smith 2012c: 167). For the former, they evaluated whether each of the organizations 'meets the institutional goals for which it was created, as reflected in the relevant enabling law or formal regulation' (Portes and Smith 2012b: 33). For the latter, they looked at 'the extent to which each organization makes a contribution to the socioeconomic development of the nation in its sphere of activity' (Portes and Smith 2012c: 167). Our definition of 'effectiveness' is very close to their concept of 'institutional adequacy', which is why we focus on this particular outcome below.

Portes and Smith compare these institutions to each other based on the 'common historical origins and culture' and the 'comparable levels of development' (ibid.: 26) of the countries they are located in. However, the case studies show clearly that with regard to the context that we have chosen as relevant for organizational performance, the politico-administrative environment, their cases differ significantly. While Chile's system can be categorized as a presidential democracy with a fairly effective bureaucracy in which laws and formal rules are generally observed, the case study authors for Colombia and the Dominican Republic stress that the polities of these countries are dominated by clientelism. From their way of using the concept 'clientelism', and from how they describe the country context, it is obvious that they refer to similar features like the ones we encountered in the politico-administrative environments of PoE, such as a powerful head of state, the prevalence of patronage and personal relations, and a largely dysfunctional public sector (see chapter 2). The World Bank indicators for the overall effectiveness of government and the public sector for the years concerned support this comparative assessment (see table 9.4).[55] When we now apply our criteria for PoE, we see that the organizations that provide public goods and services effectively in these two countries qualify as PoE, which is why we focus on them in the following discussion.

All organizations that perform well on Portes and Smith's outcome variable 'institutional adequacy' in Colombia and the Dominican Republic are organizations with rather high specificity tasks: the civil aviation agencies in both countries, the stock exchange in Colombia and the tax agency in the Dominican Republic.[56] According to our analysis, it is not specificity per se but specificity mediated by a substantive interest of the head of state or the ruling coalition, and their belief that the organizations can deliver quick and

226   *Michael Roll*

Table 9.4 Government effectiveness in the countries covered in Portes and Smith (2012a)

Country (Organization)	Years of interest	World Bank Government Effectiveness indicator (Percentile rank)
Colombia	1996	-0.19 (48.8)
(Civil aviation and stock exchange)[a]	2002	-0.41 (39.5)
	2011	0.06 (56.4)
Dominican Republic	2006	-0.58 (32.2)
(Civil aviation and tax agency)[b]	2011	-0.58 (34.1)
Chile	1996	1.28* (87.8)
	2011	1.26* (85.8)
Argentina	1996	0.27 (62.4)
	2011	-0.14 (48.8)
Mexico	1996	0.07 (59.0)
	2011	0.31 (63.5)

Notes: * More than one standard deviation above or below the mean of zero.

According to the World Bank, the Government Effectiveness indicator is 'capturing perceptions of the quality of public services, the quality of the civil service and the degree of its independence from political pressures, the quality of policy formulation and implementation, and the credibility of the government's commitment to such policies' (Kaufmann, Kraay and Mastruzzi 2009: 6). The Worldwide Governance Indicators (WGI) are aggregate indicators which, for the countries included in the table, are based on between three data sources in the earlier years up to a maximum of 11 data sources in more recent years. The units of measurement follow a normal distribution with a mean of zero and a standard deviation of one. Almost all scores therefore lie between -2.5 and 2.5, with higher scores indicating better, and lower scores poorer outcomes. For the percentile rank each country is ranked among all other countries included in that particular year. It ranges from 0 until 100 with 0 corresponding to the lowest and 100 corresponding to the highest rank. We argue that, notwithstanding the many shortcomings of this indicator for our purposes and more generally, it provides a useful approximation.

The earliest year for which the WGI data are available is 1996. Our years of interest are the years in which the organizations were either established or reformed. For Colombia and the Dominican Republic, we selected the two organizations that qualified as PoE, respectively. While they were established relatively recently and we can therefore report the indicators for these years, we report the 1996 and the latest available indicator at the time of writing (2011) for all other countries. For an overview of the years of establishment and reform of all the organizations covered in their study, see Portes and Smith (2012b: 30-31).

[a] Colombia's stock exchange was established in 2001. However, since WGI data are not available for this particular year, we used the data for 2002.

[b] In the Dominican Republic the civil aviation authority and the tax agency were both established in 2006.

Source: World Bank (n.d.).

tangible results, that makes them more likely to be established as PoE compared to other organizations.

The results from these four organizations and the overall study offer broad support for our analysis. Almost all effective organizations score high on the three internal determinants that the research team included (meritocracy, immunity to corruption, no 'islands' of power) (see table 9.5). This corresponds to some degree although not perfectly to our factors of staff deployment, performance-orientation and inclusive leadership (see table 9.6). In general, it confirms the importance of what we call organizational strength and culture.

Beyond that, the study provides insights into and support for the recruitment strategies for PoE we discovered, the importance of creative pragmatism and political management and finally our choice of the politico-administrative system as the appropriate context dimension for comparing PoE to each other. We begin with the unusual case of the Dominican Republic's effective tax agency. In contrast to the high scores of most effective organizations on the internal determinants referred to above, it scores low on meritocracy and immunity to corruption (see table 9.5). However, on meritocracy the case study reveals a different story. Lozano (2012) writes that the organization has 'two types of staff positions: those based on "trust", without benefit of meritocratic competition, and those that are part of the regular career service' (Lozano 2012: 119–20). Moreover, the organization has a 'technical nucleus with strong meritocratic capacities that the management takes into account and protects' (ibid.: 123). This shows three things. First, meritocratic

Table 9.5 Truth table scores for selected institutions in Colombia and the Dominican Republic

Country Institution	Determinants Crisp set score (fuzzy set score)*						Result
	Internal			External			
	Meritocracy	Immunity to corruption	No 'islands' of power'	Proactivity	Technological flexibility	External allies	Institutional adequacy
Colombia							
Civil aviation	1 (4)	1 (3)	1 (3.5)	0 (2)	1 (5)	0 (2.5)	1 (4)
Stock exchange	1 (4)	1 (3.5)	1 (3.5)	0 (2)	1 (3.5)	1 (4)	1 (4)
Dominican Republic							
Civil aviation	1 (3.5)	1 (3.5)	1 (3.5)	1 (5)	1 (3.5)	1 (4)	1 (4)
Tax agency	0 (3)	0 (3)	1 (4)	1 (4)	1 (5)	1 (4)	1 (4)

Notes: *Crisp set score key: *1* = *Presence;* *0* = *Absence;* Fuzzy set score key: *1* = *'Entirely outside the conceptual set defined by the variable';* *2* = *'More outside than inside';* *3* = *'Neither';* *4* = *'More inside than outside';* *5* = *'Entirely inside'* For the fuzzy score of 3 ('neither'), the crisp score can be either 0 or 1. The case studies in Portes and Smith (2012a) provide detailed analyses of these organizational features.
Source: Portes and Smith (2012b: 34-35).

228   *Michael Roll*

Table 9.6 Factors that explain how PoE emerge and corresponding factors from Portes and Smith (2012a)

Category Factors	Corresponding factors from Portes and Smith (2012)

Organizational strength
  Focussed powers
  Staff deployment
  Standardization
	Meritocracy, immunity to corruption

Organizational culture
  Inclusive leadership
  Performance-orientation
  Organizational identity
	No 'islands' of power

Organizational proactivity
  Political management
  Autonomy
  Outreach & cooperation*
	External allies, proactivity
	External allies, immunity to corruption
	Proactivity

Work mode of PoE Creative pragmatism	
Non-necessary other factors Embedded technology	Technological flexibility

Note: *Necessary only for scale effectiveness.
Source: Corresponding factors from Portes and Smith (2012b: especially 34–35).

principles *did* indeed apply to a sizable portion of staff, but second and more importantly, it reveals a division of staff that mirrors one of our findings. We saw that while meritocratic principles were applied for the rank and file staff, appointments to higher management positions were made based on criteria such as acquaintance and personal trust, usually in combination with some kind of informal or implicit meritocratic assessment. That is also the case in the Dominican Republic.

The apparent absence of an organizational immunity to corruption also merits a closer look. Lozano informs us that external experts generally assess the organization which acquired operational autonomy in 2004 to be 'generally honest but with a strong tendency to *interpret rules and take discretionary action*; this tendency ends up facilitating agreements in favour of the most important and powerful taxpayers' (ibid.: 120, with reference to Guzmán 2008; our emphasis). He also reports that the agency was successful in making powerful groups enter into formal agreements with the authorities for reducing their tax payments, instead of using fraud or evading taxes on a massive scale (ibid.: 119). And some pages later, we learn that 'there is considerable immunity to corruption' (ibid.: 123). How can these apparently contradictory statements be reconciled?

Without having more empirical details, we suggest the following interpretation. Bribery and corruption do not seem to be major issues any more in the agency. Moreover, through the standardization of its procedures it has established a reputation for non-corruptibility and predictability that has led 'powerful groups' to shift to negotiations within the legal framework, rather than informal and personalized settlements. The importance of 'interpreting rules' and using discretionary room for manoeuver confirms our observation that the working mode of PoE is one of 'creative pragmatism'. In challenging environments this may be frequently necessary for PoE to be able to carry out their task in a sustained and effective manner.

The research project also confirms the importance of the factor we have termed 'political management' for triggering top level political protection and support. The authors of the case studies from Colombia and the Dominican Republic point out that the respective directors had direct access to the president or ministers and, focussing more on processes, that they 'also achieved alliances with political elites' (Lozano 2012: 127, 123–24; Rodríguez-Garavito 2012: 93) for three of the four successful organizations. They emphasize the importance of this factor for the organization's effectiveness. Colombia's civil aviation authority does not seem to fit into this pattern, since it scored low on the importance of 'external allies' for its effectiveness. This may be explained by the civil aviation authority's questionable status as a PoE. Rodríguez-Garavito states that the organization's effectiveness 'has been much more limited [compared to the strengthening of staff training] in terms of its airport management function' (ibid.: 89).[57] A somewhat weaker explanation may be Columbia's generally 'fragmented state apparatus that provides no reliable allies' (ibid.: 93), with the exception of the stock exchange authority, in whose existence the finance ministry and the financial sector had an interest (ibid.: 93).

The last conclusion that we can draw from this project confirms our reasoning for, and our choice of the politico-administrative system as the appropriate context dimension for comparing PoE. We argued in the introduction that for answering our research questions, we can meaningfully compare PoE in *similar* politico-administrative environments or systems. Meaningful comparisons of effective public organizations may *not* be possible if the respective politico-administrative systems differ fundamentally. What would we expect to find in the data to confirm the latter hypothesis? When looking at the determinants of organizational effectiveness or, in Portes and Smith's term, institutional adequacy, we should expect to see a systematic difference between the determinants of effective organizations in countries with a politico-administrative system based on formal legal rules and countries in which informal and personalized relations dominate. Since Portes and Smith included both types of countries in their study, they provide us with the opportunity to test this hypothesis.

Leaving out Colombia's civil aviation authority, we compare the three undisputed PoE from Colombia and the Dominican Republic (see table 9.5) to the five organizations included in their study from Chile (Wormald and Brieba 2012; Portes and Smith 2012b: 34–35). Their truth table (ibid.: 34–35) shows that all five Chilean organizations included in the study scored high on

230   *Michael Roll*

institutional adequacy, which indicates that they are all effective public organizations. However, because they exist within a politico-administrative environment that is largely based on formal rules and laws and is therefore also fairly effective, these organizations are no 'pockets'. The only systematic difference that we find between the three PoE and the Chilean organizations is that, while all PoE score high on 'external allies' (see table 9.5), three out of the five Chilean public organizations score low on this factor (see Portes and Smith 2012b: 34–35). For achieving institutional adequacy or organizational effectiveness, having external allies does *not* seem to be a necessary factor in formal legal rule-based environments, while it apparently *is* in politico-administrative systems characterized by informal and personalized relations.[58] Different types of environment seem to require different kinds of engagement of organizations with external allies to become and remain effective. Therefore, while political management is apparently essential for PoE in countries like Nigeria, it may be beneficial but is not necessary in Chile.[59] This finding confirms our assumption that there is indeed a systematic difference between the factors that explain the emergence and persistence of effective organizations in different politico-administrative environments.

Overall, together with the other studies, Portes and Smith's (2012c, 2012a) findings provide strong support for many of the factors we have identified in our analysis. The case studies from Colombia and the Dominican Republic are particularly instructive, and offer evidence that confirms our findings on how particular mechanisms work. While more systematic comparisons of our findings with the results from other PoE studies are necessary to be able to claim that our analysis has external validity and our findings are generalizable to a certain degree, our first attempts clearly point into that direction. We now turn to our fourth and last research question.

Trigger effects, reform and state-society bargaining

So far, we have held back the answer to our fourth research question on the potential triggering effect of PoE on other public organizations and the broader governance environment. We provide the answer in this section, and combine it with a discussion of the potential contribution of PoE to public sector reform and renewed state-society bargaining in the type of politico-administrative environments in which PoE exist.

Compared to the other questions, our empirical foundation for answering the 'trigger' question, is thin. It is mainly restricted to the historical case studies of the Sino-Foreign Salt Inspectorate in Republican China and Brazil's National Bank for Economic Development. In both cases we found evidence for attempts to model other public organizations on the PoE. In Republican China, several politicians clearly admired the bureaucratic effectiveness of the salt inspectorate and tried to introduce some of the inspectorate's organizational principles in other public organizations (see chapter 3). However, while we lack the data to arrive at a more informed assessment of these attempts,

Comparative analyisis: deciphering PoE   231

we can safely say that the inspectorate did not trigger a broader reform of administrative institutions in China at that time. The same is true for the rural reconstruction reforms in Taiwan.

We have more evidence for the triggering effects of Brazil's BNDE. Eliza Willis describes how the organization actively disseminated its high technical standards and expertise, combined with administrative professionalism, to other organizations (see chapter 4). The bank did so by offering its expertise and advise to other ministries, using its power as a lender to improve technical standards in state-owned enterprises, sending staff to other state organizations, having staff from other organizations working with them on a temporary basis and, although often unsuccessfully, by establishing regional and state-based development banks throughout the country. The analysis of these paths includes all three of the triggering mechanisms proposed in chapter 2 (demonstration mechanism, contagion mechanism, transplantation mechanism), but goes beyond them by suggesting that the bank used its power as a lending agency in a much more deliberate way, and generally was much more proactive and 'missionary' than we had imagined when developing these abstract mechanisms. It was not so much that other organizations were impressed by the PoE's success and then tried to mimic certain features in this case, but rather that those 'infected' with the 'PoE virus' tried to spread it. This interpretation is confirmed by Ben Ross Schneider's finding that the bank 'took on this modernizing role and fought traditionalism and personalism where it could' (Schneider 1991: 37). Overall, this fits very well with our analysis, in which organizational culture, identity and public service commitment feature so prominently.

While the case studies from Republican China and Brazil offer some evidence for the importance of PoE and some of the channels through which they worked, overall we cannot conclude that, on their own, they triggered broader administrative reforms. Acknowledging both the limitations of our data and the external contributions these organizations *did* make, it is fair to say that, for a long period of time, these PoE generally remained what they were in the first place: fairly isolated pockets of public sector performance in otherwise ineffective and non-bureaucratic politico-administrative systems. While they may have played a facilitating role in a broader institutional reform process at some point, they themselves did not trigger such a process. This suggests an interpretation of PoE as either function-specific instruments motivated by personal or political interests of the head of state, or isolated 'second-best' solutions in environments in which there is insufficient collective interest in more comprehensive reforms.

That leads us to the question of whether PoE may be able to facilitate public sector reform in today's developing countries. Our findings from Republican China, Taiwan and Brazil above suggest a negative answer. Does this hold true for all types of PoE? With the exception of Republican China, all our case studies cover PoE that were not externally induced but emerged as a result of primarily domestic political and administrative processes. In

232   *Michael Roll*

recent years, international development organizations have increasingly suggested and supported the establishment of semi-autonomous executive agencies. In line with a more general governance trend towards 'agencification' that began in the late 1980s and early 1990s, the rationale behind this model is to isolate selected executive agencies from the broader civil service and from political influence.[60] These organizations are granted semi- or full autonomous status with regard to staff recruitment and management, income generation and salary structure. The most common examples are semi-autonomous revenue agencies (SARAs) that have been established in many developing countries in recent years (see Fjeldstad and Moore 2008: 249–55 and with a focus on sub-Saharan Africa, Ayee 2008: 134–37 and Fjeldstad and Moore 2009).

In international development cooperation donor agencies work together with the respective governments for establishing such agencies. For a limited period of time, they usually provide technical assistance, funding and expatriate personnel. The government of the country concerned awards these agencies a semi-autonomous status with regard to key procedures, as outlined above, which makes them independent of the regular civil service rules and procedures. Function-specific rights are also often granted, and private sector performance management instruments are introduced. Comparative studies of the effect of the introduction of these agencies that include developing countries are rare (see Talbot and Caulfield 2002; Pollitt and Talbot 2004; Fjeldstad and Moore 2009; Sulle 2010). In general their conclusions are similar to those that studies of the introduction of agencies in OECD countries have arrived at (Pollitt et al. 2004; Talbot 2004; Pollitt 2009). They show that, while some progress has been made with regard to internal management processes and sometimes staff commitment, there is little evidence that the introduction of agencies has improved service delivery (Caulfield 2002: 215; Therkildsen 2008: 25; Prado 2008), except for a short 'honeymoon period' immediately after the agency has been established (Therkildsen 2004; Laking 2005: 13–14; Robinson 2007).

Based on our analysis of PoE this finding is not surprising. The idea to establish such semi-autonomous agencies is often the result of intergovernmental negotiations or agreements with development agencies. Furthermore, establishing such agencies with donor support takes a long time. Due to these reasons these agencies tend to lack precisely what enables PoE to emerge and to persist: genuine domestic interest from political key actors and embeddedness in the political system and process. This leads to weak incentives for heads of states and political elites to provide these organizations with sufficient political support, respond to political management and maintain or extend the autonomy of these organizations. One could assume that, to the extent that a strong political interest and embeddedness are given, e.g. due to an interest in additional financial resources provided by an effective tax agency, the organization might have a much better chance of performing well. However, in agreement with studies from the International Monetary Fund

(Gupta and Tareq 2008), Fjeldstad and Moore (2009), conclude that, apart from a few exceptions, the semi-autonomous revenue agencies that have been introduced in Africa in recent decades have *not* increased government revenues substantially. It is beyond the scope of this chapter to assess the performance of donor-supported semi-autonomous executive agencies in developing countries in more detail. However, based on our findings on why and how PoE emerge and persist, we can see many reasons why it is difficult for external actors to make a meaningful contribution to establishing truly effective and sustainable semi-autonomous agencies.

In our analytical framework we introduced a political sociology perspective, and argued that the provision of basic public goods and services may be crucial for bridging the trust and legitimacy gap that exists between state and society in many developing countries. We went on to argue that effective public service provision may then contribute to facilitating state-society bargaining, increasing accountability and eventually to state building. While we did not explicitly test this claim in our case studies, our findings allow us to comment on whether the PoE contributed to such a process. Our answer is short and clear: no, they did not. Citizens in developing countries clearly distinguish between the different state actors and agencies. They know which organizations or officials they can or cannot trust. Overall, they are very much aware that the large majority of those acting in the name of the state either try to extract money from them without providing adequate public services or simply ignore them. The occasional effective public organization is a pleasant surprise and exception for them but only serves to prove the general rule.

Based on the analysis of our case studies, we can also conclude that with regard to the legitimacy of the state, PoE do little, if anything at all, to improve it. For better understanding why this is the case we use David Easton's distinction between diffuse and specific support for a state or government (Easton 1965: 267–79). While 'specific support' is a function of the output of the system, 'diffuse support' is not based on what the system does, but on what it represents and whether or not that corresponds with what is considered 'right and proper' (ibid.: 279). The latter is therefore usually the product of experiences cumulated over a longer period of time and measured against expectations and principles.[61] Once established, it is to a certain degree independent of short-term fluctuations in government performance and is passed on through socialization. For the developing countries we are looking at, that implies that it will take strong general public sector performance over a sustained period of time, or at least a government's credible commitment to it to strengthen the legitimacy of the state and to create diffuse support.

We have now concluded that PoE do not offer an alternative route to public sector reform in developing countries, that the lack of trust between state and society is unlikely to be bridged by isolated PoE and that, on their own, they cannot produce state legitimacy. This is not a fair overall assessment of PoE

234 *Michael Roll*

for two reasons. First, their very existence in a hostile environment is a remarkable, important and for many people life-saving achievement. Even if PoE 'only' manage to survive and continue to effectively provide public goods and services they deserve to be studied and celebrated. They send out the message that has long been ignored and underestimated in development studies and political economy more broadly that indeed 'there *is* scope for improving the functioning of institutions, even in relatively hostile environments' (Banerjee and Duflo 2011: 254, our emphasis). Apart from service provision these exceptional organizations are also of significant symbolic importance that should not be underestimated. They signify to citizens, progressive civil servants and politicians, civil society, the media and international observers that a different mode of governance and public sector management, and therefore state action, is indeed possible. In environments in which patronage politics and captured bureaucracies abound, pockets of effectiveness are also pockets of hope for a better future. All these are significant contributions. Simply because these organizations manage to beat the odds and are effective under adverse circumstances they are no magic bullets, and should not be expected to solve all the other political and institutional problems that exist in their countries. In most cases they are busy enough surviving.

There is a second reason why the above assessment presents a distorted picture. It may well be that it is not the features of a PoE as such that determine whether it can have a broader transformative effect or not. The particular task that the organization is responsible for may be just as important. We give two examples for public organizations that share several features with PoE and *did* have a transformative effect. The first example is the economic policy 'pilot' or 'nodal' agency that was key in East Asia's developmental states.[62] Unlike the public organizations we have analysed in this book, the primary task of these agencies was to promote international competitiveness and domestic growth, through the implementation and coordination of industrial and trade policy in close collaboration with both the government and private enterprises.[63] From our sample, only Brazil's BNDE had a somewhat similar but much more limited role in economic policy. It could well be that one of the most powerful ways through which this particular type of PoE can contribute to public sector reform in developing countries is indirectly, by facilitating sustained economic growth.

A second group of a very different kind of PoE that may have transformative qualities are the public organizations running conditional cash transfer programmes for poverty alleviation (see Hanlon, Barrientos and Hulme 2010). Since the end of the 1990s these social welfare programmes have been implemented across Latin America, starting with Mexico's *Progresa* (later *Oportunidades*) and then Brazil's well-known *Bolsa Família*.[64] Many of these programmes are quite effective and target a significant proportion of poor families that have not previously benefitted much from government services. In addition to that, these programmes may indeed succeed in bridging the trust gap between state and society and earn the state legitimacy, because they respond to some of the most pressing needs of these people. Based on this new trust and legitimacy, citizens could feel encouraged to take the state seriously and demand public services and accountability, while politicians on the other hand may switch the way they relate to citizens and voters, from a clientelist relationship to one based on political programmes, and from personal to institutional benefits. While many organizations in our sample performed tasks that were of broad relevance to citizens, they did not address the most urgent priorities of the majority of the poor people in these countries. That is one of the reasons why they could not bridge the trust gap more effectively or earn the state significant legitimacy. Whether or not PoE have transformative effects is therefore not only a function of the effectiveness with which public goods and services are provided, but also of the relevance of these goods and services to a large share of the population that has previously been neglected.

Taking an 'upside-down view of governance' (Centre for the Future State 2010a), that is non-normative but rather explorative for empirically and analytically capturing actual social processes, has proved to be a fruitful approach for this study. The comparative analysis of our case studies across time and space has allowed us to come up with a model of why and how PoE emerge, how they manage to persist and has enabled us to provide a preliminary assessment of their broader transformative potential. We have confirmed previous findings from some of the pioneers in PoE research, and have in turn found our results supported by theirs and those of others. Along the way, new puzzles and potential research questions have emerged. One of the most important challenges that remains is to identify the *sufficient* factors for the emergence and persistence of PoE.[65] Overall, PoE are counterintuitive and fascinating phenomena that we can still learn a lot from, in terms of structure, agency and power as well as institutional change and development. Especially with regard to their broader transformative potential and their limitations, our knowledge is still in its infancy. We hope that our analytical framework, the empirical analysis and theoretical discussion will inspire future researchers to refine, challenge and go beyond our conclusions.

Notes

1 While this book is a collective enterprise and this chapter in particular is based on all case studies, I alone am responsible for the comparative analysis. The authors of the case studies may or may not agree with it.

2 Since most of the public organizations we looked at in this study were not pre-existing organizations that were reformed but newly established organizations, we will refer to 'established' organizations only in the remainder of this chapter, claiming that the same arguments apply to those that were reformed.

3 In our cases, these heads of state were mostly strong presidents. However, in principle a sufficiently small and coherent ruling elite could act in similar ways. The reader may therefore choose to substitute 'coherent ruling elite' for 'head of state' throughout this chapter.

236 *Michael Roll*

4 This idea is based on the 'trader's dilemma' as formulated by Hans-Dieter Evers (1994). Based on research in Southeast Asia, he argues that small traders or trader minorities frequently face the dilemma that on the one hand, they need to accumulate capital, while on the other hand they face strong moral obligations to share their profits with kin and neighbours. Geddes's 'politican's dilemma' argument, as a conflict between the short-term need to ensure political survival through clientelism and a long-term interest in national development which would require a professional civil service, also comes to mind (Geddes 1994).

5 For easier reading we use the masculine form only in the remainder of this chapter. Of course, the analysis holds for both men and women.

6 Throughout this chapter we use the term 'chief executive' to refer to the head of a PoE or another public organization.

7 According to Granovetter 'the strength of a tie is a (probably linear) combination of the amount of time, the emotional intensity, the intimacy (mutual confiding), and the reciprocal services which characterize the tie' (Granovetter 1973: 1361). He uses the concept to focus on how the tie between two individuals who belong to otherwise separate and, each for itself, more close-knit groups serve as 'bridging' (weak) ties (Granovetter 1983: 202) between these different social circles. He illustrated the 'strength' of these weak ties by showing that in a study of job seekers, the majority of them got information that led to new jobs, not through strong but through weak ties (Granovetter 1973: 1371–76 and Granovetter 1974).

8 However, some of the chief executives had been involved in community development and subnational politics before to some degree (e.g. NAFDAC's Dora Akunyili). Staatsolie's Eddy Jharap in Suriname was a co-founder of the leftist *Volkspartij*. However, based on his qualification as a geologist, he was appointed as the head of the Surinamese oil commission under the military regime, before he became the state oil company's first president.

9 This resonates well with the point that Hertog makes about 'regime autonomy' in his contribution (chapter 8).

10 A potential alternative to this first factor that we did, however, not observe, is a situation in which either the president is weak or the risk is generally high, but where the establishment of a PoE is supported by a large enough group of politicians across groups and parties in response to a major crisis. Such an extraordinary situation could produce a temporary overarching interest that could lead to a short moment of collective decision-making.

11 Four cases from our sample require further clarification in addition to the information given in table 1.1. First, the driving force behind the establishment of Republican China's tax inspectorate was not the government but a consortium of foreign banks. The second clarification concerns the Republic of China/Taiwan's Joint Commission on Rural Reconstruction. After Japan had been defeated and surrendered in 1945, the Chinese civil war between forces led by the Kuomintang (Chinese Nationalist Party), loyal to the government of the Republic of China, and the Communist Party of China continued. Taiwan was legally and administratively 'returned' to the Republic of China by Japan in September 1945, but the period between then and January 1949 were months of brutal decolonization from Japan and political mismanagement. It was during this period of civil war and fragile government that the Joint Commission on Rural Reconstruction was established first on the mainland, and then transferred its activities to Taiwan in late 1949. The third case is Suriname's state oil company Staatsolie. It was established on 13 December 1980, several months after the coup d'état on 25 February in the same year. Fourth, Nigeria's anti-trafficking agency NAPTIP started work on 26 August 2003, after the respective trafficking prohibition act had been passed and Olusegun Obasanjo had been re-elected for a second and final term in office in April the same year.

12 The ruling Dominican Liberation Party won the absolute majority in the May 2006 legislative elections as the leading member of the electoral alliance 'Progressive Bloc'.

13 As part of the same larger and comparative project on institutional performance in Latin America (Portes and Smith 2012a), research in Colombia showed that both the stock exchange and the civil aviation authority can be regarded as PoE, and were established less than two years after the new president came into office (Rodríguez-Garavito 2012). However, the evidence that these two cases add has to be considered carefully, since the stock exchange is a private organization and, unlike the cases in our sample, we did not examine whether it can be meaningfully compared to public organizations. Moreover, the PoE status of the Colombian civil aviation authority is questionable, as we will discuss below.

14 In our sample, only Nigeria had a two term limit legislation in place when the two public organizations that then became PoE were established. Therefore, we have not sufficient data to test whether a systematic relationship between term limitations and the emergence of PoE exists or not.

15 This happened in the context of President Vargas's policy of industrialization and nationalization and to limit the growing influence of U.S. American oil companies in the country's oil sector. While *Petrobras* was the subject of fierce political infighting after its establishment and its history is not one of consistent effectiveness, it has managed to survive in this hostile environment, and has become an unusually effective and profitable company by international standards over the past decades.

16 In her study, Grindle also finds that 'the type of task undertaken by the organization was not a good predictor of differences between good and poor performance' (Grindle 1997: 484). While claiming that the notion of specificity lacks operational relevance for their purpose, the authors of another study also do not find a link between the kind of task a public organization performs and its overall effectiveness (Barma, Huybens and Viñuela 2012: 7).

17 For an example of Israel 'objective' understanding of measurable task specificity, see his suggestions for building a 'specificity index' (Israel 1987: 68–71).

18 A critical juncture is defined as 'a period of significant change, which typically occurs in distinct ways in different countries (or other units of analysis), and which is hypothesized to produce distinct legacies' (Collier and Collier 1991: 29; see also Capoccia and Kelemen 2007). For the distinct but related concept of 'critical decisions', see Ermakoff 2008: 332.

19 We use the term 'client' with regard to public services with some unease, since they are not 'clients' in the private sector sense of the term but first and foremost citizens. However, for the lack of an alternative term that describes their role in this context precisely enough, we decided to use it.

20 Especially service delivery or regulatory public organizations started with small but targeted and effectively advertised initiatives in their first year of existence, like NAFDAC did with the drinking water producers (Akunyili 2010: 43–44). These initiatives can be seen as early attempts for building up scale effectiveness.

21 For a rare and detailed account of this initial phase in the case of NAFDAC, see Akunyili 2010: 41–55.

22 Meritocratic recruitment is one of the best known and researched factors for administrative effectiveness and the reduction of corruption. See, among many others, Evans and Rauch (1999), Owusu (2006a, 2006b) and Dahlström, Lapuente and Teorell (2012).

23 This is a common finding in PoE studies. See Grindle (1997: 484) and Owusu (2006a, 2006b), for example.

24 We also note that, especially with regard to the factors discussed in this section, there are interesting similarities between our analysis and the classical

238   *Michael Roll*

organizational sociology literature, such as Selznick (1957), or the classical comparative public administration literature (e.g. Riggs 1964), that we cannot discuss in this chapter due to space limitations.

25 Grindle also makes the point that higher salaries may contribute but, on their own, do not lead to improved organizational performance (Grindle 1997: 484).

26 Kovach's work is interesting because he looks at what motivates workers most, based on survey results from 1946, 1981, 1986 and 1995. Factors such as 'interesting work', 'full appreciation of work done' and 'feeling on being in on things' consistently rank higher than 'good wages' (Kovach 1987, 1995). A recent representative survey on what motivates workers in Germany produced almost identical results (Hay Group 2012).

27 The focus of research on the state-owned enterprises in the Middle East and Suriname was not on the inner workings of the organizations. This is why the analysis of the degree to which organizational identity was important for performance and effectiveness is less clear in these chapters than in others. However, both authors confirmed that organizational identity was an important factor for effectiveness in both cases.

28 However, while there were organizational shortcomings before 2001, one has to keep in mind that the agency also operated in a very difficult environment of military dictatorship and political instability, and had to grapple with problems such as a lack of political support, inadequate funding and poorly policed borders, which made the import of counterfeit drugs very easy.

29 It is important to note that such chief executives do not necessarily have to be charismatic personalities, in the common understanding of the term. While many of the chief executives in our case studies were, others were clearly not. However, this latter group of leaders was still authentic and focussed enough to communicate their mission so powerfully and convincingly as to earn their staff's loyalty and support. Moreover, for some organizations the motivation to perform well came only partly from a framing of the organization's task with reference to broader overall goals or values. It also came from a narrower but equally strong 'technical' or 'bureaucratic ethos' (see the case of Brazil's BNDE, chapter 4).

30 In the medium to long run it was also essential for the motivations of members of staff that they knew the organization had strong and focussed powers that minimized the need for external cooperation with other public organizations. An official who knows that the evidence he or she is collecting will definitely be used for the prosecution of a perpetrator by his colleagues in another department, will work more diligently than another one who later has to hand over the case to an external agency that is notorious for its dysfunctionality.

31 NAFDAC's new chief executive reported that she had to reign in '"going to the bank", a common practice by public service employees in Nigeria' (Akunyili 2010: 48).

32 On the importance of bureaucratic socialization – among many other things – see Herbert Kaufman's *Forest Ranger* (1967) and Steinmetz (1993: 104–107). On collective alignment and realignment processes, see Ermakoff (2008: 181–210).

33 One could even go further and claim that PoE most closely resemble minority elite groups, which tend to be even more closely integrated due to their minority status.

34 Such attacks occurred frequently in our case studies, especially to the regulatory agencies in Nigeria.

35 We do not argue that every member of staff began to regard his or her job as a personal 'mission'. It was probably only a minority of rank and file staff. But such a 'core group' that does not necessarily have to occupy a formal leadership position is sufficient for providing drive and motivation for the organization as a whole. Other officials may still identify with the organization's mission but simply carry out their responsibilities in a more business-like manner in the 'shadow' of these others.

Comparative analyisis: deciphering PoE   239

36 For just two out of a large number of examples and case studies, see Prado (2008) on more or less independent regulatory agencies in Brazil and Joshi and Ayee (2009) on Ghana's internal revenue service. Apart from showing that the restructuring of Ghana's revenue authorities along the lines of the model of the semi-autonomous revenue authority (SARA) in 1986 did *not* lead to more independence, they argue that the revenue collection increase that still occurred since the early 1990s was primarily due to organizational design reforms rather than to more autonomy, as is often assumed.

37 James Q. Wilson's (1989) notion of autonomy in his classic study of government agencies in the United States is actually quite similar to ours. In more casual terms, he writes: 'No agency has or can have complete autonomy, but all struggle to get and keep as much as they can' (Wilson 1989: 28; see also 188–92).

38 However, like for organizational autonomy and political management, some of the features we have discovered as necessary conditions for PoE in developing countries are also found in public organizations in established bureaucracies in Europe and the United States (see, for example, Wilson 1989: chapter 11 and, for an overview, 27–28; see also Carpenter 2001b). A discussion of the similarities and differences of these bureaucratic features in very different institutional contexts would be insightful, but is beyond the scope of this paper.

39 While we argue throughout this study that the state-owned enterprises in our sample can be meaningfully compared to the public goods and service delivery public organizations, this is probably least true with regard to outreach and cooperation. The major difference is that the relationship of these organizations with their clients is market-based and profit-driven. We therefore exclude the Suriname and Middle East case studies from our analysis on this particular point.

40 A recent comparative study of institutions in Latin America that we will discuss in more detail below (Portes and Smith 2012a), provides additional empirical support for this conclusion. Our definition of organizational effectiveness is close to what they define as 'institutional adequacy' (Portes and Smith 2012c: 167). For the two organizations from their sample in Colombia (Rodríguez-Garavito 2012) which meet our PoE criteria (civil aviation and stock exchange authorities), the determinant 'proactivity' was absent (see Portes and Smith 2012b: 34–35 and table 9.5). Since these are both clearly core effectiveness organizations, their finding is in line with our analysis. However, as we will discuss further below, there are doubts whether Colombia's civil aviation authority really qualifies as a PoE and whether the country's stock exchange agency, which is a private organization, can be compared to public organizations.

41 Akunyili writes that, between 2001 and 2007 alone, NAFDAC managed to resolve 65 out of 80 company disputes (Akunyili 2010: 75).

42 The advantages of incrementalism for public organizations have been analysed long ago by Charles Lindblom as 'muddling through' (1959).

43 Although unusual, it also helps if the organization benefits from some sort of 'benign neglect' on the part of the government. The organization may then be able to quietly build an administrative structure and obtain a strong position, because the politicians are not really paying attention to it. This happened in the case of Suriname's state oil company *Staatsolie*, which was not regarded as a priority compared to companies in other major rent-producing sectors from the 1980s until the mid-1990s (see chapter 7).

44 Gernot Klantschnig's study of drug law enforcement in Nigeria and the country's National Drug Law Enforcement Agency (NDLEA) provides an example for a shift of political interests (Klantschnig 2009). According to him the 'war on illegal drugs has been replaced by the war against corruption and fake drugs' (ibid.: 541) with the transition to democratic rule in Nigeria. He shows how this shift led to a decline in political support and government funding for the NDLEA, while

NAFDAC was one of the organizations that benefitted from it. However, Klantschnig also argues that, contrary to the dominant narrative, even while NDLEA did enjoy political support under military rule, its fight against illegal drugs was not really effective (ibid.: 541).

45 In NAPTIP's case there was concern that the controversial then Minister of Justice and Attorney General of the Federation Michael Kaase Aondoakaa, under whose authority NAPTIP was, had retired Ndaguba to install a confidant and take control of the agency (see American Embassy Abuja 2009).

46 For more information and analyses of this gripping incident of Nigerian politics, see the insight account by Adeniyi (2011: 16–42) as well as Lawson (2009: 87–92) and Adebanwi and Obadare (2011).

47 It is difficult to tell whether the BNDE can still be considered a 'pocket' in the early 1990s, since the overall bureaucratic quality may have improved between the 1980s and then. The World Bank Government Effectiveness indicator that is presented in table 1.2 is not of much help here, since the first year for which it is available is 1996.

48 One could argue that our analysis was influenced by our prior knowledge of the findings of these authors. However, not all researchers were familiar with these findings to the same degree. More importantly, our research approach was deliberately open and explorative, so that contradictory or different kinds of evidence did not escape our attention. Our results confirm this, since we emphasize factors differently and introduce new distinctions and factors.

49 While I had read Leonard's book when research in Nigeria was ongoing, I deliberately decided not to look at it again after that, to minimize the risk of it influencing the analysis. Due to the complexity of Leonard's account, the inclusion of other case studies, and by analysing our data using an approach that required the 'grounding' of the analysis in the data and the constant control of the emerging theory by the data, I argue that this analysis was developed in sufficient independence from Leonard's study to justify a meaningful ex post comparison of the findings.

50 Joe Abah is currently transforming his dissertation into a book. Using a matched pair design, he analysed why one of these organizations in each of the three pairs he is looking at performed well while the other did not. He studied public organizations in Nigeria, one of which is NAFDAC. Barma, Huybens and Viñuela (2012) studied nine successful public agencies in Lao PDR, Sierra Leone, The Gambia and Timor-Leste, while McDonnell (2012) studied effective 'subcultural bureaucracy' in Ghana. See also Owusu (2012) and some of the contributions in Bierschenk and Olivier de Sardan (forthcoming).

51 Current research programmes on PoE, state effectiveness and closely related issues in the developing world include Princeton University's *Innovations for Successful Societies* programme, directed by Jennifer Widner, with a fascinating digital archive of case studies of reform efforts (www.princeton.edu/successfulsocieties). Also at Princeton, there is the *State Building in the Developing World* network, organized by Miguel Centeno, Atul Kohli and Deborah Yashar (www.princeton. edu/statebuilding). The international research initiative *Developmental Leadership Program* was led by Adrian Leftwich (www://dlprog.org). At the University of Manchester, David Hulme directs the *Effective States and Inclusive Development Research Centre* (www.effective-states.org). Lant Pritchett, Matt Andrews and Michael Woolcock lead the *Building State Capability* project at Harvard University (http://www.hks.harvard.edu/centers/cid/programs/building_state_capability). Another programme is the *Developmental Regimes in Africa* programme, that partly grew out of the *Africa Power and Politics* programme discussed in chapter 1 and is based at the Overseas Development Institute, where it is coordinated by David Booth, Ton Dietz, David Henley, Tim Kelsall and André Leliveld (http://www.

institutions-africa.org/page/initiating-developmental-regimes). Of course, this list is by no means complete and is just intended to give a brief overview.

52 The authors also specify a sociological understanding of 'institutions' and, through their study, want to demonstrate the empirical usefulness of this concept (Portes and Smith 2012a).

53 In short, the conditions they derived from the literature prior to research and then tested, are: meritocracy; immunity to corruption; no 'islands' of power (internal factors); proactivity; technological flexibility, and external allies (external factors) (Portes and Smith 2012b).

54 QCA should not be used for samples with very low numbers of cases, e.g. less than ten (Schneider and Wagemann 2012: 317), which is why we did not make use of it for our study.

55 Compare these indicators with the indicators in table 1.2 for the countries in which the PoE covered in this book are located.

56 Neither Portes and Smith nor the case study authors use Israel's concept of 'specificity'. Alternatively, they distinguish between mostly economic, mostly technical and mostly socially oriented organizations (Portes and Smith 2012b: 28). For them, stock exchange and tax authorities fall into the economic category and civil aviation authorities fall 'in between as a mostly technical organization' (ibid.: 28).

57 At this point, it is difficult for the reader to comprehend how the scoring of the outcome 'institutional adequacy' relates to the qualitative analysis, and how exactly the two outcome variables are distinguished.

58 Describing Brazil's BNDE as a PoE, Ben Ross Schneider makes a similar point when he warns that 'we should not confuse this institutionalization with a Weberian legal-rational bureaucracy' (Schneider 1991: 36), and thereby overlook its fundamentally political nature, foundation and need for political support (ibid.: 36).

59 It could well be that it is not political management as such but the organizational autonomy it helps to negotiate that is the original 'causal' factor here.

60 The focus of the 'agencification' literature is still largely on OECD countries, but case studies of experiences in developing countries are sometimes included. For more information, see OECD (2002), van Donge (2002), James (2003), Pollitt and Talbot (2004), Pollitt et al. (2004), Larbi (2006: 31–33), Ayee (2008: 134–37) and critically Moynihan (2006).

61 Narr and Offe (1975) make a similar point and introduce the term 'mass loyalty' to replace 'legitimacy'.

62 The classic case study of Japan's Ministry of International Trade and Industry (MITI) is Johnson (1982). See also Amsden (1989), Wade (1990), Evans (1995, 1998), Cheng, Haggard and Kang (1998), Woo-Cumings (1999), Chibber (2002), Kohli (2004) and, more recently, Edigheji (2010).

63 Again, it pays off to assume variation rather than homogeneity. The organizations that we refer to here in generalizing terms as 'pilot agencies' were organized and worked very differently in different contexts, as Cheng, Haggard and Kang's (1998) comparative analysis of South Korea's and Taiwan's bureaucracies shows.

64 Of course one would first have to assess whether, based on our definition, these programmes are PoE at all. The fact that they are government programmes rather than organizations would not be a major issue, since these programmes are being implemented by government organizations. Of greater concern would be the question of whether these programmes and the organizations that implement them are really 'pockets' in hostile politico-administrative environments, or whether their implementation is just an expression and element of overall institutional reform. For the case of Mexico, Portes and Smith's account (Portes and Smith 2012c: 185; see also Velasco 2012), as well as the indicators for Mexico in table 9.4, suggest the latter.

65 See Portes and Smith (2012c) for some leads in that direction.

Bibliography

Abah, Joe (2012) 'Strong Organisations in Weak States. Atypical Public Sector Performance in Dysfunctional Environments', doctoral dissertation, Maastricht University.

Abbott, Andrew (1997) 'On the Concept of Turning Point', *Comparative Social Research* 16: 85–105.

Achebe, Chinua (1958): *Things Fall Apart*, London: Heinemann.

——(1984/1998): *The Trouble with Nigeria*, London: Heinemann.

Adamolekun, Ladipo (1986) *Politics and Administration in Nigeria,* Ibadan: Spectrum Books.

Adamolekun, Ladipo, Erero, John and Oshionebo, Basil (1991) '"Federal Character" and Management of the Federal Civil Service and the Military', *Publius*, 21: 75–88.

Adebanwi, Wale and Obadare, Ebenezer (2011) 'When corruption fights back: democracy and elite interest in Nigeria's anti-corruption war', *Journal of Modern African Studies* 49: 185–213.

Adejumobi, Said (ed.) (2011) *State, Economy and Society in Post-Military Nigeria*, New York: Palgrave Macmillan.

Adeniyi, Olusegun (2011) *Power, politics and death: a front-row account of Nigeria under the late President Yar'Adua*, Lagos: Prestige.

Adshead, Samuel A. (1970) *The Modernization of the Chinese Salt Administration, 1900–1920,* Cambridge: Harvard University Press.

Africa Power and Politics Programme, Developmental Leadership Programme, Elites, Production and Poverty: A Comparative Analysis, Political Economy of Agricultural Policy in Africa, Tracking Development (2012) 'The political economy of development in Africa. A joint statement from five research programmes'.

African Development Bank (2005): *African Development Report 2005: Public Sector Management in Africa*, Oxford: African Development Bank and Oxford University Press.

Agbaje, Adigun, Akande, Adeolu and Ojo, Jide (2007) 'Nigeria's ruling party: A complex web of power and money', *South African Journal of International Affairs* 14: 79–97.

Aharoni, Yair (1986) *The Evolution and Management of State Owned Enterprises*, Cambridge: Ballinger.

Ahmad, Ehtisham and Mottu, Eric (2002) *Oil Revenue Assignments: Country Experiences and Issues*, Washington D.C.: International Monetary Fund.

Ake, Claude (eds) (1985) *Political Economy of Nigeria*, London: Longman.

Akindele, S.T., Olaopa, O.R. and Ajisafe, R.A. (2001) 'Public Enterprises Management in Nigeria', in F. Omotoso (ed.) Contemporary Issues in Public Administration, Lagos: Bolabay: 156–65.

Bibliography 243

Akunyili, Dora Nkem (2010) *The war against counterfeit medicine. My story*, Ibadan: Safari Books.

Alessi, Louis de (1969) 'Implications of Property Rights for Government Investment Choices', *American Economic Review*, 59: 13–24.

Allen, Douglas W. (2002) 'The British Navy Rules: Monitoring and Incompatible Incentives in the Age of Fighting Sail', *Explorations in Economic History* 39: 204–31.

al-Naqeeb, Khaldoun Hasan (1990) *Society and State in the Gulf and Arab Peninsula*, London: Routledge.

American Embassy Abuja (2009) 'Nigeria: NAPTIP's new leader causes concern', email from 23 February 2009, made available through wikileaks. Online. Available: wikileaks.org/cable/2009/02/09ABUJA326.html (accessed: 3 March 2013).

Amsden, Alice H. (1989) *Asia's next giant: South Korea and late industrialization*, New Oxford: Oxford University Press.

Amuzegar, Jahangir (1999) *Managing the Oil Wealth: OPEC's Windfalls and Pitfalls*, London: I.B. Tauris.

Anders, Gerhard (2010) *In the shadow of good governance: An ethnography of civil service reform in Africa*, Leiden: Brill.

Appelbaum, Eileen and Batt, Rosemaryt (1994) *The new American workplace: transforming work systems in the United States*, Ithaca: Cornell University Press.

Ayee, Joseph R. A. (2008) *Reforming the African Public Sector: Retrospect and Prospects*, Dakar: CODESRIA.

Ayubi, Nazih N. (1992) 'Withered Socialism or Whether Socialism? The Radical Arab States as Populist-Corporatist Regimes', *Third World Quarterly*, 13: 89–105.

Bach, Daniel (2011) 'Patrimonialism and neopatrimonialism: comparative trajectories and readings', *Commonwealth and Comparative Politics* 49: 275–94.

Bach, Daniel and Gazibo, Mamoudou (eds) (2012) *Neopatrimonialism in Africa and Beyond*, London: Routledge.

Baer, Werner and Villela, Annibal (1980) 'The Changing Nature of Development Banking in Brazil', *Journal of Inter-American and World Affairs* 22: 23–34.

Banco Nacional de Desenvolvimento Econômico (1954) *Exposição Sobre o Programa e Reaparelhamento Econômico: Exercício de 1954*', Rio de Janeiro.

——(1956) *Exposição Sobre o Programa e Reaparelhamento Econômico: Exercício de 1955*', Rio de Janeiro.

——(2009) *Annual Report for 2009*, Rio de Janeiro. Online. Available HTTP: http://www.bndes.gov.br/SiteBNDES/export/sites/default/bndes_en/Galerias/RelAnu alEnglish/ra2009/Rel_Anual_2009_ingles.pdf (accessed 14 July 2011).

——(2012) *Annual Report for 2011*, Rio de Janeiro. Online. Available HTTP: http:// www.bndes.gov.br/SiteBNDES/bndes/bndes_en/Hotsites/Annual_Report_2011/ (accessed 15 July 2011).

Banerjee, Abhijit V. and Duflo, Esther (2011) *Poor Economics: Barefoot Hedge-fund Managers, DIY Doctors and the Surprising Truth about Life on Less Than $1 a Day*, London: Penguin Books.

Bangura, Yusuf and Larbi, George A. (2006a) 'Introduction: Globalization and Public Sector Reform', in Yusuf Bangura and George A. Larbi (eds) *Public Sector Reform in Developing Countries: Capacity Challenges to Improve Services*, Basingstoke: Palgrave Macmillan and UNRISD: 1–24.

Bangura, Yusuf and Larbi, George A. (eds) (2006b) *Public Sector Reform in Developing Countries: Capacity Challenges to Improve Services*, Basingstoke: Palgrave Macmillan and UNRISD.

244 *Bibliography*

Barma, Naazneen H., Huybens, Elisabeth and Viñuela, Lorena (2012) 'Institutions Taking Root: Building State Capacity in Challenging Contexts', paper presented at the International Research Society for Public Management XVI Conference, Rome, April 11–13.

Barnes, Philip (1995) *Indonesia: The Political Economy of Energy*, Oxford: Oxford University Press for the Oxford Institute for Energy Studies.

Barriaux, Marianne (2007) 'The Friday interview: Dora Akunyili. Indomitable woman in the front line of the other war on drugs', *The Guardian*. Online. Available HTTP: http://www.guardian.co.uk/business/2007/nov/09/7 (accessed: 29 April 2010).

Barth, Fredrik (1969) *Ethnic groups and boundaries. The social organization of culture difference*. Oslo: Universitetsforlaget.

Batley, Richard (1999) 'Policy arena: The new public management in developing countries: Introduction', *Journal of International Development* 11: 755–60.

Batley, Richard and Larbi, George A. (2004) *The Changing Role of Government: The Reform of Public Services in Developing Countries*, Basingstoke: Palgrave Macmillan.

——(2006) 'Capacity to Deliver? Management, Institutions and Public Services in Developing Countries', in Yusuf Bangura and George A. Larbi (eds) *Public Sector Reform in Developing Countries: Capacity Challenges to Improve Services*, Basingstoke: Palgrave Macmillan and UNRISD: 99–130.

Bayat, Assef (1983) 'Workers' Control after the Revolution', *MERIP Reports* 113: 19–34.

Bebbington, Anthony and McCourt, Willy (eds) *Development Success: Statecraft in the South*, Basingstoke: Palgrave Macmillan.

Beblawi, Hazem (1987) 'The Rentier State in the Arab World', in Hazem Beblawi and Giacomo Luciani (eds) *Nation, State, and Integration in the Arab World*, London: Croom Helm.

Beekers, Daan and van Gool, Bas (2012) 'From patronage to neopatrimonialism. Postcolonial governance in Sub-Saharan Africa and beyond', ASC Working Paper 101/2012, Leiden, African Studies Centre.

Behdad, Sohrab (2000) 'From Populism to Economic Liberalism: The Iranian Predicament', in Parvin Alizadeh (ed.) *The Economy of Iran: Dilemmas of an Islamic State*, London: I.B. Tauris.

Belev, Boyan (2001) 'Privatization in Egypt and Tunisia: Liberal Outcomes and/or Liberal Policies?', *Mediterranean Politics*, 6: 68–103.

Bevan, David, Gunning, Jan and Collier, Paul (1999) *Nigeria and Indonesia*, Oxford: Oxford University Press.

Bevilaqua, Alfonso S. and Márcio G. P. Garcia (2002) 'Banks, Domestic Debt and Crises: The Recent Brazilian Experience', *Journal of Brazilian Political Economy* 22: 85–103.

Bienen, Henry (1985) *Political Conflict and Economic Change in Nigeria*, London: Cass.

Bierschenk, Thomas (forthcoming) 'States at Work in West Africa: Sedimentation, Fragmentation and Normative Double-Binds', in Thomas Bierschenk and Jean-Pierre Olivier de Sardan (eds) *States at Work. Dynamics of African Bureaucracies*, Leiden: Brill.

Bierschenk, Thomas and Olivier de Sardan, Jean-Pierre (2003) 'Powers in the village: rural Benin between democratisation and decentralisation', *Africa* 73: 145–73.

Bierschenk, Thomas and Olivier de Sardan, Jean-Pierre (eds) (forthcoming) *States at Work. Dynamics of African Bureaucracies*, Leiden: Brill.

Blundo, Giorgio and Le Meur, Pierre-Yves (eds) (2009) *The governance of daily life in Africa. Ethnographic explorations of collective and public services*, Leiden: Brill.

Booth, David (2011a) 'Turning Governance Upside Down', *Development Policy Review* 29: 115–24.

——(2011b) 'Governance for development in Africa: building on what works', Policy Brief No. 1, Africa Power and Politics Programme, London: Africa Power and Politics Programme.

——(2012) *Development as collective action problem. Addressing the real challenges of African governance*, London: Africa Power and Politics Programme.

Booth, David and Golooba-Mutebi, Frederick (2012) 'Developmental patrimonialism? The case of Rwanda', *African Affairs* 111: 379–403.

Boycko, Maxim, Shleifer, Andrei and Vishny, Robert W. (1996) 'A Theory of Privatisation', *Economic Journal*, 106: 309–19.

Boyne, George A., Farrell, Catherine, Law, Jennifer, Powell, Martin and Walker, Richard M. (2003) *Evaluating Public Management Reforms: Principles and Practice*, Buckingham: Open University Press.

Bratton, Michael and Lewis, Peter (2007) 'The Durability of Political Goods? Evidence from Nigeria's New Democracy', *Commonwealth & Comparative Politics* 45: 1–33.

Bratton, Michael and van de Walle, Nicolas (1994) 'Neopatrimonial Regimes and Political Transitions in Africa', *World Politics* 46: 453–89.

Bräutigam, Deborah, Fjeldstad, Odd-Helge and Moore, Mick (eds) (2008): *Taxation and State-Building in Developing Countries: Capacity and Consent*, Cambridge: Cambridge University Press.

Bresnan, John (1993) *Managing Indonesia: The Modern Political Economy*, New York: Columbia University Press.

Buddingh', Hans (2000) *Geschiedenis van Suriname* [History of Suriname] (3rd ed.), Utrecht: Het Spectrum.

Byman, Daniel and Green, Jerrold (1999) 'The Enigma of Political Stability in the Persian Gulf Monarchies', *Middle East Review of International Affairs*, 3. Online. Available HTTP: http://meria.idc.ac.il/journal/1999/issue3/jv3n3a3.html (accessed 12 September 2009).

Campos, Roberto (1969) 'A Retrospect over Brazilian Development Plans', in Howard Ellis (ed.) *The Economy of Brazil*, Berkeley: University of California Press.

——(1994) *A Laterna na Popa: Memórias*. Rio de Janeiro: Editora Topbooks.

Capoccia, Giovanni and Kelemen, R. Daniel (2007) 'The Study of Critical Junctures. Theory, Narrative, and Counterfactuals in Historical Institutionalism', *World Politics* 59: 341–69.

Carothers, Thomas (2002) 'The End of the Transition Paradigm', *Journal of Democracy* 13: 5–21.

Carothers, Thomas and de Gramont, Diane (2011) 'Aiding Governance in Developing Countries: Progress Amid Uncertainties' (The Carnegie Papers, Democracy and Rule of Law), Washington D.C.: Carnegie Endowment for International Peace.

Carpenter, Daniel P. (2000) 'State Building through Reputation Building: Coalitions of Esteem and Program Innovation in the National Postal System, 1883–1913', *Studies in American Political Development* 14: 121–55.

——(2001a) 'The Political Foundations of Bureaucratic Autonomy: A Response to Kernell', *Studies in American Political Development* 15: 113–122.

——(2001b) *The Forging of Bureaucratic Autonomy: Reputations, Networks, and Policy Innovation in Executive Agencies, 1862–1928*, Princeton: Princeton University Press.

——(2010) *Reputation and Power: Organizational Image and Pharmaceutical Regulation at the FDA*, Princeton: Princeton University Press.

246 Bibliography

Carpenter, Daniel P. and Krause, George A. (2011) 'Reputation and Public Administration', *Public Administration Review* 72: 26–32.

Caulfield, Janice (2002) 'Executive agencies in Tanzania: Liberalization and third world debt', *Public Administration and Development* 22: 209–20.

Centre for the Future State (2010a) *An Upside-down View of Governance*, Brighton: Institute of Development Studies.

——(2010b) 'Societies, States and Citizens: A policymaker's guide to the research', Brighton: Institute of Development Studies.

Chaudhry, Kiren Aziz (1997) *The Price of Wealth: Economics and Institutions in the Middle East*, Ithaca: Cornell University Press.

Chen, P.T. (1936) 'Public Finance', in Kwei Chungshu (ed.) *The Chinese Yearbook, 1936*, Shanghai: Commercial Press.

Cheng, Tun-Jen, Haggard, Stephan and Kang, David (1998) 'Institutions and Growth in Korea and Taiwan: The Bureaucracy', *Journal of Development Studies* 34: 87–111.

Cheriet, Boutheina (1992) 'The Resilience of Algerian Populism', *Middle East Report*, no. 174: 9–34.

Chibber, Vivek (2002) 'Bureaucratic Rationality and the Developmental State', *American Journal of Sociology* 107: 951–89.

——(2003) *Locked in Place: State-Building and Late Industrialization in India*, Princeton, N.J: Princeton University Press.

Chin, Henk E. and Buddingh', Hans (1987) *Surinam: Politics, Economics and Society*, London: Pinter.

Clapham, Christopher (ed.) (1982) *Private Patronage and Public Power. Political Clientelism in the Modern State*, New York: St. Martin's Press.

Collier, David and Levitsky, Steven (1997) 'Democracies with Adjectives: Conceptual Innovations in Comparative Research', *World Politics* 49: 430–51.

Collier, David, Mahoney, James and Seawright, Jason (2004) 'Claiming too much: warnings about selection bias' in Henry E. Brady and David Collier (eds) *Rethinking Social Inquiry: Diverse Tools, Shared Standards*, Lanham: Rowman and Littlefield.

Collier, Ruth Berins and Collier, David (1991) *Shaping the Political Arena. Critical Junctures, the Labor Movement, and Regime Dynamics in Latin America*, Princeton: Princeton University Press.

Croissant, Aurel (2002) 'Einleitung: Demokratische Grauzonen – Konturen und Konzepte eines Forschungszweigs', in Petra Bendel, Aurel Croissant and Friedbert W. Rüb (eds) *Zwischen Demokratie und Diktatur. Zur Konzeption und Empirie demokratischer Grauzonen*, Opladen: Leske + Budrich: 9–53.

Crook, Richard (1989) 'Patrimonialism, Administrative Effectiveness and Economic Development in Côte D'Ivoire', *African Affairs* 88: 205–28.

——(2010) 'Rethinking civil service reform in Africa: "Islands of effectiveness" and organisational commitment', *Commonwealth & Comparative Politics* 48: 479–504.

Croome, J.D. (n.d.) Microfilm in United States Department of State Records with Special Reference to the Internal Affairs of China, 1930–39, Washington DC, DS 893.51/150;.

Crystal, Jill (1990) *Oil and Politics in the Gulf: Rulers and Merchants in Kuwait*, Cambridge: Cambridge University Press.

d'Avila, Viana (1981) 'O BNDE e a Industrialização Brasileira, 1952–61', unpublished Masters thesis, Universidade de Campinas.

Bibliography 247

Dahl-Østergaard, Tom, Unsworth, Sue, Robinson, Mark, Jensen, Rikke Ingrid (2005): 'Lessons learned on the use of power and drivers of change analyses in development cooperation' (Review commissioned by the OECD DAC network on governance [GOVNET]).

Dahlström, Carl, Lapuente, Victor and Teorell, Jan (2012) 'The Merit of Meritocratization: Politics, Bureaucracy, and the Institutional Deterrents of Corruption', *Political Research Quarterly* 65: 656–68.

Daland, Robert (1981) *Exploring Brazilian Bureaucracy: Performance and Pathology,* Washington D.C.: University Press of America.

Davidson, Christopher (2005) *The United Arab Emirates: A Study in Survival,* Boulder, CO: Lynne Rienner Publishers.

——(2008) *Dubai: The Vulnerability of Success,* London: Hurst & Company.

Davis, John (1987) *Libyan Politics: Tribe and* Revolution, London: I.B. Tauris.

Derveld, Rick (1999) 'Veranderingen in de Surinaamse politiek, 1975–98' [Changes in Surinamese Politics, 1975–88], *Oso: Tijdschrift voor Surinaamse Taalkunde, Letterkunde, Cultuur en Geschiedenis* 18: 5–21.

DFID (Department for International Development) (2009) 'Why tax matters for international development' (DFID Briefing Note), London: Department for International Development.

Di John, Jonathan (2006) 'The Political Economy of Industrial Policy in Venezuela', paper presented at conference on Venezuelan Economic Growth 1975–2000, Center for International Development, Harvard University, 28–29 April.

Diamond, Larry (2002) 'Thinking about Hybrid Regimes', *Journal of Democracy* 13: 21–35.

Diamond, Larry and Plattner, Marc F. (eds) (1996) *The Global Resurgence of Democracy,* Baltimore: John Hopkins University Press.

Dilulio Jr., John D. (1994) 'Principled Agents: The Cultural Bases of Behavior in a Federal Government Bureaucracy', in J*ournal of Public Administration Research and Theory* 4: 277–318.

Ding, Changqing, and Foding, Liu (1990) *Minguo Yanwu Shigao* [Draft History on Salt Affairs in the Republican Period], Beijing: Renmin Chubanshe.

Dion, Douglas (1998) 'Evidence and Inference in the Comparative Case Study', *Comparative Politics* 30: 127–45.

Dornbusch, Rudiger and Edwards, Sebastian (eds) (1991) *The Macroeconomics of Populism in Latin America*, Chicago: University of Chicago.

Easton, David (1965) *A Systems Analysis of Political Life*, New York: John Wiley & Sons.

Ebigbo, Peter O. (2000) 'Child trafficking in Nigeria: the state of the art', study for the International Labour Organization/International Programme on the Elimination of Child Labour, Abidjan.

Economic Commission for Africa (2003): *Public Sector Management Reforms in Africa: Lessons Learned*, Addis Ababa: Economic Commission for Africa.

Edigheji, Omano (ed.) (2010) *Constructing a democratic developmental state in South Africa: potentials and challenges*, Pretoria: Human Sciences Research Council Press.

Ehteshami, Anoushiravan and Murphy, Emma (1996) 'Transformation of the Corporatist State in the Middle East', *Third World Quarterly*, 17: 753–72.

Ehteshami, Anoushiravan and Wright, Steven (2007) 'Political change in the Arab Oil Monarchies: From Liberalization to Enfranchisement', *International Affairs*, 83: 913–32.

248   *Bibliography*

Eisenstadt, Shmuel N. (1973) *Traditional Patrimonialism and Modern Neo-Patrimonialism*, Beverly Hills: Sage.

Eisenstadt, Shmuel N. and Lemarchand, René (eds) (1981) *Political Clientelism, Patronage and Development*, Beverly Hils: Sage.

Eisenstadt, Shmuel N. and Roninger, Luis (1984) *Patrons, clients, and friends: Interpersonal relations and the structure of trust in society*, Cambridge: Cambridge University Press.

Ellner, Steve (2003) 'The Contrasting Variants of the Populism of Hugo Chávez and Alberto Fujimori', *Journal of Latin American Studies*, 35: 139–62.

Ellsworth, Brian and Parra-Bernal, Guillermo (2011) 'Brazil BNDES to receive $27 billion from government' *Reuters*, February 15. Online. Available HTTP: http://www.reuters.com/article/2011/02/15/pg-brazil-bndes-loans-idUSN1514589120110215 (accessed 20 July 2011).

Elman, Benjamin (1991) 'Social, Political, and Cultural Reproduction via Civil Service Examinations in Late Imperial China', *Journal of Asian Studies*, 51: 7–28.

——(2000) *A Cultural History of Civil Examinations in Late Imperial China*, Berkeley: University of California Press.

Elwert, Georg (1989) 'Nationalismus und Ethnizität. Über die Bildung von Wir-Gruppen', *Kölner Zeitschrift für Soziologie und Sozialpsychologie* 41: 440–64.

Entelis, John (1999) 'SONATRACH: The Political Economy of an Algerian State Institution', *Middle East Journal*, 53: 9–27.

Erdmann, Gero and Engel, Ulf (2007) 'Neopatrimonialism Reconsidered: Critical Review and Elaboration of an Elusive Concept', *Commonwealth and Comparative Politics* 45: 95–119.

Ermakoff, Ivan (2008) *Ruling oneself out. A theory of collective abdications.* Durham: Duke University Press.

Ertman, Thomas (1997) *Birth of the Leviathan. Building States and Regimes in Medieval and Early Modern Europe*, Cambridge: Cambridge University Press.

Esman, Milton J. and Uphoff, Norman T. (1984) *Local Organizations: Intermediaries in Rural Development*, Ithaca, NY: Cornell University Press.

Esther Morrisson (1959) 'The Modernization of the Confucian Bureaucracy', unpublished doctoral dissertation, Radcliffe College.

Evans, Peter B. (1989) 'Predatory, Developmental, and Other Apparatuses: A Comparative Political Economy Perspective on the Third World State', *Sociological Forum* 4: 561–87.

——(1992) 'The State as Problem and Solution: Predation, Embedded Autonomy, and Structural Change', in Steven Haggard (ed.) *The Politics of Economic Adjustment: International Constraints, Distributive Conflicts, and the State*, Princeton: Princeton University Press: 140–81.

——(1995) *Embedded Autonomy: States and Industrial Transformation*, Princeton: Princeton University Press.

——(1997) *State-Society Synergy: Government and Social Capital in Development*, Berkeley: University of California at Berkeley, International and Area Studies.

——(1998) 'Transferable Lessons? Re-examining the Institutional Prerequisites of East Asian Economic Policies', *Journal of Development Studies* 34(6): 66–86.

Evans, Peter B. and Rauch, James E. (1999) 'Bureaucracy and Growth: A Cross-National Analysis of the Effects of "Weberian" State Structures on Economic Growth', *American Sociological Review* 64: 748–65.

Evers, Hans-Dieter (1994) 'The trader's dilemma – a theory of the social transformation of markets and society', in Hans-Dieter Evers and Heiko Schrader (eds) *The moral economy of trade: ethnicity and developing markets*, London: Routledge: 9–14.

Falola, Toyin and Heaton, Matthew M. (2008) *A History of Nigeria*, Cambridge: Cambridge University Press.

Fasano, Ugo, and Goyal, Rishi (2004) *Emerging Strains in GCC Labor Markets*, IMF Working Paper WP/04/71, Washington D.C.: International Monetary Fund.

Field, Michael (1984) *The Merchants: The Big Business Families of Arabia*, London: J. Murray.

Fippin, William (1953) *The Joint Commission on Rural Reconstruction: Its Policies, Procedures and Program*, Joint Commission on Rural Reconstruction.

Fischer, Wolfram and Lundgren, Peter (1975) 'The Recruitment and Training of Administrative and Technical Personnel', in Charles Tilly (ed.) *The Formation of National States in Western Europe*, Princeton: Princeton University Press: 456–561.

Fjeldstad, Odd-Helge and Moore, Mick (2008) 'Tax reform and state-building in a globalised world', in Deborah Bräutigam, Odd-Helge Fjeldstad and Mick Moore (eds) (2008) *Taxation and State-Building in Developing Countries: Capacity and Consent*, Cambridge: Cambridge University Press: 235–60.

——(2009) 'Revenue authorities and public authority in sub-Saharan Africa', *Journal of Modern African Studies* 47: 1–18.

Fjeldstad, Odd-Helge and Therkildsen, Ole (2008) 'Mass taxation and state-society relations in East Africa', in Deborah Bräutigam, Odd-Helge Fjeldstad and Mick Moore (eds) (2008) *Taxation and State-Building in Developing Countries: Capacity and Consent*, Cambridge: Cambridge University Press: 114–34.

Font, Mauricio (2003) *Reforming Brazil: A Reform Era in Perspective*, Lanham, MD: Rowman & Littlefield Publishers.

Freedom House (2012) 'Country Ratings and Status, FIW 1973–2012'. Online. Available HTTP: http://www.freedomhouse.org/sites/default/files/FIW%20All%20Scores%2C%20Countries%2C%201973–2012%20%28FINAL%29.xls (accessed 13 December 2012).

Fukuyama, Francis (1992) *The end of history and the last man*, New York: Free Press.

——(2005) *State Building: Governance and World Order in the Twenty-First Century*, London: Profile Books.

Gause, F. Gregory (1994) *Oil Monarchies: Domestic and Security Challenges in the Arab Gulf* States, New York: Council on Foreign Relations Press.

Geddes, Barbara (1990a) 'Building "State" Autonomy in Brazil, 1930–64', *Comparative Politics* 22: 217–35.

——(1990b) 'How the cases you choose affect the answers you get: selection bias in comparative politics', *Political Analysis* 2: 131–150.

——(1994) *Politician's Dilemma: Building State Capacity in Latin America*, Berkeley: University of California Press.

——(2003) *Paradigms and Sand Castles: Theory Building and Research Design in Comparative Politics*, Ann Arbor: University of Michigan Press.

George, Alexander L. and Bennett, Andrew (2005) *Case Studies and Theory Development in the Social Sciences*, Cambridge: MIT Press.

Germono, G. (2001) 'Human trafficking as a transnational problem, the responses of destination countries', proceedings of the first Pan-African Conference on Human Trafficking, Abuja, Nigeria, 19–23 February.

250 *Bibliography*

Gerring, John (2004) 'What Is a Case Study and What Is It Good for?', *American Political Science Review* 98: 341–54.

Gillies, Alexandra (2007) 'Obasanjo, the donor community and reform implementation in Nigeria', *The Round Table*, 96: 569–86.

Girgis, Maurice and Diwan, Ishac (2002) *Labour Force Development in Saudi Arabia*, Riyadh: Ministry of Planning.

Granovetter, Mark (1973) 'The Strength of Weak Ties', *American Journal of Sociology* 78: 1360–80.

——(1974) *Getting a Job: A Study of Contacts and Careers*, Cambridge: Harvard University Press.

——(1983) 'The Strength of Weak Ties: A Network Theory Revisited', *Sociological Theory* 1: 201–33.

Grant, Ursula, Hudson, Alan and Sharma, Bhavna (2009) 'Exploring "development success": Indicators, stories and contributing factors'. Online. Available HTTP: http://www.odi.org.uk/sites/odi.org.uk/files/odi-assets/publications-opinion-files/4227. pdf (accessed 7 September 2011).

Grindle, Merilee S. (1997) 'Divergent Cultures? When Public Organizations Perform Well in Developing Countries', *World Development*, 25: 481–95.

——(2004) 'Good Enough Governance: Poverty Reduction and Reform in Developing Countries', *Governance* 17: 525–48.

——(2007) 'Good Enough Governance Revisited', *Development Policy Review* 25: 553–74.

——(2010) 'Good Governance: The Inflation of an Idea', Center for International Development Working Paper No. 202, Harvard University.

Gupta, Sanjeev and Tareq, Shamsuddin (2008) 'Mobilizing Revenue', Finance and Development 45: 44–47.

Hall, Peter A. and Lamont, Michèle (2009) *Successful Societies: How Institutions and Culture Affect Health*, Cambridge: Cambridge University Press.

Hanlon, Joseph, Barrientos, Armando, Hulme, David (2010) *Just Give Money to the Poor: The Development Revolution from the Global South*, Sterling: Kumarian Press.

Hawkins, Kirk (2003) 'Populism in Venezuela: the rise of Chavismo', *Third World Quarterly*, 24: 1137–60.

Hay Group (2012) 'Mitarbeiter sind käuflich, ihre Motiation nicht: Ergebnisse einer aktuellen Studie zur Arbeitsmotivation'. Online. Available HTTP: http://www. haygroup.com/downloads/de/Mitarbeiter_sind_kauflich_Ihre_Motivation_nicht.pdf (accessed 18 February 2013).

Henry, Clement M. (2004) 'Algeria's Agonies: Oil Rent Effects in a Bunker State', *Journal of North African Studies*, 9: 68–81.

Henry, Clement M. and Springborn, Robert (2001) *Globalization and the Politics of Development in the Middle East*, Cambridge: Cambridge University Press.

Herb, Michael (1999) *All in the Family: Absolutism, Revolution, and Democracy in Middle Eastern Monarchies*, Albany: State University of New York Press.

——(2009) 'A Nation of Bureaucrats: Political Participation and Economic Diversification in Kuwait and the United Arab Emirates', *International Journal of Middle East Studies*, 41: 375–95.

Heredia, Blanca and Schneider, Ben Ross (2003) 'The Political Economy of Administrative Reform in Developing Countries', in Ben Ross Schneider and Blanca Heredia (eds) *Reinventing Leviathan: The Politics of Administrative Reform in Developing Countries*, Miami: North-South Center Press: 1–29.

Hertog, Steffen (2010a) 'Defying the Resource Curse: Explaining Successful State-Owned Enterprises in Rentier States', *World Politics*, 62: 261–301.

——(2010b) *Princes, Brokers and Bureaucrats: Oil and the State in Saudi Arabia*, Ithaca: Cornell University Press.

Hilderbrand, Mary E. and Grindle, Merilee S. (1997) 'Building Sustainable Capacity in the Public Sector: What Can Be Done?', in Merilee, S. Grindle (ed.) *Getting Good Government: Capacity Building in the Public Sectors of Developing Countries*, Cambridge: Harvard University Press: 31–62.

Hippler, Jochen (ed.) (2005) *Nation-Building: A Key Concept for Peaceful Conflict Transformation?* London: Pluto Press.

Hira, Sandew (2007) *Eddy Jharap, Vertrouwen in eigen kunnen: Een biografisch interview over de ontwikkeling van Staatsolie Maatschappij Suriname NV* [Eddy Jharap, Confidence in Our Own Abilities: A Biographical Interview on the Development of the State Oil Company of Suriname, Ltd], The Hague/Paramaribo: Amrit.

Holden, David, and Johns, Richard (1981) *The House of Saud*, London: Sidgwick & Jackson.

Holmberg, Sören and Rothstein, Bo (2012) *Good Government. The Relevance of Political Science*, Cheltenham: Edward Elgar.

Hood, Christopher (1991) 'A Public Management for All Seasons?', *Public Administration* 69: 3–19.

Hooglund, Eric (1992) 'Iranian Populism and Political Change in the Gulf', *Middle East Report*, no 174: 19–21.

Hough, Richard Lee (1968) 'Models of Rural Development Administration: The JCRR Experiment in Taiwan', SEADAG Papers on Problems of Development in Southeast Asia, 37.

Hout, Wil (2007) 'Development under Patrimonial Conditions: Suriname's State Oil Company as a Development Agent', *Journal of Development Studies* 43: 1331–50.

Houtzager, Peter P. (2003) 'Introduction: From Polycentrism to the Polity', in Peter P. Houtzager and Mick Moore (eds): *Changing Paths: International Development and the New Politics of Inclusion*, Ann Arbor: University of Michigan Press: 1–31.

Human Rights Watch (2010) *'Everyone's in on the Game'. Corruption and Human Rights Abuses by the Nigeria Police Force*, New York: Human Rights Watch.

——(2012) *Spiraling Violence: Boko Haram Attacks and Security Force Abuses in Nigeria*, United States of America: Human Rights Watch.

Huntington, Samuel P. (1991) *The Third Wave: Democratization in the Late Twentieth Century*, Oklahoma City: University of Oklahoma Press.

Hutchcroft, Paul D. (1998) *Booty Capitalism: The Politics of Banking in the Philippines*, Ithaca: Cornell University Press.

Ibrahim, Jibrin (1997) *Expanding Democratic Space in Nigeria*, Dakar: CODESRIA.

Iliffe, John (2011) *Obasanjo, Nigeria and the World*, Woodbridge: James Currey.

ILO/IPEC (International Labour Organization/International Programme on the Elimination of Child Labour) (2000) *Combating trafficking in children for labour in West and Central Africa*, Geneva: International Labour Organization.

Inter-American Development Bank (2001) *Governance in Suriname. Economic and Sector Study Series*, No. RE3–01-001. Washington, D.C.: Inter-American Development Bank.

International Labour Organization (1994) *World Labor Report 1994*, Geneva: International Labour Organization.

Inusantara Networks (2007) *The Politics of Privatization of the State-Owned Enterprises in Indonesia*, Singapore.

252 Bibliography

Israel, Arturo (1987) *Institutional Development: Incentives to Performance*, Washington D.C. and Baltimore: The World Bank and John Hopkins University Press.

Jackson, Robert H. (1990) *Quasi-states: International relations, sovereignty and the third world*, Cambridge: Cambridge University Press.

Jackson, Robert H. and Rosberg, Carl G. (1982) 'Why Africa's weak states persist: the empirical and the juridical in statehood', *World Politics* 35: 1–24.

Jaffe, Amy and Elass, Jareer (2007) 'Saudi Aramco: National Flagship with Global Responsibilities', Working Paper, Baker Institute, Rice University. Online. Available HTTP: http://www.rice.edu/energy/publications/docs/NOCs/Papers/Sau diAramco_Jaffe-Elass.pdf (accessed 12 September 2009).

Jain, Pankaj S. (1994) 'Managing for success: Lessons from Asian development programs', *World Development* 22: 1363–77.

James, Oliver (2003): *The Executive Agency Revolution in Whitehall: Public Interest versus Bureau-Shaping Perspectives*, Basingstoke: Palgrave Macmillan.

Jega, Attahiru M. (2007) *Democracy, Good Governance and Development in Nigeria: Critical Essays*, Ibadan: Spectrum Books Limited.

Jharap, Sirahmpersad E. (1998) 'De weg van Staatsolie: Het verwerven van expertise in techniek en management' [Staatsolie's Way: The Acquisition of Expertise in Engineering and Management], lecture delivered at the Dies Natalis of the Anton de Kom University of Suriname, 31 October 1997, Paramaribo: Staatsolie Maatschappij Suriname.

——(2006) 'Ervaringen met 25 jaar Staatsolie' [25 years of experience in Staatsolie]. Rotary Lecture, 25 January and 15 February, Paramaribo: mimeo.

——(2010a) 'De back story bij "De realisatie van een droom (Staatsolie)" [The Back Story of 'The Realisation of a Dream (Staatsolie)']. Online. Available HPPT: http://www.staatsolie.com/pdf/backstory_realisatie_van_een_droom_eddy_jharap.pdf (accessed 13 December 2012).

——(2010b) 'Realization of a Dream: Staatsolie, a Model for the Development of Natural Resources in Suriname'. Online. Available HTTP: http://www.staatsolie.com/pdf/realization_of_a_dream.pdf (accessed 13 December 2012).

Johnson, Chalmers (1982) *MITI and the Japanese Miracle: The Growth of Industrial Policy, 1925–1975*, Stanford: Stanford University Press.

Joint Brazil-United States Economic Development Commission (1954) *The Development of Brazil*, Washington, D.C.: Institute of Inter-American Affairs.

Joint Commission on Rural Reconstruction (1950) *General Report (I)*, Joint Commission on Rural Reconstruction.

Joseph, Richard A. (1987) *Democracy and Prebendal Politics in Nigeria: The Rise and Fall of the Second Republic*, Cambridge: Cambridge University Press.

Joshi, Anuradha (2006) 'Institutions and Service Delivery in Asia', *IDS Bulletin* 37: 115–26.

Joshi, Anuradha and Ayee, Joseph (2009) 'Autonomy or Organisation? Reforms in the Ghanaian Internal Revenue Service', *Public Administration and Development* 29: 289–302.

Joshi, Anuradha and Moore, Mick (2004) 'Institutionalised Co-production: Unorthodox Public Service Delivery in Challenging Environments', *Journal of Development Studies* 40: 31–49.

Kapiszewski, Andrzej (2008) 'Elections and Parliamentary Activity in the GCC States', in Abdulhadi Khalaf and Giacomo Luciani (eds) *Constitutional Reform and Political Participation in the Gulf*, Dubai: Gulf Research Center.

Karbassian, Akbar (2000) 'The Islamic Revolution and the Management of the Iranian Economy', *Social Research*, 67: 621–40.

Bibliography 253

Karl, Terry Lynn (1986) 'Petroleum and Political Pacts', in Guillermo O'Donnell, Philippe Schmitter and Laurence Whitehead (eds) *Transitions from Authoritarian Rule*, Baltimore: Johns Hopkins University Press.

——(1997) *The Paradox of Plenty: Oil Booms and Petro-States*, Berkeley: University of California Press.

Karshenas, Massoud (1990) *Oil, State and Industrialization in Iran*, Cambridge: Cambridge University Press.

Kaufman, Herbert (1967) *The Forest Ranger: A Study in Administrative Behavior*, Washington: Resources for the Future.

Kaufmann, Daniel, Kraay, Aart, Mastruzzi, Massimo (2009) 'Governance Matters VIII. Aggregate and Individual Governance Indicators 1996–2008', Policy Research Working Paper 4978, Washington, D.C.: The World Bank.

Kelsall, Tim (2011) 'Rethinking the Relationship between Neo-patrimonialism and Economic Development in Africa', *IDS Bulletin* 42: 76–87.

Kelsall, Tim (with David Booth, Diana Cammack, Brian Cooksey, Mesfin Grebemichael, Fred Golooba-Mutebi, Sarah Vaughan) (2013) *Business, Politics, and the State in Africa: Challenging the Orthodoxies on Growth and Transformation*, London: Zed Books.

Khalaf, Abdulhadi (2003) 'A King's Dilemma – Obstacles to Political Reforms in Bahrain', paper presented at the Fifth Mediterranean Social and Political Research Meeting, Montecatini, Italy, April 2004.

Khan, Mushtaq H. (2010) 'Political Settlements and the Governance of Growth-Enhancing Institutions'. Online. Available HTTP: http://eprints.soas.ac.uk/9968/1/Political_Settlements_internet.pdf (accessed 2 April 2012).

Khan, Mushtaq H. and Jomo, Kwame Sundaram (2000) *Rents, Rent-Seeking and Economic Development*, Cambridge: Cambridge University Press.

King, Gary, Keohane, Robert O., Verba, Sidney (1994) *Designing Social Inquiry: Scientific Inference in Qualitative Research*, Princeton: Princeton University Press.

Klantschnig, Gernot (2009) 'The politics of law enforcement in Nigeria: lessons from the war on drugs', *Journal of Modern African Studies*, 47: 529–49.

Koch, Christian (2000) *Politische Entwicklung in einem Arabischen Golfstaat: Die Rolle von Interessengruppen im Emirat Kuwait*, Berlin: Klaus Schwarz.

Kohli, Atul (2004) *State-Directed Development: Political Power and Industrialization in the Global Periphery*, Cambridge: Cambridge University Press.

Kornai, Janos (1979) 'Resource-Constrained versus Demand-Constrained Systems', *Econometrica*, 47: 801–19.

Kovach, Kenneth A. (1987) 'What motivates employees? Workers and supervisors give different answers', *Business Horizons* 30: 58–65.

——(1995) 'Employee motivation: addressing a crucial factor in your organization's performance', *Employment Relations Today* 22: 93–107.

Krishna, Anirudh, Uphoff, Norman and Esman, Milton J. (eds) (1997) *Reasons for Hope: Instructive Experiences in Rural Development*, West Hartford: Kumarian Press.

Lafer, Celso (1975) 'O Planejamento no Brasil—Observações Sobre O Plano de Metas (1956–61)', in Betty Mindlin Lafer (ed.) *Planejamento no Brasil*, São Paulo: Editora Perspectiva.

Laking, Rob (2005) 'Agencies: Their benefits and risks', *OECD Journal on Budgeting* 4: 7–25.

Larbi, George A. (2006): 'Applying the New Public Management in Developing Countries', in Yusuf Bangura and George A. Larbi (eds): *Public Sector Reform in*

254 *Bibliography*

Developing Countries: Capacity Challenges to Improve Services, Basingstoke: Palgrave Macmillan and UNRISD: 25–52.

Larbi, George A. and Bangura, Yusuf (2006) 'Public Sector Reform: What are the Lessons from Experience?', in Yusuf Bangura and George A. Larbi (eds) *Public Sector Reform in Developing Countries: Capacity Challenges to Improve Services*, Basingstoke: Palgrave Macmillan and UNRISD: 275–87.

Lawson, Colin (1994) 'The Theory of State-Owned Enterprises in Market Economies', *Journal of Economic Surveys*, 8: 283–309.

Lawson, Fred (1989) *Bahrain: The Modernization of Autocracy*, Boulder, Colo.: Westview.

Lawson, Letitia (2009): 'The politics of anti-corruption reform in Africa', *Journal of Modern African Studies* 47: 73–100.

Lazzarini, Sergio G., Musacchio, Aldo, Bandeira-de-Mello, Rodrigo and Marcon, Rosilene (2011) 'What Do Development Banks Do? Evidence from Brazil, 2002–9', Harvard Business School Working Paper 12–047. Online. Available HTTP: http://hbswk.hbs.edu/item/6915.html (1 December 2012).

Leftwich, Adrian (2000) *States of development: on the primacy of politics in development*, Cambridge: Polity Press.

——(2002) 'Forms of the Democratic Developmental State: Democratic Practices and Development Capacity', in Mark Robinson and Gordon White (eds) *The Democratic Developmental State: Political and Institutional Design*, Oxford: Oxford University Press: 52–83.

——(2010) 'Beyond Institutions: Rethinking the Role of Leaders, Elites and Coalitions in the Institutional Formation of Developmental States and Struggles', *Forum for Development Studies* 37: 93–111.

Lemonick, Michael D. (2005) 'Drug Warrior', *Time*. Online. Available HTTP: http://www.time.com/time/magazine/article/0,9171,1124289,00.html (accessed 29 April 2010).

Leonard, David K. (1991) *African Successes: Four Public Managers of Kenyan Rural Development*, Berkeley: University of California Press.

——(2008) 'Where Are 'Pockets' of Effective Agencies Likely in Weak Governance States and Why? A Propositional Inventory', Institute of Development Studies Working Paper 306, Brighton: Institute of Development Studies at the University of Sussex.

——(2010) '"Pockets" of effective agencies in weak governance states: Where are they likely and why does it matter?', *Public Administration and Development* 30: 91–101.

Levi, Margaret (1988) *Of Rule and Revenue,* Berkeley: University of California Press.

Levine, Daniel (1973) *Conflict and Political Change in Venezuela*, Princeton: Princeton University Press.

Levitsky, Steven and Way, Lucan (2002) 'The Rise of Competitive Authoritarianism', *Journal of Democracy* 13: 51–65.

Lewis, Peter (1992) 'The Political Economy of Public Enterprise in Nigeria', unpublished doctoral dissertation, Princeton University.

——(2007) *Growing Apart: Oil, Politics, and Economic Change in Indonesia and Nigeria*, Ann Arbor: University of Michigan Press.

Lin, Justin Yifu, Fang Cai and Zhou Li (1998) 'Competition, Policy Burdens, and State-Owned Enterprise Reform', *American Economic Review*, 88: 422–27.

Lindblom, Charles (1959) 'The "Science" of Muddling Through', *Public Administration Review* 19: 79–88.

Lipsky, Michael (1980) *Street-Level Bureaucracy. Dilemmas of the Individual in Public Service*, New York: Russel Sage Foundation.

Bibliography 255

Long, Norman and Jan Douwe van der Ploeg (1989) 'Demythologizing planned intervention: An actor perspective', *Sociologia Ruralis* 29: 226–49.

Looney, Robert (1994) *Manpower Policies and Development in the Persian Gulf Region*, Westport, Conn.: Praeger.

Lotens, Walter (2004) *Omkijken naar een 'revolutie': Surinaamse intellectuelen onder militairen* [Looking Back to a 'Revolution': Surinamese Intellectuals under the Military], Paramaribo: Faranaz.

Lozano, Wilfredo (2012) 'Development Opportunities: Politics, the State, and Institutions in the Dominican Republic in the Twenty-First Century', in Alejandro Portes and Lori D. Smith (eds) *Institutions Count: Their Role and Significance in Latin American Development*, Berkeley: University of California Press: 113–29.

Luciani, Giacomo (2005) 'Saudi Arabian Business: From Private Sector to National Bourgeoisie', in Paul Aarts and Gerd Nonneman (eds) *Saudi Arabia in the Balance: Political Economy, Society, Foreign Affairs*, London: Hurst.

Luhmann, Niklas (1983) *Legitimation durch Verfahren*, Frankfurt am Main: Suhrkamp.

Mahdavy, Hussein (1970) 'The Patterns and Problems of Economic Development in Rentier States: the Case of Iran', in M. A. Cook (ed.) *Studies in the Economic History of the Middle East*, London: Oxford University Press.

Maicibi, N. Alhas (2005) *Education: 'The Iron Curtain'*, Kampala, Netmedia Publications Ltd.

——(2006) 'Centrality of education in the pull, push and stop factors of trafficking in humans: perspective from Africa', paper presented at the International Conference on Security, Human Rights and Democracy, Amman, Jordan, 10–12 July.

Maicibi, N. Alhas, Babandede, Muhammed and Gyong, John E. (2007) *A Study on Causes and Patterns of Trafficking in Human Commodities in Nigeria*, Kampala: United Nations African Institute for the Prevention of Crime and the Treatment of Offenders (UNAFRI).

Mainwaring, Scott and Scully, Timothy (2008) 'Latin America: Eight Lessons for Governance', *Journal of Democracy* 19: 113–26.

Malley, Robert (1996) *The Call from Algeria: Third Worldism, Revolution and the Turn to Islam*, Berkeley: University of California Press.

Maloney, Suzanne (2000) 'Agents or Obstacles? Parastatal Foundations and Challenges for Iranian Development', in Parvin Alizadeh (ed.) *The Economy of Iran: Dilemmas of an Islamic State*, London: I.B. Tauris.

Manning, Nick (2001) 'The Legacy of the New Public Management in Developing Countries', *International Review of Administrative Sciences* 67: 297–312.

Manor, James (ed.) (2007) *Aid That Works: Successful Development in Fragile States*, Washington D.C.: The World Bank.

March, James G. and Simon, Herbert A. (1958) *Organizations*, New York: Wiley.

Mares, David, and Altamirano, Nelson (2007) 'Venezuela's PDVSA and World Energy Markets', Working Paper, Baker Institute, Rice University. Online. Available HTTP: http://www.rice.edu/energy/publications/docs/NOCs/Papers/NOC_PDVSA_Mares-A ltamirano.pdf (accessed 12 September 2009).

Martin, Dougal (2001) 'Macroeconomic Developments during the 1990s', in Pitou van Dijck (ed.) *Suriname, the Economy: Prospects for Sustainable Development*, Kingston: Ian Randle Publishers: 43–90.

Martin, Isaac William, Mehrotra, Ajay K. and Prasad, Monica (eds) (2009) *The New Fiscal Sociology: Taxation in Comparative and Historical Perspective*, Cambridge: Cambridge University Press.

256 Bibliography

McCourt, Willy and Bebbington, Anthony (2007) 'Introduction: A Framework for Understanding Development Success', in Anthony Bebbington and Willy McCourt (eds) *Development Success: Statecraft in the South*, Basingstoke: Palgrave Macmillan: 1–29.

McCourt, Willy and Minogue, Martin (eds) (2001) *The Internationalization of Public Management: Reinventing the Third World State*, Cheltenham: Edward Elgar.

McDonnell, Erin (2012) 'Subcultural Bureaucracy', doctoral dissertation, Northwestern University.

Médard, Jean-François (1982) 'The Underdeveloped State in Tropical Africa: Political Clientelism or Neo-Patrimonialism?', in Christopher Clapham (ed.) *Private Patronage and Public Power. Political Clientelism in the Modern State*, New York: St. Martin's Press: 162–92.

——(1991) 'L'État néo-patrimonial en Afrique noire' in Jean-François Médard (ed.) *États d'Afrique noire: formation, mécanismes et crises*, Paris: ed. Karthala: 323–53.

Melo, Marcus Andre, Ng'ethe, Njuguna and Manor, James (2012) *Against the Odds: Politicians, Institutions and the Struggle Against Poverty*, London: C. Hurst & Co.

Menke, Jack (1991) 'The State in the Development Process of Suriname, 1948–90', in Henry Jeffrey and Jack Menke (eds) *Problems of Development of the Guianas*, Paramaribo: Anton de Kom University of Suriname: 55–77.

Merkel, Wolfgang (2004) 'Embedded and Defective Democracies', *Democratization* 11: 33–58.

Merton, Robert K. (1936) 'The Unanticipated Consequences of Purposive Social Action', *American Sociological Review* 1: 894–904.

Minogue, Martin, Polidano, Charles and Hulme, David (eds) (1999) *Beyond the New Public Management: Changing Ideas and Practices in Governance*, Cheltenham: Edward Elgar.

Moore, Mick (1998) 'Death Without Taxes: Democracy, State Capacity, and Aid Dependency in the Fourth World', in Mark Robinson and Gordon White (eds) *The Democratic Developmental State. Politics and Institutional Design*, Oxford: Oxford University Press: 84–121.

——(2001) 'Political Underdevelopment: What Causes "Bad Governance"?', *Public Management Review* 1: 385–418.

——(2002) 'Death without Taxes: Democracy, State Capacity, and Aid Dependence in the Fourth World', in Mark Robinson and Gordon White (eds) *The Democratic Developmental State: Political and Institutional Design*, Oxford: Oxford University Press: 84–121.

——(2004) 'Revenues, State Formation, and the Quality of Governance in Developing Countries', *International Political Science Review* 25: 297–319.

Moore, Mick and Rakner, Lise (2002) 'Introduction: The New Politics of Taxation and Accountability in Developing Countries', *IDS Bulletin* 33: 1–9.

Moore, Mick and Schneider, Aaron (2004) 'Taxation, Governance, and Poverty: Where do Middle Income Countries Fit In?', *IDS Working Paper 230*, Sussex: Institute of Development Studies.

Moynihan, Donald P. (2006) 'Ambiguity in Policy Lessons: The Agencification Experience', *Public Administration*, 84: 1029–50.

Mustapha, Abdul Raufu (2007) 'Institutionalising ethnic representation: How effective is the Federal Character Commission in Nigeria?', CRISE Working Paper no. 43, Oxford: Centre for Research on Inequality, Human Security and Ethnicity (CRISE), University of Oxford.

Bibliography 257

NAFDAC (n.d. a) 'NAFDAC Organisation', Online. Available HTTP: http://www.nafdac.gov.ng/index.php?option=com_content&view=article&id=46:nafdac-organisation (accessed 15 December 2012).

——(n.d. b) 'Our Vision, Mission', Online. Available HTTP: http://www.nafdac.gov.ng/index.php/mission-a-vision (accessed 15 December 2012).

Nakamoto, Michiyo and Leahy, Joe (2011) 'BNDES eyes opening of Asian office', *Financial Times,* June 22. Online. Available HTTP: http://www.ft.com/intl/cms/s/0/335d41a2–9cd0–11e0-bf57–00144feabdc0.html#axzz2NGzWhj4v (accessed 31 July 2011).

NAPTIP (2005a) *Situation assessment of child trafficking in eleven Southern Nigerian states,* Abuja: NAPTIP.

——(2005b) 'NAPTIP News', Abuja: NAPTIP.

——(2009a) 'NAPTIP News', no. 3, Abuja: NAPTIP.

——(2009b) 'NAPTIP News', no. 4, Abuja: NAPTIP.

Narr, Wolf-Dieter and Offe, Claus (eds) (1975) *Wohlfahrtsstaat und Massenloyalität,* Köln: Kiepenheuer & Witsch.

Naur, Maja (1986) *Political Mobilization and Industry in Libya,* Uppsala: Akademisk Forlag.

Nduwugwe, Justus (2008) 'DFID, PATHS launch N13.2 Billion Health Support Programme', *Leadership.* Online. Available HTTP: http://allafrica.com/stories/200806160800.html (accessed: 15 April 2010).

Niblock, Tim (2007) *The Political Economy of Saudi Arabia,* London: Routledge.

Niethammer, Katja (2006) 'Voices in Parliament, Debates in Majlis, and Banners on Streets: Avenues of Political Participation in Bahrain', EUI Working Paper 2006/27, Florence: European University Institute.

NOI Polls (2009): 'Perceptions of Effectiveness, Confidence & Corruption in Government Institutions/Agencies 2007, 2008 & 2009', printout, Abuja: NOI Polls.

Nwogu, Vicky (2005) 'Trafficking in Persons to Europe: The Perspective of Nigeria as a Sending Country', paper presented at the ASI and OIKOS Conference on Trafficking and Migration: A Human Rights Approach, Lisbon, Portugal.

Nwokeji, G Ugo (2007) 'Nigerian National Petroleum Corporation', Working Paper, Baker Institute, Rice University. Online. Available HTTP: http://www.rice.edu/energy/publications/docs/NOCs/Papers/NNPC_Ugo.pdf (accessed 12 September 2009).

O'Donell, Guillermo A. (1994) 'Delegative Democracy', *Journal of Democracy* 5: 55–69.

OECD (Organisation for Economic Co-operation and Development) (2002): *Distributed Public Governance: Agencies, Authorities and other Government Bodies,* Paris: OECD.

——(2005), *Paris Declaration on Aid Effectiveness,* Paris: OECD.

——(2010) *Citizen-State Relations. Improving Governance Through Taxation,* Paris: OECD.

OECD-DAC (Organisation for Economic Co-operation and Development, Development Assistance Committee) (2007) *Principles for Good International Engagement in Fragile States and Situations,* Paris: OECD DAC.

Okonjo-Iweala, Ngozi (2012) *Reforming the Unreformable: Lessons from Nigeria,* Cambridge: The MIT Press.

Olaoye, E.O. (2005): *Public Management in Nigeria,* Akure: Adeyemo Publishers.

Olowu, Dele (2002) *Africa Development* 27 (special issue 'New Public Sector Management Approaches in Africa').

258   *Bibliography*

Olurode, 'Lai (ed.) (2010) *Reflections on a decade of democratization in Nigeria*, Abuja: Friedrich-Ebert-Stiftung (FES).

Olurode, 'Lai and Anifowose, Remi (eds) (2005) *Rich but Poor: Corruption and Good Governance in Nigeria*, Lagos: Faculty of Social Sciences, University of Lagos.

Olurode, 'Lai and Akinboye, S.O. (eds) (2005) *Democracy, Good Governance and Corruption in Nigeria*, Lagos: Friedrich-Ebert-Stiftung (FES).

Onoh, J. K (1983) *The Nigerian Oil Economy: From Prosperity to Glut*, London: Croom Helm.

Oostindie, Gert and Klinkers, Inge (2001) *Het Koninkrijk in de Caraïben: Een korte geschiedenis van het Nederlandse dekolonisatiebeleid, 1940–2000* [The Kingdom in the Caribbean: A Short History of Dutch Decolonisation, 1940–2000], Amsterdam: Amsterdam University Press.

Osaghae, Eghosa E. (1998) *Crippled Giant: Nigeria Since Independence*, Bloomington: Indiana University Press.

——(1999) 'Exiting from the state in Nigeria', *African Journal of Political Science* 4: 83–98.

Ostrom, Elinor (1997) 'Crossing the Great Divide: Coproduction, Synergy, and Development', in Peter Evans (ed.) *State-Society Synergy: Government and Social Capital in Development*, Berkeley: University of California at Berkeley, International and Area Studies: 85–118.

Ottaway, Marina (2003) *Democracy Challenged: The Rise of Semi-Authoritarianism*, Washington D.C.: Carnegie Endowment for International Peace.

Ovadje, Franca and Utomi, Pat (2009) 'Dora Akunyili at NAFDAC: The Challenge of Changing a Government Agency', unpublished paper, Lagos: Lagos Business School.

Owusu, Francis (2006a) 'On Public Organisations in Ghana: What Differentiates Good Performers from Poor Performers?', *African Development Review* 18: 471–85.

——(2006b) 'Differences in the Performance of Public Organisations in Ghana: Implications for Public-Sector Reform Policy', *Development Policy Review* 24: 693–705.

——(2012) 'Organizational culture and public sector reform in a post-Washington consensus era: Lessons from Ghana's good reformers', *Progress in Development Studies* 12: 135–51.

Oxford English Dictionary (n.d.) Online version. Available HTTP: www.oed.com/view/Entry/59674 (accessed 13 February 2012).

Oyekanmi, Felicia A.D. and Soyombo, Omololu (eds) (2007) *Society and Governance: The Quest for Legitimacy in Nigeria*, Lagos: Friedrich-Ebert-Stiftung (FES).

Panter-Brick, Keith (1978) *Soldiers and Oil: The Political Transformation of Nigeria*, London: Frank Cass.

Peters, Thomas J. and Waterman, Robert H. (1982) *In Search of Excellence: Lessons from America's Best-Run Companies*, New York: Harper & Row.

Pitcher, Anne, Moran, Mary H. and Johnston, Michael (2009) 'Rethinking Patrimonialism and Neopatrimonialism in Africa', *African Studies Review* 52: 125–56.

Polidano, Charles (2001) 'Why civil service reforms fail', *Public Management Review* 3: 345–62.

Pollitt, Christopher (2009) 'Decentralized management: Agencies and "arm's length" bodies', in Tony Bovaird and Elke Löffler (eds): *Public management and governance*, London: Routledge: 249–60.

Pollitt, Christopher and Bouckaert, Geert (eds) (2004) *Public Management Reform: A Comparative Analysis*, Oxford: Oxford University Press.

Bibliography   259

Pollitt, Christopher and Talbot, Colin (eds) (2004) *Unbundled Government: A Critical Analysis of the Global Trend to Agencies, Quangos, and Contractualisation*, London: Routledge.

Pollitt, Christopher, Talbot, Colin, Caulfield, Janice and Smullen, Amanda (2004) *Agencies: How governments do things through semi-autonomous organizations*, New York: Palgrave Macmilan.

Pollitt, Christopher, Van Thiel, Sandra and Homburg, Vincent (eds) (2007) *New Public Management in Europe: Adaptation and Alternatives*, Basingstoke: Palgrave Macmillan.

Portes, Alejandro and Smith, Lori D. (eds) (2012a) *Institutions Count: Their Role and Significance in Latin American Development*, Berkeley: University of California Press.

Portes, Alejandro and Smith, Lori D. (2012b) 'The Comparative Study of Institutions: The "Institutional Turn" in Development Studies', in Alejandro Portes and Lori D. Smith (eds) *Institutions Count: Their Role and Significance in Latin American Development*, Berkeley: University of California Press: 24–38.

Portes, Alejandro and Smith, Lori D. (2012c) 'Conclusion: The Comparative Analysis of the Role of Institutions in National Development', in Alejandro Portes and Lori D. Smith (eds) *Institutions Count: Their Role and Significance in Latin American Development*, Berkeley: University of California Press: 167–90.

Prade, Hans (1999) 'Overheidsbestedingen en politieke machtsverhoudingen in Suriname tussen 1975 en 1998' [Government Spending and Political Power Relations in Suriname between 1975 and 1998], *Oso: Tijdschrift voor Surinaamse Taalkunde, Letterkunde, Cultuur en Geschiedenis* 18: 36–43.

Prado, Mariana Mota (2008) 'The Challenges and Risks of Creating Independent Regulatory Agencies: A Cautionary Tale from Brazil' *Vanderbilt Journal of Transnational Law* 41: 435–503.

President of the Republic of Suriname (2010) *'Kruispunt': Samen naar betere tijden* [At the Crossroads: Together Heading for a Better Era], policy statement 2010–15, delivered to the National Assembly, 1 October 2010. Online. Available HTTP: http://www.starnieuws.com/index.php/beyond_files/get_file/be9b66dfda484b3ec78ad32afcdceab6.pdf (accessed 13 December 2012).

Prichard, Wilson (2009) 'The Politics of Taxation and Implications for Accountability in Ghana 1981–2008' (IDS Working Paper No. 330), Brighton: Institute of Development Studies.

——(2010) 'Taxation and State Building: Towards a Governance Focused Tax Reform Agenda' (IDS Working Paper No. 341), Brighton: Institute of Development Studies.

Prichard, Wilson and Leonard, David K. (2010) 'Does reliance on tax revenue build state capacity in sub-Saharan Africa?', *International Review of Administrative Sciences* 76 (4): 653–75.

Ragin, Charles C. (2000) *Fuzzy-Set Social Science*, Chicago: University of Chicago Press.

Rainey, Hal G. and Bozeman, Barry (2000) 'Comparing Public and Private Organizations: Empirical Research and the Power of the A Priori', *Journal of Public Administration Research and Theory* 10: 447–69.

Ramsoedh, Hans (2001) 'Playing Politics: Ethnicity, Clientelism and the Struggle for Power', in Rosemarijn Hoefte and Peter Meel (eds) *Twentieth-Century Suriname: Continuities and Discontinuities in a New World Society*, Kingston/Leiden: Ian Randle Publishers/KITLV Press: 91–110.

Rawksi, Thomas (1989) *Economic Growth in Pre-War China*, Berkeley: University of California Press.

260 *Bibliography*

Reno, William (1998) *Warlord politics and African states*, Boulder: Lynne Rienner Publishers.

Renzler, Nick (2012) 'Brazil's Belo Monte Move: Will National Development Banks Start Taking Human Rights and Environmental Concerns More Seriously?', *Corporate Responsibility and the Law*, 13 December. Online. Available HTTP: http://www.csrandthelaw.com/2012/12/brazils-belo-monte-move-will-national-development-banks-start-taking-human-rights-and-environmental-concerns-more-seriously/ (accessed 19 December 2012).

Riggs, Fred W. (1964) *Administration in Developing Countries. The Theory of Prismatic Society*, Boston: Houghton Mifflin Company.

Robinson, Mark (2007) 'The political economy of governance reforms in Uganda', *Commonwealth & Comparative Politics* 45: 452–74.

Robinson, Mark (2007) 'The Politics of Successful Governance Reforms: Lessons of Design and Implementation', *Commonwealth and Comparative Politics* 45: 521–48.

Rodríguez-Garavito, César (2012) 'The Colombian Paradox: A Thick Institutionalist Analysis', in Alejandro Portes and Lori D. Smith (eds) *Institutions Count: Their Role and Significance in Latin American Development*, Berkeley: University of California Press: 85–112.

Roll, Michael (2004) 'Autonomous politicians and the local state in Sri Lanka: on the social organisation of politics and administration', *Internationales Asienforum* 35: 263–93.

——(forthcoming) 'The state that works: "pockets of effectiveness" as a perspective on stateness in Nigeria and beyond', in Thomas Bierschenk and Jean-Pierre Olivier de Sardan (eds) *States at Work. Dynamics of African Bureaucracies*, Leiden: Brill.

Ross, Michael L. (1999) 'The Political Economy of the Resource Curse', *World Politics* 51: 297–322.

——(2004) 'Does Taxation Lead to Representation?', *British Journal of Political Science* 34: 229–49.

Rotberg, Richard I. (2003) *When states fail: causes and consequences*, Princeton: Princeton University Press.

Rothstein, Bo and Teorell, Jan (2008) 'What is Quality of Government? A Theory of Impartial Government Institutions', *Governance* 21: 165–90.

Ruppert, Elizabeth (1999) 'The Algerian Retrenchment System: A Financial and Economic Evaluation', *The World Bank Economic Review*, 13: 155–84.

Saeidi, Ali (2001) 'Charismatic Political Authority and Populist Economics in Post-Revolutionary Iran', *Third World Quarterly*, 22: 219–36.

Schedler, Andreas (2002) 'The Menu of Manipulation', *Journal of Democracy* 13: 37–50.

Schick, Allen (1998) 'Why Most Developing Countries Should Not Try New Zealand's Reforms', *The World Bank Research Observer* 13: 123–31.

Schneider, Ben Ross (1987) 'Framing the State: Economic Policy and Political Representation in Post-authoritarian Brazil', in John D. Wirth, Edwon de Oliveira Nunes and Tomas E. Bogenschild (eds) *State and Society in Brazil: Continuity and Change*, Boulder: Westview Press: 214–55.

——(1991) *Politics within the State: Elite Bureaucrats and Industrial Policy in Authoritarian Brazil*, Pittsburgh: University of Pittsburgh Press.

——(1999) 'The *Desarrollista* State in Brazil and Mexico', in Meredith Woo-Cumings (ed.) *The Developmental State*, Ithaca: Cornell University Press: 276–305.

Schneider, Carsten Q. and Wagemann, Claudius (2012) *Set-Theoretic Methods for the Social Sciences: A Guide to Qualitative Comparative Analysis*, Cambridge: Cambridge University Press.

Schumpeter, Joseph A. (1918) *Die Krise des Steuerstaates*, Graz und Leipzig.

Sedney, Jules (1997) *De toekomst van ons verleden: Democratie, etniciteit en politieke machtsvorming in Suriname* [The Future of our Past: Democracy, Ethnicity and Political Power Formation in Suriname], Paramaribo: Vaco.

Selznick, Philip (1957) *Leadership in Administration. A Sociological Interpretation*, New York: Harper & Row Publishers.

Shafer, D. Michael (1994) *Winners and Losers: How Sectors Shape the Developmental Prospects of States*, Ithaca: Cornell University Press.

Shen, T.H. (1970) *The Sino-American Joint Commission on Rural Reconstruction: Twenty Years of Cooperation for Agricultural Development*, Ithaca: Cornell University Press.

Sikkink, Kathryn (1991) *Ideas and Institutions: Developmentalism in Brazil and Argentina*, Ithaca, NY: Cornell University Press.

Silos, Maureen (2002) 'Leiderschap in de organisatie van armoede' [Leadership in the Organisation of Poverty], Seventh Multatuli Lecture, 1 November 2002. Online. Available HTTP: www.multatuli-lezing.nl/download/Silos.doc (accessed 13 December 2012).

Smith, Benjamin (2007) *Hard Times in the Lands of Plenty: Oil Politics in Iran and Indonesia*, Ithaca: Cornell University Press.

Smith, Daniel Jordan (2008) *A Culture of Corruption: Everyday Deception and Popular Discontent in Nigeria*, Princeton: Princeton University Press.

Soyinka, Wole (1996) *The Open Sore of a Continent: A Personal Narrative of the Nigerian Crisis*, Oxford: Oxford University Press.

State Oil Company of Suriname (2006) 'Press Release, 21 March'. Online. Available HTTP: http://www.staatsolie.com/press_releases/Persberichten%202006/Staatsolie%20bedrijfsbreed%20ISO%20gecertificeerd.pdf (accessed 13 December 2012).

——(2009) *Half-Year Report 2009*, Paramaribo: State Oil Company of Suriname.

——(2010a) *Annual Report 2009*, Paramaribo: State Oil Company of Suriname.

——(2010b) *Half-Year Report 2010*, Paramaribo: State Oil Company of Suriname.

——(2012a) *Annual Report 2011*, Paramaribo: State Oil Company of Suriname.

——(2012b) 'Company Profile 2012'. Online. Available HTTP: http://www.staatsolie.com/pdf/company_profile2012.pdf (retrieved 13 December 2012).

——(2012c) 'Staatsolie Petroleum Opportunities'. Online. Available HTTP: http://www.staatsolie.com/pio (accessed 13 December 2012).

——(2012d) 'The Suriname-Guyana Basin: The Next Giant. Suriname 2013 International Bidding Round'. Online. Available HTTP: http://www.staatsolie.com/pio/images/stories/PDF/aapg-international-conference-exhibition-singapore2012.pdf (accessed 13 December 2012).

Steinmetz, George (1993) *Regulating the Social: The Welfare State and Local Politics in Imperial Germany*, Princeton: Princeton University Press.

——(2005) 'The Epistemological Unconscious of U.S. Sociology and the Transition to Post-Fordism: The Case of Historical Sociology', in Julia Adams, Elisabeth S. Clements and Ann Shola Orloff (eds) *Remaking Modernity: Politics, History, and Sociology*, Durham: Duke University Press: 109–57.

Stevens, Mike and Teggemann, Stefanie (2004) 'Comparative Experience with Public Sector Reform in Ghana, Tanzania, and Zambia', in Brian Levy and Sahr Kpundeh

262 *Bibliography*

(eds) *Building State Capacity in Africa: New Approaches, Emerging Lessons*, Washington, D.C.: The World Bank: 43–86.

St-Hilaire, Aonghas (2001) 'Ethnicity, Assimilation and Nation in Plural Suriname', *Ethnic and Racial Studies* 24: 998–1019.

Strauss, Anselm L. (1998) *Grundlagen qualitativer Sozialforschung*, München: Fink.

Strauss, Julia C. (1998) *Strong Institutions in Weak Polities: State Building in Republican China, 1927–1940*, Oxford: Oxford University Press.

Strauss, Julia C. (2008) 'Rethinking Institutional Capacity and Tax Regimes: The Case of the Sino-Foreign Salt Inspectorate in Republican China' in Mick Moore, Deborah Brautigam and Odd-Helge Fjeldstad (eds) *Capacity and Consent: Taxation and State-Building in Developing Countries*, Cambridge: Cambridge University Press.

Strauss, Julia C. (2009) 'Forestry Reform and the Transformation of State Capacity in fin-de-siècle China', *Journal of Asian Studies*, 68: 1168–88.

Sulle, Andrew (2010) 'The application of new public management doctrines in the developing world: An exploratory study of the autonomy and control of executive agencies in Tanzania', *Public Administration and Development* 30: 345–54.

Talbot, Colin (2004) 'Executive agencies: Have they improved management in government?', *Public Money and Management* 24: 104–12.

——(2010) *Theories of Performance: Organizational and Service Improvement in the Public Domain*, Oxford: Oxford University Press.

Talbot, Colin and Caulfield, Janice (2002) (eds) *Hard agencies in soft states: A study of agency creation programmes in Jamaica, Latvia and Tanzania*, Pontypridd: University of Glamorgan.

Talierco, Jr., Robert (2004) 'Administrative Reform as Credible Commitment: The Impact of Autonomy on Revenue Authority Performance in Latin America', *World Development*, 32: 213–32.

Tang, Hui-Sun (1954) *Land Reform in Free China*, Joint Commission on Rural Reconstruction.

Tavares, Maria da Conceiçao, de Melo, Hildete Pereira, Caputo, Ana Claudia, da Costa, Gloria Maria Morais and de Araujo, Victor Leonardo (2010) 'O papel do BNDE na industrialização do Brasil: Os anos dourados de desenvolvimento, 1952–80', *Memórias de Desenvolvimento* 4: 1–338.

Tendler, Judith (1997) *Good Government in the Tropics*, Baltimore: John Hopkins University Press.

Tétreault, Mary Ann (1995) *The Kuwait Petroleum Corporation and the Economics of the New World Order*, Westport, Conn.: Quorum Books.

——(2000) *Stories of Democracy: Politics and Society in Contemporary Kuwait*, New York: Columbia University Press.

The Economist (2007) 'Too little, too late', 7 July. Online. Available HTTP: http://www.economist.com/node/18929248 (accessed 20 July 2011).

The Guardian (2011) 'Development banks still have a role to play, as Brazil's success shows', March 29. Online. Available HTTP: http://www.guardian.co.uk/global-development/poverty-matters/2011/mar/29/development-banks-role-brazil-success (accessed 7 July 2011).

Therkildsen, Ole (2004) 'Autonomous tax administration in sub-Saharan Africa: The case of the Uganda Revenue Authority', *Forum for Development Studies* 31: 59–88.

——(2005) 'Understanding public management through neopatrimonialism: A paradigm for all African seasons?', in Ulf Engel and Gorm Rye Olsen (eds) *The African exception*, Aldershot: Ashgate: 35–52.

——(2006) 'Elusive Public Sector Reforms in East and Southern Africa', in Yusuf Bangura and George A. Larbi (eds) *Public Sector Reform in Developing Countries: Capacity Challenges to Improve Services*, Basingstoke: Palgrave Macmillan and UNRISD: 53–81.

——(2008) 'Public Sector Reforms and the Development of Productive Capacities in the LDCs' (UNCTAD, The Least Developed Countries Report 2009: The state and development governance, Background Paper No. 1).

——(forthcoming) 'Working in neopatrimonial settings: perceptions of public sector staff in Tanzania and Uganda', in Thomas Bierschenk and Jean-Pierre Olivier de Sardan (eds) *States at Work. Dynamics of African Bureaucracies*, Leiden: Brill.

Thompson, James D. (1967) *Organizations in Action: Social Science Bases of Administrative Theory*, New York: McGraw-Hill.

Tilly, Charles (ed.) (1975) *The Formation of National States in Western Europe*, Princeton: Princeton University Press.

——(1990) *Coercion, Capital, and European States, AD 990–1992*, Malden: Blackwell Publishing.

Tsai, Lily L. (2007) *Accountability Without Democracy: Solidarity Groups and Public Goods Provision in Rural China*, Cambridge: Cambridge University Press.

Turner, Mark and Hulme, David (eds) (1997) *Governance, Administration and Development: Making the State Work*, West Hartford, Conn.: Kumarian Press.

U.S. Department of State (2009) *Trafficking in Persons Report 2009*, Washington D.C.: U.S. Department of State Publication.

——(2012) *Trafficking in Persons Report 2012*, Washington D.C.: U.S. Department of State Publication.

Ugorji, Ebenezer C. (1995) 'Privatization/Commercialization of State-Owned Enterprises in Nigeria: Strategies for Improving the Performance of the Economy', *Comparative Political Studies*, 27: 537–60.

UNAFRI (United Nations African Institute for the Prevention of Crime and the Treatment of Offenders) (2003) 'Workshop Report on Trafficking of Women and Children: The Situation in Africa', Kampala: UNAFRI.

UNESCO (United Nations Educational, Scientific and Cultural Organization) (2006) 'Human Trafficking in Nigeria: Root Causes and Recommendations', Policy Paper, no. 14.2 (E), Paris: UNESCO.

UNICEF (United Nations Children's Fund) (2005) *The State of the World's Children 2006: Excluded and Invisible*, New York: UNICEF.

——(2007) 'UNICEF congratulates the Government of Nigeria for achieving Universal Salt Iodization'. Online. Available HPPT: http://www.unicef.org/media/media_39607.html (accessed: 15 December 2012).

UNICRI (United Nations Interregional Crime and Justice Research Institute) (2004) 'Trafficking of Nigerian Girls to Italy', report, UNICRI.

UNODC (United Nations Office on Drugs and Crime) (2004) *United Nations Convention against Transnational Organized Crime and the Protocols thereto*, New York: United Nations.

Uphoff, Norman (ed.) (1994) *Puzzles of Productivity in Public Organizations*, San Francisco: ICS Press.

264   *Bibliography*

Uphoff, Norman, Esman, Milton J. and Krishna Anirudh (1998) *Reasons for Success: Learning form Instructive Experiences in Rural Development*, West Hartford: Kumarian Press.

Van Dijck, Pitou (2001) 'Continuity and Change in a Small Open Economy: External Dependency and Policy Inconsistencies', in Rosemarijn Hoefte and Peter Meel (eds) *Twentieth-century Suriname: Continuities and Discontinuities in a New World Society*, Kingston/Leiden: Ian Randle Publishers/KITLV Press: 48–70.

Van Dijck, Pitou (2004) 'Hulp, beleid en economische groei' [Aid, Policy and Economic Growth], in Pitou van Dijck (ed.) *De toekomst van de relatie Nederland–Suriname* [The Future of the Dutch–Surinamese Relationship], Amsterdam: Rozenberg Publishers: 39–68.

van Donge, Jan Kees (2002): 'Agencification', in Colin Kirkpatrick (ed.): *Handbook on Development Policy and Management*, Cheltenham: Edward Elgar: 315–22.

Vandewalle, Dirk (1986) 'Libya's Revolution Revisited', *MERIP Middle East Report*, no. 143: 30–43.

——(1998) *Libya since Independence: Oil and State-Building*, Ithaca: Cornell University Press.

Velasco, José Luis (2012) 'The Uneven and Paradoxical Development of Mexico's Institutions', in Alejandro Portes and Lori D. Smith (eds) *Institutions Count: Their Role and Significance in Latin American Development*, Berkeley: University of California Press: 130–66.

Vernon, Raymond (1984) 'Linking Managers with Ministers: Dilemmas of the State-Owned Enterprise', *Journal of Policy Analysis and Management*, 4: 39–55.

Vitalis, Robert (2007) *America's Kingdom: Mythmaking on the Saudi Oil Frontier*, Stanford, Calif.: Stanford University Press.

von Soest, Christian (2007) 'How Does Neopatrimonialism Affect the African State? The Case of Tax Collection in Zambia', *Journal of Modern African Studies* 45: 621–45.

——(2009) *The African State and Its Revenue. How Politics Influences Tax Collection in Zambia and Botswana*, Baden-Baden: Nomos.

von Soest, Christian, Bechle, Karsten and Korte, Nina (2011) 'How Neopatrimonialism Affects Tax Administration: A Comparative Study of Three World Regions', *Third World Quarterly* 32: 1307–29.

Wade, Robert (1990) *Governing the Market: Economic Theory and the Role of Government in East Asian Industrialization*, Princeton: Princeton University Press.

Waterbury, John (1993) *Exposed to Innumerable Delusions: Public Enterprise and State Power in Egypt, India, Mexico, and Turkey*, Cambridge: Cambridge University Press.

Weick, Karl E. (1969) *The Social Psychology of Organizing*, Reading: Addison-Wesley.

——(1982/2001) 'Management of organizational change among loosely coupled elements', in Karl E. Weick: *Making sense of the organization*, Malden: Blackwell Publishing: 380–403.

Weiland, Heribert, Wehr, Ingrid and Matthias Seifert (eds) (2009) *Good Governance in der Sackgasse?* Baden-Baden: Nomos.

Werenfels, Isabelle (2002) 'Obstacles to Privatisation of State-Owned Industries in Algeria: The Political Economy of a Distributive Conflict', *Journal of North African Studies*, 7: 1–28.

Weyland, Kurt (2001) 'Clarifying a Contested Concept: Populism in the Study of Latin American Politics', *Comparative Politics*, 34: 1–22.

White, Gordon and Robinson, Mark (1998) 'Towards synergy in social provision: Civic organizations and the state', in Martin Minogue, Charles Polidano and David Hulme (eds) *Beyond the New Public Management: Changing Ideas and Practices in Governance*, Cheltenham: Edward Elgar: 94–116.

Willis, Eliza (1986) 'The State as Banker: The Expansion of the Public Sector in Brazil', unpublished doctoral dissertation, University of Texas at Austin.

——(1995) 'Explaining Bureaucratic Independence in Brazil: The Experience of the National Economic Development Bank', *Journal of Latin American Studies* 27: 625–61.

Wilson, James Q. (1989) *Bureaucracy: What Government Agencies Do and Why They Do It*, New York: Basic Books.

Women's Consortium of Nigeria (2000) 'Research on Trafficking in Women and Children in Nigeria: Report', Lagos: WOCON.

Woo-Cumings, Meredith (ed.) (1999): *The Developmental State*, Ithaca: Cornell University Press.

Wood, D. (2010) 'Company Presentation', Bank of America Merrill Lynch 2010 Global Energy Conference, Miami Beach, Florida, 10–12 November 2010. Online. Available HTTP: http://docsearch.derrickpetroleum.com/files/08525/Murphy%202010%20Bank%20of%20America%20Merrill%20Lynch%202010%20Global%20Energy.pdf (accessed 13 December 2012).

World Bank (1989) *Sub-Saharan Africa: From Crisis to Sustainable Growth*, Oxford: Oxford University Press.

——(1992) *Governance and Development*, Washington D.C.: The World Bank.

——(1994) 'Algeria Country Economic Memorandum: The Transition to a Market Economy', Economic Report 12048, Washington, DC: World Bank.

——(1997) *World Development Report 1997: The State in a Changing World*, Oxford and Washington, D.C.: Oxford University Press and The World Bank.

——(2003a) *World Development Report 2004: Making Services Work for Poor People*, Washington, D.C.: The World Bank and Oxford University Press.

——(2003b) 'Algeria: A Medium-Term Macroeconomic Strategy', Country Economic Memorandum 26005, Washington, DC: World Bank.

——(2006) 'Socialist People's Libyan Arab Jamahiriya', Country Economic Report 30295, Washington, DC: World Bank.

——(2008) *Public Sector Reform: What Works and Why? An IEG Evaluation of World Bank Support*, Washington D.C.: The World Bank.

——(2012a) *The World Bank's Approach to Public Sector Management 2011–2020: "Better Results from Public Sector Institutions"*, Washington D.C.: The World Bank.

——(2012b) 'World Development Indicators 2012'. Online. Available HTTP: http://data.worldbank.org/data-catalog/world-development-indicators/wdi-2012 (accessed 13 December 2012).

——(n.d.) Worldwide Governance Indicators. Online. Available HTTP: http://info.worldbank.org/governance/wgi/index.asp (accessed 2 April 2013).

Wormald, Guillermo and Brieba, Daniel (2012) 'Institutional Change and Development in Chilean Market Society', in Alejandro Portes and Lori D. Smith (eds) *Institutions Count: Their Role and Significance in Latin American Development*, Berkeley: University of California Press: 60–84.

Yager, Joseph (1988) *Transforming Agriculture in Taiwan*, Ithaca: Cornell University Press.

266 Bibliography

Yizraeli, Sarah (1997) *The Remaking of Saudi Arabia: The Struggle Between King Sa'ud and Crown Prince Faysal, 1953-1962*, Tel Aviv: Moshe Dayan Center.

Zakaria, Fareed (1997) 'The Rise of Illiberal Democracy', *Foreign Affairs* 76: 22–43.

Zartman, I. William (ed.) (1995) *Collapsed States: The Disintegration and Restoration of Legitimate Authority*, Boulder: Lynne Rienner Publishers.

Index

Abah, Joe 240
accountability 30; state-society
bargaining 4, 39, 40, 233, 235
Africa Power and Politics Programme
4–5, 20, 240
agency 35; agencification 126, 232, 241;
Staatsolie 149
ARAs/SARAs (autonomous/semi-
autonomous revenue authorities) 50,
53, 60, 72, 232–33
Attoh, Franca C. 128–46
autonomy 35; a bargaining relationship
213–14, 239; BNDE 77, 78–79, 80,
81, 89 (*autarquia* 78); financial
autonomy 14, 214; Gulf SOEs 174,
176, 179–80 (autonomy from
bureaucratic/political predation 174,
179–80; managerial autonomy 174,
179, 181; regime autonomy 187–88,
189, 190, 199); JCRR 47, 66, 71;
NAFDAC, autonomous powers 121,
122, 123, 214 (autonomy 98–99, 105,
108–9, 111, 114–16, 125; focussed
powers 108, 114, 116); NAPTIP 133,
136, 139, 145; OECD 126, 213;
organizational autonomy 32, 39, 200,
210, 213–14, 217, 218, 220, 224, 239,
241; Sino-Foreign Salt Inspectorate
47, 48, 55, 62–63, 64, 71; SOE, lack of
autonomy 175–76, 182, 183;
Staatsolie 150, 151, 165, 170
(autonomy from political influence
149, 150–51, 161, 164–67, 169, 213,
220, 239)
Ayee, Joseph R. A. 7, 239

Banerjee, Abhijit V. 40, 196, 234
Barma, Naazneen H. 240
Batley, Richard 6–7, 20

Bebbington, Anthony 26
BNDE (National Bank for Economic
Development) 16, 17, 19, 74–96, 150,
241; autonomy 77, 78–79, 80, 81, 89
(*autarquia* 78); BNDES 75, 96;
bureaucracy 80, 81 (insulation 79, 82,
83, 86, 88, 89); capacity and flexibility
76, 81, 85; criticism 77, 95; ECLA 85,
87, 89; effectiveness 74, 75–77, 81, 82,
86, 87, 94, 95, 223 (challenges 83,
89–93, 95); *esprit de corps* 76, 77, 83,
85–86, 87, 88, 92, 95, 96; favourable
environment 74, 81–83, 94–95; FRE
79, 80, 92–93; function specificity 74,
75, 76, 77, 80–81, 86, 90, 94; funding
76, 77, 78, 79, 83, 89, 90, 92–93;
Government Effectiveness indicators
18; historical case study 16, 26, 74;
incorruptibility 76–77; Joint
Commission 77–79, 82–84, 86–87, 90,
94; legislation 77, 78–81; meritocracy
77, 83, 84, 85, 87, 95; organizational
culture 83, 95, 96; origins and
expansion 74, 75–76, 77–80, 88–89;
persistence 74, 75, 80, 94; SANBRA
91–92; staff (commitment 74, 76, 95;
growing size of 88, 95, 96, 223;
training 85, 86, 96); technocracy 77,
80, 82, 83–88, 89, 90, 91–92, 94, 95,
223; triggering effect 75, 93–94, 230,
231, 234; turning points 87–89, 223;
World Bank 77, 79, 81, 82, 83, 87, 94;
see also entries below for BNDE;
Brazil
BNDE, Brazilian presidents' influence
79–80, 82–83, 89–91, 94–95, 212–13;
Kubitschek, Juscelino 80–95 *passim*
(Targets Plan 81, 82, 83, 87–93
passim, 95); Lula da Silva, Luiz

268   *Index*

Inácio 76; Vargas, Getúlio 78, 79, 80, 82–85, 89–90, 92–94, 198; *see also* BNDE

BNDE, leadership 74, 77, 82, 83–86, 87, 90, 93, 95, 212–13; Campos, Roberto 82, 84–86, 87, 88, 90, 91, 92–93, 95; Paiva Teixeira, Glycon de 84, 85, 86, 87, 90; political management 210, 212–13; *see also* BNDE

Bratton, Michael 42

Brazil 16, 19, 74–96; developmentalism 82; economic populism 199–200; patrimonial state 75, 80, 86; patronage 80, 84, 86, 90, 91; *Petrobras* 168, 198, 237; petrochemical sector 150; *Petroquisa* 150; *see also* BNDE

Buddingh', Hans 147, 155

bureaucracy 43; BNDE 80, 81 (insulation 79, 82, 83, 86, 88, 89); bureaucratic standardization 205; effectiveness 63; impersonal bureaucracy 48, 54, 56, 59, 62, 63; Sino-Foreign Salt Inspectorate 48, 52–57, 60, 62, 63, 71 (insulation 52, 53–54, 55, 56, 57, 58, 60, 71; strategies of goal achievement 52, 54, 56; technocratic bureaucracy 63, 71); technocratic bureaucracy 63, 71

Carpenter, Daniel P. 213, 220, 239n38

case study 9, 10, 16–19; comparative analysis of case studies 11, 14, 15, 19, 194–241; Government Effectiveness indicators 16, 18, 21; historical case study 12, 13, 16, 26, 74; politico-administrative system 12, 19, 24; selection of 11–14, 15; *see also* BNDE; Gulf SOEs; JCRR; methodology and research; NAFDAC; NAPTIP; Sino-Foreign Salt Inspectorate; *Staatsolie*

Centre for the Future State 4, 9, 19, 39–40

China 45–73; Chinese Communist Party 45–46, 47, 67–70, 236; civil war 13, 46, 51, 53, 58, 64, 67, 70, 236; corruption 46, 48, 50, 52; environment 72; Guomindang 45–47, 51, 52, 56, 60, 62, 63, 67–69, 236; historical case study 26; patrimonialism 48; patronage 13, 47; politico-administrative system 13; Sino-Japanese War 47, 52, 62, 71;

taxation 47, 49–50; tree planting campaign 44–45; weak state 45–46, 47, 48, 56; Yuan Shikai 45, 50, 51, 55; *see also* JCRR; Sino-Foreign Salt Inspectorate

civil service 6, 20, 39, 207; patrimonial use of 24; patronage and prebends 24; Sino-Foreign Salt Inspectorate 56, 57–61 (staff commitment 71; training 57); *see also* meritocracy; organizational culture; staff

civil society 3, 30, 133, 142, 209, 211, 234; *see also* NGO

clientelism 183, 197, 225, 236; state 152, 161, 169; Suriname 19, 151, 153, 154–55, 156, 162, 169, 170; *see also* patronage

Colbert, Jean-Baptiste 62

Collier, David 2, 237

Collier, Ruth 237

corruption 39, 43; BNDE, incorruptibility 76–77; China 46, 48, 50, 52; Dominican Republic 227, 228–29; GCC 180; Gulf SOEs 176, 178; NAFDAC, anti-corruption regime 104, 108, 112–13 (whistle blowing 104, 119–20); NAPTIP, anti-corruption measures 140–41, 144; Nigeria 14, 97, 102, 112; reduction of 237; Sino-Foreign Salt Inspectorate 58, 72; SOE 175; Suriname 155, 171

Daland, Robert 1, 23

democracy 1–3, 5, 17, 39, 153, 154; democracies with adjectives 2

developing country: development 152–53; failure to transform into developmental state 152; governance 2–3; public sector 6–7, 111; taxation 40, 71–72; weak state 1

development 3; ARAs/SARAs 232–33; developing country 152–53; developmental patrimonialism 5; developmental state 151–52, 174, 191, 192; governance, public sector and development 1–9; rentier state, politics of development 175; state in development 151–53

DFID (British Department for International Development) 3

Dion, Douglas 15–16

donor organization 3, 7, 29, 115, 143, 232

Duflo, Esther 40, 196, 234

Index 269

Easton, David 233
economic populism 174, 181–85, 186, 188, 190, 199–200; Gulf SOEs, non-populism 183–84, 187, 190, 191; *see also* SOE
effectiveness 25, 43, 70, 71; BNDE 74, 75–77, 81, 82, 86, 87, 94, 95, 223 (challenges 83, 89–93, 95); bureaucracy 63; committed leadership 71; 'core' effectiveness 201, 215; effectiveness strategy 219, 220–21; environment 72; Gulf SOEs 173, 174, 176–81, 190, 238; institutional adequacy 225, 229–30, 239; insulation and buffering 70; JCRR 47, 66–67, 69–70, 71; leadership 71, 95, 202, 223; measurement 45; NAFDAC 100–101, 110–11, 125, 207, 237; NAPTIP 129, 133, 134–35, 137, 143; organizational effectiveness 239; PoE 25, 36, 43–44; 'scale' effectiveness 200, 201, 210, 214, 217, 218, 228, 237; Sino-Foreign Salt Inspectorate 47, 48, 51, 52, 53, 57, 59–60, 62, 63–64, 71; SOE 190, 191; *Staatsolie* 148–49, 156–60, 238; staff 70, 71, 203; standardization 204; technology 205; *see also* PoE
efficiency 43–44; measurement 45
enforcement: NAFDAC 99, 100, 103, 111, 114, 116, 120, 126; NAPTIP 132, 134, 145; standardization 203–4
environment 35; China 72; effectiveness 72; favourable environment (BNDE 74, 81–83, 94–95; JCRR in Taiwan 67, 70, 72); hostile environment 10, 25, 72, 124, 209, 222, 234 (NAFDAC 100, 118, 124, 238; NAPTIP 144; Sino-Foreign Salt Inspectorate 48, 51–52, 59, 60–61, 63; *Staatsolie* 148, 150, 167–68, 169, 170); organizational identity 209; *see also* politico-administrative system
Ermakoff, Ivan 237n18, 238n32
Evans, Peter B. 23, 150, 151–52, 169, 192
Evers, Hans-Dieter 236

Fjeldstad, Odd-Helge 233
focussed powers 200, 202, 217, 218, 220, 238; NAFDAC 108, 114, 116; *see also* PoE, how does it emerge?
Font, Mauricio 77
function/task-related factors: BNDE, function specificity 74, 75, 76, 77, 80–81, 86, 90, 94; Gulf SOEs 176,

179, 184, 191; Israel, Arturo: task specificity 27–28, 34, 199, 201, 224, 225, 241; NAFDAC 19, 98, 100, 107, 125; NAPTIP 133–34, 144; PoE, emergence 34, 196, 197, 199, 217, 237; PoE, persistence 220–21; *Staatsolie* 149, 157–59

GCC (Gulf Cooperation Council) 17, 18, 19, 21; corruption 180; developmental state 191; Government Effectiveness indicators 18, 21; member countries 18, 21; patronage 180, 184, 188; PoE 191; politico-administrative system 13; rent-seeking 180; *see also* Gulf SOEs
Geddes, Barbara 1, 23, 236
Ghana 42, 239
governance 2; complexity of 3; crisis of 19; developing country 2–3; development debate on 3, 5; good governance 2, 4, 6, 23; governance, public sector and development 1–9; governance, state and politics 1–5, 8–9; World Bank 2
Granovetter, Mark 197, 236
Grindle, Merilee S. 27, 31–32, 33, 34, 103, 207, 224, 237
Grounded Theory 14–15
Gulf SOEs 14, 19, 176–81, 187–88, 190, 191; autonomy 174, 176, 179–80 (autonomy from bureaucratic/political predation 174, 179–80; managerial autonomy 174, 179, 181; regime autonomy 187–88, 189, 190, 199); Bahrain 174, 177, 178, 187 (Alba 177, 180, 192); corruption 176, 178; effectiveness 173, 174, 176–81, 190, 238; emergence as PoE 180, 195; function/task-related factors 176, 179, 184, 191; government principals 174, 176, 178–80, 187, 193 (unified principals 179, 181, 189); institutional context 178–81, 191; Kuwait 174, 176, 185, 186, 187, 188–90, 193; meritocracy 178; non-populism 183–84, 187, 190, 191; political economy context 174, 179–81, 187; Qatar 173, 174, 177; Saudi Arabia 174, 176, 178 (Aramco 179, 180; SABIC 173, 176–77, 178, 179, 180); staff 178 (training 178); technology 176; United Arab Emirates 173, 174, 177, 180 (Dubai 177, 180; Emirates

270 *Index*

Airlines 177, 192); *see also* GCC; SOE

head of state 12, 13, 24, 194, 235; PoE, emergence 195–200, 211–12, 217, 218, 235 (appointment of chief executive 197–98, 200, 217; breaking with patronage rationale 197–98, 200, 217; quick and politically tangible results 198–99, 218, 225, 227; strong head of state/low risk constellation 198, 218; timing/critical juncture 198, 200, 218, 237); PoE, persistence: president's strategy 219, 220
Heredia, Blanca 41
Hertog, Steffen 21, 173–93, 199
Hilderbrand, Mary E. 27, 31–32, 34, 103, 207
Hout, Wil 147–72
human rights 13, 26
human trafficking 19, 128–29; forced labour 128, 129, 130–31; internal/trans-border 129, 130–31; prostitution 129, 130–31, 145; *see also* NAPTIP; Nigeria and human trafficking
Hutchcroft, Paul D. 152, 153
Huybens, Elisabeth 240

IMF (International Monetary Fund) 20, 50, 232
Israel, Arturo 27–28, 31, 32, 41; task specificity 27–28, 34, 199, 201, 224, 241

JCRR (Joint Commission on Rural Reconstruction) 16, 17, 46, 47, 64–70; autonomy 47, 66, 71; civil war 13, 46, 47, 64, 67–70; Cornell School of Agronomy 65–66, 68, 71; effectiveness 47, 66–67, 69–70, 71; emergence as PoE 195; exporting the JCRR model 72; functions 64–65; land reform 46, 65, 66, 67, 68–69; leadership 65–66; New Deal 64, 65, 66; origins 64–65, 236; rural development projects 46, 64–70; staff commitment 71; Taiwan 66, 68, 70 (exile to Taiwan 47, 236; hospitable environment 67, 70, 72); technocracy 65, 67, 70; *see also* China; Taiwan
Joshi, Anuradha 40, 239

Karl, Terry Lynn 153, 170–71, 185
Kelsall, Tim 5, 240

Klantschnig, Gernot 239–40
Kovach, Kenneth A. 238

Larbi, George A. 6–7, 20
Latin America 14, 224–30, 234, 237, 239, 241; Argentina 225, 226; Chile 225, 226, 229–30; Colombia 225, 226, 227, 229, 230, 237, 239; Dominican Republic 198, 204, 221–30 *passim*, 237 (corruption 227, 228–29; meritocracy 227–28; political management 229; standardization 229); ECLA 85, 87, 89, 93; how do PoE emerge? 227–29; institutional adequacy 225, 229–30, 239; Mexico 190, 225, 226, 234 (*Progresa/ Oportunidades* 234–35, 241); politico-administrative system 229–30; Venezuelan SOEs 174, 175, 176, 182–83, 185, 190, 192; *see also* BNDE; Brazil
leadership: appointment of chief executive 197–98, 236 ('insider's dilemma' 197, 200, 236; weak/strong ties 197, 200, 236); committed leadership 71, 95; creative pragmatism 218–19, 227; effectiveness 71, 95, 202, 223; environment 35; founding chief executive 55, 136–37, 143, 202, 217, 223; inclusive leadership 102, 105–6, 122, 200, 206, 207, 216, 217–18, 227, 228; JCRR 65–66; leadership change 38, 221; Leonard, David K. 28–29, 31; meritocracy 200; NAPTIP 136–39, 143–44, 145 (Ndaguba, Carol 132, 136–39, 143–44, 145, 221, 240); organizational identity 207–8, 238; personality cult 37; PoE 34, 37–38 (PoE as incremental process, not predefined blueprint 219); political management 210–13, 217, 220; second guard/second row leadership 222, 223; Sino-Foreign Salt Inspectorate 55, 56 (Dane, Sir Richard 51, 55, 56, 59, 206, 219); *Staatsolie* 149, 150–51, 161, 168, 169 (Jharap, Eddy 147, 156–57, 162–67, 172, 236); *see also* BNDE, leadership; NAFDAC, leadership
Leftwich, Adrian 149, 152
Leonard, David 1, 23, 27, 28–29, 31, 33, 41, 224, 240; leadership 28–29, 31
Levitsky, Steven 2
Lewis, Peter 42
Lozano, Wilfredo 204, 221, 223, 227–29

Maicibi, N. Alhas 129, 131
Mainwaring, Scott 74
March, James G. 204
McCourt, Willy 26
McDonnell, Erin 24, 224, 240n50
MDGs (Millennium Development Goals) 3, 7
media 30, 36, 38, 39; NAFDAC 107, 110, 113, 117; NAPTIP 142, 144; Nigerian human trafficking (Adenuga, Wale: *Itohan: A Call to Action* 142, 146; *Glamour Girls II: The Italian Connection* 131); positive media reporting 30, 113, 199, 209, 211
meritocracy 34, 103, 156, 164, 203, 221, 227–28, 237; BNDE 77, 83, 84, 85, 87, 95; Dominican Republic 227–28; Gulf SOEs 178; leadership 200; NAFDAC 103–4; NAPTIP 138–39; organizational identity 207, 209; Sino-Foreign Salt Inspectorate 57–59, 60; *Staatsolie* 156, 164; *see also* civil service; staff
methodology and research 9–16, 23, 194, 240; causation 11; cross-country analysis 4, 21, 22; Grounded Theory 14–15; Latin America, research on 225 (QCA 225, 241); NAFDAC 97–98, 101, 125; NAPTIP 129–30; processes and mechanisms 11, 15, 194, 200; research approach 14; research questions 10–11; *see also* case study
Moore, Mick 9, 152, 233

NAFDAC (National Agency for Food and Drug Administration and Control) 17, 19, 97–127, 218; autonomous powers 121, 122, 123, 214 (autonomy 98–99, 105, 108–9, 111, 114–16, 125; focussed powers 108, 114, 116); counterfeit drugs and products 99, 111–12, 116–17, 119, 124–25, 126; effectiveness 100–101, 110–11, 125, 207, 237; emergence as PoE 101, 121–23, 124, 195, 196; enforcement 99, 100, 103, 111, 114, 116, 120, 126; Government Effectiveness indicators 18; hostile environment 100, 118, 124, 238; media 107, 110, 113, 117; methodology and research 97–98, 101, 125; NDLEA 98, 124, 239–40; Obasanjo, Olusegun 107, 108, 111–13,

126; operational factors 102, 107–11, 122 (institutionalization of procedures 110–11, 124; registration and control regime 108–9, 123; strategic decisions on land/air/sea import of drugs 108, 114; technology 107, 109, 124, 205); organization 98–99 (Governing Council 98, 113, 114, 124, 125, 214); origins 98–99, 207; outreach and cooperation 102, 116–21, 122, 215 (domestic cooperation 118–20, 121, 122, 123–24; international cooperation 120–21, 122, 127; public communication 116–17); persistence as PoE 101, 123–24; political factors 100, 102, 111–14, 122 (political interest 111–13, 123; political management 111, 113–14, 118, 122, 123, 124; political protection 111, 114, 118, 122–23, 127); standardization 110–11, 204; triggering effect 100–101; WHO 101, 103, 109; *see also entries below for* NAFDAC; Nigeria
NAFDAC, leadership 97, 98, 100, 102, 104, 105–6, 112–13, 214, 219; Akunyili, Dora 97–121 *passim*, 124, 125, 126, 204, 207, 214, 219, 222, 239 (*The War Against Counterfeit Medicine. My Story* 101, 125); *see also* NAFDAC
NAFDAC, organizational culture 121, 122, 123, 126; anti-corruption regime 104, 108, 112–13 (whistle blowing 104, 119–20); function/mission 19, 98, 100, 107, 125; meritocracy 103–4; organizational factors 102–7, 122 (functional restructuring 103); public service commitment 106–7; staff 97 (integrity and commitment 103, 105, 107; training and performance regime 103, 104–5, 109, 120, 125); *see also* NAFDAC
NAPTIP (National Agency for the Prohibition of Traffic in Persons) 17, 19, 128–46, 215; 2003 Trafficking in Persons (Prohibition) Law Enforcement and Administration Act 132, 133, 136, 143, 236; Abubakar, Amina Titi 132, 133, 136, 143; Adenuga, Wale: *Itohan: A Call to Action* 142, 146; anti-corruption measures 140–41, 144; autonomy 133, 136, 139, 145; budget allocations 139, 140, 143, 144, 145; effectiveness 129,

272   Index

133, 134–35, 137, 143;
emergence/persistence as PoE 136–44,
195, 196; enforcement 132, 134, 145;
external collaboration 137, 142–43,
144; functions 133–34, 144;
Government Effectiveness indicators
18; hostile environment 144;
international support 137, 139, 143,
144; leadership and management
136–39, 143–44, 145 (Ndaguba, Carol
132, 136–39, 143–44, 145, 221, 240);
meritocracy 138–39; methodology
and research 129–30; NGO 134, 135,
138, 142, 144; Operation Koolvis 135,
143, 145; operational powers and
independence 137, 139–40;
organizational culture 137–38, 144;
origins 132–33, 136, 236; political
factors 136; staff 137, 139, 140–42,
145 (commitment 141–42, 144;
training 137, 139, 143, 144); structure
133–34, 145; United Nations 128,
133, 196; WOTCLEF 132, 133, 136,
142; *see also* human trafficking;
Nigeria and human trafficking
NGO (non governmental organization)
214; human trafficking 130, 132, 134,
138, 142, 144; *see also* civil society
Nigeria 14, 21, 26; Babangida, Ibrahim
Badamasi 98, 132–33; corruption 14,
97, 102, 112; counterfeit drugs and
products 99, 111–12, 116–17, 119,
124–25, 126; EFCC 125, 222;
NDLEA 98, 124, 239–40;
neopatrimonial country 14; nepotism
104; Obasanjo, Olusegun 107, 108,
111–13, 126, 133, 136, 221, 222, 236;
patronage 186; pharmaceutical
industry 99, 100–101, 118–19; Pockets
of Effectiveness in Nigeria 11, 97–127,
128–46; political goods 42; public
sector failure 97; Yar'Adua, Umaru
Musa 221, 222; *see also* NAFDAC;
NAPTIP; Nigeria and human
trafficking
Nigeria and human trafficking 130–32,
143; Benin City/Edo state 131, 141,
144–45; causes 131, 145;
destinations for trafficked Nigerians
130–31; IRRRAG 132; Nigeria as
'source' country 129, 130, 136;
organized crime 131, 146; US
Trafficking Victims Protection Act
135–36, 145

OECD (Organisation for Economic
Co-operation and Development) 30,
48, 111, 213; agencification 126, 232,
241; autonomy 126, 213; *Paris
Declaration on Aid Effectiveness* 3
Oladeji, Abubakar O. 128–46
organizational culture: BNDE 83, 95,
96, 125 (*esprit de corps* 76, 77, 83,
85–86, 87, 88, 92, 95, 96); 'elite'
organization 141, 209, 238; Grindle,
Merilee S. 31–32, 103, 121, 205, 224;
Hilderbrand, Mary E. 31–32, 103,
121, 205; How do PoE emerge? 200,
201–2, 205–10, 217–18, 224, 227;
inclusive leadership 102, 105–6, 122,
200, 206, 207, 216, 217–18, 227, 228;
individual factors 126; mission/
mystique 32, 107, 125, 126, 202, 207,
209–10, 224, 238; NAPTIP 137–38,
144; organizational identity 200,
206–9, 217, 218, 222–23, 224, 238
(environment 209; leadership 207–8,
238; positive feedback 209);
participation 31, 137; performance
orientation 200, 206, 217, 218, 227;
Staatsolie 150, 162–63; *see also* civil
service; NAFDAC, organizational
culture; PoE, how does it emerge?;
staff
outreach and cooperation 200, 210,
214–15, 216, 218, 228, 239; NAFDAC
102, 116–21, 122; *see also* PoE, how
does it emerge?
Owusu, Francis 42, 103

patrimonialism 72, 149, 168–69; China
48; civil service 24; developmental
patrimonialism 5; 'neopatrimonial'
system 14, 41, 43; Nigeria 14;
patrimonial state 152; Suriname 149,
150, 153, 154, 155
patronage 152, 169, 212, 234; Brazil 80,
84, 86, 90, 91; China 13, 47; civil
service 24; emergence of PoE 197;
GCC 180, 184, 188; head of state 197;
Nigeria 186; public sector 12, 13, 19,
25, 111; SOE 175, 176; Suriname 19,
151, 154–55, 156, 162, 169, 170;
Taiwan 13; *see also* clientelism
Peters, Thomas J. 22
PoE (pockets of effectiveness): criteria
for PoE 23, 25–26, 41 (capacity to
provide public good or service
throughout the country 25, 26; human

rights and laws of the country concerned 25, 26; persistence 25, 26; relative effectiveness 25); definition 1, 24; effectiveness 25, 36, 43–44; efficiency 43–44; hostile environment 10, 25; importance of 9, 22; 'islands of excellence' 1, 23; 'pockets of efficiency' 1, 23; 'pockets of productivity' 1, 23; politico-administrative system 12, 22, 24, 36, 38, 209, 210, 218, 227, 229–30; productivity 43, 44; terminology 23–25; *see also entries below for* PoE; effectiveness

PoE, analytical framework 11, 19, 35–41, 233; autonomy and agency 35; dynamic lifecycle perspective and turning points 36–37, 221; emergence and persistence 36; leadership 37–38; organizational sociology 35–38; organizations and environments 35; political sociology 35, 38–41, 233; relative effectiveness and internal variation 36; triggering change and state society-bargaining 38–41, 233 (politico-administrative system 38–39; rebuilding state-society relations 39–40); *see also* PoE, emergence; PoE, persistence

PoE, emergence 10–11, 16, 32–33, 36, 194–219; factors behind the establishment of PoE 195; head of state 195–200, 211–12, 217, 218, 235; international factors 196; Leonard, David K. 33–35, 206; mega-hypotheses 33–35 (external or political economy factors 34, 174; function or task-related factors 34, 196, 197, 199, 217, 237; internal factors 34); model 122–23, 124, 194, 215–18, 235 (generalizability 223–30, 235); motivations 195–97; patronage 197; regime autonomy 199; result of deliberate decision 24, 194; top-down political decision 24, 194; why do PoEs emerge? 11, 194–200, 216, 224; *see also* civil service; environment; function/task-related factors; head of state; leadership; PoE emergence, case studies; PoE, how does it emerge?; staff

PoE emergence, case studies: BNDE 80, 195, 196; Gulf SOEs 180, 195; JCRR 195; NAFDAC 101, 121–23, 124, 195,

196; NAPTIP 136–44, 195, 196; Sino-Foreign Salt Inspectorate 195, 236; *Staatsolie* 150, 156–66, 169–70, 195, 196; *see also* PoE, emergence; PoE, how does it emerge?

PoE, how does it emerge? 11, 200–215, 224; characteristics of process and approach 218–19; core/scale effectiveness 201, 214; founding features 201–2, 219; organizational culture 200, 201–2, 205–10, 217–18, 224, 227; organizational proactivity 200, 210–15, 217–18; organizational strength 200, 202–5, 217–18, 224, 227; Portes and Smith's study 227–28; *see also* focussed powers; organizational culture; outreach and cooperation; political management; standardization

PoE, literature on 12, 21, 26–33, 224, 240; commonalities 32–33; current research programmes 240–41; marginal monologues 26–27; scarcity of comparative studies of 10, 22–23; *see also* Grindle, Merilee S.; Hilderbrand, Mary E.; Israel, Arturo; Leonard, David; Portes, Alejandro; Smith, Lori D.; Tendler, Judith

PoE, persistence 10–11, 16, 33, 36, 216, 219–23; BNDE 74, 75, 80, 94; criteria for PoE 25, 26; foundational legacy 219–20; function/task-related factors 220–21; model for how PoEs persist 123–24, 216; NAFDAC 101, 123–24; NAPTIP 136–44; political management 210; Sino-Foreign Salt Inspectorate 59, 60, 62, 63–64; *Staatsolie* 19, 166–68, 169–70; strategies 219–22, 223 (effectiveness strategy 219, 220–21; legitimate referencing strategy 219, 221; president's strategy 219, 220)

PoE, trigger effects 10, 16, 26, 33, 38–41, 230–35; Brazil (BNDE 75, 93–94, 230, 231, 234; *Bolsa Família* 234–35, 241); contagion mechanism 38–39, 231; demonstration mechanism 38, 231; Mexico, *Progresa/Oportunidades* 234–35, 241; NAFDAC 100–101; 'pilot agency' 234; PoE contribution to public sector reform 9, 230, 231, 233–34; Sino-Foreign Salt Inspectorate 61–64, 230–31; state legitimacy 39, 40, 233, 235; state-society bargaining 39–40,

274 *Index*

230, 233; transplantation mechanism 39, 231

Pogoson, Aituaje Irene 97–127

political economy 42; economic populism 174, 181–85, 186, 188, 190, 199–200; Gulf SOEs, political economy context 174, 179–81, 187; Suriname 151–56

political management 200, 210–13, 214, 217, 218, 220, 223, 224, 227, 228, 229, 230, 232, 239, 241; BNDE 210, 212–13; NAFDAC 111, 113–14, 118, 122, 123, 124; purposes of 211–13; *see also* PoE, how does it emerge?; politics

political science 2, 11, 182

politico-administrative system: based on personal loyalty and informal networks 22, 24, 194, 211; China 13; formal rules and laws 24, 194; GCC 13; Latin America 229–30; PoE 12, 22, 24, 36, 38, 209, 210, 218, 227, 229–30; public organization 24–25; Suriname 19, 154, 170; Taiwan 13; *see also* environment; politics

politics: governance, state and politics 1–5, 8–9; NAFDAC 100, 102, 111–14, 122; NAPTIP 136; negotiating political interference 212 (legitimate referencing strategy 221); political elites and fragile states 4; political protection 36, 111, 114, 118, 122–23, 127, 212, 213, 220, 229 (NAFDAC 111, 114, 118, 122–23, 127); political underdevelopment 148, 152; rentier state, politics of development 175; SOE, politicization 161, 174, 175, 176, 182, 192; *see also* autonomy; political economy; political management; politico-administrative system

Portes, Alejandro 14, 21, 224–30, 237, 239, 241; *see also* Latin America

public organization 35; as unit of analysis 24; patronage 25; politico-administrative system 24–25; power 25; SOE/public organization distinction 14, 24, 239; *see also* state

public sector 1; developing country 6–7, 111; dysfunctional public sector 12, 24; economic populism 182; governance, public sector and development 1–9; NPM/New Public Management 6–7, 20; patronage 12,

13, 19, 111; public authority 4, 9–10, 20, 40; public sector reform 5–9, 20–21, 32, 194 (major flaws 7; PoE contribution to public sector reform 9, 230, 231, 233–34; technocratic reform approach 7); sub-Saharan Africa 6; Suriname 154–55, 156; World Bank 6, 7, 8, 9, 20–21; *see also* state

Ragin, Charles 193

rentier state 152–53, 161, 168–69; politics of development 175; rent-seeking 149, 152–53, 161, 169, 176, 179–80; rentier SOE, pathologies 175–76 (autonomy, lack of 175–76, 182, 183; corruption 175; cronyism 175, 176, 185; overstaffing 175, 180, 182, 183, 189; patronage 175, 176; political principals' manipulation 175, 182; politicization 161, 174, 175, 176, 192; price manipulation 175, 182, 183; rent-seeking, 161, 176, 180; unprofitability 175); Suriname 148, 150, 152, 153–54, 156, 169; *see also* SOE; state

Roll, Michael 1–42, 97–127, 194–241

Schneider, Ben Ross 41, 150, 151, 231, 241

Scully, Timothy 74

Shafer, D. Michael 153

SIDA (Swedish Development Cooperation Agency) 3

Simbine, Antonia T. 128–46

Simon, Herbert A. 204

Sino-Foreign Salt Inspectorate 16, 17, 46–47; autonomy 47, 48, 55, 62–63, 64, 71; bureaucracy 48, 52–57, 60, 62, 63, 71 (insulation 52, 53–54, 55, 56, 57, 58, 60, 71; strategies of goal achievement 52, 54, 56; technocratic bureaucracy 63, 71); civil service system 56, 57–61, 71 (staff commitment 71; training 57); Consolidated Tax Administration 61–62; corruption 58, 72; cultural resonance 58–59; de-personalization 48, 54, 56, 59, 62, 63; effectiveness 47, 48, 51, 52, 53, 57, 59–60, 62, 63–64, 71; emergence as PoE 195, 236; Fourteen Principles 55, 59; hostile environment 48, 51–52, 59, 60–61, 63; leadership 55, 56 (Dane, Sir Richard 51, 55, 56, 59, 206, 219); meritocracy

57–59, 60; nationalist government 60–64, 73; origins 50–51, 53, 55; persistence 59, 60, 62, 63–64; Reorganization Loan 53, 55, 60, 61; rule boundedness 48, 54–55, 56, 58, 71; salt tax regime 46, 49–50; standardization 54, 60, 61, 63, 203; technocracy 63, 71; trigger effects 61–64, 230–31; *see also* China

Smith, Lori D. 14, 21, 224–30, 237, 239, 241; *see also* Latin America

sociology: organizational sociology 35–38; political sociology 35, 38–41, 233

SOE (state-owned enterprise) 161, 169, 173; Algeria 174, 175, 176, 177, 182–83, 185–86, 188, 190, 192; economic populism 174, 181–85, 186, 188, 190, 199–200; effectiveness 190, 191; Indonesia 174, 175, 176, 184, 190, 193; Iran 174, 175, 182–83, 185, 186, 188, 190, 193; Iraq 191; Libya 174, 176, 177, 182–83, 185, 190, 192, 193; Nigeria 174, 175, 176, 177, 185, 186–87, 188, 190; regime autonomy 185–87, 189–90, 199; rent dependence 181; rentier SOE, pathologies 175–76; Russia 191; SOE/public organization distinction 14, 24, 239; Suriname 155, 190 (*Staatsolie* 14, 19, 148, 149–50, 169); Venezuela 174, 175, 176, 182–83, 185, 190, 192; *see also* Gulf SOEs

Staatsolie 17, 19, 147–72; agency 149; autonomy 150, 151, 165, 170 (autonomy from political influence 149, 150–51, 161, 164–67, 169, 213, 220, 239); Bouterse, Desiré Delano 147, 156, 166, 167; challenges 167–68, 170; double strategy 161–68, 169; effectiveness 148–49, 156–60, 238; emergence as PoE 150, 156–66, 169–70, 195, 196; formal-legal position 149, 161, 166, 169; function/task-related factors 149, 157–59; Government Effectiveness indicators 18; hostile environment 148, 150, 167–68, 169, 170; independence 150, 165; leadership 149, 150–51, 161, 168, 169 (Jharap, Eddy 147, 156–57, 162–67, 172, 236); meritocracy 156, 164; military regime 147, 156, 162, 164–65; organizational culture 150, 162–63; origins 156–57, 162, 236; persistence as PoE 19,

166–68, 169–70; SOE 14, 19, 148, 149–50, 169; staff 149, 163–64 (training 157, 163, 164); technological and management skills 149, 150, 157, 161, 163, 166, 170; *Volkspartij* 162, 164, 171, 236; Wijdenbosch, Jules 147–48, 166–67; *see also* Suriname

staff: BNDE (commitment 74, 76, 95; growing size of 88, 95, 96, 223; training 85, 86, 96); commitment 70, 126, 206, 209–10, 224; effectiveness 70, 71, 203; Gulf SOEs 178 (training 178); high salary 14, 56, 57, 60–61, 105, 106, 139, 140, 141, 206, 207, 208, 238; JCRR 71 (Cornell School of Agronomy 65–66, 68, 71); NAFDAC 97 (integrity and commitment 103, 105, 107; training and performance regime 103, 104–5, 109, 120, 125); NAPTIP 137, 139, 140–42, 145 (commitment 141–42, 144; training 137, 139, 143, 144); socialization 71; SOE, overstaffing 175, 180, 182, 183, 189; *Staatsolie* 149, 163–64 (training 157, 163, 164); staff deployment 200, 202, 203, 217, 218, 227; training and capacity building 31, 103, 126, 203, 207; *see also* civil service; meritocracy; organizational culture

standardization 200, 202, 203–5, 218, 221; bureaucratic standardization 205; Dominican Republic 229; effectiveness 204; enforcement 203–4; NAFDAC 110, 204; Sino-Foreign Salt Inspectorate 54, 60, 61, 63, 203; *see also* PoE, how does it emerge?

state: accountability 4, 39, 40, 233, 235; clientelism 152, 161, 169; developmental state 151–52, 174, 191, 192; governance, state and politics 1–5, 8–9; legitimacy 39, 40, 42, 233, 235, 241; patrimonial state 152; petro-state 149, 153, 170–71; predatory state 151; provision of basic public goods and services 39–40; regime autonomy 185–87, 198; state building 2, 4, 9, 39, 40, 47, 74, 233; state capacity 4, 9, 17, 71; state in development 151–53; state-society bargaining 39–40, 230, 233; strong state 47; taxation 39–40, 47; weak/fragile state 1, 2, 4, 48 (China 45–46, 47, 48, 56; political elites and fragile states 4); *see also* head of state;

276 *Index*

patrimonialism; patronage; rentier state; SOE
Stevens, Mike 7
Strauss, Julia C. 43–73
sub-Saharan Africa 7, 45; *Sub-Saharan Africa: From Crisis to Sustainable Growth* 19
Suriname 14, 147–72; Bouterse, Desiré Delano 147, 155–56, 166, 167, 171; clientelism 19, 151, 153, 154–55, 156, 162, 169, 170; corruption 155, 171; foreign aid 153–54; NDP 147, 155, 167; non-developmental mining state 149, 153, 156, 170–71; patrimonial state 149, 150, 153, 154, 155; patronage 19, 151, 154–55, 156, 162, 169, 170; political economy 151–56; politico-administrative system 19, 154, 170; population and ethnic diversity 154, 171; public sector 154–55, 156; rentier state 148, 150, 152, 153–54, 156, 169; SOE 155; state and economy 153–56; Wijdenbosch, Jules 147, 155, 166, 167; *see also Staatsolie*

Taiwan 13, 66–67, 70, 236; *see also* JCRR
taxation 42, 62; China 47, 49–50; developing country 40, 71–72; Dominican Republic 198, 204, 227–28; state-building 39, 40, 47; state society-bargaining 39–40; weak state 48; *see also* Sino-Foreign Salt Inspectoratetechnocracy: appointment of chief executive 198, 200; BNDE 77, 80, 82, 83–88, 89, 90, 91–92, 94, 95, 223; JCRR 65, 67, 70; public sector

reform 7; Sino-Foreign Salt Inspectorate 63, 71; technocratic bureaucracy 63, 71; *see also* leadership
technology 205; effectiveness 205; Gulf SOEs 176; NAFDAC 107, 109, 124, 205; *Staatsolie* 149, 150, 157, 161, 163, 166, 170
Teggemann, Stefanie 7
Tendler, Judith 27, 30–31, 32–33, 34, 37, 205, 224
Therkildsen, Ole 1, 23, 42
Tilly, Charles 44

United Nations, human trafficking: 196; 2000 Palermo protocol 133; UNAFRI 128
United States 66, 81; Trafficking Victims Protection Act 135–36, 145

Van Dijck, Pitou 153, 154
Viñuela, Lorena 240

Waterbury, John 161, 184, 188
Waterman, Robert H. 22
WHO (World Health Organization) 101, 103, 109
Willis, Eliza J. 74–96
Wilson, James Q. 239
World Bank 81; 1997 World Development Report 7; BNDE 77, 79, 81, 82, 83, 87, 94; governance 2; Government Effectiveness indicators 16, 18, 21, 225, 226; public sector 6, 7, 8, 9, 20–21; *Sub-Saharan Africa: From Crisis to Sustainable Growth* 19